THE PURIFYING POWER

OF LIVING BY FAITH IN...

FUTURE GRACE

JOHN PIPER

MULTNOMAH PUBLISHERS, INC.
SISTERS, OREGON

INTER-VARSITY PRESS
LEICESTER, ENGLAND

FUTURE GRACE

published by Multnomah Publishers, Inc.
and
published in Britain by
Inter-Varsity Press

© 1995 by John Piper

U.S. International Standard Book Number: 1-57673-337-8
British International Standard Book Number: 0-85111-162-9

Edited by Steve Halliday
Cover design by David Carlson

Unless otherwise noted, the Scripture quotations are from
the *New American Standard Bible,* The Lockman Foundation, ©1988.

For information:

MULTNOMAH PUBLISHERS, INC.
POST OFFICE BOX 1720
SISTERS, OREGON 97759

INTER-VARSITY PRESS
38 DE MONTFORT STREET
LEICESTER LEI TGP, U.K.

98 99 00 01 02 03 04 — 10 9 8 7 6 5 4 3 2

To

Ruth Eulalia Piper
1918 - 1974

TABLE OF CONTENTS

Preface

I have dedicated this book to my mother, who was killed in a bus accident in Israel in 1974. I was 28 years old when she died. For the last 10 years of her life she wrote to me about once a week, first in Illinois during college, then in California during seminary, then in Germany during graduate school, then in Minnesota as I began my ministry of teaching. She was relentless in her love. Scarcely a letter would be without a quote from the Scriptures. She had saturated me as a boy. She would go on saturating me as a man. Of all the texts that she quoted, one predominated. I think it must have been her favorite. At least it was the one she believed I needed most often, Proverbs 3:5-6 (in her version, KJV):

> Trust in the LORD with all thine heart;
> and lean not unto thine own understanding.
> In all thy ways acknowledge him,
> and he shall direct thy paths.

Over the years I have come to see that this passage is a call to live by *faith in future grace*. The call to live by *faith* is in the words, "*Trust* in the Lord with all thine heart." The reference to future grace is in the words, "He *shall* direct thy paths." Month after month my mother counseled me to live by faith in future grace. She called me to trust the Lord and she showed me that the focus of my trust is what God promised to do for me in the future: "Son, the Lord will direct your paths; trust him, trust him." This book is a tribute to the legacy of my mother's exhortation.

She taught me to live my life between two lines of "Amazing Grace." The first line: "'Tis *grace* has brought me safe thus far." The second line: "And *grace* will lead me home." Before I could explain it, I learned that believing the first line fortifies faith in the second line; and believing the second line empowers radical obedience to Jesus. That's what this book is about.

The book is also an evidence of grace poured out on me through the staff and elders and congregation of Bethlehem Baptist Church in Minneapolis. I have been loved and cared for and chastened and inspired in this fellowship for fifteen years. They have not begrudged me the seasons of solitude to think and pray and write. They refined my understanding as I taught this material on Wednesday nights during the 1994-1995 school year. I love them and cherish the pleasures of living together by faith in future grace.

Jon Bloom, my assistant and Administrator of *Desiring God Ministries,* carries a huge load for me and frees my mind from the crushing weight of countless details. But best of all is his passion for the truth we serve together —that God is most glorified in us when we are most satisfied in him.

Daniel Fuller's vision of the Christian life as an "obedience of faith" is the garden in which the plants of my ponderings have grown. Almost three decades of dialogue on the issues in this book have left a deep imprint. If I tried to show it with footnotes, they would be on almost every page. His major work, *The Unity of the Bible* (Zondervan Publishing House, 1992), is explanatory background to most of what I write.

Tom Schreiner, Professor of New Testament at Bethel Theological Seminary, St. Paul, and a comrade at Bethlehem, has been an extraordinary partner in this project. Not only has he helped me teach the material, but he has read it all, and saved me from errors by his keen exegetical eye.

To my great relief, Carol Steinbach stepped forward again (I think we've teamed up on five books) and willingly took on the task of making the book more navigable with the text index. In the process her editor's eye rescued my wording just in time.

Editor, advocate, encourager and friend, Steve Halliday pressed gently to make the book better. What I owe him for ten years of partnership is immense. Perhaps best of all is that he understands. When he reads he gets it.

Finally, for almost twenty-seven years Noël has stood by me in the rugged grace of marriage. I lean on her more than anyone knows. Perhaps I can best thank her with the following lines composed for Mother's Day, 1995:

I used to dream about becoming old,
And leaning on your heart so long I'd fold
It into mine, like that old hickory tree
Along the cottage path, that after three,
Or four, or maybe five decades, has pressed
Itself against the fencing wire with rest
Unceasing, till, without a drop of blood,
The pith is pierced, and every barb a bud.

Now, barely shy of half a century,
And long since pierced with fierce fidelity,
I dream about becoming older still,
And how, some day, beside the Brightwood mill,
Between the watercourse and stream, four sons
And faithful wives, and all their little ones,
Will rise and bless the velvet steel where I,
And they, have leaned, and will until we die.

God is most glorified in us
when we are most satisfied in him.

We shall bring our Lord most glory
if we get from Him much grace.
If I have much faith, so that I can take God at His Word...
I shall greatly honor my Lord and King.
CHARLES SPURGEON

Why and How
This Book Was Written

The ultimate purpose of this book is that God be *prized* above all things. I could also say that the ultimate purpose is the *praise* of the glory of God's grace. The reason both are aims, and both are ultimate, is that *prizing* is the authenticating essence of *praising*. You can't praise what you don't prize. Or, to put it another way, God is most glorified in us when we are most satisfied in him.

On the other side of the coin, the aim of this book is to emancipate human hearts from servitude to the fleeting pleasures of sin. Sin is what you do when your heart is not satisfied with God. No one sins out of duty. We sin because it holds out some promise of happiness. That promise enslaves us until we believe that God is more to be desired than life itself (Psalm

63:3). Which means that the power of sin's promise is broken by the power of God's. All that God promises to be for us in Jesus stands over against what sin promises to be for us without him. This great prospect of the glory of God is what I call *future grace*. Being satisfied with that is what I call *faith*. And therefore the life I write about in this book is called *Living by Faith in Future Grace*.

A CRISIS IN SPIRITUALITY

Alister McGrath, the Oxford theologian and penetrating observer of American Evangelicalism, describes a "Crisis of Spirituality in American Evangelicalism."[1] He says that Evangelicalism, particularly American Evangelicalism, is failing the church.

> *Evangelicals have done a superb job of evangelizing people, bringing them to a saving knowledge of Jesus Christ as Savior and Lord, but they are failing to provide believers with approaches to living that keep them going and growing in spiritual relationship with him... Many start the life of faith with great enthusiasm, only to discover themselves in difficulty shortly afterward. Their high hopes and good intentions seem to fade away. The spirit may be willing, but the flesh proves weak... People need support to keep them going when enthusiasm fades.*[2]

My aim and prayer is that this book will give that kind of support, and will provide an "approach to living that will keep believers going and growing." It has been forged in the furnace of pastoral ministry where the mingled fires of suffering and ecstasy make every joy deeper and every burden lighter. It is the fruit of unremitting meditation on the Word of God in relation to what David Powlinson calls "the existential and situational realities of human experience in the trenches of life."[3]

WRONG THINKING BEHIND WRONG LIVING

The book has grown out of the conviction that behind most wrong living is wrong thinking. Jesus calls us, for example, to a radical purity. But I find that many Christians have no categories for thinking clearly about the commands and warnings and promises of Jesus. When he says that we should pluck out our lusting eye, he backs it up with a warning: "It is better for you that one of the parts of your body perish, than for your whole body to be thrown into hell" (Matthew 5:29). Threats of going to hell because of lust are simply not the way contemporary Christians usually talk or think. This is not because such warnings aren't in the Bible, but because we don't know how to fit them together with other thoughts about grace and faith and eternal security. We nullify the force of Jesus' words because our conceptual framework is disfigured. Our Christian living is lamed by sub-Christian thinking about living.

I have found in twenty years of preaching and teaching and struggling with people who want to be authentic Christians, that the way they think about Christian living is often absorbed from the cultural air we breathe rather than learned from categories of Scripture. Not only that, some of the inherited categories of "Christian" thinking are so out of sync with the Bible that they work against the very obedience they are designed to promote.

THE PLACE OF GRATITUDE IN MOTIVATION

For example, one of the main claims of this book is that the Bible rarely, if ever, motivates Christian living with gratitude. Yet this is almost universally presented in the church as the "driving force in authentic Christian living." I agree that gratitude is a beautiful and utterly indispensable Christian affection. No one is saved, who doesn't have it. But you will search the Bible in vain for *explicit* connections between gratitude and obedience. If, as I will try to show in Chapters One and Two, gratitude was never designed as the primary motivation for radical Christian obedience, perhaps that is one reason so many efforts at holiness abort. Could it be that *gratitude for bygone grace* has been pressed to serve as the power for holiness, which only *faith in future grace* was designed to perform? That conviction is one of the main driving forces behind this book.

UNMERITED, CONDITIONAL GRACE

I have also found that some popular notions of grace are so skewed and so pervasive that certain biblical teachings are almost impossible to communicate. For example, the biblical concept of unmerited, *conditional* grace is nearly unintelligible to many contemporary Christians who assume that *unconditionality* is the essence of all grace.

To be sure, there is unconditional grace. And it is the glorious foundation of all else in the Christian life. But there is also *conditional* grace. For most people who breathe the popular air of grace and compassion today, *conditional grace* sounds like an oxymoron—like heavy feathers. So, for example, when people hear the promise of James 4:6, that God "gives grace *to the humble,"* many have a hard time thinking about a grace that is conditional upon humility. Or, if they hear the precious promise that "all things work together for good *to them that love God, to them who are the called according to his purpose"* (Romans 8:28, KJV), they scarcely allow themselves to ponder that this promise of grace is conditional upon our being called and our loving God.

And yet conditional promises of grace are woven all through the New Testament teaching about how to live the Christian life. "If you forgive men for their transgressions, your heavenly Father will also forgive you" (Matthew 6:14). "Pursue...sanctification without which no one will see the Lord" (Hebrews 12:14). "If we walk in the light as He Himself is in the light...the blood of Jesus His Son cleanses us from all sin" (1 John 1:7). I find that the biblical thinking behind these kinds of conditional promises is uncommon in the minds of Christians today. Some popular conceptions of grace cannot comprehend any role for conditionality other than legalism. But if God meant these teachings to help us live radical lives of Christian love, is it any wonder that we so often fall short? As a culture and as a church we are not given to much serious reflection. The consequence is that we are often molded by popular notions, rather than permeated by biblical ones. And the church looks very much like the world.

But this book is driven by the conviction that right thinking shapes right living. What shall we *think* when someone treats the *commandments* of God as contrary to a life empowered by the *grace* of God? How is it that John says, "For this is the love of God, that we keep His commandments; and His commandments are not burdensome" (1 John 5:3)? What shall we *think* when we hear Jesus say, on the one hand, "My yoke is easy, and my burden is light," but, on the other hand, "The gate is narrow and the way is hard, that leads to life" (Matthew 11:30; 7:14, RSV)? How can Christian living be both easy and hard? What shall we think when we read that justification is by grace through faith alone (Romans 3:28), and yet also read that the kingdom has been promised "to those who *love* him" (James 2:5)? How do faith and love relate as prerequisites for final salvation? This book is a response to questions like these.

At the heart of the book is the conviction that the promises of future grace are the keys to Christ-like Christian living. The hand that turns the key is faith, and the life that results is called *living by faith in future grace*. By *future* I do not merely mean the grace of heaven and the age to come. I mean the grace that begins now, this very second, and sustains your life to the end of this paragraph. By *grace* I do not merely mean the pardon of God in passing over your sins, but also the power and beauty of God to keep you from sinning. By *faith* I do not merely mean the confidence that Jesus died for your sins, but also the confidence that God will "also with him freely give us all things" (Romans 8:32). Faith is primarily a future-oriented "assurance of things hoped for" (Hebrews 11:1). Its essence is the deep satisfaction with all that God promises to be for us in Jesus—beginning now!

WHAT MADE MOSES FREE?

This understanding of faith accounts for why faith works through love (Galatians 5:6). The transforming power of faith in future grace is owing to liberating satisfaction that future grace sustains in the heart. Consider, for example: by what power did Moses break free from the "fleeting pleasures of sin" in the courts of Egypt? The answer of Hebrews 11:24-26 is that he was set free by the power of faith in future grace. "By *faith* Moses...[chose] rather to share ill-treatment with the people of God, than to enjoy the fleeting pleasures of sin. He considered abuse suffered for the Christ greater wealth than the treasures of Egypt, for *he looked to the reward*" (RSV). The promise of God overpowered the promise of sin, and produced a lifetime of sacrificial love. This book is an attempt to understand and apply that power —the purifying power of prizing God over sin.

THOMAS CHALMERS'
"THE EXPULSIVE POWER OF A NEW AFFECTION"

Thomas Chalmers was a great preacher and professor at the University of St. Andrews, Scotland. After seven years of ineffective rural ministry, he had a deep encounter with Christ that changed his heart and set his preaching ablaze. One of his most famous sermons begins with words that express profoundly the aim of this book:

> *There are two ways in which a practical moralist may attempt to displace from the human heart its love of the world—either by a demonstration of the world's vanity, so that the heart shall be prevailed upon simply to withdraw its regards from an object that is not worthy of it; or,* by setting forth another object, even God, as more worthy of its attachment, *so that the heart shall be prevailed upon not to resign an old affection, which shall have nothing to succeed it, but to exchange an old affection for a new one. My purpose is to show that from the constitution of our nature, the former method is altogether incompetent and ineffectual, and that the latter method will alone suffice for the rescue and recovery of the heart from the wrong affection that domineers over it.*[4]

My aim is the same as Chalmers', namely, to displace from the human heart its love for the world "by setting forth another object, even God, as more worthy of its attachment." And in this way I hope and pray to magnify (like a telescope, not a microscope) the infinite value of God.

One difference from Chalmers is that I do not make my case mainly "from the constitution of our nature," but mainly from the teachings of Scripture. I will try to show from Scripture that saving faith means, in its essence, *prizing the superior worth of all that God is for us in Jesus.* And I will try to show that *this* faith is not just the key to heaven, but also the key to holiness. Which is why the Bible can teach that there is no heaven without practical holiness (Hebrews 12:14), and yet heaven is reached "by grace through faith" (Ephesians 2:8).

This book is an extended meditation on the biblical testimony that the human heart is "cleansed...*by faith*" (Acts 15:9 RSV); that every act of obedience to Christ is a *"work of faith"* (1 Thessalonians 1:3; 2 Thessalonians 1:11); that the aim of all biblical instruction is "love *from...sincere faith"* (1 Timothy 1:5); that Abel and Noah and Abraham and Rahab were empowered for obedience *"by faith"* (Hebrews 11:4, 7, 8, 31); that "sanctification [is] *by...faith in the truth"* (2 Thessalonians 2:13; Acts 26:18); *that "faith [works] through love"* (Galatians 5:6); and that the whole law of God was meant to be pursued not "as though it were by works," but "by faith" (Romans 9:32).

J. C. RYLE'S AMAZEMENT AT THE PROMISES OF GOD

This amazingly effectual faith has the power it does because it looks to the future and embraces the promises of God as more satisfying than the promises of sin. Which means that the promises of God are of central importance in this book. I share the wonder of J.C. Ryle as he looks out over the panorama of promises in the Word of God. I marvel with him at the way God has so wisely and lovingly given them for our "inducement" to listen and obey.

> God is continually holding out inducements to man to listen to Him, obey Him, and serve Him... He has...shown His perfect knowledge of human nature, by spreading over the Book a perfect wealth of promises, suitable to every kind of experience and every condition of life...Their name is legion. The subject is almost inexhaustible. There is hardly a step in man's life, from childhood to old age, hardly any position in which man can be placed, for which the Bible has not held out encouragement to every one who desires to do right in the sight of God. There are "shalls" and "wills" in God's treasury for every condition. About God's infinite mercy and compassion,—about His readiness to receive all who repent and believe,—about His willingness to forgive, pardon, and absolve the chief of sinners,—about His power to change hearts and alter our corrupt nature,—about the encouragements to pray, and hear the gospel, and draw near to the throne of grace,—about strength for duty, comfort in trouble, guidance in perplexity, help in sickness, consolation in death, support under bereavement, happiness beyond the grave, reward in

*glory,—about all these things there is an abundant supply of promises
in the Word. No one can form an idea of its abundance unless he carefully searches the Scriptures, keeping the subject steadily in view. If any
one doubts it, I can only say, "Come and see."[5]*

That is what I would like the reader to do with this book: "Come and
see." To help navigate the way, I offer now an overview that explains how
the book is organized.

WHY DOES THE BOOK HAVE THIRTY-ONE CHAPTERS?

It is not accidental that there are 31 chapters. This was intentional from the
start, and was inspired by Andrew Murray's *Abide in Christ* and C. S. Lewis'
Screwtape Letters, both of which have 31 chapters—one for each day of the
month. Murray explained the structure of his book like this:

*It is only by continuously fixing the mind for a time on some one of the
lessons of faith, that the believer is gradually helped to take and thoroughly assimilate them. I have the hope that to some…it will be a help
to come and for a month, day after day, spell over the precious words,
"abide in me."[6]*

My hope is that even people who do not have extended periods of time
for reading will be able to spend some time each day for a month reading
one chapter of *Living by Faith in Future Grace.* I have kept the chapters relatively short for that purpose. The advantage of this daily reading is not only,
as Murray says, "thorough assimilation," but also unrushed reflection. O the
riches of understanding that come from lingering in thought over a new
idea—or a new expression of an old idea! I would like this book to be read
in the same way that St. Paul wanted his letters to be read by Timothy:
"*Think* over what I say, for the Lord will grant you understanding in everything" (2 Timothy 2:7 RSV). Every book worth reading beckons with the
words, "*Think over* what I say." I do not believe that what I have written is
hard to understand—if a person is willing to think it over. When my sons
complain that a good book is hard to read, I say, "Raking is easy, but all you
get is leaves; digging is hard, but you might find diamonds."

I have tried to write as I preach—with a view to instructing the mind and moving the heart. I do not take lightly the challenges of reading. For example, I would not copy John Owen, the seventeenth century Puritan pastor and theologian. He began one of his books with an almost disdainful warning to the reader, "READER,...if thou art, as many in this pretending age, *a sign or title gazer,* and comest into books as Cato into the theater, to go out again,—thou hast had thy entertainment; farewell!"[7] Virtually everyone I know who has read John Owen complains that he writes in a cumbersome and unhelpful way, and that his thoughts are difficult to grasp. But he does have one formidable defense: twenty-four volumes of his books are still in print three hundred years after his death. People are still struggling through his difficult diction in search of treasure. What's the lesson here? The lesson is that biblical substance feeds the church, not simplicity. Whether there is nutritional substance for the church in these pages is not finally for me to judge. But that is my design.

AN OVERVIEW OF THE BOOK

If right thinking nourishes right living, then it seems that truth should precede application in the writing of a book. But life is more complex than that. Most of us need some evidence that what we read is not only true but helpful. There are many true things that are not significant. We only have one life to live, and perhaps a few hours (or less!) in the week for reading. It simply must be *helpful* as well as true.

For this reason, I have not waited until the end of the book to set forth some of the practical effects of living by faith in future grace. Mingled with the foundations are applications. There are eight interspersed chapters called "Applying the Purifying Power." In these chapters I take eight areas of human struggle with evil, and try to show how living by faith in future grace is the way to prevail over the deceptive promises of sin. In one sense, this arrangement is less than ideal because some application comes *before* pertinent foundation. But in another sense this is the way life is. We learn and live and refine and learn some more. I think the benefits of early and repeated exposure to the practical application outweigh the drawbacks.

I said at the beginning of this Introduction that the aim of this book is to emancipate human hearts from servitude to the fleeting pleasures of sin. These "Applying the Purifying Power" chapters are where that aim reaches its sharpest focus. How does faith in future grace triumph over anxiety, pride, shame, impatience, covetousness, bitterness, despondency and lust? That is the question these interspersed chapters try to answer.

The book begins with two chapters that distinguish *living by faith in future grace* from living by gratitude for past grace. My argument is that the backward look of gratitude is not designed by God as the primary empowerment of obedience. The future look of faith is (Chapters One and Two). Then follow two chapters (Chapters Four and Five) that explain what is meant by the "futureness" and the "graciousness" of *future grace*. They answer the question: Does the Bible really make so much of future grace? Is this a central biblical concept?

At this point I can feel the tension building in those who, like me, cherish the magnificence of bygone grace. In Chapters Seven through Nine I try to relieve that tension. The aim here is to show that the great redemptive works of past grace—for example, the death and resurrection of Jesus—are indispensable foundations for our faith in future grace. But their power resides precisely in that—they purchase and certify the future grace in which we hope. The life and death of Jesus were God's Yes to all his promises (2 Corinthians 1:20). Christ came into the world "to confirm the promises given to the Fathers" (Romans 15:8). Because of Christ's death, God will "with him freely give us all things" (Romans 8:32). Those whom God *has* justified, he *will* most certainly glorify (Romans 8:30). Past grace is the foundation of life-transforming faith in future grace.

Chapters Eleven and Twelve survey the Old and New Testaments to answer the question, "Why did obedience sometimes languish and why did it sometimes flourish?" My conclusion is that obedience rises and falls in proportion to faith in future grace. Both the law of God in the Old Testament and the teachings of Jesus and the apostles in the New Testament were meant to be pursued, as Paul said in Romans 9:32, not "by works," but by faith in future grace. This forces us to press the question, "Why is it that faith yields obedience? Why has God designed it this way? What is it about faith that necessarily bears the fruit of righteousness and love?" Chapters Fourteen through Sixteen tackle these questions under the heading, "The Nature of Faith in Future Grace." What emerges here is that faith is the God-appointed means of justification and sanctification because, better than any other act, it highlights the freedom of grace and magnifies the glory of God. It does that because, at its heart, faith in future grace means being satisfied with all that God promises to be for us in Jesus. This kind of faith magnifies God because God is most glorified in us when we are most satisfied in him.

After seventeen chapters of looking at the biblical dynamics of living by faith in the promises of God, we are compelled at this point to deal directly with the conditionality of many of those promises. How does one actually trust a conditional promise (Chapter Eighteen)? Who are the beneficiaries of the promises (Chapter Nineteen)? What is the bottom line condition of the promises of future grace (Chapter Twenty)? I conclude from these three chapters that faith and love are the conditions a Christian meets in order to go on enjoying the benefits of future grace. But faith and love are not conditions in the same way. Faith perceives the glory of God in the promises of future grace, and embraces all that God promises to be for us in Jesus. This spiritual apprehension and delight in God is the self-authenticating evidence that God has called us to be beneficiaries of his grace. This evidence frees us to bank on the promise as our own. And this banking on the promise empowers us to love others, which in turn confirms that our faith is real. Thus faith is the bottom line condition that unites us to the power of future grace; and love is a condition only in confirming the reality of this faith.

With this grasp of how faith apprehends the power of future grace, we are now prepared to unfold how faith *works through love,* as Paul says in Galatians 5:6 (Chapter Twenty-Two); and how it empowers us for all kinds of practical ministries (Chapter Twenty-Three). What becomes evident as we describe the links between faith and love is that living by faith in future grace is not a life of coasting and ease. It is a lifelong battle against unbelief, or, as Paul calls it in 1 Timothy 6:12, "the good fight of faith" (Chapter Twenty-Five). Which means that we must take heed to the great enemy of faith, Satan, and expose his strategies to undo our confidence in future grace (Chapter Twenty-Six).

As the book draws to a close I reckon with the fact that, as long as this age lasts, every one of us will have to suffer and die. "Through many tribulations we must enter the kingdom of God" (Acts 14:22). This poses a great threat to faith in future grace. But here too the promises abound. God makes plain that suffering and death are themselves agents of more grace, and will lead, in the end, to everlasting and ever-increasing joy (Chapters Twenty-Eight and Twenty-Nine). We will be given new bodies on a new earth, and God will spend eternity exhausting the treasures of his immeasurable grace on us (Chapter Thirty).

The final chapter is for people who like to see the roots and relationships of things. Here I try to show how my thinking about faith in future grace coheres with the thinking of Jonathan Edwards, the eighteenth century theologian and pastor. And I try to show how the ideas of this book are of one piece with the vision of God and life developed in my earlier books, *Desiring God* and *The Pleasures of God*.

WHERE YOU END IS WHAT MATTERS

With this understanding of how the chapters fit together, you are, of course, free to begin reading anywhere you like. My concern is not primarily where you begin, but where you end. Will it be with deeper faith in future grace? I pray that it will be. I pray that you will hear and follow the call to find your joy in all that God promises to be for you in Jesus. And I pray that the expulsive power of this new affection will go on freeing you from the fleeting pleasures of sin and empower you for a life of sacrificial love. If, in this way, we prove that God is prized above all things, then living by faith in future grace will be to the praise of his glory. For God is most glorified in us when we are most satisfied in him.

Is it by the instrumentality of faith
we receive Christ as our justification,
without the merit of any of our works? Well.
But this same faith, if vital enough to embrace Christ,
is also vital enough to 'work by love,' 'to purify our hearts.'
This then is the virtue of the free gospel, as a ministry of sanctification,
that the very faith which embraces the gift
becomes an inevitable and a divinely powerful
principle of obedience.

ROBERT L. DABNEY

For Theologians

N ot everyone needs to read this section. But it may be helpful for some, if I orient the book in the history and the categories of more formal theology. From this angle I would say that the aim of this book is to explore how the faith that justifies also sanctifies. Or to be more precise (since I am here talking to theologians), the aim is to examine how the faith, which is alone the means through which *pardoning grace* justifies, is also the faith through which[1] *empowering grace* sanctifies. In its popular form, the classic Reformed, Protestant expression of faith's relation to sanctification goes like this: "It is faith alone which justifies, but the faith which justifies is not alone." That is, justifying faith is always accompanied by good works. But the Reformed Confessions go further than this. They say that justifying faith is not only accompanied by good works, but also is, in some way, the instrumental cause of those works.

THE AUGSBURG CONFESSION

The historic Lutheran Augsburg Confession was written by Philipp Melancthon (1497-1560), sanctioned by Martin Luther and presented by the German Protestants to Charles V in 1530. It describes the relationship between justifying faith and the subsequent life of obedience in the following terms:

> (IV) *[The churches with common consent among us] teach that men can not be justified before God by their own powers, merits, or works; but are justified freely for Christ's sake through faith, when they believe...*
> *(VI) Also they teach that this faith should bring forth good fruits, and that men ought to do the good works commanded of God, because it is God's will, and not on any confidence of meriting justification before God by their works.*

Thus far, the Augsburg Confession simply says that justifying faith "*should* bring forth good fruits." But in Article XX it goes deeper in explaining this connection:

> *Because the Holy Spirit is received by faith, our hearts are now renewed, and so put on new affections, so that they are able to bring forth good works. For thus saith Ambrose: "Faith is the begetter of a good will and of good actions." ... Hereby every man may see that this doctrine [of justification by faith alone] is not to be accused, as forbidding good works; but rather is much to be commended, because it showeth after what sort we must do good works. For without faith the nature of man can by no means perform the works of the First or Second Table. Without faith, it can not call upon God, hope in God, bear the cross; but seeketh help from man, and trusteth in man's help. So it cometh to pass that all lusts and human counsels bear sway in the heart so long as faith and trust in God are absent.*[2]

The doctrine of justification by faith "showeth after what sort [i.e., way] we must do good works." I take this to mean that the Augsburg Confession is not content to say that good works merely exist alongside justifying faith, but also arise from that faith. "Faith is the begetter of...good actions." The power of "lusts and human counsels" is broken where this faith is present. This book is an attempt to understand why and how faith has that sanctifying power.

A SWISS CONFESSION

The First Helvetic Confession was composed by Swiss theologians (Heinrich Bullinger, Simon Grynaeus, Oswald Myconius, etc.) at Basel, Switzerland in 1536. It represented the faith of all the cantons of Switzerland at that period of the Reformation. Article XIII is entitled, "How the grace of Christ and his merit are imparted to us and what fruit comes from them." It reads, "We come to the great and high deeds of divine grace and the true sanctifying of the Holy Spirit not through our merit or powers, but through faith, which is a pure gift and favor of God." Then Article XIV explains the connection between this faith and works:

> This same faith is a certain, firm, yes, undoubting ground, and a grasping of all things that one hopes from God. From it love grows as a fruit, and, by this love, come all kinds of virtues and good works. And, although the pious and believing practice such fruit of faith, we do not ascribe their piety or their attained salvation to such works, but to the grace of God. This faith comforts itself with the mercy of God, and not its works, even though it performs innumerable good works. This faith is the true service which pleases God.[3]

Thus the Helvetic Confession affirms that love grows from faith and produces all virtues. Faith does not simply exist alongside the fruit of obedience, but itself "performs innumerable good works."

THE THIRTY-NINE ARTICLES OF THE CHURCH OF ENGLAND

The Thirty-Nine Articles of Religion of the Church of England were published as an expression of Anglican Reformed faith in 1571. Its teaching on justification and good works is refreshingly straightforward and clear:

> We are accounted righteous before God, only for the merit of our Lord
> and Saviour Jesus Christ by Faith, and not for our own works or deserv-
> ings. Wherefore, that we are justified by Faith only, is a most wholesome
> Doctrine, and very full of comfort… Albeit that Good Works, which are
> the fruits of Faith, and follow after Justification, can not put away our
> sins, and endure the severity of God's judgment; yet are they pleasing
> and acceptable to God in Christ, and do spring out necessarily of a true
> and lively Faith; insomuch that by them a lively Faith may be as evi-
> dently known as a tree discerned by the fruit.[4]

A life of obedience "springs out necessarily" from a true and lively faith. Good works "are the fruits of Faith." Justifying faith is not merely alongside good works, but is also the agency employed by the grace of God to give rise to good works. Thus good works are the evidence of authentic faith.

THE WESTMINSTER CONFESSION OF FAITH

Perhaps the best known Confession of the Reformed faith is the Westmin-ster Confession of Faith, published in England in 1647. Chapter XI of the Confession says:

> (1) Those whom God effectually calleth he also freely justifieth; not by
> infusing righteousness into them, but by pardoning their sins, and by
> accounting and accepting their persons as righteous: not for anything
> wrought in them, or done by them, but for Christ's sake alone… (2)
> Faith, thus receiving and resting on Christ and his righteousness, is the
> alone instrument of justification; yet is it not alone in the person jus-
> tified, but is ever accompanied with all other saving graces, and is
> not dead faith, but worketh by love.[5]

Thus the Confession boldly declares that the faith which is the "instru-ment of justification" also "work[s] by love." It affirms, therefore, that justifying faith is also sanctifying faith. It "works by love." The Confession makes explicit (by its footnotes) that the words, "work[s] by love," are a ref-erence to Galatians 5:6, "For in Christ Jesus neither circumcision nor uncircumcision means anything, but *faith working through love.*" This text will be central to the argument of this book.

A CLASSIC ON JUSTIFICATION

Numerous other witnesses could be called in to show that the historic viewpoint of the Reformed confessions is that justifying faith is also sanctifying faith.[6] The faith that justifies gives rise to lives of obedience—not perfection, but growing holiness. Thus in a classic restatement of the doctrine of justification, James Buchanan invites us to:

> consider how Good Works stand related to Faith, and to Justification, respectively. They are the effects of faith, and, as such, the evidences both of faith, and of justification. That they are the effects of faith is clear; for "whatsoever is not of faith is sin" [Romans 14:23]; and "without faith it is impossible to please God" [Hebrews 11:6]; and "the end of the commandment is charity, out of a pure heart, and of a good conscience, and faith unfeigned" [1 Timothy 1:5]. It is equally clear that, being the effects, they are also the evidences, of a true and living faith; for "a man may say, Thou hast faith, and I have works: show me thy faith without thy works, and I will show thee my faith by my works" [James 2:18]; and all the good works, which are ascribed to believers under the Old Testament, are traced to the operation of faith [Hebrews 11:4, 7, 8, 23, 32].[7]

SCARCE REFLECTIONS ON HOW FAITH SANCTIFIES

One of the remarkable things about this unified stream of thinking is that comparatively little attention is given to the spiritual dynamics of *how* faith sanctifies. I could be wrong about this, since I am not an expert in the history of doctrine. But my sense is that both historically and currently, the claim that justifying faith "*is not alone in the person justified, but is ever accompanied with all other saving graces*" is usually left dangling without any extended reflection on *why* this is the case, and *how* it works out in the spiritual dynamics of real Christian living. Such an extended reflection is what this book is meant to be.

My aim is to understand and explain how it is that justifying faith works through love (Galatians 5:6). My argument is that the reason justifying faith is never alone, is that it is the nature of faith to sanctify. There is something about the essence of justifying faith which makes it a morally transforming agency. Or, to put it more precisely, there is something about the faith through which pardoning grace justifies, that makes it a suitable and efficient means through which empowering grace always sanctifies.

JUSTIFICATION AND SANCTIFICATION ARE DISTINCT

In no way do I mean to confound justification and sanctification. They are distinct. Justification is not a human behavior of soul or body. But sanctification is a (divinely effected) human behavior of soul and body. Both justification and sanctification are brought about by God, but they are not brought about in the same way. Justification is an act of God's reckoning; sanctification is an act of God's transforming. Thus the function of faith in regard to each is different. In regard to justification, faith is not the channel through which a power or a transformation flows to the soul of the believer, but rather faith is the occasion of God's forgiving and acquitting and reckoning as righteous. These justifying acts of God do not in themselves touch the soul of man. They are *extra nos*—outside ourselves. Paul speaks of the justification of the "ungodly" (Romans 4:5). We do not remain ungodly, but we do begin as "justified ungodly." However, in regard to sanctification, faith is indeed the channel through which divine power and transformation flow to the soul; and the work of God through faith does indeed touch the soul, and change it.

THREE ASSUMPTIONS

My point in this book is that the faith, which is the occasion of justification, is the same faith through which sanctifying power comes to the justified sinner. There are three assumptions here. The first assumption is that justifying faith[8] is persevering faith. As Jonathan Edwards explained with careful and nuanced language, "Perseverance in faith is, in one sense, the condition of justification; that is, the promise of acceptance is made only to a persevering sort of faith, and the proper evidence of it being that sort is its actual perseverance."[9] Thus it is proper to speak of the moral effectiveness of justifying faith not merely because it brings us into a right standing with God at the first moment of its exercise, but also because it is a persevering sort of faith, whose effectiveness resides also in its daily embrace of all that God is for us in Jesus.

A second assumption is that justifying faith is not only a trusting in the past grace of God, but also a trusting in the future grace of God, secured by the past grace of Christ's death and resurrection. Justifying faith embraces the finished work of Christ's atonement, in the sense that it rests in all that this atonement means for our past, present *and future*. As the First Helvetic Confession affirms "Faith is...a grasping of all things that one hopes from God." Or as John Calvin says in his sermon on Ephesians 3:14-19, "If we come to Christ, with belief in him, *that is to say, if we receive the promises of the gospel,* let us assure ourselves that he will dwell in our hearts, even by means of faith."[10] Standing on the bygone grace of Christ's death and resurrection, justifying faith is a future-oriented trust in the promises of God.

A third assumption is that the essence (though not the sum total) of justifying faith is *being satisfied with all that God is (and promises to be) for us in Jesus.* As other theologians have said, it is the embracing of Jesus in every office in which he is presented in the Word of God. Justifying faith is not selective, embracing Christ as he is offered by God in one role, while rejecting him as he is offered in another. "True faith embraces Christ in whatever ways the Scriptures hold him out to poor sinners."[11] Justifying faith, embraces all that God promises to be for us in Jesus. And this embracing is not a mere intellectual assent to a teaching, but is also a vital heartfelt satisfaction with God.

These three assumptions about the nature of justifying faith (which I will try to develop and justify biblically) account for why and how justifying faith necessarily sanctifies. This book is an extended reflection on the biblical underpinnings and practical spiritual dynamics of the sanctifying power of justifying faith. I call these dynamics *living by faith in future grace.*

PART I

A FOE
TO
FAITH IN FUTURE GRACE

And how long will they not believe in Me,
despite all the signs which I have performed in their midst?

NUMBERS 14:11

Gratitude exults in the past benefits of God and says to
faith, "Embrace more of these benefits for the future, so that
my happy work of looking back on God's deliverance may
continue."

The Debtor's Ethic: Should We Try to Pay God Back?

WHAT IS GRATITUDE?

L ike most precious things, gratitude is vulnerable. We easily forget that gratitude exists because sometimes things come to us *"gratis"*—without price or payment. When that happens, we should feel a pleasant sense of the worth of what we've received and the goodwill behind it. This *pleasant sense* is what we call gratitude. Then, spontaneously rising from this pleasant sense, come expressions of delight. We feel constrained with joy to acknowledge the gift and the goodwill behind it, and to express how good we feel about the gift and the heart of the giver.

Gratitude corresponds to grace (*"gratis"*). This is true even when we feel thankful for something we have paid for. We sense that what we bought might have been disappointing in spite of our having enough money to buy it. It might not have been in such good condition; or it might not have been the exact one we wanted; or someone might have bought it before we did; or the transaction might have been harsh; or the timing might have been wrong for our intended use; or the price might have gone up just after we bought it. In other words, gratitude is not the feeling that we have been shrewd in the way we get things. It is the emotion that rises joyfully in response to something *"gratis,"* even in our purchases.

The Birthplace of the Debtor's Ethic

But right at this point there lurks a danger. There is an impulse in the fallen human heart—all our hearts—to forget that gratitude is a spontaneous response of joy to receiving something over and above what we paid for. When we forget this, what happens is that gratitude starts to be misused and distorted as an impulse to pay for the very thing that came to us "gratis." This terrible moment is the birthplace of the "debtor's ethic."

The debtor's ethic says, "Because you have done something good for me, I feel indebted to do something good for you." This impulse is *not* what gratitude was designed to produce. God meant gratitude to be a spontaneous expression of pleasure in the gift and the good will of another. He did not mean it to be an impulse to return favors. If gratitude is twisted into a sense of debt, it gives birth to the debtor's ethic—and the effect is to nullify grace.

Don't misunderstand me. Gratitude itself does not nullify grace. It exults in grace. It was created by God to echo grace. Even the thought that it can be twisted to serve evil shocks some people and makes them shrink back. Make no mistake, I exalt gratitude as a central biblical response of the heart to the grace of God. The Bible commands gratitude to God as one of our highest duties. "Enter His gates with *thanksgiving,* and His courts with praise. Give *thanks* to Him, bless His name" (Psalm 100:4). God says that gratitude *honors* Him: "He who offers a sacrifice of thanksgiving *honors* Me" (Psalm 50:23). In spite of being vulnerable to misuse in the debtor's ethic, gratitude is not guilty.

We all know what the debtor's ethic is, even if we've never called it this. Suppose you invite me over for dinner. It is certainly right for me to feel gratitude. But O, how easily we distort this spontaneous response of joy into an impulse to pay back. You gave me an invitation and now I *owe* you one. When our virtue—toward other people, or toward God—is born out of this sense of "paying back," we are in the grip of the debtor's ethic.

What's gone wrong? It's not wrong to feel gratitude when someone gives us a gift. The trouble starts with the impulse that now we *owe* a "gift". What this feeling does is turn gifts into legal currency. Subtly the gift is no longer a gift but a business transaction. And what was offered as free grace is nullified by distorted gratitude.

SHOULD WE PAY GOD BACK?

It is remarkable how widespread and durable the debtor's ethic is among Christians. Recently I heard a well-known evangelical leader deliver a powerful message about the need for Americans to recover the call of duty and devotion to Christ. He used a compelling illustration about self-sacrifice. But his explanation of the spiritual dynamics of the sacrifice focused entirely on gratitude for what Christ had done. I sat there longing to hear a strong word about the essential role of *hope* as the sustaining power of laying your life down. But it didn't come.

This way of motivating duty and devotion seems harmless, even noble. Its appeal is strong. It speaks in words that are almost above criticism. For example, it might say, "God has done so much for you; now what will you do for him?" Or: "He gave you his very life; now how much will you give to him?" The refrain of Francis Havergal's old hymn "I Gave My Life for Thee," is hazardous language. In it Christ says, "I gave, I gave My life for thee, what hast thou given for me?" And: "I bring, I bring rich gifts to thee, what hast thou brought to Me?" I don't mean that sentences like these *must* express the debtor's ethic. I only mean that they easily can, and often do.

In the debtor's ethic the Christian life is pictured as an effort to pay back the debt we owe to God. Usually the concession is made that we can never fully pay it off. But "gratitude" demands that we work at it. Good deeds and religious acts are the installment payments we make on the unending debt we owe God. This debtor's ethic often lies, perhaps unintentionally, beneath the words, "We should obey Christ *out of gratitude*."

This appeal to gratitude as a way of motivating Christians is so common it may come as a shock when I question whether it has much biblical support. But consider this for a moment. How many places in the Bible can you think of where gratitude or thankfulness is *explicitly* made the motive of moral behavior? I mean behaviors like treating people with love, and doing your business with integrity, and taking risks in the obedience of missions. Does the Bible tell us that these things are to be done "out of gratitude," or "in the power of thankfulness" or "because we owe Jesus so much"?

This is not nit-picking or incidental; it is amazing. If you ask Christians today, "What is the biblical motive for Christian obedience?" great numbers would say, "Gratitude to God." And yet this way of thinking seems almost totally lacking in the Bible. The Bible rarely, if ever, explicitly makes gratitude the impulse of moral behavior, or ingratitude the explanation of immorality.

This is stunning when you let it sink in. This most common way of talking about motivating Christian obedience is scarcely mentioned in the Bible. This fact comes like a punch in the belly; it takes your breath away. Is this really so? You will need to search for yourself to be completely sure.

WAS INGRATITUDE THE PROBLEM?

In the Old Testament the people of God often sinned against him despite all the good things he had done for them. But the reason given for this sin is not their *ingratitude* but, for example, their lack of *faith:* "How long will they not *believe* in me despite all the signs which I have performed in their midst?" (Numbers 14:11). The ethical problem troubling Moses is not ingratitude. What troubles him is that God's past grace did not move the people to *trust* in God's future grace. Faith in future grace, not gratitude, is the missing ethical power to overcome rebellion and motivate obedience.

Just when today's Christian would probably say the problem is lack of gratitude, the biblical writers again and again say that the problem is a lack of *faith* in God's future grace. Moses rebukes the people, "You saw how the Lord your God carried you just as a man carries his son…but for all this you did not *trust* the Lord your God" (Deuteronomy 1:31-32).

The psalmist gives the same reason for why God's people sinned in spite of all his blessings: although God "split the rocks in the wilderness, and gave them abundant drink…yet still they continued to sin against Him…because they did not *believe* in God, and did not *trust* in His salvation" (Psalm 78:15, 17, 22).

It's true that the disobedient people must have lacked gratitude. But that's not how the Bible explains their rebellion and disobedience. Repeatedly the explanation given is lack of faith in God's future grace. The missing channel of motivating power between past grace and future obedience was not past-oriented gratitude, but future-oriented faith. You will read the Old

Testament in vain for texts that make gratitude the explicit motive or power for obedience.

THE FEAR OF THE LORD AND FAITH IN FUTURE GRACE

There are other Old Testament motives for obedience, such as love to God and fear of the Lord. We will deal in coming chapters with the relationship between faith in future grace and love for God.[1] But this is a good place to say a word about the fear of the Lord and its relationship to obedience and to faith in future grace.

Moses taught Israel that the fear of the Lord would give rise to obedience: "Fear the Lord your God, to keep all his statutes and his commandments" (Deuteronomy 6:2). Solomon summed up his own teaching in Ecclesiastes, "The conclusion, when all has been heard, is: *fear* God and keep his commandments" (Ecclesiastes 12:13). Nehemiah told the nobles and rulers in Jerusalem to "*walk* in the *fear* of our God" (Nehemiah 5:9). And Proverbs 23:17 says, "*Live* in the *fear* of the Lord always." Right "walking" and right "living" flow from fearing God. But to my knowledge there are no expressions corresponding to these which link gratitude and obedience in the same way.

And even these expressions about fearing the Lord are probably the flip side of trusting the Lord's future grace.[2] In other words, "fear the Lord" means "fear the terrible insult it would be to God if you do not trust his gracious promises of power and wisdom on your behalf." That's probably why Psalm 115:11 says, "You who *fear* the Lord, *trust* in the Lord; He is their help and their shield." In other words, if fear is not mingled with trust it will not be pleasing to the Lord. "Without faith it is impossible to please [God]" (Hebrews 11:6). The obedience that comes from fearing God *without faith in his future grace* will not be free, but servile.

The interconnectedness of fear and faith is probably why people looked at the grace given to David in distress, and felt fear and trust rising side by side in their hearts. "And He put a new song in my mouth, a song of praise to our God; many will see and *fear,* and will *trust* in the Lord" (Psalm 40:3). The same thing had happened at the Red Sea. "When Israel saw the great power which the Lord had used against the Egyptians, the people *feared* the

Lord, and they *believed* in the Lord" (Exodus 14:31). Fear and faith happen together in response to God's mighty power and his promise of future grace.

To fear the Lord is to tremble at the awareness of what a terrible insult it is to a holy God if we do not have faith in his future grace after all the signs and wonders he has performed to win our obedient trust. It's this faith in future grace that channels the power of God into obedience. We search the Old Testament in vain for the explicit teaching that gratitude is a channel of this power.

PAY YOUR VOWS TO THE MOST HIGH

One possible exception to this observation in the Old Testament is the teaching that we should "pay our vows" to God. Thinking about this "exception" has taken me deeper into the relationship between gratitude and faith in future grace.

One of the most significant vows I ever made to the Lord was prompted by stage fright. I was in college and almost paralyzed by the prospect of public speaking.[3] I was asked by Chaplain Evan Welch at Wheaton College to give a brief prayer of invocation at a summer school chapel. That meant speaking, perhaps for 30 seconds, to several hundred people. That may seem like a small thing to most people, but to me it was a watershed moment in my life. Against all my natural inclinations I said yes. Then I began to wrestle with God in the hope that he would help me so that I would not get so choked up with paralyzing fear that I couldn't speak— which had happened all through high school whenever I had to make a little presentation.

So I made a vow. I said, "Lord, if you will bring me through this one prayer in front of all those students and faculty, I will never again turn down a speaking opportunity out of fear." God helped me, and, to the best of my knowledge, I have kept my vow to this day. But was I right to do this? Or is the making and keeping of vows a part of the debtor's ethic?

Vows are promises that a person makes to God, usually in times of distress. For example, Absalom said to David, "Your servant vowed a vow while I was living at Geshur in Aram, saying, 'If the Lord shall indeed bring me back to Jerusalem, then I will serve the Lord'" (2 Samuel 15:8). The

Lord is not against making vows.[4] In fact it seems that Hezekiah is criticized for *not* making one: "In those days Hezekiah became mortally ill; and he prayed to the Lord, and the Lord spoke to him and gave him a sign. But Hezekiah gave no return for the benefit he received, because his heart was proud; therefore wrath came on him and on Judah and Jerusalem" (2 Chronicles 32:24-25). It seems that Hezekiah should have made a vow of service to the Lord and fulfilled it. Moreover, God gives instructions for keeping vows: "When you make a vow to the Lord your God, you shall not delay to pay it, for it would be sin in you, and the Lord your God will surely require it of you" (Deuteronomy 23:21).

Sometimes the keeping of vows is connected with gratitude. For example, Psalm 50:14 says, "Offer to God a sacrifice of *thanksgiving*, and *pay your vows* to the Most High." Probably the vows in this context are vows to offer sacrifices of thanksgiving. This seems to be the case in Psalm 66:13-14, "I shall come into Thy house with burnt offerings; I shall pay Thee my vows, which my lips uttered and my mouth spoke when I was in distress." When he was in distress he vowed that he would offer burnt offerings to the Lord. So the "sacrifice of thanksgiving" is a fulfillment of the vow.

It may well be that other things are vowed from time to time besides acts of worship like burnt offerings. So it seems fair to say that some moral commitments find their impulse in the desire to render back to God some good because of the help he has given in distress. The Old Testament does not say explicitly that this behavior is "from gratitude" or is even an expression of gratitude. But the connection is obviously very close. How are we to understand this connection and its relationship to faith in future grace? And why is rendering back to God the payment of our vows not an example of the debtor's ethic?

IS PAYING VOWS AN EXAMPLE OF THE DEBTOR'S ETHIC?

What keeps the paying of vows from the dangers of the debtor's ethic is that the "payment" is, in reality, not an ordinary payment, but another act of receiving which magnifies the ongoing grace of God. It does not magnify our resourcefulness. We can see this in two Psalms. First, in Psalm 116:12-14, the psalmist says, "What shall I render to the Lord for all His benefits toward me? I shall lift up the cup of salvation, and call upon the name of the Lord. I shall pay my vows to the Lord." The psalmist's answer to his own question, "What shall I render to the Lord for all his benefits?" is, in essence, that he will go on receiving from the Lord so that the Lord's inexhaustible goodness will be magnified. First, *lifting up the cup of salvation* signifies taking the Lord's satisfying salvation in hand and drinking it and expecting more. This is why I say that "paying" back to God in these contexts is not an ordinary payment. It is an act of receiving.

Second, this is also the meaning of the next phrase: "I shall call upon the name of the Lord." What shall I render to God for graciously answering my call? Answer: I shall call again. I will render to God the praise and the tribute that he is never in need of me, but is always overflowing with benefits when I need him (which I always do). Then the psalmist says, in the third place, "I will pay my vows to the Lord." But how will they be paid? They will be paid by holding up the cup of salvation and by calling on the Lord. That is, they will be paid by faith in future grace.

FAITH IN FUTURE GRACE PROTECTS GRATITUDE FROM THE DEBTOR'S ETHIC

Faith in future grace is the secret that keeps impulses of gratitude from turning into the debtor's ethic. True gratitude exults in the riches of God's grace as it looks back on the benefits it has received. By cherishing past grace in this way, it inclines the heart to trust in future grace. We might say that gratitude has a strong appetite for the enjoyment of looking back on the outpourings of God's grace. Since God does this future outpouring *through faith,* therefore gratitude sends its impulses of delight into faith in future grace. This is expressed in the words: lift up the cup of salvation and call on the name of the Lord. Gratitude exults in the past benefits of God and says to faith, "Embrace more of these benefits for the future, so that my happy work of looking back on God's deliverance may continue."

The same kind of thought is found in Psalm 50. God warns against a wrong kind of payment when he says in verse 12-13, "If I were hungry, I would not tell you; for the world is Mine, and all it contains. Shall I eat the flesh of bulls, or drink the blood of male goats?" In other words, "Don't view your 'payments' as ordinary payments that meet my needs or add anything to me. I own your 'payments' already."

What then? Verse 14-15 answers, "Offer to God a sacrifice of *thanks-giving,* and *pay your vows* to the Most High. And call upon Me in the day of trouble; I shall rescue you, and you will honor Me." Here again, the way to pay vows is explained as calling on the Lord in the day of trouble so that he will do the rescuing and he will get the honor. This makes clear that "paying" vows in the Old Testament is not part of the debtor's ethic. It is an act of faith in future grace. Pay your vow, that is, call on me in the day of trouble, and I will rescue you with future grace. And you will give me honor.

In sum, we can say that true gratitude does not give rise to the debtor's ethic because it gives rise to faith in future grace. With true gratitude there is such a delight in the worth of God's past grace, that we are driven on to experience more and more of it in the future. But this is not done by "payments" of a debt in any ordinary sense. Rather, it is done by transforming gratitude into faith as it turns from contemplating the pleasures of past grace and starts contemplating the promises of the future.

If this is the direction the Old Testament points, then what about the New Testament? What direction does it lead us in thinking about the debtor's ethic? For that we turn to Chapter Two.

The effort to repay God, in the ordinary way we pay creditors,
would nullify grace and turn it into a business transaction.
If we see acts of obedience as installment payments,
we make grace into a mortgage...
Let us not say that grace creates debts;
let us say that grace pays debts.

Past grace is glorified by intense and joyful gratitude.
Future grace is glorified by intense and joyful confidence.
This faith is what empowers us
for venturesome obedience
in the cause of Christ.

CHAPTER TWO

When Gratitude Malfunctions

A FILIPINO INSIGHT

While this book was being written I taught a lesson on the debtor's ethic at our church. In the audience there happened to be a visiting missionary to the Philippines who came up to me afterwards and said, "Did you know that you were talking about something extremely important for Filipino culture?" He explained that in the Filipino mind-set there is something called *utang na loob*. He showed me later an essay that explained what he meant.

Evelyn Miranda-Feliciano has written a book in which she defines *utang na loob* as "debt of volition." "It is an interior law which dictates that the recipient of a good act or deed behave generously towards his benefactor as long as he lives."[1]

She goes on to say that "To a Filipino, to show a lack of due gratitude is outrageous; being grateful is almost second nature to him. His sense of *utang na loob* defines his integrity as a person in the context of social relationships."[2] But there are negative aspects to this mind-set.

Generally, the lifetime indebtedness aspect of utang na loob *draws from the fact that it is difficult to measure one's debt of gratitude. It is an indebtedness that is harder to pay than money owed. Nothing is said about it. Nothing is counted or quantified. Everything is played by ear and the poor recipient is never sure whether what he had done suffices to repay his debt. Thus, he is bound to be at the beck and call of his benefactor. Unless the benefactor outrightly tells him to stop, or releases him from the burden of a self-imposed obligation.*

Evidently, an unquestioning form of utang na loob *tends to create a patron-client relationship that is oppressive. It creates a kind of dependency and mendicancy detrimental to the formation of a truly free, self-respecting individual, or nation for that matter.*[3]

IT'S A HUMAN ISSUE, NOT A FILIPINO ONE

This awareness of the reality of *utang na loob* in Filipino culture, and the problems it creates for the Christian mission, has raised the stakes of my concern higher than ever. I don't think the spiritual dangers of *utang na loob* are unique to the Philippines. They are present in every human heart. We are spring-loaded, it seems, to conceive of our relationship to God in terms that focus on what he has done for us in the past and what we must now do for him in the future by way of repayment.

What we saw in the last chapter is that living by faith in future grace is the biblical antidote to this debtor's ethic—the negative aspects of *utang na loob*. God has promised grace for tomorrow. Whatever returns we make to him for all his past goodness to us, we make by relying on his future grace. The only debt that grace creates is the "debt" of relying on more grace for all that God calls us to be and do. That is what we saw in the last chapter from our pondering the Old Testament. It is also what we will see now from our meditation on the New Testament.

ALL OBEDIENCE IS TO BE BY FAITH

In the New Testament the prevalence of faith in future grace as the impulse of Christian obedience is even clearer and more explicit than in the Old Testament. The apostle Paul faulted Israel for failing to pursue the law "from faith." But he never faulted them for not pursuing it "from gratitude." For example, he says, "Israel, pursuing a law of righteousness, did not arrive at that law. Why? Because they did not pursue it *by faith*, but as though it were by works" (Romans 9:31-32).

Similarly, in Hebrews 11 we find the saints of the Old Testament commended again and again because their obedience was motivated *by faith*. "By faith" Abraham "obeyed" (11:8); "by faith" Noah "prepared an ark" (11:7); "by faith" Moses "left Egypt" (11:27); "by faith" others "performed acts of righteousness" (11:33). But we find no expression in the Bible like, "by gratitude they obeyed," or "by thankfulness they performed acts of righteousness."

Furthermore we find Christian obedience called the "work of faith," never of the "work of gratitude" (1 Thessalonians 1:3; 2 Thessalonians 1:11). We find expressions like "live by faith" (Galatians 2:20) and "walk by faith" (2 Corinthians 5:7), but never any expression like "live by gratitude" or "walk by gratitude." We find the expression "faith working through love" (Galatians 5:6), but not "gratitude working through love." We read that "the goal of our instruction is love from a pure heart and a good conscience and a sincere faith" (1 Timothy 1:5), but not "from sincere gratitude." We read that sanctification is by "faith in the truth" (2 Thessalonians 2:13), not that it is "by gratitude." We read that "faith without works is dead" (James 2:26), but not that "gratitude without works is dead." And when Jesus deals with the disciples' hesitancy to seek the kingdom first because they were worried about food and clothing, he did not say, "O men of little gratitude"; he said, "O men of little faith" (Matthew 6:30). Faith in future grace, not gratitude, is the source of radical, risk-taking, kingdom-seeking obedience.

As I said before, this is not nit-picking or incidental; it is amazing. Gratitude is not set forth in the Bible as a primary motive for Christian living. Gratitude is a beautiful thing. There is no Christianity without it. It is at the heart of worship. It should fill the heart of every believer. But when it comes to spelling out the spiritual dynamics of how practical Christian obedience happens, the Bible does not say that it comes from the backward gaze of gratitude, but that it comes from the forward gaze of faith.

A POSSIBLE EXCEPTION

One possible exception in the New Testament would be Hebrews 12:28-29, "Since we receive a kingdom which cannot be shaken, let us show *gratitude, by which we may offer to God an acceptable service* with reverence and awe; for our God is a consuming fire." Notice that it says, "By which—that is, by gratitude—we offer to God acceptable service." This seems to make gratitude the impulse of our service. That may well be the meaning. If it is, then the way gratitude empowers service is probably by feeding faith with the joyful expectation of future grace on the basis of past experience. I say this because the book of Hebrews, more than any other book in the New Testament, is explicitly insistent that obedience comes "by faith" (Hebrews 11).

But, in fact, Hebrews 12:28 might mean something different. The King James Version translates it like this: "Wherefore we receiving a kingdom which cannot be moved, *let us have grace,* whereby we may serve God." The phrase "let us have grace" is a literal rendering which is taken usually to mean "have gratitude." But if the literal rendering is accurate, what the verse is saying is precisely, "Let's keep trusting in future grace which will give us the power to serve God." In that case it would not be a word about gratitude, but about faith in future grace. In either case this verse does not nullify the point we are making: neither the Old Testament nor the New treats gratitude as a prominent impulse for obedience. Faith in future grace is much more prominent. And what we will see at the end of this chapter is that the interplay of gratitude and faith makes gratitude the servant of faith in future grace.

COULD GRATITUDE NULLIFY GRACE?

It seems that gratitude is so vulnerable to misuse as a debtor's ethic that God has not ordained for it to function as a prominent motive in Christian living. This is a remarkable thing. And we can see more clearly why God would lead us in this way when we see what is at stake. If the impulses of gratitude slip over into the debtor's ethic, grace soon ceases to be grace. The effort to repay God, in the ordinary way we pay our creditors, would nullify grace and turn it into a business transaction. If we see acts of obedience as installment payments, we make grace into a mortgage.

Picture salvation as a house that you live in. It provides you with protection. It is stocked with food and drink that will last forever. It never decays or crumbles. Its windows open onto vistas of glory. God built it at great cost to himself and to his Son, and he gave it to you. The "purchase" agreement is called a "new covenant." The terms read: "This house shall become and remain yours if you will receive it as a gift and take delight in the Father and the Son as they inhabit the house with you. You shall not profane the house of God by sheltering other gods nor turn your heart away after other treasures." Would it not be foolish to say yes to this agreement, and then hire a lawyer to draw up an amortization schedule with monthly payments in the hopes of somehow balancing accounts. You would be treating the house no longer as a gift, but a purchase. God would no longer be the free benefactor. And you would be enslaved to a new set of demands that he never dreamed of putting on you. If grace is to be free—which is the very meaning of grace—we cannot view it as something to be repaid.

"O, TO GRACE HOW GREAT A DEBTOR"?

What does this mean for respected and loved hymns like Robert Robinson's Come Thou Fount? The last verse says,

> O to grace how great a debtor
> Daily I'm constrained to be!
> Let Thy goodness, like a fetter,
> Bind my wand'ring heart to Thee:
> Prone to wander, Lord, I feel it,
> Prone to leave the God I love;
> Here's my heart, O take and seal it;
> Seal it for Thy courts above.

I don't deny that we are debtors to God. Jesus taught us to pray, "Forgive us our debts" (Matthew 6:12), and he called people "debtors" because of their sins (Luke 13:4). In other words, when the Bible focuses on our being in debt to God it has reference to our sins that need to be forgiven, not our obedience that needs to be paid.

It would seem more appropriate to say that we are debtors to God's justice, not to his grace. That is, if we deal with him in payments of debt, he will deal with us in terms of justice: value for value (see Romans 4:4). We will not get very far in this transaction. That is why we plead for forgiveness of our debts instead of proposing a schedule of payments. To be more biblical, let us not say that grace *creates* debts; let us say that grace *pays* debts. As a more recent song says,

> O be ye glad, O be ye glad
> Ev'ry debt that you ever had
> Has been paid up in full by the grace of the Lord
> Be ye glad, be ye glad, be ye glad.[4]

I think Robinson uses the phrase "debtor to grace" very loosely to mean that everything he has is "owing" to grace. It all comes from grace. Therefore he is absolutely dependent on grace for everything now and forever. His "debt" does not imply a pattern of repayment, but an eternity of childlike dependence.

Perhaps Robinson might say—I hope he would say—the only debt you can pay to grace without nullifying grace is dependence on future grace. What honors never-ending, inexhaustible future grace is moment-by-moment "payments" (not a good word) of trust. I hope that's what Robinson was praying for when he wrote, "Bind my wandering heart to Thee...Seal it for Thy courts above." That is, keep me close to you and trusting you rather than wandering off in search of something more reliable and more satisfying.

NOT ALL GOD'S GLORY IS IN THE PAST

There's another problem with the debtor's ethic. It runs the risk of minimizing the glory of grace by its limited past-orientation. Gratitude looks back. This is not bad. The Bible commands us to remember the past grace of God: "Remember His wonders which He has done, His marvels, and the judgments uttered by His mouth" (Psalm 105:5). Vast stretches of God's grace and glory would be degraded if we forgot the past. It is the function of gratitude to call up this glory in worship.

WHEN GRATITUDE MALFUNCTIONS

But we do not live in the past. None of our potential obedience can happen in the past. All of our life will be lived in the future. Therefore when we try to make gratitude empower this future obedience, something goes wrong. Gratitude is primarily a response to the past grace of God; it malfunctions when forced to function as motivation for the future—unless it is transformed into faith in future grace.

There is a divine power for future obedience. But gratitude is not designed for carrying this high voltage current of future grace. Faith is. When gratitude is thrust into this role, what tends to happen is that a debtor's ethic emerges that tries to produce future obedience with the power of past grace. It won't work. It is past. So poor gratitude does the best it can, although out of its element: it appeals to the will to make returns to God for the past grace that it knows so well. Thus, inspired by past grace (but not empowered by future grace), the will tries to do good things for God in the power of gratitude—that is, in the power of remembered past grace. If faith in future grace does not come in to rescue gratitude at this point, the debtor's ethic takes over and subtle forms of religious self-reliance develop. We call them legalism.

The main problem here is that the past-orientation of the debtor's ethic tends to blind us to the infinite, never-ending, inexhaustible, uninterrupted flow of future grace from this moment to eternity. This grace is there in the future to be trusted and lived on. It is there to give the motivation and power for our obedience. This infinite overflow of God's grace is dishonored when we fail to appropriate it by faith in future grace. Gratitude is not designed for this. Faith is. Past grace is glorified by intense and joyful gratitude. Future grace is glorified by intense and joyful confidence. This faith is what frees us and empowers us for venturesome obedience in the cause of Christ.

THE DEBTOR'S ETHIC IS NOT NEW

As I was working on this chapter I happened to pull off the shelf a little book by Andrew Murray titled *Abide in Christ*. Murray was a Dutch Reformed pastor and writer who ministered in South Africa until his death in 1917.

A moment's inspection revealed that in his own day he shared a concern about the way the gratitude ethic limits our grasp of God's grace.

> *The idea [many Christians] have of grace is this: that their conversion and pardon are God's work, but that now, in gratitude to God, it is their work to live as Christians and follow Jesus... No, wandering one, as it was Jesus who drew thee when He spake "Come," so it is Jesus who keeps thee when He says "Abide." The [past] grace to come and the [future] grace to abide are alike from Him alone.*[5]

The act of the soul designed to receive the power of this grace and convey it into a new way of life is not gratitude, but faith in future grace. Thus Murray says, "By faith you became partakers of the initial grace; by that same faith you can enjoy the continuous grace of abiding in Him."[6] In this way we maximize the glory of grace. We glory in past grace through gratitude, and we bank our future, by faith, on the inexhaustible flow of future grace.

A TRIBUTE TO GRATITUDE

Gratitude is such a great and wonderful thing in Scripture that I feel constrained to end this chapter with a tribute. There are ways that gratitude helps bring about obedience to Christ. One way is that the spirit of gratitude is simply incompatible with some sinful attitudes. I think this is why Paul wrote, "There must be no filthiness and silly talk, or coarse jesting, which are not fitting, but rather *giving of thanks*" (Ephesians 5:4). Gratitude is a humble, happy response to the good will of someone who has done or tried to do you a favor. This humility and happiness cannot coexist in the heart with coarse, ugly, mean attitudes. Therefore the cultivation of a thankful heart leaves little room for such sins.

There is a sense in which gratitude and faith are interwoven joys that strengthen each other. As gratitude joyfully revels in the benefits of past grace, so faith joyfully relies on the benefits of future grace. Therefore when gratitude for God's past grace is strong, the message is sent that God is supremely trustworthy in the future because of what he has done in the past. In this way faith is strengthened by a lively gratitude for God's past trustworthiness.

On the other hand, when faith in God's future grace is strong, the message is sent that this kind of God makes no mistakes, so that everything he has done in the past is part of a good plan and can be remembered with gratitude. In this way gratitude is strengthened by a lively faith in God's future grace. Surely it is only the heart of faith in future grace that can follow the apostle Paul in "giving thanks for *all things* in the name of our Lord Jesus Christ" (Ephesians 5:20). Only if we trust God to turn past calamities into future comfort can we look back with gratitude for *all things*.

It seems to me that this interwovenness of future-oriented faith and past-oriented gratitude is what prevents gratitude from degenerating into the debtor's ethic. Gratitude for bygone grace is constantly saying to faith, "Be strong, and do not doubt that God will be as gracious in the future as I know he's been in the past." And faith in future grace is constantly saying to gratitude, "There is more grace to come, and all our obedience is to be done in reliance on that future grace. Relax and exult in your appointed feast. I will take responsibility for tomorrow's obedience."

Or, as Jesus would say, "O ye of little faith. Do not be anxious" (Matthew 6:30-31, KJV). Ponder for a few moments with me in the next chapter how faith in future grace purifies us from anxiety.

When I am afraid,

I put my trust in Thee.

PSALM 56:3 (RSV)

Cast all your anxieties on Him,

for He cares about you.

1 PETER 5:7, (RSV)

Do not be anxious then, saying,

"What shall we eat?" or

"What shall we drink?" or

"With what shall we clothe ourselves?"

For all these things the Gentiles eagerly seek;

for your heavenly Father knows that you need all these things.

MATTHEW 6:31-32

CHAPTER THREE

Applying the Purifying Power

Faith in Future Grace
vs.
Anxiety[1]

A PERSONAL TRIUMPH THROUGH FUTURE GRACE

When I was in junior and senior high school, I could not speak in front of a group. I became so nervous that my voice would completely choke up. It was not the common butterflies that most people deal with. It was a horrible and humiliating disability. It brought immense anxiety into my life. I could not give oral book reports in school. I couldn't run for any class offices at school, because I would have had to make campaign speeches. I could only give very short—several word—answers to the questions teachers would ask in class. In algebra class I was ashamed of how my hands shook when doing a problem on the blackboard. I couldn't lead out on the Sundays when our church gave the service over to the youth.

There were many tears. My mother struggled with me through it all, supporting me and encouraging me. We were sustained by God's grace, even though the "thorn" in my flesh was not removed. I managed to make it to college without any significant public speaking. But the battle with anxiety was intense. I knew that my life would be incredibly limited if there were no breakthrough. And I suspected that I would not be able to get through college without public speaking. In fact, Wheaton College required a speech class in those days. It loomed in front of me like a horrible concrete barricade.

In all these years, the grace of God had driven me deeper into God in desperation, rather than driving me away from God in anger. I thank God for that, with all my heart. Out of that maturing relationship came the sense that there just had to be a breakthrough.

One crucial opportunity came in Spanish class my freshman year. All of us had to give a short speech in Spanish in front of the rest of the class. There was no way around it. I felt like this was a make-or-break situation. Even as I write about it now, I don't laugh. I memorized the speech cold. I thought that memorizing would mean that I wouldn't have to look down at notes, and possibly lose my place, and have one of those horrible, paralyzing pauses. I also arranged to speak from behind a large tree-stump lectern that I could hold onto so that my shaking might be better controlled. But the main thing I did was cry out to God and lay hold on his promises of future grace. Even now the tears come to my eyes as I recall walking back and forth on Wheaton's front campus, pleading with God for a breakthrough in my life.

I don't remember those three moments of Spanish very clearly. I only remember that I made it through. Everyone knew I was nervous. There was that terrible silence that falls when people feel bad for you, and don't know how to respond. But they didn't snicker, as so many kids had done in previous years. And the teacher was kind with his comments. But the overwhelming thing was, I got through it. Later I poured out my thanks to God in the autumn sunshine. Even now I feel deep gratitude for the grace God gave me that day.

Perhaps the most decisive event of the breakthrough came over a year later. I was staying at college for summer school. Chaplain Evan Welch invited me to pray in the summer school chapel. Several hundred students and faculty would be present. My first reaction was immediate rejection of the idea. But before I could turn it down, something stopped me. I found myself asking, "How long does the prayer have to be?" He said it didn't matter. It should just be from my heart.

Now this I had never even tried—to speak to *God* in front of hundreds of people. I amazed myself by saying I would do it. This prayer, I believe, proved to be a decisive turning point in my life. For the first time, I made a vow to God. I said, "Lord, if you will bring me through this without letting my voice break, I will never again turn down a speaking opportunity for you out of anxiety." That was 1966. The Lord answered with precious grace again, and to my knowledge, I have kept my vow.

There is more to the story as one future grace has been lavished on another. I do not presume to understand fully all the purposes of God in his timing. I would not want to relive my high-school years. The anxiety, the humiliation and shame, were so common, as to cast a pall over all those years. Hundreds of prayers went up, and what came down was not what I wanted at the time—the grace to endure. My interpretation now, thirty years later, is that God was keeping me back from excessive vanity and worldliness. He was causing me to ponder weighty things in solitude, while many others were breezily slipping into superficial patterns of life.

The Bible my parents gave me when I was 15 is beside me right now on the table. It is well marked. The assurance of Matthew 6:32 is underlined in red: "Your heavenly father knoweth that ye have need of all these things" (KJV). Already in those early teen years I was struggling to live by faith in future grace. The victories were modest, it seems. But, O, how faithful and kind God has been.

THE ASSOCIATES OF ANXIETY

In the decades that have followed I have learned much more about the fight against anxiety. I have learned, for instance, that anxiety is a condition of the heart that gives rise to many other sinful states of mind. Think for a moment how many different sinful actions and attitudes come from anxiety. Anxiety about finances can give rise to coveting and greed and hoarding and stealing. Anxiety about succeeding at some task can make you irritable and abrupt and surly. Anxiety about relationships can make you withdrawn and indifferent and uncaring about other people. Anxiety about how someone will respond to you can make you cover over the truth and lie about things. So if anxiety could be conquered, a mortal blow would be struck to many other sins.

THE ROOT OF ANXIETY

I have also learned something about the root of anxiety and the ax that can sever it. One of the most important texts has been the one I underlined when I was 15—the whole section of Matthew 6:25-34. Four times in this passage Jesus says that his disciples should not be anxious. Verse 25: "For this reason I say to you, do not be anxious for your life." Verse 27: "And which of you by being anxious can add a single cubit to his life's span?" Verse 31: "Do not be anxious, saying, 'What shall we eat?'" Verse 34: "Therefore do not be anxious for tomorrow."

Anxiety is clearly the theme of this text. It makes the *root* of anxiety explicit in verse 30: "But if God so arrays the grass of the field, which is alive today and tomorrow is thrown into the furnace, will He not much more do so for you, O men of little *faith?*" In other words, Jesus says that the root of anxiety is inadequate faith in our Father's future grace. As unbelief gets the upper hand in our hearts, one of the effects is anxiety. The root cause of anxiety is a failure to trust all that God has promised to be for us in Jesus.

I can think of two kinds of disturbed responses to this truth. Let me tell you what they are and then give a biblical response to each of them, before we look more closely at the battle against the unbelief of anxiety.

IS THIS GOOD NEWS?

One response would go like this: "This is not good news! In fact, it is very discouraging to learn that what I thought was a mere struggle with an anxious disposition is rather a far deeper struggle with whether I trust God." My response to this is to agree, but then to disagree. Suppose you had been having pain in your stomach and had been struggling with medicines and diets of all kinds, to no avail. And then suppose that your doctor tells you, after a routine visit, that you have cancer in your small intestine. Would that be good news? You say, emphatically not! And I agree.

But let me ask the question another way: Are you glad the doctor discovered the cancer while it is still treatable, and that indeed it can be very successfully treated? You say, yes, I am very glad that the doctor found the real problem. Again I agree. So the news that you have cancer is not good news. But, in another sense, it is good news, because knowing what is really wrong is good, especially when your problem can be treated successfully.

That's what it's like to learn that the real problem behind anxiety is unbelief in the promises of God's future grace. In a sense it's not good news, because the unbelief is a very serious cancer. But in another sense it is good news because knowing what is really wrong is good, especially because unbelief can be treated so successfully by our Great Physician. He is able to work in wonderfully healing ways when we cry out, "I do believe! Help my unbelief!" (Mark 9:24).

So I want to stress that finding out the connection between our anxiety and our unbelief is, in fact, very good news, because it is the only way to focus our fight on the real cause of our sin and get the victory that God can give us by the therapy of his Word and his Spirit. When Paul said, "Fight the *good* fight of faith," (1 Timothy 6:12), he called it *good* because the fight is focused on exactly the right cancer: unbelief.

HOW CAN I HAVE ANY ASSURANCE AT ALL?

There is another possible response to the truth that our anxiety is rooted in our failure to live by faith in future grace. It goes like this: "I have to deal with feelings of anxiety almost every day; and so I feel like my faith in God's grace must be totally inadequate. So I wonder if I can have any assurance of being saved at all."

My response to this concern is a little different. Suppose you are in a car race and your enemy, who doesn't want you to finish the race, throws mud on your windshield. The fact that you temporarily lose sight of your goal and start to swerve, does not mean that you are going to quit the race. And it certainly doesn't mean that you are on the wrong race track. Otherwise the enemy wouldn't bother you at all. What it means is that you should turn on your windshield wipers and use your windshield washer.

When anxiety strikes and blurs our vision of God's glory and the greatness of the future that he plans for us, this does not mean that we are faithless, or that we will not make it to heaven. It means our faith is being attacked. At first blow, our belief in God's promises may sputter and swerve. But whether we stay on track and make it to the finish line depends on whether, by grace, we set in motion a process of resistance—whether we fight back against the unbelief of anxiety. Will we turn on the windshield wipers and will we use our windshield washer?

Psalm 56:3 (RSV) says, "When I am afraid, I put my trust in thee." Notice: it does not say, "I never struggle with fear." Fear strikes, and the battle begins. So the Bible does not assume that true believers will have no anxieties. Instead the Bible tells us how to fight when they strike. For example, 1 Peter 5:7 (RSV) says, "Cast all your anxieties on Him, for He cares about you." It does *not* say, you will never feel any anxieties. It says, when you have them, cast them on God. When the mud splatters your windshield and you temporarily lose sight of the road and start to swerve in anxiety, turn on your wipers and squirt your windshield washer.

So my response to the person who has to deal with feelings of anxiety every day is to say: that's more or less normal. At least it is for me, ever since my teenage years. The issue is: How do we fight them?

THE TWO GREAT FAITH BUILDERS

The answer to that question is: we fight anxieties by fighting *against* unbelief and fighting *for* faith in future grace. And the way you fight this "good fight" is by meditating on God's assurances of future grace and by asking for the help of his Spirit. The windshield wipers are the promises of God that clear away the mud of unbelief, and the windshield washer fluid is the help of the Holy Spirit. The battle to be freed from sin, as we have seen, is "by the *Spirit* and *faith* in the truth" (2 Thessalonians 2:13). The work of the Spirit and the Word of truth. These are the great faith-builders.

Without the softening work of the Holy Spirit, the wipers of the Word just scrape over the blinding clumps of unbelief. Both are necessary—the Spirit and the Word. We read the promises of God and we pray for the help of his Spirit. And as the windshield clears so that we can see the welfare that God plans for us (Jeremiah 29:11), our faith grows stronger and the swerving of anxiety smooths out.

SEVEN PROMISES OF FUTURE GRACE AGAINST ANXIETY

How does this actually work in practice? Here in Matthew 6 we have the example of anxiety about food and clothing. Even in America, with its extensive welfare system, anxiety over finances and housing can be intense. But Jesus says in verse 30 that this stems from inadequate faith in our Father's promise of future grace: "O men of *little faith.*" And so this paragraph has at least seven promises designed by Jesus to help us fight the good fight against unbelief and be free from anxiety.

PROMISE #1:

> For this reason I say to you, do not be anxious for your life, as to what you shall eat, or what you shall drink; nor for your body, as to what you shall put on. Is not life more than food, and the body more than clothing? (Matthew 6:25)

Since your body and your life are vastly more complex and difficult to provide, than food and clothing are, and yet God has, in fact, created and provided you with both, then surely he will be able and willing to provide you with food and clothing. Moreover, no matter what happens God will raise your body some day and preserve your life for his eternal fellowship.

PROMISE #2:

> Look at the birds of the air, that they do not sow, neither do they reap, nor gather into barns, and yet your heavenly Father feeds them. Are you not worth much more than they? (Matthew 6:26)

If God is willing and able to feed such insignificant creatures as birds who cannot do anything to bring their food into being—as you can by farming—then he will certainly provide what you need, because you are worth a lot more than birds.

PROMISE #3:

> And which of you by being anxious can add a single cubit to his life's span? And why are you anxious about clothing? (Matthew 6:27-28)

This is a promise of sorts—the simple promise of reality: anxiety will not do you any good. It's not the main argument, but sometimes we just have to get tough with ourselves and say, "Soul, this fretting is absolutely useless. You are not only messing up your own day, but a lot of other people's as well. Leave it with God and get on with your work." Anxiety accomplishes nothing worthwhile.

PROMISE #4:

> *Observe how the lilies of the field grow; they do not toil nor do they spin,*
> *yet I say to you that even Solomon in all his glory did not clothe himself*
> *like one of these. But if God so arrays the grass of the field, which is alive*
> *today and tomorrow is thrown into the furnace, will He not much more*
> *do so for you, O men of little faith?* (Matthew 6:28-30)

Compared to the flowers of the field you are a much higher priority for God, because you will live forever, and can thus bring him eternal praise. Nevertheless, God has such an overflow of creative energy and care, he lavishes it on flowers that last only a matter of days. So he will certainly take that same energy and creative skill and use it to care for his children who will live forever.

PROMISE #5:

> *Do not be anxious then, saying, "What shall we eat?" or "What shall we*
> *drink?" or "With what shall we clothe ourselves?" For all these things*
> *the Gentiles eagerly seek; for your heavenly Father knows that you need*
> *all these things.* (Matthew 6:31-32)

Do not think that God is ignorant of your needs. He knows all of them. And he is your "heavenly Father." He does not look on, indifferently, from a distance. He cares. He will act to supply your need when the time is best.

PROMISE #6:

> *But seek first His kingdom and His righteousness; and all these things*
> *shall be added to you.* (Matthew 6:33)

If you will give yourself to his cause in the world, rather than fretting about your private material needs, he will make sure that you have all you need to do his will and give him glory. This is similar to the promise of Romans 8:32, "Will [God] not also with [Christ] freely give us all things?" (For an explanation of what "all things" means, see Chapter Eight.)

PROMISE #7:

Therefore do not be anxious for tomorrow; for tomorrow will care for itself. Each day has enough trouble of its own. (Matthew 6:34)

God will see to it that you are not tested in any given day more than you can bear (1 Corinthians 10:13). He will work for you, so that "as [your] days, so shall [your] strength be" (Deuteronomy 33:25, KJV). Every day will have no more trouble than you can bear; and every day will have mercies sufficient for that day's stress (Lamentations 3:22-23).

"MY GOD WILL SUPPLY ALL YOUR NEEDS"

Paul learned these lessons from Jesus and applied them to the battle against anxiety in the church at Philippi. In Philippians 4:6 he said, "Be anxious for nothing, but in everything by prayer and supplication with thanksgiving let your requests be made known to God." And then in verse 19 he gives the liberating promise of future grace, just as Jesus did: "My God shall supply all your needs according to his riches in glory in Christ Jesus." If we live by faith in this promise of future grace, it will be very hard for anxiety to survive. God's "riches in glory" are inexhaustible. He really means for us not to worry about our future.

WHEN I AM ANXIOUS

We should follow the pattern of Jesus and Paul. We should battle the unbelief of anxiety with the promises of future grace. When I am anxious about some risky new venture or meeting, I battle unbelief with one of my most often-used promises, Isaiah 41:10. The day I left for three years in Germany my father called me long distance and gave me this promise on the telephone. For three years I must have quoted it to myself five hundred times to get me through periods of tremendous stress. "Fear not for I am with you, be not dismayed for I am your God, I will strengthen you, I will help you, I will uphold you, with My victorious right hand" (Isaiah 41:10, RSV). When the motor of my mind is in neutral, the hum of the gears is the sound of Isaiah 41:10.

When I am anxious about my ministry being useless and empty, I fight unbelief with the promise of Isaiah 55:11. "So shall My word be which goes forth from My mouth; it shall not return to Me empty, without accomplishing what I desire, and without succeeding in the matter for which I sent it."

When I am anxious about being too weak to do my work, I battle unbelief with the promise of Christ, "My grace is sufficient for you, for power is perfected in weakness" (2 Corinthians 12:9).

When I am anxious about decisions I have to make about the future, I battle unbelief with the promise, "I will instruct you and teach you in the way which you should go; I will counsel you with My eye upon you" (Psalm 32:8).

When I am anxious about facing opponents, I battle unbelief with the promise, "If God is for us, who is against us!" (Romans 8:31).

When I am anxious about the welfare of those I love, I battle unbelief with the promise that if I, being evil, know how to give good things to my children, how much more will the "Father who is in heaven give what is good to those who ask Him!" (Matthew 7:11). And I fight to maintain my spiritual equilibrium with the reminder that everyone who has left house or brothers or sisters or mother or father or children or farms, for Christ's sake "shall receive a hundred times as much now in the present age, houses and brothers and sisters and mothers and children and farms, along with persecutions; and in the age to come, eternal life" (Mark 10:29-30).

When I am anxious about being sick, I battle unbelief with the promise, "Many are the afflictions of the righteous but the Lord delivers him out of them all" (Psalm 34:19). And I take the promise with trembling: "Tribulation brings about perseverance; and perseverance, proven character; and proven character, hope; and hope does not disappoint, because the love of

God has been poured out within our hearts through the Holy Spirit who was given to us" (Romans 5:3-5).

When I am anxious about getting old, I battle unbelief with the promise, "Even to your old age, I shall be the same, and even to your graying years I shall bear you! I have done it, and I shall carry you; and I shall bear you, and I shall deliver you" (Isaiah 46:4).

When I am anxious about dying, I battle unbelief with the promise that "not one of us lives for himself and not one of us dies for himself; for if we live, we live for the Lord, or if we die, we die for the Lord; therefore whether we live or die, we are the Lord's. For to this end Christ died and lived again that He might be Lord both of the dead and of the living" (Romans 14:7-9).

When I am anxious that I may make shipwreck of faith and fall away from God, I battle unbelief with the promises, "He who began a good work in you will perfect it until the day of Christ" (Philippians 1:6); and, "He is able to save forever those who draw near to God through Him, since He always lives to make intercession for them" (Hebrews 7:25).

This is the way of life that I am still learning as I approach my fiftieth year. I am writing this book in the hopes, and with the prayer, that you will join me. Let us make war, not with other people, but with our own unbelief. It is the root of anxiety, which, in turn, is the root of so many other sins. So let us turn on our windshield wipers and use the washer fluid, and keep our eyes fixed on the precious and very great promises of God. Take up the Bible, ask the Holy Spirit for help, lay the promises up in your heart, and fight the good fight—to *live by faith in future grace.*

PART II

FREE AND
FUTURE GRACE

The life which I now live in the flesh
I live by faith in the Son of God.

GALATIANS 2 : 20

My hope for future goodness and future glory
is future grace.

Grace be with you.

ALL OF ST. PAUL'S LETTERS

CHAPTER FOUR

The Life
That's Left
Is Future Grace

The only life I have left to live is future life. The past is not in my hands to offer or alter. It is gone. Not even God will change the past. All the expectations of God are future expectations. All the possibilities of faith and love are future possibilities. And all the power that touches me with help to live in love is future power. As precious as the bygone blessings of God may be, if he leaves me only with the memory of those, and not with the promise of more, I will be undone. My hope for future goodness and future glory is future grace.

But does the New Testament really make that much of future grace? Is it true that the life we have left to live—from now to eternity—will be lived by future grace, or will be lost?

LETTERS ENCOMPASSED WITH FUTURE GRACE

Let's start with a simple and remarkable observation. Without exception the apostle Paul begins and ends each of his thirteen New Testament letters by blessing his Christian readers with future grace.[1] What he usually says at the beginning of his letters is, *"Grace* to you and peace from God our Father, and the Lord Jesus Christ." At the end he usually says something like, "The *grace* of the Lord Jesus be with you."

Nothing else in Paul's letters comes close to this kind of unbroken focus on future grace at the beginning and ending of every letter. The blessing of "peace" comes close. It's there alongside grace at the beginning of every letter. But it falls away from every blessing at the end of all the letters.[2] Future grace alone stands at the beginning *and* the ending of every letter.

What is Paul doing when he begins and ends his letters with words like these? He is blessing his readers, including us! A biblical blessing happens when we say something like, "May God bless you with grace." That's what Paul is saying at the beginning and ending of his letters, even though he doesn't use the word "bless".

Blessings are peculiar. They focus on the persons spoken to ("Grace to you"). But they also appeal to God to do something ("Grace to you *from God* our Father"). The person who blesses takes a position between God and others, and makes his words a conduit of blessing between the two. Blessings are not quite the same as prayers, because the person addressed is not God but other people. You look them in the eye, as it were, and say, "Grace be to you." There is however a prayer-like quality, because implicit in the blessing is the appeal, "O God, make these very words of mine a means of grace from you."

There is another remarkable thing about these blessings of future grace. Without exception the blessings *at the beginning* of Paul's letters say "Grace [be] *to* you," while the blessings *at the end* of the letters say, "Grace [be] *with* you."[3] This is so consistent through thirteen letters that it must mean something.

The meaning I would suggest is this: at the beginning of his letters Paul has in mind that the letter itself is a channel of God's grace *to* the readers. Grace is about to flow "from God" through Paul's writing *to* the Christians. So he says, "Grace *to* you." That is, grace is now active and is about to flow from God through my inspired writing *to* you as you read—"grace [be] *to* you."

But as the end of the letter approaches, Paul realizes that the reading is almost finished and the question rises, "What becomes of the grace that has been flowing to the readers through the reading of the inspired letter?" He answers with a blessing at the end of every letter: "Grace [be] *with* you." *With* you as you put the letter away and leave the church. *With* you as you go home to deal with a sick child and an unaffectionate spouse. *With* you as you go to work and face the temptations of anger and dishonesty and lust. *With* you as you muster courage to speak up for Christ over lunch.

What then do we learn from Paul's unbroken pattern of beginning and ending his letters in this way ("Grace be *to* you." "Grace be *with* you.")? We learn that grace is an unmistakable priority in the Christian life. We learn that it is from God the Father and the Lord Jesus Christ, but that it can come through people. We learn that grace is ready to flow *to* us every time we take up the inspired Scriptures to read them. And we learn that grace will abide *with* us when we lay the Bible down and go about our daily living.

In other words, we learn that grace is not merely a past reality but a *future* one. Every time I reach for the Bible, God's grace is a reality that *will* flow to me. Every time I put the Bible down and go about my business, God's grace *will* go with me. This is what I mean by *future grace*.

EVERY STEP BY FUTURE GRACE

The reason future grace is so important is that everything in the Christian life depends on it. You can't be a Christian without faith in future grace. Jesus said, "The way is narrow that leads to life, and few are those who find it" (Matthew 7:14). Every turn in that narrow way is planned by future grace and empowered by future grace. At every point on the way, true saints sing, "'Tis grace has brought me safe thus far, and grace will lead me home." Every glance backward sparks gratitude for bygone grace; every look forward casts the soul onto faith in future grace.

When Paul ends every letter with the words "Grace be with you," he is blessing the believers with what they will need to be Christians from that moment on—future grace. No one became a Christian without past grace. And no one can be a Christian moment by moment without future grace. Our standing as Christians is as secure as God's supply of future grace. Consider some of the things that hang on this supply.

FUTURE GRACE FOR WEARY SAINTS

Again and again the Christian heart grows weak and begins to falter. Where will we find strength of heart? I don't mean physical strength. God doesn't demand physical strength, or health, or even life for that matter. But he does call us to be "strengthened…in the inner man" (Ephesians 3:16). How does this happen? One answer is very plain: "It is good for the heart to be *strengthened by grace,* not by foods" (Hebrews 13:9). The heart is strengthened *by grace. "Be strong in the grace* that is in Christ Jesus" (2 Timothy 2:1). Daily grace is to the heart what daily bread is to the body. It gives strength. Without it we can't live and we can't work.

Someone might ask, "But doesn't Ephesians 3:16 itself say that the strength of the 'inner man' comes with power *through his Spirit?"* Yes it does. And we will see in just a moment that those words are almost a perfect definition of future grace. The Holy Spirit is called "the Spirit of grace" (Hebrews 10:29) and the power he brings, as we will see, is the power of grace.

FUTURE GRACE FOR SUFFERING SAINTS

The need for this inner strength arises not just from the depletions of everyday stress, but from the suffering and afflictions that come from time to time. And they do come. "Through many tribulations we must enter the kingdom of God" (Acts 14:22; cf. 1 Thessalonians 3:4; 2 Timothy 3:12). Suffering is inevitably added to heart-weariness on the way to heaven. When it comes, the heart wavers and the narrow way that leads to life looks impossibly hard. It's hard enough to have a narrow road and tiring hills that test the jalopy's strength to the limit. But what shall we do when the car breaks down?

Paul cried out three times with this question because of some affliction in his life. But future grace did not come in the form he asked. It came in another form. Christ answered, "My *grace* is sufficient for you, for power is perfected in weakness." Here we see grace given in the form of Christ's sustaining power in unrelieved affliction—one grace given in the circle of another grace denied. And Paul responded with faith in the sufficiency of this future grace: "Most gladly, therefore, I will rather boast about my weaknesses, that the power of Christ may dwell in me" (2 Corinthians 12:9).

God often blesses us with a "grace given" in the circle of "grace denied." For example, on a beastly hot day in July the water pump on our car stopped working and twenty miles from any town we were stranded on the Interstate in Tennessee. I had prayed that morning that the car would work well and that we would come to our destination in safety. No one was stopping as we stood around our car. Then my son Abraham (about eleven at the time) said, "Daddy, we should pray." So we bowed behind the car and asked God for some future grace—a help in time of need. When we looked up, a pickup truck had pulled over. The driver was a mechanic who worked about twenty miles away. He said he would be willing to go get the parts and come back and fix the car. I rode with him to town and was able to share the gospel with him. We were on our way in about five hours.

Now the remarkable thing about that answer to our prayer is that it came inside the circle of a prayer denied. We asked for a trouble-free trip. God gave us trouble. But in the midst of a grace denied we got a grace supplied. And I am learning to trust God's wisdom in giving the grace that is best for me and for unbelieving mechanics and for the faith of eleven-year-old boys. We should not be surprised that God gives us wonderful graces in the midst of suffering that we had asked him to spare us. He knows best how to apportion his grace for our good and for his glory.

THE POWER OF THE SPIRIT AND THE WORKING OF GRACE

I said above that the heart-strengthening power that comes from the Holy Spirit (Ephesians 3:16) is virtually the same as what I mean by future grace. What we have just seen in 2 Corinthians 12 is the evidence of this. Christ said, "My *grace* is sufficient for you." Then he added by way of explanation that "*[his] power* is perfected in weakness." So Christ's *power,* acting to sustain and strengthen believers, is also his grace. And since "the Lord is the Spirit" (2 Corinthians 3:17), it is not wrong to say that the power of the Spirit is also the working of the Lord's grace.

We cannot survive as Christians if we do not find strength to endure affliction. God's answer to this necessity on the narrow road is future grace. And future grace is the power of Christ perfected in our weakness. Make sure you don't miss the point here. The grace for endurance—even glad boasting in weakness—is not primarily looking back to bygone grace. It is looking forward to the next moment's and next month's arrival of the power of Christ to do for us what we absolutely despair of doing ourselves. This is future grace.

FUTURE GRACE AND THE CALL TO ENDURE

Sometimes in the midst of these afflictions and ordinary stresses of daily life we may cry out, "How long, O Lord? I can't see beyond today's pain. What will tomorrow bring? Will you be there for that affliction too?" This question is utterly urgent, because Jesus said, "The one who endures to the end, he shall be saved" (Mark 13:13). We tremble at the thought of being among "those who shrink back to destruction" (Hebrews 10:39). We are not playing games. Suffering is a horrible threat to faith in future grace.

Therefore it is a wonderful thing to hear Peter promise the afflicted and weary Christians, "After you have suffered for a little while, the *God of all grace,* who called you to His eternal glory in Christ, will Himself perfect, confirm, strengthen and establish you" (1 Peter 5:10). The assurance that he will not delay beyond what we can endure and that he will abolish the flaws we bemoan and that he will establish forever what has tottered so long —that assurance comes from "all grace." God is not the God of *some* grace —like bygone grace. He is the God of "all grace"—including the infinite, inexhaustible stores of *future* grace. Faith in that grace is the key to enduring on the narrow and hard way that leads to life.

FUTURE GRACE AND THE LIFE OF LOVE

But endurance is not the best word to describe the Christian life. That's part of it. But the way that leads to life is a way of love, not just endurance— love for other people. This too is a matter of tremendous urgency since Jesus said, "By this will all men know that you are My disciples, if you have love for one another" (John 13:35). And John said, "We know that we have passed out of death into life, because we love the brethren" (1 John 3:14). We may not achieve perfection in this life, but we *must* change direction. The way that leads to life is the way of love.

How shall we live a life of love—love for people we don't know, and even for our enemies? There is a real-life illustration that answers this question. Paul had gone through Macedonia planting churches in Philippi and

Thessalonica and Berea. In the process he was also teaching the new churches to care for the poor—to love them. Part of his plan was to have the churches make contributions for the poor Christians in the mother church in Jerusalem. What happened as he did this was so astonishing that he used it as an example when he wrote to the church in Corinth to inspire them to give as the Macedonian churches had done. Here's what he wrote to them. Watch for the power of future grace.

> *Now, brethren, we wish to make known to you the* grace of God *which has been given in the churches of Macedonia, that in a great ordeal of affliction their abundance of joy and their deep poverty overflowed in the wealth of their liberality. For I testify that according to their ability, and beyond their ability they gave of their own accord, begging us with much entreaty for the favor of participation in the support of the saints.* (2 Corinthians 8:1-4)

This response of the Macedonians took Paul's breath away. What makes it so spectacular is that their poverty was not taken away when they became Christians: their deep poverty overflowed in liberality (v. 2). In fact it seems that becoming Christians had made their lives not easier, but harder: their generosity flowed out of a great ordeal of affliction (v. 2). Nevertheless there was a wealth of liberality (v. 2). They gave "beyond their ability" (v. 3). They gave "of their own accord" (v. 3). And they even begged for "the *favor* of participation in the support of the saints" (v. 4). The word "favor" in that sentence is "grace." Keep that in mind for a moment.

How did such countercultural and counter-natural behavior come about? How were the Christians freed from the natural love of money and comfort? Part of the answer in verse 2 is that their abundance of joy overflowed. Joy in something else had severed the root of joy in money. They had been freed by joy to give to the poor. But where did this powerful, unearthly joy come from?

The answer is that it came from the *grace of God.* Paul's explanation of this incredible love was *"the grace of God* which has been given in the churches of Macedonia" (v. 1). What the Corinthians are supposed to learn from this story is that the same grace that was given in Macedonia is available now in Corinth. Paul is saying in effect that the key to this kind of joyful, sacrificial generosity is faith in future grace. When you trust in future grace the way the Macedonians did, your life becomes a grace. Paul calls their giving a *"grace* of participation in the support of the saints" (v. 4).

We know that faith in future grace is the key because later on in this section of 2 Corinthians Paul holds out this wonderful promise: "God is able to make *all grace* abound to you, that always having all sufficiency in every-thing, you may have an abundance for every good deed" (2 Corinthians 9:8). In other words, if you want to be free from the need to stash away your money—if you want to overflow with an abundance (of grace!) for every good work (like the poor in Jerusalem)—then put your faith in future grace. Trust the promise that "God is able to make all grace abound to you" in every future moment for this very purpose.

Again, don't miss the point. The key to love and generosity is not pri-marily looking back on bygone grace and how much God has done for you —as precious and indispensable as that is. The key is to turn from the glory and guarantee of bygone grace and put your faith firmly in future grace— that "God is able (in the future) to make all (future) grace abound to you," so that your needs are met and so that you will be able, like the amazing Macedonians, to overflow with the love of liberality. Freedom from greed comes from faith in future grace.

EVERY FUTURE GOOD FROM FUTURE GRACE

What we have seen is that the New Testament really does make much of future grace. The life that's left for us to live from now to eternity will be lived by future grace, or will be lost. We are not left to ourselves, nor even to the precious memories of bygone grace. We are not left at all. Today and tomorrow and for the rest of eternity "He gives a greater grace" (James. 4:6). This is not decoration on the permanent structure of the Christian life. It is what makes the Christian life permanent. We live moment by moment from the strength of future grace. If it were not there, we would perish. But it is there. And every future good that we enjoy, in this life and the next, will come from future grace.

I will be gracious to whom I will be gracious,
and will show compassion on whom I will show compassion.

EXODUS 33:19

But if it is by grace,
it is no longer on the basis of works,
otherwise grace is no longer grace.

ROMANS 11:6

Grace would not be grace
if it were a response to resources in us.
Grace is grace because it highlights
God's own overflowing resources of kindness.
Grace is eternal because it will take that long for God
to expend inexhaustible stores of goodness on us.
Grace is free because God would not be
the infinite, self-sufficient God he is
if he were constrained by
anything outside himself.

CHAPTER FIVE

The Freest
of All
God's Acts

I f God were not a self-replenishing, all-sufficient, everlasting fountain of future grace, there would be no hope for sinners. If God has been gracious only in the past, but will not be in the future, Christians are of all people most to be pitied. Our life hangs on future grace. Understanding this and living in the freedom and power of it is what I hope this book advances.

So we must ask again, *What is future grace?* We have seen that it is grace that carries me from this moment on. It is one millisecond away and ten billion ages of ages away. All of God's goodness and power that will be exerted for me before I finish this sentence, and all the goodness and power that will sustain me beyond the grave forever is future grace. But now we ask, more precisely, what makes grace grace? Granted that it is there for us in the future, and granted that it is the strength to live by (1 Corinthians 15:10)— what is it?

DEFINING GRACE AND MERCY

Common definitions of God's grace and mercy go like this: *grace* is the goodness of God shown to people who don't deserve it; *mercy* is the goodness of God shown to people who are in a miserable plight.[1] These definitions help us see that although grace and mercy are different, they also overlap in meaning.

GRACE BEFORE THE FALL

Before sin entered the world, Adam and Eve experienced God's goodness not as a response to their demerit (since they didn't have any) but still without deserving God's goodness. You can't deserve to be created. You can't deserve, as a non-being, to be put into a lavish garden where all your needs are met by a loving Father. So even before they sinned, Adam and Eve lived on grace. And God's will for them was that they live by faith in future grace —God's daily, fatherly care and provision. This is important because it is customary among some theologians to give the erroneous impression that God wanted Adam and Eve to relate to him in terms of meritorious works rather than childlike faith.

In Genesis 2:16-17, "The Lord God commanded the man, saying, 'From any tree of the garden you may eat freely; but from the tree of the knowledge of good and evil you shall not eat, for in the day that you eat from it you shall surely die.'" I think John Sailhamer is right when he says that the point of these verses is

> that God alone knows what is good for human beings and God alone knows what is not good for them. To enjoy the "good" we must trust God and obey him. If we disobey, we will have to decide for ourselves what is good and what is not good. While to modern men and women such a prospect may seem desirable, to the author of Genesis it is the worst fate that could have befallen humanity.[2]

In other words, not eating of the tree of the knowledge of good and evil was meant by God to be an act of trust in his gracious wisdom and his readiness to lead Adam and Eve in what is good and to meet all their needs. "The snake speaks only twice, but that is enough to offset the balance of trust and obedience between the man and the woman and their Creator."[3] Their disobedience was a breach of trust in their Father's love and a forsaking of faith in his future grace.

EVERY ACT OF GRACE AN ACT OF MERCY

Since sin entered the world the experience of grace has been different for all of us. Adam and Eve did not deserve grace, but their lack of desert was not yet accompanied by misery. Now that sin has entered the world, however, everyone who does not deserve God's goodness is also in a miserable plight. "The wages of sin is *death*" (Romans 6:23).

Since sin always brings misery, and misery is always experienced by sinners, therefore all of God's acts of grace are also acts of mercy, and all his acts of mercy are also acts of grace. Every act of *grace* shown to a person because he is a sinner is also an act of *mercy* because his sin brings misery. And every act of *mercy* shown to a person because of his miserable plight is also an act of *grace* because he doesn't deserve it. It never makes sense to say that sometimes God shows us mercy and sometimes he shows us grace. Whenever he shows one he is showing the other. The difference is whether the act of goodness is viewed in relation to our sin or in relation to our misery.

In a courtroom you might look at the same act of acquittal from two angles. From behind the judge you might see his black robe and huge bench and all the papers with convicting evidence spread out before him. This would make the acquittal look like an amazing act of *grace*. Sin and justice call for conviction, not acquittal. But if you moved around to the front of the bench and saw the tears in the judge's eyes and noticed the utterly miserable plight of the criminal, this would make the acquittal look like an act of *mercy*. The act of goodness is one act, not two. What changes is the angle from which we view it.

The fact that all God's acts of mercy are also acts of grace probably has resulted in a partial merging of their meanings in the Bible. The common distinction I have described does not seem to be carried through totally in Scripture. For example, contrary to our definitions, people sometimes cry out to God for *grace* because they are *sufferers* (for example, Psalm 6:2); and people sometimes receive *mercy* because they are guilty *sinners* (for example, 1 Timothy 1:13; Romans 11:32). But in general the distinction is evident in the Bible and helps us grasp the largeness of God's heart.[4]

GRACE LOOKS MORE FREE THAN MERCY

This distinction between grace (toward the one who sins) and mercy (toward the one who suffers) implies another helpful distinction. Mercy, by its very nature, does not seem as free as grace. When we show mercy, it looks as if we are responding to pain and being constrained by a painful condition outside ourselves. It is a beautiful constraint. But it does not seem to be as free as grace. Grace, however, contemplates the ugliness of sin, and, contrary to all expectation, acts beneficently. This looks more free. Pain seems to constrain mercy, but guilt does not seem to constrain grace. Grace looks more free.

I don't mean that God's mercy is in fact less free than his grace. No one deserves God's mercy. And God is not bound to be merciful to any of his creatures. What I do mean is that "freeness" lies closer at the heart of the meaning of grace. Grace, by definition, is free and unconstrained. It even lacks the *seeming* constraint of naturalness that exists between suffering and mercy. If God's grace is "natural" in response to sin, it is owing entirely to something amazing in God, not in the constraining power of sin. Suffering constrains pity; but sin kindles anger. Therefore grace toward sinners is the freest of all God's acts.

FREE, UNMERITED, CONDITIONAL GRACE

However, *free* doesn't always mean unconditional. Many of God's acts of grace are conditional. For example, when Paul says, "Grace be with all those who love our Lord Jesus Christ with a love incorruptible" (Ephesians 6:24), he means that there is a grace that comes to those who love Jesus, but does not come to those who don't. This grace is conditional. And when James says, "[God] gives a greater grace…God is opposed to the proud, but gives grace to the humble" (James. 4:6), he means that there is a grace that comes to those who are humble, but does not come to the proud.

But conditional grace is not earned grace. It is not merited. "Earned grace" is an oxymoron. Grace cannot be earned. The very meaning of grace is that the one receiving the grace does not deserve it—has not earned it. If a philanthropist pays $80,000 for your college education on the condition that you graduate from high school, you have not earned the gift, but you have met a condition. It is possible to meet a condition for receiving grace and yet not earn the grace. Conditional grace does not mean earned grace. How can this be?[5]

The part of the answer that needs to be said here is that when God's grace is promised based on a condition, that condition is also a work of God's grace. This guarantees the absolute freeness of grace. The philanthropist mentioned above may even become the personal tutor for a failing high school student to insure that he does get his diploma and so meets the condition for the $80,000 grant. A biblical example would be that repentance is the condition we must meet in order to receive the grace of forgiveness. "Repent therefore and return that your sins may be wiped away" (Acts 3:19). But repentance itself is a gift of God's grace. "God has *granted* to the Gentiles also the repentance that leads to life" (Acts 11:18; see also 5:31). "God may *grant* them repentance leading to a knowledge of the truth" (2 Timothy 2:25). John Calvin quotes Augustine in this regard: "Man's good will precedes many of God's gifts, but not all. The very will that precedes is itself among these gifts."[6] God's freedom is not reduced when he makes some of his graces depend on conditions that he himself freely supplies. Grace responding to grace is still grace.

Freedom is at the heart of the meaning of biblical grace. This freedom is emphasized in at least four ways.

TO BE GOD IS TO BE FREE

First, when God reveals himself to Moses he virtually defines himself as an absolutely free giver of grace. In Exodus 33:18 Moses says to God, "I pray Thee, show me Thy glory!" God's first response to this prayer is to give Moses a verbal revelation instead of a visual one. He says in effect, Here is my glory: "*I will be gracious to whom I will be gracious,* and will show compassion on whom I will show compassion" (Exodus 33:19).[7]

When God says, "I will be gracious to whom I will be gracious," he means: I am free in showing grace. If you ask, "Who are those to whom you show grace?" the answer is: "Those on whom I show grace." In other words, God does not look outside his own will for an impulse to move his grace. Ultimately grace is not constrained by anything outside God himself.

Soon after I finished graduate school in 1974 I devoted about seven years to studying the freedom of God's grace, preparing to write a book on Romans 9, where this Old Testament text is quoted in verse 15: "For [God] says to Moses, 'I will have mercy on whom I have mercy, and I will have compassion on whom I have compassion.'" I tried to be fair to all the differing views and to give all the necessary evidence for my conclusions. One of the most important conclusions goes like this: "[Exodus 33:19] is a solemn declaration of *the nature of God*, or (which is the same thing) a proclamation of his *name and glory*... It is the glory of God and his essential nature mainly to dispense mercy on whomever he pleases apart from any constraint originating outside his own will. This is the essence of what it means to be God. This is his name."[8]

So right at the center of God's self-revelation is the declaration that he is free in the way he dispenses his grace. And this freedom belongs to the very essence of what it means to be God. God is gracious to whom he will be gracious. He is not limited by anyone's wickedness. He is never trapped by his own wrath. His grace may break out anywhere he pleases. Which is a great encouragement to the worst of sinners to turn from futile hopes and put their trust in future grace.

LIFE-GIVING GRACE IS FREE GRACE

Second, the freedom of God's grace is emphasized by the way Paul describes its role in salvation. In Ephesians 2:4-6 he says,

> *(4) But God, being rich in mercy, because of His great love with which He loved us, (5) even when we were dead in our transgressions, made us alive together with Christ (by grace you have been saved), (6) and raised us up with Him, and seated us with Him in the heavenly places, in Christ Jesus.*

The decisive act of God in conversion is that he "made us alive together with Christ" even when "we were dead in our transgressions." In other words, we were dead to God. We were unresponsive; we had no true spiritual interest; we had no taste for the beauties of Christ; we were simply dead to all that mattered. Then God acted—unconditionally—before we could do anything to be fit vessels of grace. He made us alive. He sovereignly awakened us to see the glory of Christ (2 Corinthians 4:4). The spiritual senses that were dead miraculously came to life.

Verse 4 says that this was an act of "mercy." That is, God saw us in our deadness and pitied us. God saw the terrible wages of sin leading to eternal death and misery. And the riches of his mercy overflowed to us in our need. But what is so remarkable about this text is that Paul breaks the flow of his own sentence in order to insert, "by grace you have been saved." "God made us alive together with Christ—*by grace you have been saved*—and raised us up with Him."

Paul is going to say this again in verse 8. So why does he break the flow in order to add it here? What's more, the focus is on God's *mercy* responding to our miserable plight of deadness; so why does Paul go out of his way to say that it is also by *grace* that we are saved?

I think the answer is that Paul recognizes here a perfect opportunity to emphasize the freeness of grace. As he describes our dead condition before conversion, he realizes that dead people can't meet conditions. If they are to live, there must be a totally unconditional and utterly free act of God to save them. This freedom is the very heart of grace. Paul wants to emphasize this and so he breaks into the sentence and virtually shouts, "You see, it was grace! All grace! You were dead. You could do nothing. Mercy it was, indeed, because your plight was pitiable. But the freeness of it is the heart of what I mean by grace. What act could be more one-sidedly free and non-negotiated than one person raising another from the dead!" This is the meaning of grace.

ELECTING GRACE IS FREE GRACE

Third, the freedom of God's grace is emphasized by its relation to God's election and man's works. In Romans 11:5 Paul says that "at this present time also there is a remnant according to *the election of grace*" (KJV). In other words, the existence of a remnant of believers and those destined to become believers is owing to God's election—his choosing them. And this election is an "election *of grace*." God's choosing was free. He gives grace to whom he will give grace. The elect are elect because of free and unconditional grace and not because of anything in themselves. That's the meaning of the phrase "election of grace."

The next verse emphasizes this again. Paul adds, "But if it is by grace, it is no longer on the basis of works, otherwise grace is no longer grace" (Romans 11:6). In other words, if the existence of a saved remnant were owing to works, then it would not be owing to the "election of grace." Because grace is free, but works imply earning or meriting, as Paul said in Romans 4:4, "To the one who *works*, his wage is not reckoned according to *grace*, but according to debt."[9] So Paul spotlights the freedom of grace by contrasting it with works. If human works earn salvation and create a remnant, the grace of election would no longer be grace. What began as grace in free and unconditional election would cease to be grace.

THE INEXHAUSTIBLE GOD AND THE FREEDOM OF GRACE

Finally, the freedom of grace is emphasized by the inexhaustibility of its source and the eternity of its outpouring. Grace is free because God is jealous to be seen as an inexhaustible fountain of self-replenishing life and power and joy. "I will *have mercy* on the whole house of Israel; and I shall *be jealous* for My holy name" (Ezekiel 39:25). He is jealous for the world to see that he has no deficiencies which we humans could supply with our works or our distinctives. He is always the benefactor and we are always the beneficiary. He is never constrained by what he has made. He remains free. This is what it means to be God. This is what he is jealous to preserve and display for the endless enjoyment of all who trust him.

Paul speaks of the "riches of His grace." His point is that the free overflow of God's inexhaustible, self-replenishing fullness is immeasurably great. There is no end to grace because there is no bottom to the well from which it comes. This is what Paul is getting at in Ephesians 2:6-7, "[God] raised us up with Him, and seated us with Him in the heavenly places, in Christ Jesus, *in order that in the ages to come He might show the surpassing riches of His grace* in kindness toward us in Christ Jesus."

There are two astonishing things here. One is that the purpose of our salvation is for God to lavish the riches of his grace on us. The other is that it will take him forever to do it. This is a mighty thought. God made us alive and secured us in Christ so that he could make us the beneficiaries of ever-lasting kindness from infinite riches of grace. This is not because we are worthy. Quite the contrary, it is to show the infinite measure of *his* worth. Grace would not be grace if it were a response to resources in us. Grace is grace because it highlights God's own overflowing resources of kindness. Grace is eternal because it will take that long for God to expend inexhaustible stores of goodness on us. Grace is free because God would not be the infinite, self-sufficient God he is if he were constrained by anything outside himself.

GLORY IS DULY PRAISED WHERE GRACE IS DULY PRIZED

It should be obvious from this why future grace is so utterly crucial in God's great plan to glorify himself and satisfy his people. Most of our experience of God's active grace lies in the future. The grace that I have already experienced from God—from a quantitative standpoint—is infinitesimally small compared to the future grace that I will experience from now to eternity. This means that the great wealth of glory that God means to display for the enjoyment of his people is duly praised where future grace—in all its freedom—is duly prized.

In exalting the freedom of God, faith in future grace very practically nullifies the power of pride. We will pause in the next chapter to ponder how this works. How does prizing the freedom of God's grace purify us from the corruption of pride?

Thus says the LORD,

"Let not a wise man boast of his wisdom,

and let not the mighty man boast of his might,

let not a rich man boast of his riches;

but let him who boasts boast of this,

that he understands and knows Me,

that I am the LORD who exercises

lovingkindness, justice, and righteousness on earth;

for I delight in these things," declares the LORD.

JEREMIAH 9:23–24

The pleasure of pride is like the pleasure of scratching.

If there is an itch one does want to scratch;

but it is much nicer to have neither the itch nor the scratch.

As long as we have the itch of self-regard

we shall want the pleasure of self-approval;

but the happiest moments are those when we forget our

precious selves and have neither but have everything else

(God, our fellow humans, animals, the garden and the sky) instead.

C.S. LEWIS

Humble yourselves...under the mighty hand of God

that He may exalt you at the proper time.

1 PETER 5:6

CHAPTER SIX

Applying the Purifying Power

Faith in Future Grace
vs.
Pride

THE SHADOW OF GOD

Humility is not a popular human trait in the modern world. It's not touted in the talk shows or celebrated in valedictory speeches or commended in diversity seminars or listed with corporate core values. And if you go to the massive self-help section of your sprawling mall bookstore, you won't find many titles celebrating humility.

The basic reason for this is not hard to find: humility can only survive in the presence of God. When God goes, humility goes. In fact you might say that humility follows God like a shadow. We can expect to find humility applauded in our society about as often as we find God applauded.

In my local newspaper recently a guest editorial captured the atmosphere of our time that asphyxiates humility:

> *There are some who naively cling to the nostalgic memory of God. The average churchgoer takes a few hours out of the week to experience the sacred... But the rest of the time, he is immersed in a society that no longer acknowledges God as an omniscient and omnipotent force to be*

loved and worshiped… Today we are too sophisticated for God. We can stand on our own; we are prepared and ready to choose and define our own existence.[1]

In this atmosphere humility cannot survive. It disappears with God. When God is neglected, the runner-up god takes his place, namely man. And that, by definition, is the opposite of humility, namely, the haughty spirit called pride. So the atmosphere we breathe is hostile to humility.

AN APPETITE FOR GOD IN THE HEART

The point of this chapter is that a haughty spirit is a form of unbelief and that the way to battle the unbelief of pride is by faith in future grace. Trusting God and being arrogant are opposites: "An *arrogant* man stirs up strife, but he who *trusts* in the Lord will prosper" (Proverbs 28:25). That's why Stephen Charnock said, "A proud faith is as much a contradiction as a humble devil."[2] To see why faith and pride are opposites we need to remind ourselves what faith is.

We will see in Chapter Sixteen that the heart of biblical faith in Jesus is coming to him for the satisfaction of all that God is for us in him. Jesus said in John 6:35, "I am the bread of life; he who *comes* to me shall not hunger, and he who *believes* in me shall never thirst." From this we have drawn out the truth that *belief* in Jesus means coming to Jesus for the satisfaction of all that God is for us in him. And *unbelief* is a turning away from Jesus in order to seek satisfaction in other things.

Belief is not merely an *agreement* with facts in the head; it is also an *appetite* for God in the heart, which fastens on Jesus for satisfaction. "He who comes to me shall not hunger and he who believes in me shall never thirst!" Therefore eternal life is not given to people who merely *think* that Jesus is the Son of God. It is given to people who *drink* from Jesus as the Son of God. "The water that I shall give him shall become in him a well of water springing up to eternal life" (John 4:14). He is also the bread of life, and those who *feed* on him for nourishment and satisfaction live by him. "I am the living bread that came down out of heaven; if anyone *eats* of this bread, he shall live forever" (John 6:51). The point of these images of *drinking* and *eating* is to make clear the essence of faith. It is more than believing that there is such a thing as water and food; and it is more than believing that Jesus is life-giving water and food. Faith is coming to Jesus and *drinking* the water and *eating* the food so that we find our hearts satisfied in him.

TURNING FROM SATISFACTION IN GOD
TO SATISFACTION IN SELF

With this background we will see more clearly that pride is a species of unbelief. *Unbelief* is a turning away from God and his Son in order to seek satisfaction in other things. *Pride* is a turning away from God specifically to take satisfaction in *self*. So pride is one specific form of unbelief. And its antidote is the wakening and strengthening of faith in future grace.

In Chapter Seventeen we will see that *covetousness* is turning away from God, usually to find satisfaction in things. In Chapter Twenty-Seven we will see that *lust* is turning away from God to find satisfaction in sex. We will see that *bitterness* is turning away from God to find satisfaction in revenge (Chapter Twenty-One). *Impatience* is turning away from God to find satisfaction in your own uninterrupted plan of action (Chapter Thirteen). *Anxiety, misplaced shame* and *despondency* are various conditions of the heart when these efforts of unbelief miscarry (Chapters Three, Ten, Twenty-Four).

But deeper than all these forms of unbelief is the unbelief of pride, because self-determination and self-exaltation lie behind all these other sinful dispositions. Every turning from God—for anything—presumes a kind of autonomy or independence that is the essence of pride. Turning from God assumes that one knows better than God. Thus pride lies at the root of every turning from God. It is the root of every act of distrust toward God. Or, more accurately, pride is not so much the *root* as it is the *essence* of unbelief, and its remedy is faith in future grace. Thus the battle against pride is the battle against unbelief; and the fight for humility is the fight of faith in future grace.

Biblical references to pride can be categorized as different ways of distrusting God. Each text on pride reveals what we refuse to trust God for. Or, more specifically, each one shows what we prefer to find in ourselves.

GOD'S GREAT COMPETITORS

In Jeremiah 9:23 God says, "Let not a wise man boast of his *wisdom*, and let not the mighty man boast of his *might*, let not a rich man boast of his *riches.*" In those three phrases God names his great competitors for the boast of the human heart. Each one—wisdom, might, and riches—tempts us to take satisfaction in ourselves—our intelligence, our strength, our material resources. Each one lures us away from trusting God as the superior satisfaction above them all. It is radically humbling to confess that the source of all our joy resides outside ourselves.

WHEN KNOWLEDGE PUFFS UP

Take wisdom and intelligence, for example. The apostle Paul warns that "knowledge makes arrogant, but love edifies" (1 Corinthians 8:1). This does not mean he favors ignorance and irrationality: "Do not be children in your *thinking;* yet in evil be babes, but in your *thinking* be mature" (1 Corinthians 14:20). G. K. Chesterton, the British Catholic journalist-author who died in 1936, warned that in the Twentieth Century we are not clear about the relationship between intellectual conviction and pride.

> *What we suffer from…is humility in the wrong place. Modesty has moved from the organ of ambition. Modesty has settled upon the organ of conviction; where it was never meant to be. A man was meant to be doubtful about himself, but undoubting about the truth; this has been exactly reversed. Nowadays the part of a man that a man does assert is exactly the part he ought not to assert—himself. The part he doubts is exactly the part he ought not to doubt—the Divine Reason.[3]*

Paul is not calling into question the necessity of firm conviction and true knowledge. Nevertheless he is keenly aware that what we know—or think we know—can lure us from resting in God's wisdom and lead us toward boasting in our own.

The organ of knowledge was given to us that we might know God and how the world relates to God. One of the first things we learn, when we know him as we ought, is the Word of Jesus: "Flesh and blood did not reveal this to you, but my Father who is in heaven" (Matthew 16:17). All true knowing depends on God. "Who has been [God's] counselor…for from him and through him and to him are all things" (Romans 11:34, 36, RSV). God gave us minds not only to know, but to know how we ought to know. We know the way we ought to know when we boast in the Source of all knowing, not in our fragile little chip, with its tiny, God-designed circuitry. God has not chosen many wise, says the apostle. And the reason he gives is "that no man should boast before God." But: "Let him who boasts, boast in the Lord" (1 Corinthians 1:26, 29, 31).

When we boast in our wisdom we show that we have turned from God to trust in ourselves. We disclose that our satisfaction is not first in God's infinite, primary wisdom, but in our derivative, secondary capacities. It is a failure of faith in future grace—the promise of God to use his infinite wisdom to keep on managing the universe for the good of all who hope in him.

BLOWING THE BUBBLE OF OUR RESOURCES

Similarly, we are prone to boast in our might. When God graciously blesses us, we leap to take credit for the gift—as if there were more satisfaction in blowing the bubble of our resourcefulness than in benefiting from God's. We have been duly warned in Deuteronomy 8:11-17,

> Beware…lest, when you have eaten and are satisfied, and have built good houses and lived in them, and when your herds and your flocks multiply, and your silver and gold multiply, and all that you have multiplies, then your heart becomes proud, and you forget the Lord your God who brought you out from the land of Egypt, out of the house of slavery… In the wilderness He fed you manna which your fathers did not know, that He might humble you and that He might test you, to do good for you in the end. Otherwise, you may say in your heart, "My power and the strength of my hand made me this wealth."

If the people built their houses and tended their flocks and gathered their gold by faith in future grace, it would not enter their minds to say, "My power and my strength have gotten me this wealth." When you live by faith in future grace, you know that all the products of your living are the products of grace.

GOD WILL NOT SHARE HIS GLORY WITH THE PROUD

The king of Assyria illustrates the pride that rises in the heart when both wisdom *and* power conspire to lure the heart from God to self. God made the king the rod of his righteous wrath against the people of Israel (Isaiah 10:5). Yet the king did not delight in God's enabling power and guidance, but took credit for himself and said, "By the power of my hand and by my wisdom I did this, for I have *understanding;* and I removed the boundaries of the peoples, and plundered their treasures, and like *a mighty man* I brought down their inhabitants" (Isaiah 10:13). This is not smart. God will not share his glory with the proud. In fact, he promises, "I will punish the fruit of the arrogant heart of the king of Assyria and the pomp of his haughtiness" (Isaiah 10:12). The antidote to the king's pride is to believe this threat and find his gladness in God's power and God's wisdom, not his own.

WHEN THE PROUD EAT GRASS LIKE AN OX

Not too much later in Israel's history the king of Babylon, Nebuchadnezzar, was brought low for his proud boast: "Is this not Babylon the great, which I myself have built as a royal residence by the might of my power and for the glory of my majesty?" (Daniel 4:30). For that pride, God humbled him and made him eat grass like an ox in the open field (Daniel 4:33), until he learned to exult in God's sovereign power far above his own:

> *All the inhabitants of the earth are accounted as nothing, but He does according to His will in the host of heaven and among the inhabitants of earth; and no one can ward off His hand or say to Him, 'What hast Thou done?' Now I Nebuchadnezzar praise, exalt, and honor the King of heaven, for all His works are true and His ways just, and He is able to humble those who walk in pride. (Daniel 4:35, 37)*

The antidote to Nebuchadnezzar's pride was not merely a new knowledge in the head, but a new exultation in the heart. His "praise" and "exultation" reveal the wakening of faith, and the gladness that God ruled the future with the omnipotent grace to establish his plan and humble the proud. He was satisfied with God's prerogative to do as he pleases in the sovereign freedom of his justice and grace.

WHY BOAST AS IF IT WERE NOT A GIFT?

Alongside wisdom and might, perhaps the greatest tempter to pride is money. With it we can purchase the resources of intelligence and power that we may not have in ourselves. So wealth is the great symbol of self-sufficiency. If we have savvy in the stock market or luck in the lottery, it makes up for any lack of other skills or power, because now we control the resources to satisfy our desires—so we think. And the result is described by God in Hosea 13:6, "As they had their pasture, they became satisfied, and being satisfied, their heart became proud; therefore, they forgot Me." Pride is an issue of where your *satisfaction* is. "As they had their pasture, they became *satisfied.*" Which is another way of saying, pride is an issue of what you are trusting in for your future. Hence God uses the language of trust to indict Israel's pride in Jeremiah 49:4, "How boastful you are about the valleys! Your valley is flowing away, O backsliding daughter who *trusts in her treasures,* saying, 'Who will come against me?'"

Israel trusts in treasures to make her future secure from invading armies. Her faith is not in God's future grace. And that's the problem. She has been lured into a delusion of false delights: treasures, which themselves are gifts of God's grace. Therefore they will pierce the hand if they lean on them instead of God. The apostle Paul would ask these people, as he did the Corinthians, "What do you have that you did not receive? But if you did receive it, why do you boast as if you had not received it?" (1 Corinthians 4:7). Everything we have we have received from God. It lies in his hand to leave or to take, to turn for us or against us.

This is why the Bible never tires of telling us, "The king is not saved by a mighty army; a warrior is not delivered by great strength. A horse is a false hope for victory; nor does it deliver anyone by its great strength" (Psalm 33:16-17). You can buy armies and warriors and horses with your wealth, but unless the Lord decides to give you deliverance and victory, they will be useless in the day of battle. Future grace, not military force, is the final hope of kings and warriors—and everyone else. That's why the next verses in Psalm 33 point to an alternative treasure for our trust: "Behold, the eye of the Lord is on those who fear Him, on those who hope for His loving kindness...He is our help and our shield. For our heart rejoices in Him, because we trust in His holy name" (Psalm 33:18, 20–21). This trust that looks away from our own resources and rests in God is what I mean by faith in future grace. This is the remedy for pride.

THE ULTIMATE PRIDE: ATHEISM

When you take all three categories of temptation to self-reliance—wisdom, might and riches—they form a powerful inducement toward the ultimate form of pride, namely, atheism. The safest way to stay supreme in our own estimation is to deny anything above us. This is why the proud preoccupy themselves with looking down on others. "A proud man is always looking down on things and people: and, of course, as long as you are looking down, you cannot see something that is above you."[4] But to preserve pride it may be simpler to proclaim that there is nothing above to look at. "The wicked, in the *haughtiness* of his countenance, does not seek Him. All his thoughts are, 'There is no God'" (Psalm 10:4). Ultimately, the proud must persuade themselves that there is no God.

One reason for this is that God's reality is overwhelmingly intrusive in all the details of life. Pride cannot tolerate the intimate involvement of God in running even the ordinary affairs of life. For example, James, the brother of Jesus, diagnoses pride behind the simple presumption of planning to go from one city to another:

> Come now, you who say, "Today or tomorrow, we shall go to such and such a city, and spend a year there and engage in business and make a profit." Yet you do not know what your life will be like tomorrow. You are just a vapor that appears for a little while and then vanishes away. Instead, you ought to say, "If the Lord wills, we shall live and also do this or that." But as it is, you boast in your arrogance; all such boasting is evil. (James 4:13-17)

Pride does not like the sovereignty of God. Therefore pride does not like the existence of God, because God is sovereign. It might express this by saying, "There is no God." Or it might express it by saying, "I am driving to Atlanta for Christmas." James says, "Don't be so sure." Instead say, "If the Lord wills, we shall live and we shall get to Atlanta for Christmas." James' point is that God rules over whether we get to Atlanta, and whether you live to the end of this page. "If the Lord wills, we will *live*..." This is extremely offensive to the self-sufficiency of pride—not even to have control over whether you get to the end of the page without having a stroke!

James says that not believing in the sovereign rights of God to manage the details of your future is arrogance. The way to battle this arrogance is to yield to the sovereignty of God in all the details of life, and rest in his infallible promises to show himself mighty on our behalf (2 Chronicles 16:9), to pursue us with goodness and mercy every day (Psalm 23:6), to work for those who wait for him (Isaiah 64:4), and to supply us with all we need to live for his glory (Hebrews 13:21). In other words, the remedy for pride is unwavering faith in future grace.

THE ITCH OF SELF-REGARD AND THE SCRATCH OF APPROVAL

One of the manifestations of pride that shows its aversion to faith in future grace is the craving it produces for human approval. C. S. Lewis explains how this craving works:

> *The pleasure of pride is like the pleasure of scratching. If there is an itch one does want to scratch; but it is much nicer to have neither the itch nor the scratch. As long as we have the itch of self-regard we shall want the pleasure of self-approval; but the happiest moments are those when we forget our precious selves and have neither but have everything else (God, our fellow humans, animals, the garden and the sky) instead...*[5]

The itch of self-regard craves the scratch of self-approval. That is, if we are getting our pleasure from feeling self-sufficient, we will not be satisfied without others' seeing and applauding our self-sufficiency. Hence Jesus' description of the scribes and Pharisees: "They do all their deeds to be noticed by men...And they love the place of honor at banquets, and the chief seats in the synagogues, and respectful greetings in the market places, and being called by men, Rabbi" (Matthew 23:5-7).

THE VOID IN SELF-SUFFICIENCY

This is ironic. Self-sufficiency should free the proud person from the need to be made much of by others. That's what "sufficient" means. But evidently there is a void in this so-called self-sufficiency. The self was never designed to satisfy itself or rely upon itself. It never can be sufficient. We are but images of God, not the real thing. We are shadows and echoes. So there will always be an emptiness in the soul that struggles to be satisfied with the resources of self.

This empty craving for the praise of others signals the failure of pride and the absence of faith in future grace. Jesus saw the terrible effect of this itch for human glory. He named it in John 5:44, "How can you *believe*, when you receive glory from one another, and you do not seek the glory that is from the one and only God?" The answer is, You can't. Itching for glory from other people makes faith impossible. Why? Because faith is being satisfied with all that God is for you in Jesus; and if you are bent on getting the satisfaction of your itch from the scratch of others' acclaim, you will turn away from Jesus. But if you would turn from self as the source of satisfaction (= repentance), and come to Jesus for the enjoyment of all that God is for us in him (= faith), then the itch would be replaced by a well of water springing up to eternal life (John 4:14).

THE IRONY OF WEAK PRIDE

The irony of this insatiable itch in the self-sufficient soul becomes even more evident when pride cannot get what it wants and begins to flounder in weakness. This calls for discernment. Weak pride is not easily recognized. It sounds like an oxymoron—like round squares. But it is not. Consider the relationship between boasting and self-pity.

> *Both are manifestations of pride. Boasting is the response of pride to success. Self-pity is the response of pride to suffering. Boasting says, "I deserve admiration because I have achieved so much." Self-pity says, "I deserve admiration because I have sacrificed so much." Boasting is the voice of pride in the heart of the strong. Self-pity is the voice of pride in the heart of the weak. Boasting sounds self-sufficient. Self-pity sounds self-sacrificing.*

> *The reason self-pity does not look like pride is that it appears to be needy.*

But the need arises from a wounded ego and the desire of the self-pitying is not really for others to see them as helpless, but heroes. The need self-pity feels does not come from a sense of unworthiness, but from a sense of unrecognized worthiness. It is the response of unapplauded pride.[6]

When pride is not strong, it begins to worry about the future. In the heart of the proud, anxiety is to the future what self-pity is to the past. What did not go well in the past gives us a sense that we deserve better. But if we could not make things go our way in the past, we may not be able to in the future either. Instead of making the proud humble, this possibility makes them anxious.

THE CAMOUFLAGED PRIDE OF ANXIETY

Here is another irony. Anxiety does not look like pride. It looks weak. It looks as though you admit you don't control the future. Yes, in a sense the proud admit that. But the admission does not kill pride until the proud heart is willing to look to the one who does control the future and rest in him. Until then, the proud are hanging onto their right of self-sufficiency even as it crumbles on the horizon of the future.

The remarkable biblical evidence for this is found in two places. The first is Isaiah 51:12-13 where God indicts anxious Israel by showing them the pride beneath their fear: "I, even I, am He who comforts you. *Who are you that you are afraid of man who dies,* and of the son of man who is made like grass; that you have forgotten the Lord your Maker, who stretched out the heavens, and laid the foundations of the earth; that you fear continually all day long...?" In other words, "Who do you think you are to be afraid of mere men? You must really think you are somebody to be afraid like this!" Now that is an odd rebuke. But the meaning is plain: your fear of man is a form of pride.

Why is anxiety about the future a form of pride? God gives the answer: "I—the Lord, your Maker—I am He who comforts you, who promises to take care of you; and those who threaten you are mere men who die. So your fear must mean that you do not trust Me. You must think that your protection hangs on you. And even though you are not sure that your own resources will take care of you, yet you opt for fragile self-reliance, rather than faith in future grace. So all your trembling—weak as it is—reveals pride." The remedy? Turn from self-reliance to God-reliance, and put your faith in the all-sufficient power of future grace.

The second place where we see anxiety as a form of pride is 1 Peter 5:6-7. "Humble yourselves, therefore, under the mighty hand of God, that He may exalt you at the proper time, (7) casting all your anxiety upon Him, because He cares for you." Notice the grammatical connection between verses 6 and 7. "Humble yourselves...under the mighty hand of God... *casting* all your anxiety upon Him." Verse 7 is not a new sentence. It's a subordinate clause. "Humble yourselves...[by] *casting* your anxieties on him." This means that casting your anxieties on God is a way of humbling yourself under God's mighty hand. It's like saying, "Eat politely...*chewing* with your mouth shut." "Drive carefully...*keeping* your eyes open." "Be generous...*inviting* someone over on Thanksgiving."

Similarly, "Humble yourselves...*casting* your anxieties on God." One way to be humble is to cast your anxieties on God. Which means that one *hindrance* to casting your anxieties on God is pride. Which means that undue worry is a form of pride. Now why is casting our anxieties on the Lord the opposite of pride? Because pride does not like to admit that it has any anxieties. And if pride has to admit it, it still does not like to admit that the remedy might be trusting someone else who is wiser and stronger. In other words, pride is a form of unbelief and does not like to trust in future grace. Faith admits the need for help. Pride won't. Faith banks on God to give help. Pride won't. Faith casts anxieties on God. Pride won't. Therefore the way to battle the unbelief of pride is to admit freely that you have anxieties, and to cherish the promise of future grace in the words, "He cares for you."

We end this chapter with a final glimpse at the counsel of God through Jeremiah. At the beginning of the chapter we heard him say, "Let not a wise man boast of his wisdom, and let not the mighty man boast of his might, let not a rich man boast of his riches." We close by hearing him finish that sentence: "'But let him who boasts boast of this, that he understands and knows Me, that I am the Lord who exercises lovingkindness, justice, and righteousness on earth; for I delight in these things,' declares the Lord" (Jeremiah 9:23–24). When all is said and done, that is the rock-bottom biblical answer to the question how to best fight pride. Be stunned and satisfied that we know God—and that he knows us.

I made the following entry in my journal December 6, 1988. It's my own confession of need and my response to Jeremiah's exhortation.

> *Is not the most effective way of bridling my delight in being made much of, to focus on making much of God? Self-denial and crucifixion of the flesh are essential, but O how easy it is to be made much of even for my self-denial! How shall this insidious motive of pleasure in being made much of be broken except through bending all my faculties to delight in the pleasure of making much of God!*

> *Christian hedonism[7] is the final solution. It is deeper than death to self. You have to go down deeper into the grave of the flesh to find the truly freeing stream of miracle water that ravishes you with the taste of God's glory. Only in that speechless, all-satisfying admiration is the end of self.*

This "all-satisfying admiration" of all that God is for us in Jesus is what I mean by faith in future grace.

PART III

THE CRUCIAL PLACE
OF
BYGONE GRACE

Remember the former things long past,
For I am God, and there is no other;
I am God, and there is no one like Me.

ISAIAH 46:9

All the promises of God find their Yes in Him.
That is why we utter the Amen through Him,
to the glory of God.

2 CORINTHIANS 1:20 (RSV)

"Amen" means, "Yes, Lord, you can do it."
It means, "Yes, Lord, you are powerful.
Yes, Lord, you are wise.
Yes, Lord, you are merciful.
Yes, Lord, all future grace comes from you
and has been confirmed in Christ."
"Amen" is an exclamation point of hope after a prayer for help.

CHAPTER SEVEN

Looking Back for the Sake of the Future

D uring the fifteen years I have served as a senior pastor we have interviewed dozens of people for vocational and lay roles of ministry—deacons, elders, teachers, secretaries, receptionists, ministry assistants, pastoral associates, etc. In every case what is at stake is the future. How will they do? Will they be pure and faithful and hard-working? Will they be team-builders? Will they have a passion for the supremacy of God? All this relates to the future. That is where their ministry will happen.

But in every interview we talk about the past. We talk about their previous jobs. We talk about the track record of their performance at work and at home. We talk about their spiritual pilgrimage and the family they grew up in. Why all this talk about the past if *the* issue now is the future? The answer is obvious: confidence in someone's future reliability is grounded in a history of past faithfulness. This is also the way it is with God.

Bygone grace is the foundation for faith in future grace. We obey the teachings of Jesus by faith in future grace; and we lay hold on future grace in the promises of God's Word. But we certify the surety of the promises with the evidence of past grace. This past grace is God's down payment on the fullness of future grace.

THE PAST-WARD FLOW OF INFINITE FUTURE GRACE

Actually that image of a one-time down payment doesn't quite work. Past grace is continually accumulating every day. The infinite reservoir of future grace is flowing back through the present into the ever-growing pool of past grace. The inexhaustible reservoir is invisible except through the promises. But the ever-enlarging pool of past grace is visible; and God means for the certainty and beauty and depth to strengthen our faith in future grace.

PAST GRACE IS THE DOWN PAYMENT OF FUTURE GRACE

But then again, the image of the down payment of past grace is not only helpful, it's biblical. For example, the Holy Spirit is called a down payment or pledge of the future grace of our entire inheritance (Ephesians 1:14; 2 Corinthians 1:22; 5:5). He has been given, and the grace of this gift is immeasurable. But there is so much more future grace yet to come; and he is the guarantee of it.

Another example is Christ himself. When he was raised from the dead, he was called the "first fruits of those who [have died]" (1 Corinthians 15:20). The "first fruits" is a portion of the whole harvest that guarantees the reaping of the rest. So the resurrection of Jesus is a great work of past grace that God wants us to remember. It is the foundation for our faith in the future grace of our own resurrection.

AN OLD TESTAMENT PATTERN LOOKING BACK
FOR THE SAKE OF THE FUTURE

This pattern of looking back in order to believe in future grace is as old as grace itself. The Old Testament tells us of times when the people of God looked back to strengthen faith in future grace and times when they didn't.

For example, we are told that soon after Gideon died "the sons of Israel again played the harlot with the Baals" (Judges. 8:33). Why did they do this? Why would they choose a second-rate foreign deity instead of trusting the future grace of the true God for their help and deliverance? The next verse gives the answer: "Thus the sons of Israel *did not remember the Lord their God, who had delivered them from the hands of all their enemies on every side*"

(Judges. 8:34). They forsook their faith in God's future grace because they stopped remembering his past grace.

Nehemiah points to another example: the time the people rejected the Lord in the wilderness and wanted to go back to Egypt. "Our fathers acted arrogantly; they became stubborn and would not listen to Thy command- ments. And they refused to listen, and *did not remember Thy wondrous deeds which Thou hadst performed among them;* so they became stubborn and appointed a leader to return to their slavery in Egypt" (Nehemiah 9:16-17). Forgetting the past grace of God's "wondrous deeds" caused the slavery of Egypt to look better than the future grace of God.

Not all the people in the Old Testament failed to cherish past grace for the sake of joyful hope. For example, David wrote, "When I *remember Thee* on my bed, I meditate on Thee in the night watches; for *Thou hast been my help,* and in the shadow of Thy wings I sing for joy." (Psalm 63:6-7). God had been his help again and again. He remembered this past grace; and the effect was that he sang for joy as he reveled in the ongoing protection of future grace under the wings of God.

God himself commands this pattern of remembering bygone grace for the sake of faith in future grace. In Isaiah 46:9 he says, *"Remember the for- mer things long past,* for I am God, and there is no other; I am God, and there is no one like Me." The reason God wants them to look back on "the for- mer things" is to increase their confidence in the future things he is planning for them. "My purpose will be established, and I will accomplish all My good pleasure" (Isaiah 46:10). Remembering the former things that God has done gives a good foundation for believing his Word when he says, "I will accomplish all My good pleasure."

NOW THE GRACE OF GOD HAS COME IN JESUS

If looking back on past grace was the way the saints of the Old Testament fought the fight of faith in future grace, it is all the more necessary for us to fight this way today; because for us the greatest grace in world history is now past. Jesus Christ, the Son of God, has come into the world. In a sense we could say that God's grace has come in person and done such a decisive work of grace that all other experiences of grace depend on it. Paul said simply, "The grace of God has appeared" (Titus 2:11).

In fact, the New Testament is explicit that all future grace hangs on the past coming of Jesus. For example, Paul says, Christ came "on behalf of the truth of God *to confirm the promises given to the fathers*" (Romans 15:8). In other words, Christ came to guarantee that the promises of the Old Testament would indeed come true. He came for the sake of future grace. From the time of Christ onwards, every look back should include a look to Jesus. Without him there would be no future grace.

ALL THE PROMISES OF FUTURE GRACE ARE YES IN CHRIST

One of the most amazing and wonderful statements of this truth goes like this: "As many as may be the promises of God, in Him they are yes" (2 Corinthians 1:20). Let's savor this extraordinary truth for a moment.

The question God is asking us in this text is this: "Are you living in the fullest enjoyment of My Yes to all my promises?" Or to put it another way, "Have you said yes to all the future grace of God's Yes to you in Christ? Is there any of God's Yes to you to which you are saying, 'No,' or, 'Maybe,' or, 'Not now'?" This text begs for immediate and radical response. It calls us to cry out to God, "I consecrate myself to forsake the 'No' and the 'Maybe' and the 'Not Now' of my unbelief. And I say 'Yes' to every future grace of every promise in your Yes to me."

Let's step back for a moment to make sure we see the full force of this verse. According to 2 Corinthians 1:15-16 Paul plans to visit Corinth twice. He is going to cross the Aegean Sea to visit the church on his way to Macedonia, and then he plans to come back by Corinth and visit them again. This is his plan, and they hear about it.

But then something happens that makes him change his mind. Evidently the rumor starts to circulate that Paul's heart is divided. Yes, he loves them and wants to see them and bless them. But No, maybe not as much as he loves his own convenience or some other church. Is Paul's heart, both Yes and No toward the Corinthians?

He answers passionately in verses 17-18: "I was not vacillating when I intended to do this, was I? Or that which I purpose, do I purpose according to the flesh, that with me there should be yes, yes and no, no at the same time? But as God is faithful, our word to you is not yes and no."

In other words, my planning and my preaching are not fickle; they are not double-minded. They are unified; they are Yes to you. I live for your good. I am *for* you and not against you. My life and ministry are a resounding Yes to your joy! Yes to your holiness! Yes to your faith and hope and love and peace and power!

And then in verses 19 and 20 Paul shows why his own life is Yes to the Corinthians: namely, because God has spoken his final, decisive Yes to them in Christ. "For the Son of God, Christ Jesus, who was preached among you by us—by me and Silvanus and Timothy—was not yes and no; but is yes in him. [Literally: "The(decisive) Yes has happened in him"—God's heart is not divided in Christ. Christ means Yes to all who will have it!] For as many as may be the promises of God, in Him they are Yes."

So Paul is saying: My heart is not divided toward you, because God's heart is not divided toward you. If you belong to Christ by faith, then everything God could possibly give you for your good he has signed over to your account in Christ. You hear the same answer at every point: Is this promise in my account? Yes. Is this gift in my account? Yes. Is this blessing in my account? Yes. Yes. Yes. All the promises of God are Yes in Christ. Christ is God's Yes to all future grace.

ALL FUTURE GRACE IS OURS IN CHRIST

In Galatians 3:29 (RSV) Paul wrote, "If you are Christ's, then you are Abraham's offspring, *heirs according to promise*" (see also Ephesians 3:6; Galatians 3:14, 22; Hebrews 9:15). All the promises of God for the good of his people are in Christ. He confirms them and secures them and purchases them for all who "are Christ's"—for all who believe and belong to him (Galatians 3:22). Every sinner who comes to God in Christ, with all his needs, finds God coming to him in Christ, with all his promises. When a sinful person meets the holy God *in Christ* what he hears is Yes. God, do you love me? Yes. Will you forgive me? Yes. Will you accept me? Yes. Will you help me change? Yes. Will you give me power to serve you? Yes. Will you keep me? Yes. Will you show me your glory? Yes.

All the promises of God—all the blessings of God in the heavenly places (Ephesians 1:3)—are Yes in Christ Jesus. Jesus is God's decisive Yes to all who believe. He is the foundation of all future grace. When we look back to strengthen our faith in future grace, we look primarily to Jesus.

THE MAGNIFICENT MEANING OF AMEN

The place where the past and future are linked repeatedly in our lives is prayer. I mention this here because Paul links prayer with God's Yes in this verse in a striking way.

In 2 Corinthians 1:20 he says (with choppy Greek, that comes through in choppy English), "Wherefore also by him is our Amen to the glory of God through us." Let's try to smooth that out. Here's what he is saying: "Therefore, because of Christ, we say AMEN to God in our prayers to show that God gets the glory for the future grace we are counting on."

If you've ever wondered why Christians say Amen at the end of our prayers and where that custom comes from, here's the answer. "Amen" is a word taken straight over into Greek from Hebrew without any translation, just like it has come into English and most other languages without any translation. In Hebrew it was a very strong affirmation (see also Numbers 5:22; Nehemiah 5:13; 8:6)—a formal, solemn, earnest "I agree," or "I affirm what you just said," or "This is true." Most simply "Amen" means a very earnest Yes in the context of addressing God.

Now notice the connection between the two halves of verse 20. The first half says, "All the promises of God find their Yes in him!" (RSV). The second half says, "That is why we utter the *Amen* through him, to the glory of God" (RSV). When you realize that "Amen" and "Yes" mean the same thing, here's what the verse says: In Jesus Christ God says his Yes to us through his promises; and in Christ we say our Yes to God through prayer.

This implies four crucial things for our faith in future grace that we express in prayer.

ALL PRAYER SEEKS GOD'S YES THROUGH JESUS

First, our prayer goes to God *through Jesus.* Paul says, *"through him* is our Amen." God's Yes comes to us *in Christ.* Therefore prayer goes to God *through Christ.* Prayer goes where the Yes is: in Christ. Everybody wants to hear a Yes when they pray, and that is what we hear in Christ, and nowhere else. This is what we mean when we say, "In Jesus' name," at the end of our prayers. He is God's Yes to all the future grace that we seek in prayer.

THE GIVER OF GRACE GETS THE GLORY

Second, we see that prayer is for God's glory. Paul says that when we pray through Christ "our Amen [is] *to the glory of God.*" "Amen" is the great affirmation that God is the bountiful Giver and I am the needy receiver. Amen affirms God's inexhaustible future grace to respond to our need in the very best way for his glory and for our good. Prayer has the wonderful capacity to highlight our emptiness and God's fullness at the same time. It is wonderfully suited to express our inadequacy and God's all-sufficiency. When prayer looks away from our flaws and deficiencies to God for his future grace, he gets the glory he deserves and we get the good that we need.

PRAYER GOES TO THE BANK CALLED FUTURE GRACE

Third, we see that prayer is a response to promises, that is, to the assurances of future grace. Prayer is drawing on the account where God has deposited all his promises of future grace. Prayer is not hoping in the dark that there might be a God of good intentions out there. Prayer goes to the bank every day and draws on promises for the future grace needed for that day.

Don't miss the connection between the two halves of this great verse. Notice the "therefore:" All the *promises* of God are Yes in Christ. *Therefore* we pray Amen through him, to God's glory. To make sure we see it, let's turn the two halves around: When we pray, we say Amen to God through Christ, *because* God has said Amen to all his promises in Christ. Prayer is the confident plea for God to make good on his promises of future grace for Christ's sake. Prayer links our faith in future grace with the foundation of it all, Jesus Christ.

"AMEN" IS OUR YES TO FUTURE GRACE

Which leads to the final point: "Amen" is a full and precious word in times of prayer. It doesn't mean primarily, "Yes, I have now said all this prayer." It means primarily, "Yes, God has made all these promises." Amen means,

"Yes, Lord, you can do it." It means, "Yes, Lord, you are powerful. Yes, Lord, you are wise. Yes, Lord, you are merciful. Yes, Lord, all future grace comes from you and has been confirmed in Christ." "Amen" is an exclamation point of hope after a prayer for help.

IN JESUS' NAME, AMEN

When we come to the end of our prayers and say the simple words, "In Jesus' name, Amen," we are really saying two Amen's. When we say, "In Jesus' name," that is God's Amen to us. All his promises are Amen in Jesus: Jesus Christ is God's Yes and Amen at the end of our prayers. Then when we say, "Amen," this is our Yes and Amen back to God for his. Which means that our Amen, and the prayer it supports, is our Yes to God's Yes to us. It is a commitment from our hearts that we will now live by faith in the Yes of God's guaranteed future grace.

FORSAKING THE NO, MAYBE AND NOT-NOW FOR YES

This brings us back to our earlier question: Are you living in the fullest enjoyment of God's Yes to you in Christ Jesus? Or to put it another way: Have you said yes to all of God's Yes to you? Are you answering God's Yes to you with a No or Maybe or Not Now?

The foundation of future grace is Jesus Christ. He is the confirmation and Yes to all God's promises. He is worthy of your fullest confidence and trust. The prayer of consecration that rises in my heart, and I hope in yours, is this: "O Lord, I promise that by your grace my future will be a future of unfailing Yes to you. I consecrate myself to forsake the No and the Maybe and the Not Now of my unbelief. And I say Yes to everything in your Yes to me. I pledge myself to a holy dissatisfaction until my thoughts and my words and my deeds express the radical holiness that comes from the wonderful, joyful freedom of living by faith in guaranteed future grace. Amen. And I do mean, AMEN."

He who did not spare His own Son,
but delivered Him up for us all,
how will He not also with Him
freely give us all things?

ROMANS 8 : 3 2

Surely if he would not spare his own Son one stroke,
one tear, one groan, one sigh, one circumstance of misery,
it can never be imagined that ever he should, after this,
deny or withhold from his people, for whose sakes all this was suffered,
any mercies, any comforts, any privilege,
spiritual or temporal, which is good for them.

JOHN FLAVEL

CHAPTER EIGHT

The Solid Logic of Heaven

R omans Eight is the most precious chapter in the Bible to me. A few years ago I memorized it during the Advent season and recited it to our congregation on Christmas Eve as a kind of Christmas present from my heart. It abounds with promises of future grace. But just as important, it shows me the solid logic of heaven that makes the most far-reaching promise of future grace as firm as God's love for his Son Jesus.

THE MOST FAR-REACHING PROMISE OF FUTURE GRACE

The most far-reaching promise of future grace is found in verse 32. "He who did not spare His own Son, but delivered Him up for us all, how will He not also with Him freely give us all things?" This is the most precious verse in the Bible to me. Part of the reason is that the promise in it is so all-encompassing that it stands ready to help me at virtually every turn in my life and ministry. There never has been and never will be a circumstance in my life where this promise is irrelevant.

By itself that all-encompassing promise would probably not make the verse most precious. There are other such sweeping promises such as Psalm 84:11, "No good thing does [God] withhold from those who walk uprightly." And 1 Corinthians 3:21-22, "For all things belong to you, whether Paul or Apollos or Cephas or the world or life or death or things present or things to come; all things belong to you, and you belong to Christ; and Christ belongs to God." It is difficult to overstate the spectacular sweep and scope of these promises.

But what puts Romans 8:32 in a class by itself is the logic that gives rise to the promise and makes it as solid and unshakable as God's love for his infinitely admirable Son. Romans 8:32 contains a foundation and guarantee that is so strong and so solid and so secure that there is absolutely no possibility that the promise could ever be broken. This is what makes it an ever-present strength in times of great turmoil. Whatever else gives way, whatever else disappoints, whatever else fails, this all-encompassing promise of future grace can never fail.

The verse has two parts. The foundation and the promise. The first part, the foundation, goes like this: "He who did not spare His own Son, but delivered Him up for us all...." If this is true, says the logic of heaven, then God will most surely give all things to those for whom he gave his Son. Which means that all future grace is founded in the first half of Romans 8:32. Dwell with me for a moment on this foundation.

One of my friends who used to be a pastor in Illinois was preaching to a group of prisoners in a state prison during Holy Week several years ago. At one point in his message he paused and asked the men if they knew who killed Jesus. Some said the soldiers did. Some said the Jews did. Some said Pilate. After there was silence, my friend said simply, "His Father killed him."

That's what the first half of Romans 8:32 says: God did not spare his own Son but handed him over—to death. "This Man [was] delivered up by the predetermined plan and foreknowledge of God" (Acts 2:23). Isaiah 53 puts it even more bluntly, "We esteemed him stricken, *smitten by God*...It was the *will of the Lord* to bruise him; *he* (his Father!) has put him to grief" (vv. 4, 10, RSV). Or as Romans 3:25 says, "*God* displayed [him] publicly as a propitiation in his blood." Just as Abraham lifted the knife over the chest of his son Isaac, but then spared his son because there was a ram in the thicket, so God the Father lifted the knife over the chest of his own Son Jesus—but did *not* spare him, because he *was* the ram; he *was* the substitute.

And my pastor friend told me later that those hardened prisoners sat there in silence for a moment and then said, "Why would he do that?" Why would God kill his own Son? Why would he not "spare" him?

WHY DID GOD NOT SPARE HIS SON?

The answer is given right here in the verse: God "did not spare His own Son, but delivered Him up *for us all.*" In another place Paul says, "[God] made Him who knew no sin to be sin *on our behalf,* that we might become the righteousness of God in Him" (2 Corinthians 5:21). Or as Isaiah saw it hundreds of years before it happened:

> *He was wounded* for our transgressions,
> *He was bruised* for our iniquities;
> *Upon him was the chastisement* that made us whole,
> *And with his stripes* we are healed.
> *All we like sheep have gone astray;*
> *We have turned every one to his own way;*
> *And the Lord has laid on him the* iniquity of us all.
> (Isaiah 53:5-6, RSV)

God did not spare his own Son, because it was the only way he could spare us. The guilt of our transgressions, the punishment of our iniquities, the curse of our sin would have brought us inescapably to the destruction of hell. But God did not spare his own Son; he gave him up to be wounded for our transgressions, and bruised for our iniquities and crucified for our sin.

This verse is the most precious verse in the Bible to me because the foundation of the all-encompassing promise of future grace is that the Son of God bore in his body all my punishment and all my guilt and all my condemnation and all my blame and all my fault and all my corruption, so that I might stand before a great and holy God, forgiven, reconciled, justified, accepted, and the beneficiary of unspeakable promises of pleasure forever and ever at his right hand.

THE GLORIOUS LOGIC OF HEAVEN

But that's not all. The logic of the verse says more. Paul reasons like this: *since* God did not spare his own Son, *then* surely he *must* and *will* freely give us all things with him. Why is that? How does this all-important logic work? There is a technical name for this kind of reasoning. It's called *"a majori ad minus."* This means arguing "from the greater to the lesser." Suppose two tasks are motivated by the same desire, but one is very improbable because the cost is so high, and one is more probable because the cost is less. If I have the desire for both tasks, and somehow manage to accomplish the costly one, then it is virtually assured the less costly one will be accomplished. Overcoming the greater obstacles assures you that I will overcome the lesser ones.

It's the logic Jesus used when he said, "If God so arrays the grass of the field, which is alive today and tomorrow is thrown into the furnace, will He not much more do so for you, O men of little faith?" (Matthew 6:30). Be careful here. Don't jump to the conclusion that Jesus is arguing from "lesser to greater." Yes grass is lesser than people. But clothing grass is *more* unlikely than clothing disciples. Jesus really is arguing from the greater to the lesser. God desires to clothe both flowers and disciples. The disciples are doubtful that he really will clothe them. How does Jesus strengthen their faith in the future grace of his promise to clothe them?

He says in effect that it is *highly improbable* that God Almighty would waste his time clothing field flowers which last only a day. This high improbability is the "greater thing" in his argument from greater to lesser. On the other hand, there is a *small amount of improbability* that God would neglect his Son's disciples and not clothe them. This small improbability is the "lesser thing" in his argument. So when God overcomes the high improbability and clothes field flowers, he proves that he can and will overcome the small improbability and clothe the disciples.

So Paul is reasoning in Romans 8:32 from the hard to the easy, or from the greater to the lesser. If God did not spare his own Son, but gave him up for us—that's the hard thing, the great thing. The reason it's the greater thing is that God loved his Son infinitely. His Son did not deserve to be killed. His Son was worthy of worship by every creature, not spitting and whipping and scorn and torture. To hand over his beloved Son (Colossians 1:13) was the incomparably great thing. The reason for this is the immensity of God's love for his Son. This is what made it so unlikely that God would hand him over. Yet God did it. And in doing it he showed that he most certainly would do all other things—all of which would be easy by comparison—to give all things to the people for whom he gave his Son.

This is why I said that the promise of Romans 8:32 is as sure as God's love for his Son. God desired two things: not to see his Son made a mockery by sinners; and not to see his people denied infinite future grace. Surely it is more likely that he will spare his Son than that he will spare us. But no. He did not spare his Son. And therefore it is impossible that he should spare us the promise for which the Son died—he will freely with him give us all things.

What a truth! Giving us all things is the easy thing! Think on that every time you fear being denied something that would be good for you. You think it is a hard thing. You see many obstacles. It looks impossible. At that discouraging moment think about this heavenly logic. Giving you what you need is the easy part. And the hard part is already done. Creating the world and running it for the good of his people is a relatively easy thing for God to do compared to handing over his Son to ridicule and torture. But he did it. And now all future grace is not only sure; it is easy.

DOES GOD REALLY GIVE US ALL THINGS?

But what does this promise mean—that God will freely with Christ give us all things? Future grace like this seems out of sync with our experience. There are many things we may not receive that we think would be gracious and wise of God to give us—health, safety, more success, a spouse, believing children, long life. What does Paul mean that God will give us *all things?*

One key is found in the immediately preceding verse (Romans 8:31). There Paul says, "If God is for us, who is against us?" Our first response to this question is: lots of people are against us! In fact, Jesus said, "You will be delivered up even by parents and brothers and relatives and friends, and they will put some of you to death and you will be hated by all on account of My name" (Luke 21:16-17). That's a lot of opposition. Paul knew that.

Just a few verses later in this chapter he said, "For Thy sake we are being put to death all day long" (Romans 8:36).

What then did Paul mean when he said, "If God is for us, who is against us?" I think he meant, "Who can be *successfully* against us?" What opposition could there ever be against us that almighty God could not transform into our benefit? And the answer is: none. This is what Paul means later when he says that in tribulation, distress, persecution, famine, nakedness, peril and sword we "overwhelmingly conquer through Him who loved us" (Romans 8:37). We *overwhelmingly conquer* not by escaping these terrible things, but by watching God turn these enemies of our joy into servants of our good.

The great promise of future grace is that God will give us all things with Christ—including *death*. This is what he says in 1 Corinthians 3:21-22, "For all things belong to you, whether...life or *death*...all things belong to you." Death is ours—it will be given to us—not as a gift we can reject, but as a triumphant gateway to glory.

The great promise of future grace, guaranteed in the logic of Romans 8:32, is that nothing will ever enter your experience as God's child that, by God's sovereign grace, will not turn out to be a benefit to you. This is what it means for God to be God, and for God to *be for* you, and for God to freely give you all things with Christ.

HE STRIPS EVERY PAIN OF DESTRUCTIVE POWER

You must believe this or you will not thrive, or perhaps even survive as a Christian, in the pressures and temptations of modern life. There is so much pain, so many setbacks and discouragements, so many controversies and pressures. I do not know where I would turn in the ministry if I did not believe that almighty God is taking every setback and every discouragement and every controversy and every pressure and every pain, and stripping it of its destructive power and making it work for the enlargement of my joy in God.

The world is ours. Life is ours. Death is ours. God reigns so supremely on behalf of his elect that everything which faces us in a lifetime of obedience and ministry will be subdued by the mighty hand of God and made the servant of our holiness and our everlasting joy in God. If God is for us, and if God is God, then it is true that nothing can succeed against us. He who did not spare his own Son but gave him up for us all, will infallibly and freely with him give us all things—all things: the world, life, death, and God himself.

Romans 8:32 is a precious friend. The promise of future grace is overwhelming. But all-important is the foundation. Here is a place to stand against all obstacles. God did not spare his own Son! How much more then will he spare no effort to give me all that Christ died to purchase—all things, all good. It is as sure as the certainty that he loved his Son.

JOHN FLAVEL'S TRIBUTE TO THE GREAT LOGIC OF HEAVEN

I am not the only one who revels in the great, solid logic of Romans 8:32. Recently I read this savoring tribute from John Flavel, a Puritan pastor from over 300 years ago. It expresses my heart (and my interpretation) exactly:

> He spared not his own Son, but delivered him up for us all; how shall he not with him freely give us all things?" (Romans 8:32). How is it imaginable that God should withhold, after this, spirituals or temporals, from his people? How shall he not call them effectually, justify them freely, sanctify them thoroughly, and glorify them eternally? How shall he not clothe them, feed them, protect and deliver them? Surely if he would not spare this own Son one stroke, one tear, one groan, one sigh, one circumstance of misery, it can never be imagined that ever he should, after this, deny or withhold from his people, for whose sakes all this was suffered, any mercies, any comforts, any privilege, spiritual or temporal, which is good for them.[1]

This quote moved me so much that I copied it into my journal and added this prayer:

> Oh, Lord, I believe, help my wretched unbelief. What a life! Free from murmuring and complaint, and full of risk and joy and love! O, to believe this! God, I want to live in this reality. Help me. O, spare me nothing that would put me in this glorious confidence.

If there is a way to live by faith in this invincible future grace, I want to know that life. I want to know how trusting this promise, rooted in the unshakable logic of heaven, can free me and empower me to love and risk and suffer and die and rise for the glory of God, and the good of my people, the good of the nations, and the good of my own soul. That's one of the main reasons I am writing this book—if by any means I might come into the deeper experience of living by faith in future grace, and take as many people with me as I can.

And we know that God causes all things to work together for good
to those who love God, to those who are called according to His purpose.
For whom He foreknew, He also predestined
to become conformed to the image of His Son,
that He might be the first-born among many brethren;
and whom He predestined, these He also called;
and whom He called, these He also justified;
and whom He justified, these He also glorified.

ROMANS 8:28-30

Grace reaches back to eternity.
And every step of the way leading to this very moment
has been a moment of grace.
Election is by grace; predestination is by grace;
effectual calling is by grace; justification is by grace;
and, because of all this glorious bygone grace,
we may now, with tremendous confidence,
stand in the great halls of Romans 8:28
and live in the freedom and love and righteousness
that come through faith in the future grace:
that God will cause all things to work together for our good.

CHAPTER NINE

Four Pillars
of a
Precious Promise

E ven though I gave Romans 8:32 the most exalted place among the promises of God in my heart, thousands of Christians would do the same for Romans 8:28. "And we know that God causes all things to work together for good to those who love God, to those who are called according to His purpose." I won't quarrel with anyone who cherishes this promise of future grace above all others. The scope of both promises is all-encompassing, each in its own way. The common phrase between them is "all things." Romans 8:32 says that God will freely give us "all things," and Romans 8:28 says that God will cause "all things" to work together for our good.

Not only is each of these promises distinctly all-encompassing, both are massively rooted in the irrevocable work of bygone grace. We saw it in Romans 8:32. And we will see it now in the verses that follow and support Romans 8:28.

BROAD ROOTS AND DEEP RETAINING WALLS

Just outside my vacation study in Georgia there is an oak tree. The two bottom limbs, which come out like great arms with gnarly elbows, probably have a girth of five or six feet. The base of the trunk is perhaps 12 feet around. The height and spread of the branches is massive, giving shade over the whole area. What is not seen is the roots. That's the way it is with roots. They support everything but they don't get much attention. The more massive the tree, the more massive the root system. It's there, and if we could see it, we would be amazed. We would understand why this tree is still standing after decades of wind and lightning and hail and heat. Our faith in the durability of the tree and the shade would be strengthened.

It's the same way with buildings. In the last 15 years I have watched from my study window as the skyline of Minneapolis has filled up with one new skyscraper after another. Their construction is a wonder to watch—especially what happens before they rise from the ground. I recall watching a mammoth mechanized scoop sit in the middle of an empty lot and dig a hole deeper than many of the other buildings were tall. The foundation wall at the edge of the hole must have been six or seven stories underground. The principle is simple: the taller the building is going to be aboveground to serve people, the deeper and stronger the foundation has to be underground to serve the building.

When it comes to the architecture of future grace and the buildings we call the promises of God, Romans 8:28 shares the tribute of being one of the two or three greatest. This structure is staggering in its size. The infinitely wise, infinitely powerful God pledges that in this building, future grace will make *everything* beneficial to his people! Not just nice things, but horrible things too—like tribulation and distress and peril and famine and slaughter (Romans 8:35-37). What brick would you lay on the top of this skyscraper promise to make it taller? "God works *all things* together for good" means *all things*.

WHAT IT'S LIKE TO LIVE IN ROMANS 8:28

If you live inside this massive promise, your life is more solid and stable than Mount Everest. Nothing can blow you over when you are inside the walls of Romans 8:28. Outside Romans 8:28 all is confusion and anxiety and fear and uncertainty. Outside this promise of all-encompassing future grace there are straw houses of drugs and alcohol and numbing TV and dozens of futile diversions. There are slat walls and tin roofs of fragile investment strategies and fleeting insurance coverage and trivial retirement plans. There are cardboard fortifications of deadbolt locks and alarm systems and antiballistic missiles. Outside are a thousand substitutes for Romans 8:28.

Once you walk through the door of love into the massive, unshakable structure of Romans 8:28 everything changes. There come into your life stability and depth and freedom. You simply can't be blown over any more. The confidence that a sovereign God governs for your good all the pain and all the pleasure that you will ever experience is an incomparable refuge and security and hope and power in your life. When God's people really live by the future grace of Romans 8:28—from measles to the mortuary—they are the freest and strongest and most generous people in the world. Their light shines and people give glory to their Father in heaven (Matthew 5:16).

THE FOUR PILLARS UNDER ROMANS 8:28

The foundation of this immense structure of future grace is equally immense. It is found in Romans 8:29-30. In fact, the foundation is so massive that all I can do in this chapter is point out some of its main supporting structures and pray that you will spend the rest of your life going further and further into the strength and depth of Romans 8:28. This would not be wasted effort because Romans 8:28 contains within itself virtually every other promise God has made to us. Therefore the foundation of Romans 8:28 is the foundation of all the promises. It is good to live aboveground in the great skyscraper of Romans 8:28; but it is also needful to know our way around in the underground rooms and halls where the massive supporting pillars go deeper than we can imagine. This will make us secure and unshakable people.

I call Romans 8:29-30 the foundation of verse 28 because it begins with "for," which means that Paul is giving the *reason* or *basis* that we can be confident in this promise. The promise says, "We know that God causes all things to work together for good to those who love God, to those who are called according to his purpose." Then comes the basis of the promise in four parts:

29) **FOR** *whom He foreknew, He also predestined to become conformed to the image of His Son, that He might be the firstborn among many brethren;*

30a) and whom He predestined, these He also called;

30b) and whom He called, these He also justified;

30c) and whom He justified, these He also glorified.

These four statements are the four massive pillars in the foundation of the future grace promised in Romans 8:28.

What's the point of a chain of statements like this? The point is certainty and confidence and assurance and security. The point is that God is the one who saves his people, really saves them. He does not just offer salvation, he saves them. From beginning to end he is the One who decisively and infallibly acts so that not one of his own is lost. The point is that the chain cannot be broken: all the foreknown are predestined; all the predestined are called; all the called are justified; and all the justified are glorified. The point is to guarantee that everyone in the chain will reach the goal of glory.

WHAT WILL IT MEAN TO BE GLORIFIED?

The end of the chain is that the justified will be "glorified." That refers to "the (future) grace...at the revelation of Jesus Christ" (1 Peter 1:13), when he comes to give us "the unfading crown of glory" (1 Peter 5:4). We "will shine forth as the sun in the kingdom of [our] Father" (Matthew 13:43), because we will be completely "conformed to the image of His Son" (Romans 8:29). He will wipe away every tear from our eyes and there will be no death or crying or pain any more (Revelation 21:4). God himself will be with us; and "fullness of joy and pleasures forever more" will be ours at his right hand (Psalm 16:11); and we will "enter into the joy of [our] Master" (Matthew 25:21).

This is the ultimate fulfillment of Romans 8:28. Being "glorified" means coming to the final, everlasting experience of seeing God work everything together for our good. The "glorified" state of verse 30 is the ultimate "good" for which God works all things together in verse 28. It is our final likeness to Christ which brings *him* glory ("the firstborn among many brethren") and brings us unspeakable joy.

ALL THE JUSTIFIED WILL BE GLORIFIED

But who may be sure of this ultimate fulfillment of Romans 8:28? Paul answers: "Whom [God] justified, these He also glorified." All those who are justified will be glorified. None drops out. This is an unshakable pillar penetrating deep into the foundation of God's promise. Justification by faith secures final glorification. God has ordained it. God accomplishes it. The future grace of glorification is guaranteed by the past grace of justification. "[We are] justified as a gift *by his grace* through the redemption which is in Christ Jesus" (Romans 3:24). If we have been justified by grace, we will be glorified. God has forged the link and it cannot be broken.

ALL THE CALLED WILL BE JUSTIFIED

But who will be justified? Paul answers: "Whom He called, these He also justified." All those who are called are justified. This is the second immovable pillar in the foundation of Romans 8:28. It is a powerful claim.

How can Paul say that all who are called are justified? He teaches elsewhere, in unmistakable terms, that justification is only by faith. "Therefore having been *justified by faith* we have peace with God" (Romans 5:1). "We maintain that a man is *justified by faith* apart from works of the law" (Romans 3:28). Only people with faith are justified. And *all* the called are justified. This must mean that the "call" Paul has in mind is not the general gospel call that goes out to all who hear the gospel each time it is preached. For we know that not all those who are called in this sense exercise faith, nor are they all justified. Many close their hearts to the gospel. Paul could never say of them, "Whom he called, he also justified." They are "called" outwardly, but it has no transforming effect on their hearts.

THE CALL CREATES THE FAITH THAT JUSTIFIES

The call that Paul has in mind must be the effective, inner call of God to the heart that actually creates what it commands, namely, faith. In other words, the call of Romans 8:30 is not like "Here, Blackie! Here, Blackie!" The dog may or may not come. Rather, God's call is like, "Lazarus, come forth" from the grave (John 11:43). Or, "Let there be light!" (see 2 Corinthians 4:6). The call creates what it commands.

Since the call is infallibly effective because of God's sovereign power, Paul is able to say, "Whom he called he also justified." All the called are justified, because all the called have faith, because the call creates the faith.[1]

TO WHOM IS THE PROMISE OF ROMANS 8:28 MADE?

Here we come to the center of the foundation of Romans 8:28. Notice that Romans 8:28 is not true for everybody. The verse says "that God causes all things to work together for good...*to those who are called.*" The beneficiaries of this promise are people who are not left to their own resources to get qualified for the promise. They are people whom God calls. And we have just seen that this call is no mere invitation that might fail, but an infallibly effective work of faith-begetting creation.

Here's the center of the foundation of Romans 8:28. Those who are called by God can be sure that God will work all things together for their good because their calling guarantees their justification; and their justification, in turn, guarantees their glorification; and glorification is the ultimate fulfillment of Romans 8:28—endless ages of seeing God make everything in the universe serve our holy joy in him.

WHO RECEIVES THIS FAITH-CREATING CALL?

But Paul is not content to stop with these two pillars in the foundation of Romans 8:28. He pushes on back to ask, "What is this calling of God founded on?" Or, "Who are the ones who experience this sovereign call of God?" And he answers: "Whom [God] *predestined,* these He also called." That's foundational pillar number three. God's act of calling is based on his act of predestining.

This is just another way of saying what Romans 8:28 says in the words, "called according to His purpose." "God causes all things to work together for the good of those...who are called according to his purpose." "According to [God's] purpose" means "according to the goal of God's predestination." In other words, God did not call us without a specific aim or purpose in mind. He had a "destiny" in mind for us and he called us "according to [that] purpose." Those whom he thus predestined, he called.

And the "purpose" or "destiny" is spelled out plainly in Romans 8:29. "He also predestined [us] to become conformed to the image of His Son, that He might be the firstborn among many brethren." So the foundation of our calling is the purpose of God to have a people who will be morally and spiritually like Jesus, and will exalt him as supreme. Our calling is as sure as God's ultimate purpose to glorify his Son.

When we add pillar number three to the foundation under the promise of Romans 8:28 it looks like this: Since our final glorification is the ultimate fulfillment of Romans 8:28, we can be utterly sure it will happen, because our glorification is guaranteed by our justification, and our justification is guaranteed by our calling, and our calling is as solid and sure as the predestination of God—that is, the eternal purpose of God to make us like his Son and to exalt his Son as Supreme—to the praise of his glory. "He predestined us to adoption as sons through Jesus Christ...*to the praise of the glory of His grace*" (Ephesians 1:5–6). Pillar after pillar of past grace gives unshakable grounding to the future grace of Romans 8:28.

DIGGING BACK TO ETERNITY IN THE HEART OF GOD

There is one more. Paul does not stop even in pressing us back as far as predestination. It's as though he is saying, "For the highest of all promises of future grace I will dig the deepest foundation of past grace. I will dig all the way back to eternity in the heart of God. What is there beneath predestination to hold it up and make it even more sure? Paul's answer: "Whom [God] foreknew, He also predestined." This is as deep as Paul digs: the foreknowledge of God. From this flows the certainty of predestination and calling and justification and glorification—and therefore the infallible fulfillment of the future grace of Romans 8:28.

Sometimes people take "foreknowledge" to mean that God simply foresees the faith that we produce by our own self-determination. Then on the basis of what we do he predestines us to sonship. That makes the whole glorious chain of salvation hang ultimately on our act, not God's.

But this interpretation will not work. It assumes that faith is something we produce by the power of self-determination rather than being a work of God's sovereign call in our lives. That does not fit with what we saw in

127

Romans 8:30—"Whom He called, these He also justified." What we saw was that if all the called are justified, as Paul says, then the call of God is not a mere *invitation* to people with the power of self-determination. Rather it is *an act of creation* in people who are spiritually dead.[2] What the call creates is faith. Therefore when God looked forward into history from his standpoint in eternity he did not see free people using powers of self-determination to believe; he saw people enslaved to sin and spiritually dead, whose only hope was that the sovereign call of God would create the faith he commands.

The meaning of "foreknowledge" in Romans 8:29 is not merely God's prior awareness of what we would produce on our own. It is the kind of knowing that in the Bible frequently means "take a special recognition of with a view to setting apart for a relationship." It is virtually the same as setting one's favor on or choosing. For example, in Amos 3:2 God says to Israel, "You only have I chosen among all the families of the earth." The word translated "choose" in the NASB is "known" in Hebrew: "You only have I known." That is, God had set his special loving awareness and attention on Israel so as to set her apart from all the nations. There are numerous instances of this meaning of "know" in the Bible.[3]

What this means then is that the final pillar in the foundation of Romans 8:28 is God's free and gracious election. It gives eternal certainty and security to the whole chain. Our glorification is guaranteed by our being justified graciously by God; and our justification is guaranteed by our being called graciously by God; and our calling is guaranteed by our being predestined graciously by God; and our predestination is guaranteed by our being freely and graciously recognized by God and chosen as a beneficiary for the awesome future grace of everything working together for our good.

THE MASSIVE PLACE FOR BYGONE GRACE

As we celebrate future grace, let it not be said that there is no place for past grace. Grace reaches back to eternity. And every step of the way leading to this very moment has been a gift of grace. Election is by grace (Romans 11:5); predestination is by grace (Ephesians 1:5-6); effectual calling is by grace (2 Timothy 1:9); justification is by grace (Romans 3:24); and, because of all this glorious bygone grace, we may now, with tremendous confidence, stand in the great halls of Romans 8:28 and live in the freedom and love and righteousness that come through faith in future grace—that God will cause all things to work together for our good. The freest life of love is the life saturated with the confidence that nothing comes to me but what is good for me. It is fitting that this greatest freedom rest on the greatest foundation.

One of the most precious experiences of this freedom is deliverance from misplaced shame. Ponder with me in the next chapter the purifying power of prizing God's grace, as it overcomes the paralyzing effects of shame.

I also suffer these things,
but I am not ashamed;
for I know whom I have believed,
I am convinced that He is able to guard
what I have entrusted to Him until that day.

2 TIMOTHY 1:12

No one who believes in Him
will be put to shame.

ROMANS 10:11 (RSV)

CHAPTER TEN

Applying the Purifying Power

Faith in Future Grace
vs.
Misplaced Shame

Though shame has been fashionable as a prevalent diagnosis for emotional dysfunction, its roots are deep in the human condition, and the pain it can bring is real. If we are to live the kind of free and radically loving and holy lives Christ calls us to, we must understand the place of shame and how to fight against its crippling effects. We start with a definition: Shame is a painful emotion caused by a consciousness of guilt or shortcoming or impropriety.[1] The pain is caused not merely by our own failures but by the awareness that others see them. Let me illustrate each of these causes.

THREE CAUSES OF SHAME

First, consider *guilt* as a cause. Suppose you act against your conscience and withhold information on your tax returns. For a couple years you feel nothing because it has been put out of your mind, and you weren't caught. Then you are called to account by the IRS and it becomes public knowledge that you lied and you stole. Your guilt is known to your church and your employer and friends. Now in the light of public censure you feel the pain of shame.

Or take *shortcoming* as a cause. In the Olympics, suppose you come from a country where you are quite good in the 3000-meter race, compared to your countrymen. Then you compete before thousands of people in the Olympics, and the competition is so tough that by the time the last lap comes up you are a whole lap behind everyone else, and you must keep running all by yourself while everyone watches. There's no guilt here. You have done nothing wrong. But, depending on your frame of mind, the humiliation and shame could be intense.

Or consider *impropriety* as a cause of shame. You are invited to a party and you find out when you get there that you dressed all wrong. Again, there's no evil or guilt. Just a social blunder, an impropriety that makes you feel foolish and embarrassed. This too is a kind of shame.

One of the things that jumps right out at you from this definition of shame is that there is some shame that is justified, and some that isn't. There are some situations where shame is exactly what we should feel. And there are some situations where we shouldn't. Most people would say that the liar *ought* to be ashamed. And most people would probably say that the long distance runner who gave it his best shot ought *not* to feel ashamed. Disappointment would be healthy, but not shame.

TWO KINDS OF SHAME

Let me illustrate from Scripture these two kinds of shame. The Bible makes very clear that there is a shame we ought to have and a shame we ought not to have. I'm going to call the one kind "misplaced shame" and the other kind "well-placed shame." Like everything else that matters, the crucial issue is how God fits into the experience of shame.

MISPLACED SHAME

Misplaced shame (the kind we ought *not* to have) is the shame you feel when there is no good reason to feel it. Biblically that means that the thing you feel ashamed of is not dishonoring to God; or that it *is* dishonoring to God, but you didn't have a hand in it. In other words, misplaced shame is shame for something that's good—something that doesn't dishonor God. Or it's shame for something that's bad, but which you didn't have any sinful hand in. That's the kind of shame we ought not have.

WELL-PLACED SHAME

Well-placed shame (the kind we *ought* to have) is the shame we feel when there is good reason to feel it. Biblically that means we feel ashamed of something because our involvement in it was dishonoring to God. We ought to feel shame when we have a hand in bringing dishonor upon God by our attitudes or actions.

I want to be sure you see how important *God* is in this distinction between misplaced shame and well-placed shame. Whether we have a hand in honoring God or dishonoring God makes all the difference. If we want to battle shame at the root, we have to know how it relates to God. And we *do* need to battle shame at the root—all shame. Because both misplaced shame and well-placed shame can cripple us if we don't know how to deal with them at the root.

It will help us in our battle, if we look at some Scriptures that illustrate misplaced shame and some that illustrate well-placed shame. We need to see that these are, in fact, biblical categories. In this day, when psychology has a tremendous influence on how we use words, we need to be sure that we can assess all language about our emotions with biblical ways of thinking and speaking. If you have learned your use of the word "shame" from contemporary psychology, be aware that I am not using it in the same way (see Note One). You may find that the Bible uses the concept of shame differently from the way it is popularly used. Once you see the biblical terms clearly, you will be in a position to assess the way contemporary people talk about shame.

BIBLICAL EXAMPLES OF MISPLACED SHAME

Paul says to Timothy that if he feels shame for testifying to the gospel, he feels misplaced shame. "Do not be ashamed of the testimony of our Lord, or of me His prisoner, but join with me in suffering for the gospel according to the power of God" (2 Timothy 1:8). We ought not to feel shame for the gospel. Christ is honored when we speak well of him. And he is dishonored by fearful silence. So it is not a shameful thing to testify, but a shameful thing not to.

The same verse says that if we feel shame that a friend of ours is in prison for Jesus' sake, then our shame is misplaced. The world may see imprisonment for Christ as a sign of weakness and defeat. But Christians know better. God is honored by the courage of his servants to go to prison for his name, if they have acted in just and loving ways. We ought not to feel shame that we are associated with something that honors God in this way, no matter how much scorn the world heaps on us.

In a well-known saying of Jesus, we learn that our shame is misplaced when we feel shame because of who Jesus is or what he says. "Whoever is ashamed of Me and My words in this adulterous and sinful generation, the Son of Man will also be ashamed of him when He comes in the glory of His Father with the holy angels" (Mark 8:38). For example, if Jesus says, "Love your enemies," and others laugh and call it unrealistic, we should not feel ashamed. If Jesus says, "Don't fornicate," and promiscuous people label this command out-of-date, we should not feel shame to stand with Jesus. That would be misplaced shame because the words of Jesus are true and God-honoring, no matter how foolish the world may try to make them look.

Suffering and being reproached and made fun of as a Christian is not an occasion for shame, because it is an occasion for glorifying God. "If anyone suffers as a Christian, let him not feel ashamed, but in that name let him glorify God" (1 Peter 4:16). In other words, in the Bible the criterion for what is well-placed shame and what is misplaced shame is not how foolish or how bad you look to men, but whether you in fact bring honor to God.

WHOSE HONOR IS AT STAKE IN OUR SHAME?

This is extremely important to grasp, because much of what makes us feel shame is not that we have brought dishonor to God by our actions, but that we have failed to give the appearance that other people admire. Much of our shame is not God-centered but self-centered. Until we get a good handle on this, we will not be able to battle the problem of shame at its root.

A lot of Christian shame comes from what man thinks rather than what

God thinks. But if we realized deeply that God's assessment is infinitely more significant than anyone else's, we would not be ashamed of things that are so amazing they are even called the very power of God: "I am not ashamed of the gospel, for it is the power of God for salvation to everyone who believes" (Romans 1:16). This verse tells us another reason that shame in the gospel would be misplaced shame. The gospel is the very power of God unto salvation. The gospel magnifies God and humbles man. To the world the gospel doesn't look like power at all. It looks like weakness—asking people to be like children and telling them to depend on Jesus, instead of standing on their own two feet. But for those who believe, it is the power of God to give sinners everlasting glory.

One of the reasons we are tempted to feel shame even at the power of Jesus is that Jesus shows his power in ways that the world does not recognize as powerful. Jesus said to Paul in 2 Corinthians 12:9, "My grace is sufficient for you, for my power is perfected in weakness." Paul responds to this strange demonstration of power, "Most gladly, therefore, I will rather boast about my weaknesses that the power of Christ may dwell in me. Therefore I am well content with weaknesses, with insults, with distresses, with persecutions, and with difficulties for Christ's sake; for when I am weak, then I am strong" (2 Corinthians 12:9-10). Ordinarily weaknesses and insults are occasions for shame. But for Paul they are occasions for exultation. Paul thinks that shame in his weaknesses and shame at his persecutions would be misplaced shame. Why? Because the power of Christ is perfected in Paul's weakness.

I conclude from this—and from all these texts—that the biblical criterion for misplaced shame is radically God-centered. The biblical criterion says, Don't feel shame for something that honors God, no matter how weak or foolish it makes you look in the eyes of unbelievers.

BIBLICAL EXAMPLES OF WELL-PLACED SHAME

The same God-centeredness is seen when we look at passages that illustrate well-placed shame. Paul says to the Corinthians who were doubting the resurrection, "Become sober-minded as you ought, and stop sinning; for some have no knowledge of God. I speak this to your shame" (1 Corinthians

15:34). Here Paul says that these people *ought* to feel shame. "I speak this to your shame." Their shame would be well-placed if they saw their deplorable ignorance of God and how it was leading to false doctrine (no resurrection) and sin in the church. In other words, well-placed shame is shame for what dishonors God—like ignorance of God, and sin against God, and false beliefs about God.

In the same church, some of the believers were going to secular courts to settle disputes among themselves. Paul rebukes them. "I say this to your shame. Is it so that there is not among you one wise man who will be able to decide between his brethren?" (1 Corinthians 6:5). Again he says they should feel shame: "I say this to your shame." Their shame would be well-placed because their behavior is bringing such disrepute upon their God. They are disputing with one another before godless judges to settle their disputes. A well-placed shame is the shame you feel because you are involved in dishonoring God.

These people were trying their best to appear strong and right. They wanted to be vindicated by men. They wanted to be winners in court. They didn't want anyone to run over them, as though they had no rights. That would look weak and shameful. So in the very act of wanting to avoid shame, as the world sees it, they fell into the very behavior that God counts shameful. The point is: when you are dishonoring God, you *ought* to feel shame, no matter how strong or wise or right you are in the eyes of the world.

When a Christian's eyes are opened to the God-dishonoring evil of his former behavior, he rightly feels ashamed. Paul says to the Roman church, "For when you were slaves of sin, you were free in regard to righteousness. Therefore what benefit were you then deriving from the things of which you are now *ashamed*? For the outcome of those things is death" (Romans 6:20-21). There is a proper place for looking back and feeling the twinge of pain that we once lived in a way that was so belittling to God. We will see in a moment that we are not to be paralyzed by dwelling on this. But a sensitive Christian heart cannot think back on the follies of youth and not feel echoes of the shame, even if we have settled it all with the Lord.

Well-placed shame can be very healthy and redemptive. Paul said to the Thessalonians, "If anyone does not obey our instruction in this letter, take special note of that man and do not associate with him, so that he may be *put to shame*" (2 Thessalonians 3:14). This means that shame is a proper and redemptive step in conversion and in a believer's repentance from a season of backsliding. Shame is not something to be avoided at all costs. There is a place for it in God's good dealings with his people.

We can conclude from what we have seen so far that the biblical criterion for misplaced shame and for well-placed shame is radically God-centered. The biblical criterion for *misplaced shame* says, Don't feel shame for something that honors God, no matter how weak or foolish or wrong it makes you look in the eyes of other people. And don't take onto yourself the shamefulness of a truly shameful situation unless you are in some way truly woven into the evil. The biblical criterion for *well-placed* shame says, Do feel shame for having a hand in anything that dishonors God, no matter how strong or wise or right it makes you look in the eyes of men.

BATTLING THE UNBELIEF OF MISPLACED SHAME

Now comes the crucial question that relates to living by faith in future grace. How do you battle this painful emotion called shame? The answer is: we battle it at the root—by battling the unbelief that feeds its life. We fight for faith in the promises of God that overcome shame and relieve us from its pain. I'll try to illustrate this battle with three instances.

FUTURE GRACE FOR A FORGIVEN HARLOT

First, in the case of well-placed shame, the pain ought to *be* there, but it ought not to *stay* there. If it does, it's owing to lack of faith in the promises of God. For example, a woman comes to Jesus in a Pharisee's house weeping and washing his feet. No doubt she felt shame as the eyes of Simon communicated to everyone present that this woman was a sinner and that Jesus had no business letting her touch him. Indeed she was a sinner. There was a place for true shame. But not for too long. Jesus said, "Your sins have been forgiven" (Luke 7:48). And when the guests murmured about this, he helped her faith again by saying, "Your faith has saved you; go in peace" (Luke 7:50).

How did Jesus help her battle the crippling effects of shame? He gave her a promise: "Your sins have been forgiven! Your faith has saved you. Your future will be one of peace." He declared that past pardon would now yield future peace. So the issue for her was faith in this future grace rooted in the authority of Jesus' forgiving work and freeing word. Would she believe the glowering condemnation of the guests? Or would she believe the reassuring words of Jesus that her shame was over—that she is now and in the future forgiven, that she may go in peace and wholeness and freedom? Whom will she trust? With whose promise will she satisfy her soul?

That is the way every one of us must battle the effects of a well-placed shame that threatens to linger too long and cripple us. We must battle unbelief by taking hold of the promises of future grace and peace that come through the forgiveness of our shameful acts. "There is forgiveness with Thee that Thou mayest be feared" (Psalm 130:4). "Seek the Lord while He may be found. Call upon Him while He is near. Let the wicked forsake his way, and the unrighteous man his thoughts. And let him return to the Lord, and He will have compassion on him; and to our God for He will abundantly pardon" (Isaiah 55:6). "If we confess our sins, He is faithful and righteous to forgive us our sins and to cleanse us from all unrighteousness" (1 John 1:9). "Through His name everyone who believes in Him receives forgiveness of sins" (Acts 10:43).

It doesn't matter whether the act of God's forgiveness is entirely past, or if there is new forgiveness in the future[2]—in both cases the issue is the liberating power of God's forgiveness for our *future*—freedom from shame. Forgiveness is full of future grace. When we live by faith in future grace, we are freed from the lingering, paralyzing effects of well-placed shame.

UNASHAMED, FOR I KNOW WHOM I HAVE BELIEVED

The second instance of battling shame is when we feel shame for something that is not even bad—like Jesus or the gospel. Second Timothy 1:12 shows how Paul battled against this misplaced shame. He says, "I also suffer these things, but I am not ashamed; for I know whom I have believed and I am convinced that He is able to guard what I have entrusted to Him until that day."

Paul makes very clear here that the battle against misplaced shame is a battle against *unbelief.* "I am not ashamed, for I know whom I have *believed"* and I am confident of his keeping power. We fight against feelings of shame in Christ and the gospel and the Christian lifestyle by fighting for faith in the future grace of God. Do we really believe that the gospel is the power of God unto salvation? Do we believe that Christ's power is made perfect in our weakness? Do we really believe that endless glory awaits us in place of ridicule? Do we believe he will keep us for that great day? The battle against misplaced shame is the battle to live by faith in the greatness and glory of future grace.

FREED FROM SHAME THAT IS NOT OURS TO BEAR

Finally, we battle shame when others try to load us with shame for evil circumstances, when in fact we had no part in dishonoring God. This is extremely common. I would guess that the most common psychological diagnosis of people's emotional disorders is that they grew up in "shame-based families." There are some detailed and sophisticated connotations of meaning in this phrase that I would not affirm. But the understanding of misplaced shame I am developing here, and the one implied in the phrase "shame-based families" overlap. There is such a thing as shame that is repeatedly put on people, but which does not belong to them. Freeing people who have been hurt deeply by carrying this misplaced shame is also what living by faith in future grace is meant to do.

It has been a great encouragement to me to realize that this kind of "shaming" happened to Jesus repeatedly. For example, they called him a drunkard and a glutton (Luke 7:34). They called him a temple destroyer (Mark 14:58). They called him a hypocrite: He saved others, but he can't save himself (Luke 23:35). In all this, the goal was to load Jesus with a shame that was not his to bear. They hoped they could discourage him and paralyze him by heaping shameful accusations on him.

The same was true in Paul's experience. They called him mad when he defended himself in court (Acts 26:24). They called him an enemy of the Jewish customs and a breaker of the Mosaic law (Acts 21:21). They said he taught that you should sin so that grace may abound (Romans 3:8). All this

his enemies said to load him with a shame that it was not his to bear.

And it has no doubt happened to you, perhaps from immature parents, and probably from others. And it will happen again. How do we battle this misplaced shame? We battle it by believing the promises of God that in the end all the efforts to put us to shame will fail. We may struggle now to know what is our shame to bear and what is not. But God has a promise for us that covers either case. Isaiah promises the people who trust in God, "You will not be put to shame or humiliated to all eternity" (Isaiah 45:17). And Paul applies the Old Testament promise to Christians: "No one who believes in Him will be put to shame" (Romans 10:11, RSV).

In other words, for all the evil and ridicule and criticism that others may use to make us feel shame, and for all the distress and emotional pain that it brings, nevertheless the promise of God stands sure: they will not succeed in the end. All the children of God will be vindicated. The truth will be known. And no one who banks his hope on the promises of God will be put to shame. Living by faith in future grace is a life of freedom from crippling shame.

PART IV

WINDOWS ON THE WORKS OF FAITH

You rebelled against the command of the Lord your God;

you neither believed Him nor listened to His voice.

DEUTERONOMY 9:23

Israel, pursuing a law of righteousness,

did not arrive at that law.

Why? Because they did not pursue it by faith,

but as though it were by works.

ROMANS 9:31–32

By faith Abel offered to God a better sacrifice than Cain...

By faith Noah...prepared an ark for the salvation of his household...

By faith Abraham, when he was tested, offered up Isaac...

By faith Moses...refused to be called the son of Pharaoh's daughter.

HEBREWS 11:4, 7, 17, 24

CHAPTER ELEVEN

A Love Affair
with
God's Law

A ll my sons have loved the Old Testament during their growing up years. This seems strange in view of how many adults, even evangelical Christian adults, don't like the Old Testament. I don't think this is because adults stop liking stories. I think it's, at least partly, because they start to believe that the Old Testament is bad news and the New Testament is good news. They sniff from the theological wind that the God of the Old Testament is a demanding God, while the God of the New Testament is a giving God. But children do not smell this odor. My sons see as many demands in the New Testament as there are in the Old—and perhaps harder ones. If good news depends on God not demanding, there is no gospel. But kids know better. And we might learn from them to enjoy the Old Testament if we see that the obedience it demands is the obedience of faith in future grace.

God is·far more to his people than One who commands. But he is not less. God is gloriously captive to the perfection of his wisdom and goodness and power. Therefore he is free from all impulses of evil and expediency and mediocrity. He is fully and freely committed to what is best. Sometimes his sovereign control of the universe may not look like it, especially when he permits and governs sin.[1] But over all the apparent mishandling of evil and pain, are written the words of Joseph: "God meant it for good" (Genesis 50:20). Since God always knows what is best, his will is always binding on all humans. His fatherly love for his children does not make him less caring that they do his will. His commandments hold fast for his children, and they are an overflow of love, not a craving for power.

A LOVE AFFAIR WITH GOD'S LAW

When Moses recorded what the Lord required of his people, he said it was "to keep the Lord's commandments... *for your good*" (Deuteronomy 10:13). It is for our good that God commands us to do his will. The saints of the Old Testament knew this. Those old men and women who loved God received his commandments as blessings not burdens. They actually seemed to have a love affair with God's law. They said things like, "I shall delight in Thy commandments, which *I love*. And I shall lift up my hands to Thy commandments, which *I love;* and I will meditate on Thy statutes... *I love Thy commandments above gold, yes, above fine gold*" (Psalm 119:47, 48, 127).

King David knew, as painfully as anyone, how the law of God could crush with guilt—like the guilt of adultery and murder (2 Samuel 12:13). But no one loved the law more than David. He reveled in its practical, spiritual value. He said that it "is perfect, restoring the soul;" it is "sure, making wise the simple;" it is "right, rejoicing the heart;" it is "pure, enlightening the eyes." It is "more desirable than gold, yes, much fine gold." It is "sweeter also than honey and the drippings of the honeycomb" (Psalm 19:7-10). In other words, he experienced profoundly the truth of Moses' words that the commandments of God are "for your good."

He also knew that the law was not a mere list of commandments. The commandments of the law are woven together with threads of grace—past grace, future grace, forgiving grace and empowering grace. These threads are part of the Old Testament law. For example, as God was about to give Moses the Ten Commandments, he reminded him of past grace: "The Lord called to him from the mountain, saying, '...You yourselves have seen what I did to the Egyptians, and how I bore you on eagles' wings, and brought you to Myself. Now then, if you will indeed obey My voice and keep My covenant, then you shall be My own possession among all the peoples, for all the earth is Mine'" (Exodus 19:3-5). God carried them with grace before he commanded them for their good.

THE LAW'S GRACIOUS PROVISION FOR LAW-BREAKING: FORGIVENESS

He also promised future grace in the very center of the law-giving revelation on Mount Sinai. When he came down to speak with Moses, he identified himself this way: "The Lord, the Lord God, compassionate and gracious, slow to anger, and abounding in lovingkindness and truth; who keeps lovingkindness for thousands, who forgives iniquity, transgression and sin; yet He will by no means leave the guilty unpunished" (Exodus 34:6-7). In other words, at the head of the law stands a future provision for failing to keep the law. The law says that God "forgives iniquity, transgression and sin." This is God's promise of future grace: I will be this kind of God to you: "compassionate and gracious, slow to anger and abounding in lovingkindness."

This future grace in the law of God is a forgiving grace. He says in effect, "I make ample provision for pardon and restoration if you stumble. I do not delight as much in punishment as in reconciliation. My wrath does not have a hair trigger—I am slow to anger. My judgment falls upon those who sin with a high hand and do not turn from their sinning to receive my abundant compassion and grace." David knew this was the heart of the law, and sang of it with all his heart.

> *The Lord is compassionate and gracious,*
> *Slow to anger and abounding in lovingkindness.*
> *He will not always strive with us;*
> *Nor will He keep His anger forever.*
> *He has not dealt with us according to our sins,*
> *Nor rewarded us according to our iniquities.*
> *For as high as the heavens are above the earth,*
> *So great is His lovingkindness toward those who fear Him.*
> *As far as the east is from the west,*
> *So far has He removed our transgressions from us.*

Just as a father has compassion on his children,
So the Lord has compassion on those who fear Him.
For He Himself knows our frame;
He is mindful that we are but dust.

Psalm 103:8–14

David learned this from the law. The evidence is in the first words cited: "The Lord is compassionate and gracious, slow to anger and abounding in lovingkindness," which is a quote from the words of God on Mount Sinai (Exodus 34:6). Thus it was plain to the saints of the Old Testament that the law offered a future grace that was forgiving.

I wonder if our children can follow this scent in the Old Testament better than we can? When my sons, who are scarcely children any more, saw the outpouring of God's compassion in Psalm 103, and heard the very words of Mount Sinai ("slow to anger and abounding in lovingkindness"), they simply could not understand why someone would say that the law was not a law of mercy and grace. David tasted the mercy of Sinai, and David is the great hero of all little boys who love slingshots and giant-slaying. For these young readers of the Old Testament, David was a better interpreter of the law than some contemporary theologians. I think they were right.

THE LAW AND THE PROPHETS PROMISE FUTURE EMPOWERMENT

The law also promised a (more distant) future grace that would give power for obedience. A measure of this grace was given to the remnant of believers already throughout the history of Israel. For example, they looked away from themselves to the grace of God for the spiritual enabling that they needed to obey God's commandments. They prayed, "Open my eyes, that I may behold wonderful things from Thy law." And they prayed, "Incline my heart to Thy testimonies, and not to dishonest gain" (Psalm 119:18, 36). They knew that without the empowering future grace of God, given in answer to prayer, they would not be able to see the wonders of God in his Word. And they knew that without the sovereign heart-inclining grace of God, they would drift away from him into the love of money.

They prayed for the future grace of joy and a clean heart and a steadfast spirit; and that God himself would make them willing to do what he commands: "Make me to hear joy and gladness, let the bones which Thou hast broken rejoice...Create in me a clean heart, O God, and renew a steadfast spirit within me...Restore to me the joy of Thy salvation, and sustain me with a willing spirit" (Psalm 51:8, 10, 12). Future grace was the key to walking in a way that pleased the Lord in the Old Testament (as well as the New).

But the future grace of empowerment for obedience was not poured out fully in Old Testament times. A far greater outpouring was promised for the "new covenant" which Christ inaugurated and sealed by the shedding of his blood (Luke 22:20; 1 Corinthians 11:25). For example, God promised through Jeremiah: "'Behold, days are coming,' declares the Lord, 'when I will make a new covenant with the house of Israel...this is the covenant which I will make with the house of Israel after those days,' declares the Lord, *'I will put My law within them, and on their heart I will write it'*" (Jeremiah 31:31, 33). The time was coming when God would give more grace for obedience than he had in the past.

In Ezekiel God promised it like this: "I shall give them one heart, and shall put a new spirit within them. And I shall take the heart of stone out of their flesh and give them a heart of flesh, that they may walk in My statutes and keep My ordinances, and do them" (Ezekiel 11:19-20; cf. 36:26-28). This is the future grace of empowerment for obedience: a new heart, and new spirit, that they may obey.

All the way back in the law itself, Moses saw that this was to be God's plan. Moses gave the law. But he knew that God had some extended lessons to teach Israel by leaving the people for a season to the meager resources of their own sinful hearts. In Deuteronomy 5 Moses recounts the Ten Commandments, forty years after giving them the first time. He tells how the people had received them gladly and how they had expressed their willingness to obey. But then Moses quotes God's foreboding words: "Who will give, so that such a heart will be theirs to fear me and keep all my commandments?" (Deuteronomy 5:29, literal translation). In other words, God knew that until the future grace of empowerment was poured out more fully, most of the people would not keep the commandments.

That outpouring of future grace was reserved for the New Testament time. So Moses soberly says to the people, forty years after the giving of the law, "To this day the Lord has not given you a heart to know, nor eyes to see, nor ears to hear" (Deuteronomy 29:4). In other words, they were left to the resources of their own sinful hearts and eyes and ears. For most of them the effectual power of transforming grace was not given. But one chapter later Moses holds out the promise that this greater future grace will indeed be given: "The Lord your God will circumcise your heart and the heart of your descendants, to love the Lord your God with all your heart and with all your soul, in order that you may live (Deuteronomy 30:6). This promise is virtually the same as the promise of the new covenant given by Jeremiah and Ezekiel. It was a promise that some day, to a far greater extent than before, future grace would give new hearts to God's people, and empower them to obey his commandments.

The fact that we live in this new day under the new covenant should fill us with joy. But our joy should not be at the expense of Old Testament truth. Sometimes, to exalt our precious privilege as beneficiaries of the new covenant, we will over-criticize the old covenant. But what we are seeing in this chapter is that the old is not deficient because it was a *commanding* covenant, or because it commanded wrong things. It was deficient because it was not accompanied, by and large, with inner, transforming, enabling divine power (see Romans 8:3). But what that means practically is that we can go back and profit immensely from the instructions of the Old Testament, since we now have this transforming, new-covenant power at work within us. In this sense, the new covenant makes the Old Testament the book of the Christian Church in practical ways that we may not have thought of. We may want to join our children in going back and giving it a fresh reading.

WHY OBEDIENCE ABORTED

If we ask what was missing from the hearts of so many who heard the law and failed to walk in it, one clear biblical answer is that *faith* was missing.[2] Hebrews 4:2 explains why the Word of God at Mount Sinai and forty years later at the Jordan River did not profit those who heard, even though the text says it was "good news." "The word they heard did not profit them, because it was not united by *faith* in those who heard."[3] The Word of God did not bear fruit in their lives because they did not trust him.

Again and again this is the missing ingredient in the Old Testament that short-circuits obedience to God's commandments. The root of disobedience is unbelief in God's future grace. Psalm 78:7 describes the way faith and obedience are supposed to work. It calls for one generation to teach the Word of God to another so "that they should *put their confidence in God,* and not forget *the works of God,* but *keep His commandments."* In other words, the memory of bygone grace in "the works of God" encourages "confidence in God" for future grace, which enables them to "keep His commandments." Deuteronomy 20:1 crystallizes for us the way bygone grace was meant by God to strengthen faith in future grace. Moses exhorts the people how to face their enemies who outnumber them: "Do not be afraid of them; for the LORD your God, who brought you up from the land of Egypt, is with you." The memory of God's power and grace in Egypt is meant to strengthen faith in future grace and free Israel for fearless obedience. But this is what, repeatedly, did not happen.

Near the end of his life, as Moses looks back over his experience with Israel, he says, "When the Lord [commanded] 'Go up and possess the land which I have given you,' then you rebelled against the command of the Lord your God; *you neither believed Him* nor listened to His voice" (Deuteronomy 9:23). In other words, the failure to believe God is the root cause of rebelling against his command. And we know from the story that what they failed to believe was the promise and power of *future grace.* Moses had given God's promise, "He will bring us into this land, and give it to us... Only do not rebel against the Lord; and do not fear the people of the land, for...their protection has been removed from them, and the Lord is with us; do not fear them" (Numbers 14:8-9). But the people did not *trust* God's mighty grace to give them the land. So they gave way to fear; and fear gave rise to rebellion against his command. As the psalmist said, "They despised the pleasant land; *they did not believe in His word,* but grumbled in their tents" (Psalm 106:24). The obedience of Israel aborted because they did not live by faith in future grace.

What was the Root of Their Sin?

After centuries of this pattern, the northern kingdom of Israel was taken captive by Assyria. The writer of 2 Kings explains why this happened. He says, "Now this came about, because the sons of Israel had sinned against the Lord their God, who had brought them up from the land of Egypt" (2 Kings17:7). The cause was sin. But what is the root of this sin? Notice that the evil of the sin against God is emphasized by mentioning how powerful and good God had been to Israel in saving them from slavery in Egypt. This might cause you to think that the cause of Israel's sins is ingratitude. But that is not what the writer goes on to say. Instead he says, "they did not listen, but stiffened their neck like their fathers, *who did not believe in the Lord their God*" (2 Kings 17:14). The point is that the past grace of salvation from Egypt should have caused the people to trust God for future grace. But instead "they did not believe in the Lord their God." And that is why they turned away and sinned against him. They did not trust him for a better future than they could make for themselves by consorting with other gods.

The lesson of the whole Old Testament could be summed up in the words of Psalm 37:3, "Trust in the Lord, and do good." That is, let the great works of past grace sustain your faith in future grace so that you always trust God rather than the offers of help and guidance that come from other gods or other counselors. The root issue behind the disobedience of Israel was lack of faith in future grace.

This is unmistakable when we listen to the New Testament explanation for why Israel failed to attain the righteousness that God required in the law. But before we look at that explanation there is a misunderstanding to remove.

Is all our Righteousness Filthy Rags?

Don't make the mistake of thinking that the only righteousness the law required was perfection. It is true that any shortcoming of God's law offends against his perfect holiness and makes us liable to judgment, since God cannot look with favor on any sin (Habakkuk 1:13; James. 2:10-11). But the Old Testament law itself provided for forgiveness and reconciliation for sins.

150

So the "requirement" of the law was perfection in one sense, but not in the sense that without it a person was lost.

What brought a person to ruin in the Old Testament was not the failure to have the righteousness of sinless perfection. Rather the ruin was caused by the failure to be righteous, first, in the sense that Abraham was "reckoned righteous" by faith in future grace;[4] and, second, in the sense of habitual (though not perfect) obedience to God which was rooted in an abiding (though not perfect) faith in his future grace. Imperfection would be forgiven; but impenitent, habitual, distrusting disobedience would not.

It is terribly confusing when people say that the only righteousness that has any value is the imputed righteousness of Christ. I agree that justification is not grounded on any of our righteousness, but only the righteousness of Christ imputed to us.[5] But sometimes people are careless and speak disparagingly of all human righteousness, as if there were no such thing that pleased God. They often cite Isaiah 64:6 which says our righteousness is as filthy rags.[6] It's true—gloriously true—that none of God's people, before or after the cross, would be accepted by an immaculately holy God if the perfect righteousness of Christ were not imputed to us (Romans 5:19; 1 Corinthians 1:30; 2 Corinthians 5:21). But that does not mean that God does not produce in those "justified" people (before and after the cross) an experiential righteousness that is *not* "filthy rags." In fact, he does; and this righteousness is precious to God and is required, not as the *ground* of our justification (which is the righteousness of Christ only), but as an *evidence* of our being truly justified children of God.[7]

Consider that Zacharias and his wife Elizabeth are described by Luke in a way that many Christians stumble over: "They were both *righteous in the sight of God*, walking *blamelessly* in all the commandments and requirements of the Lord" (Luke 1:6). Their righteousness was not filthy rags. Nor was it only the imputed righteousness of Christ. This was a life of habitual obedience and faith that receives cleansing from its imperfections through the wonderful provisions of forgiveness and restoration in the law (which all pointed to Christ as the one who would decisively carry the sins of all God's people before and after the cross, cf. Romans 3:25).

IS THERE REALLY A CONTRAST BETWEEN
THE RIGHTEOUS AND THE WICKED?

If we do not grasp that the Old Testament commands a righteousness that is really possible by faith in future grace we will simply not be able to make sense out of hundreds of texts. For example, "the righteous" are contrasted with "the wicked" again and again. And the assumption is that the "righteous" are real people who are living differently from the wicked. "The *wicked* will not stand in the judgment, nor sinners in the assembly of the *righteous.* For the Lord knows the way of the *righteous,* but the way of the *wicked* will perish" (Psalm 1:5-6). "Better is the little of the *righteous* than the abundance of many *wicked.* For the arms of the *wicked* will be broken; but the Lord sustains the *righteous*" (Psalm 37:16-17). "All the horns of the *wicked* He will cut off, but the horns of the *righteous* will be lifted up" (Psalm 75:10). The "righteous" are not sinless people. "There is no man who does not sin" (2 Chronicles 6:36). Rather, as Psalm 32 shows, the "righteous" are those "whose sin is covered" and to whom the Lord "does not impute iniquity," but "who trust in the Lord," "confess [their] transgressions to the Lord," "offer prayer to God," and yield to the Lord's commands. They hear him say, "Be glad in the Lord, and rejoice, you *righteous ones*" (Psalm 32:1-2, 5-6, 8-11).

It might be helpful to pause for a moment and let this sink in. When my sons do what I tell them to do—and do it with a spirit of gladness and trust in my wisdom and care—I do not call their obedience "filthy rags," even if it is not perfect. Neither does God. All the more because he himself is "working in us that which is pleasing in His sight" (Hebrews 13:21). He does not call his own, Spirit-wrought fruit, "rags." But if my boys had cleaned their room—angry and pouting and slamming doors—I might call that "filthy rags." And so does God. External conformity without internal change brings down some of Jesus' harshest words ("whitewashed tombs," Matthew 23:27). This difference should be a great encouragement that our Father in heaven is not impossible to please. In fact, like every person with a very big heart and very high standards, he is easy to please and hard to satisfy. We would not want it otherwise. We want the smile of his happy affection and the fierce sparkle in his eye that we can—and one day will— do, O, so much better.

WHY ISRAEL FAILED TO ATTAIN RIGHTEOUSNESS

Now we are in a better position to ask the New Testament why Israel, as a whole, failed to attain the righteousness that God required in the law. That is, why did they fall short not only of perfection (which we all do), but also of that experiential righteousness that is required in the law from all God's children? Paul poses and answers this question in Romans 9:31-32. "Israel, pursuing a law of righteousness, did not arrive at that law. Why? *Because they did not pursue it by faith,* but as though it were by works." They did not pursue the law "by faith." But that was how God meant it to be pursued. This confirms what we have seen: that the underlying cause of Israel's disobedience was lack of faith in future grace.

Paul says that they failed to pursue the law by faith. For the great majority of Israel (but not saints like Moses, Caleb, David, Zachariah and Elizabeth), when they pursued the law, they pursued it "as though it were by works." The words "as though" are Paul's way of saying that the law was not meant by God to be pursued this way. This is why he says in Romans 3:31, "Do we then nullify the Law through faith? May it never be! On the contrary, we establish the Law."

What Paul means by "works" is clear from Romans 4:4-5, "Now to the one who *works,* his wage is not reckoned as a [grace], but as what is due. But to the one who does not work, but believes in Him who justifies the ungodly, his faith is reckoned as righteousness." "Works" are any actions or attitudes that aim to highlight their own worth or merit so that the normal response to them would be an earned payment, not a free gift of grace. Therefore the reason Israel failed in its pursuit of what the law required was that it misconstrued the law as calling for "works," when in fact it was calling for the obedience that comes from faith. They failed to see that the law was calling the people to live by faith in future grace.

ALL OLD TESTAMENT OBEDIENCE WAS BY FAITH IN FUTURE GRACE

It shouldn't be surprising, then, that Hebrews 11 ascribes virtually all the obedience of the Old Testament saints to the agency of faith in future grace. The author makes clear that faith is a future-oriented, promise-trusting assurance in God's care, when he says, "Faith is the assurance of things hoped for" (v. 1). Then he gives us examples to show that this faith in future grace produced obedience.

"*By faith* Abel offered to God a better sacrifice than Cain" (v. 4). "*By faith* Noah…prepared an ark for the salvation of his household" (v. 7). "*By faith* Abraham, when he was called, obeyed by going out to a place which he was to receive for an inheritance" (v. 8). "*By faith* Abraham, when he was tested, offered up Isaac" (v. 17). "*By faith* Moses, when he had grown up, refused to be called the son of Pharaoh's daughter; choosing rather to endure ill-treatment with the people of God, than to enjoy the passing pleasures of sin" (vv. 24-26).

My conclusion is that already in the Old Testament God meant for the law to be fulfilled by faith in future grace. This was possible for the true saints even before the outpouring of the new covenant promise, because God gave foretastes of his enabling power before the coming of Christ and the outpouring of the fuller measure of the Holy Spirit.

A BOOK FOR THE CHURCH ABOUT LIVING BY FAITH IN FUTURE GRACE

What this means for us today is that we may read the Old Testament with a great deal of expectancy that it speaks more directly to our need that we may have thought. The dynamic of spiritual life that God set forth in the Old Testament is not essentially different from the dynamic of spiritual life set forth in the New Testament (as we will see in the next chapter). What God requires of his people has always been essentially the same. We may be strengthened from both the Old and New Testaments in our quest to live by faith in future grace.

Taken as a whole, the Old Testament has one great aim: "Whatever was written in earlier times was written for our instruction, that through perseverance and the encouragement of the Scriptures we might have *hope*" (Romans 15:4). The Old Testament was written to strengthen our hope in God, which is another way of saying, it was written to build our *faith in future grace.*

We pray…that our God may…
fulfill every…work of faith.

2 T H E S S A L O N I A N S   1 : 1 1

Just as the body without the spirit is dead,
so also faith without works is dead.

J A M E S   2 : 2 6

The commandments of God are not negligible
because we are under grace.
They are doable because we are under grace.
The new covenant gift of the Spirit
is the power to obey the revealed will of God;
but the path along which the Spirit comes and works
is faith in future grace.

CHAPTER TWELVE

"I Will Put My Law Within Them"

ARE COMMANDMENTS AND LOVE COMPATIBLE?

Jesus shatters many common notions. For example, one notion is that commandments and love don't mix. You don't command someone you love. And you don't tend to love one who commands. Commanding connotes military hierarchy, not relationships of love. We tend to think that commanding restricts winsomeness and willingness both ways. And this is often true. Paul wrote to his friend Philemon and said, "though I have enough confidence in Christ *to order you* to do that which is proper, yet *for love's sake* I rather *appeal to you*" (Philemon 8–9; see also 2 Corinthians 8:8). Paul probably meant his love and Philemon's love. So it's true that, for love's sake, a person in authority may choose not to command.

But Jesus shatters any absolute dissociation of commandments and love. He says, "If you love Me, you will keep My *commandments*...He who has My *commandments* and keeps them, he it is who loves Me; and he who loves Me shall be loved by My Father" (John 14:15, 21). "If you keep My *commandments,* you will abide in My love; just as I have kept My Father's *commandments,* and abide in His love" (John 15:10). Thinking in terms of commandments and obedience did not stop Jesus from enjoying the love of his Father. And he expects that our thinking of him as one who commands will not jeopardize our love relationship with him either.

This is crucial to realize because the covenant relationship that we have with God through Jesus Christ is not a covenant without commandments. The basic difference between the old covenant offered by God through the law and the new covenant offered by God through Christ is not that one had commandments and the other doesn't. The basic difference is that in the old covenant the gracious enabling power to obey was not poured out as fully as it is since Jesus. "To this day the Lord has not given you a heart to know or eyes to see or ears to hear" (Deuteronomy 29:4). What's new about the new covenant is not that there is no law, but rather God's promise, "I will put My law within them, and on their heart I will write it" (Jeremiah 31:33). "I will put my Spirit within you and cause you to walk in My statutes" (Ezekiel 36:27).

What makes love possible between us and a God who commands is that he does not speak from a distance and leave us to our own resources. He draws near and gives us Himself as he gives us his commandments. The new covenant, sealed by the blood of his Son (1 Corinthians 11:25), is a commitment to put his Spirit within us. Paul said it is a "new covenant, not of the letter, but of the Spirit; for the letter kills, but the Spirit gives life" (2 Corinthians 3:6). When the law, written on stone, meets an unwilling heart of stone, all it does is condemn and kill. But when that same law is written on hearts made soft by the Spirit, the result is life.

Therefore we do not need to shrink back from the "commandments" of God as though they were cold, distant demands from an impersonal sovereign. We can embrace the full New Testament teaching that the commandments of God are utterly crucial in living the Christian life (1 John 5:3). For example, Paul said, "Circumcision is nothing, and uncircumcision is nothing, but what matters is the keeping of the commandments of God" (1 Corinthians 7:19). Yes "keeping the commandments of God" really matters—both in the Old Testament and the New.

NOT ALL OF THE LAW IS BINDING TODAY

Of course significant parts of the law are no longer binding on Christians. You can see this in the verse just quoted, where circumcision is made optional and actually contrasted with "the commandments of God," even though circumcision was one of the "commandments" that Israel was to keep in the Old Testament times. The reason that parts of the Old Testament law are no longer binding on God's people is that there has been a great fulfillment in Christ; and the way God is pursuing his redemptive plan is very different now than it was in the Old Testament, when most of his focus was on the ethnic people of Israel.

For example, the death of Christ has brought to fulfillment and to an end all the laws relating to animal sacrifice (Hebrews 9:12). Moreover laws that were designed to keep Israel ritually distinct from the nations, like food laws, and even circumcision, no longer function in the same binding way, because God's New Testament plan is to overcome all ethnic barriers and assemble a new people from every tribe and tongue and nation (Mark 7:19; Matthew 21:43; Galatians 6:15).

Nevertheless, God has not ceased to be a God of total authority and wisdom. His will still stands as the law of Christian living. Jesus said, "Do not think that I came to abolish the Law or the Prophets; I did not come to abolish, but to fulfill. For truly I say to you, until heaven and earth pass away, not the smallest letter or stroke shall pass away from the Law, until all is accomplished" (Matthew 5:17-18). Some has been "fulfilled" and "accomplished" in a decisive, once-for-all way that brings it to an end. But the moral commandments of God abide. As Paul says, "The commandments of God matter" (see 1 Corinthians 7:19). And even though Paul renounced the right to command Philemon, he was willing to call his moral instructions "commandments" in 1 Thessalonians 4:2, "For you know what *commandments* we gave you by the authority of the Lord Jesus." The sum of all that God requires, Paul calls "the *law* of Christ" (1 Corinthians 9:21; Galatians 6:2).

THE APOSTLE OF LOVE—AND COMMANDMENTS

The apostle John is perhaps best known for being the apostle of love. He was the "beloved disciple" (John 13:23; 20:2), and he wrote about love extensively. Yet over a third of all New Testament uses of the word "commandment"[1] are in his writings. They occur not only in his gospel, as we have seen, but also in the Revelation and in his letters. "By this we know that we have come to know Him, if we keep His *commandments*. The one who says, 'I have come to know Him,' and does not keep His *commandments*, is a liar, and the truth is not in him" (1 John 2:3-4). "Whatever we ask we receive from Him, because we keep His *commandments* and do the things that are pleasing in His sight…The one who keeps His *commandments* abides in Him, and He in him" (1 John 3:22, 24).

This is important to see because John also makes it clear that *faith* is the triumphant power by which the commandments of God are kept. What we are going to see is that the same spiritual dynamics for keeping the commandments of God are active in both Old and New Testaments, namely, we obey by faith in future grace. Here is the way John deals with the relationship between faith and obedience:

Whoever believes that Jesus is the Christ is born of God; and whoever loves the Father loves the child born of Him. (2) By this we know that we love the children of God, when we love God and observe His commandments. (3) For this is the love of God, that we keep His commandments; and His commandments are not burdensome. (4) For whatever is born of God overcomes the world; and this is the victory that has overcome the world—our faith. (5)And who is the one that overcomes the world, but he who believes that Jesus is the Son of God. (1 John 5:1-5)

John says that "whatever is born of God overcomes the world" (v. 4). The "for" at the beginning of verse 4 means that this is given as the basis or ground of what he said just before that: "the commandments of God are not burdensome." So when John talks here about overcoming the world, what he has in mind is overcoming the worldly impulse to reject the commandments of God and find them burdensome. When we are born again, he says, that impulse is overcome and we do not find God's commandments burdensome.

How does being born of God make the commandments of God a delight rather than a burden? John says, "This is the victory that has overcome the world—our faith." In other words, the way that being born of God overcomes the worldly burdensomeness of God's commandments is by begetting faith. This is confirmed in verse 1 which says, literally, "Whoever *believes* that Jesus is the Christ *has been born of God.*" Faith is the evidence that we have been born of God. We do not make ourselves born again by deciding to believe. God makes us willing to believe by causing us to be born again. As Peter said in his first letter, God "caused us to be born again to a living hope" (1 Peter 1:3). Our living hope, or faith in future grace, is the work of God through new birth.

So when John says, *"Whatever is born of God* overcomes the world," and then adds, *"Our faith* is the victory that has overcome the world," I take him to mean that God enables us, by the new birth, to overcome the world— that is, to overcome our worldly disinclination to keep God's commandments. The new birth does this by creating faith, which evidently includes a disposition to be pleased, rather than put off, by God's commandments. Therefore it is faith that overcomes our inborn hostility to God and his will, and frees us to keep his commandments, and say with the psalmist, "I delight to do thy will, O my God" (Psalm 40:8).

But someone may say, "How can you attribute to faith what verse 3 attributes to love for God?" "This is the love of God, that we keep His commandments." I do not deny that love for God is the power that keeps his commandments. But I do also affirm, because of the flow of thought in what follows, that faith too is the instrument of God's power that enables us to keep his commandments. The question then is, How do they fit together?

"LOVE IS THE MAIN THING IN SAVING FAITH"

The eighteenth century pastor and theologian, Jonathan Edwards, wrestled with this text and concluded, "Saving faith implies in its nature divine love...Our love to God enables us to overcome the difficulties that attend keeping God's commands; which shows that love is the main thing in saving faith, the life and power of it, by which it produces great effects."[2] I think Edwards is right and that numerous texts in the Bible support what he says.[3] Another way to say it is that faith in Christ is not just *assenting* to what God is for us, but also *embracing* all that he is for us in Christ. "True faith embraces Christ in whatever ways the Scriptures hold Him out to poor sinners."[4] This "embracing" is loving him.

Therefore there is no contradiction between verse 3, on the one hand, which says that our love for God enables us to keep his commandments, and verse 4, on the other hand, which says that our *faith* overcomes the obstacles of the world that keep us from obeying God's commandments. Love for God is implicit in faith.

Verse 5 defines the faith that obeys as "believing that Jesus is the Son of God." Is this faith in future grace? I believe it is. John cannot mean that saving faith is simply assenting to the truth that Jesus is the Son of God, because the demons assent to that (Matthew 8:29). What he means is "embracing" the significance of that truth, and banking our hope on it. "Son of God" means that Jesus is the greatest person in the universe alongside his Father. Therefore all he taught is true, and all he promised will stand firm, and all his soul-satisfying greatness will never change. Believing that he is the Son of God means banking on all this, and being satisfied with it. And that includes faith in all the future that he graciously controls for the sake of his people.

One confirmation of this is found in 1 John 4:16. There believers are described as those who have "believed the love God has for us." This is especially significant because it says "the love God *has* for us," not, "the love God *had* for us." This means that what we trust in is the ongoing love of God, that he is there for us, moment by moment. I think this means that believing in Jesus as the Son of God includes believing in all the love of God that he embodied and obtained for us.

I conclude therefore that John's focus on keeping the commandments of God is in tune with what we saw in the last chapter: he teaches us to keep the commandments of God by faith in future grace.

In the weeks that I was editing the final stages of this book, I was also preaching a series of messages under the theme, "The Greatest of These is Love." One of the texts I took up was the command of Jesus, "I say to you, love your enemies, and pray for those who persecute you" (Matthew 5:44). At that same time the report came over my E-mail news service that two missionaries with New Tribes Mission near Bogota, Colombia, had been killed by Marxist guerrillas on Monday, June 19, 1995. Steve Welsh and Timothy Van Dyke were shot numerous times. They were both 42 years old and had been teaching at a missionary school when they were kidnapped in January, 1994.

The question I had to pose, as I preached on loving our enemies was, How do you love the men who kidnap you and then, after a year and a half, kill you? How do the wives and children of these two men love the murderers? Jesus says, "Love them. Love them. If they kill you, love them. If they take away your father, love them. If they destroy your family, love them. Love your enemies. Be that kind of person. Be so changed on the inside that this is really possible."

How can we do this? Where does power to love like this come from? Just think how astonishing this is when it appears in the real world! Could anything show the truth and power and reality of Christ more than this? I believe Jesus gives us the key to this radical, self-sacrificing love in the very same chapter.

In Matthew 5:11-12 he again talks about being persecuted: "Blessed are you when men cast insults at you, and persecute you, and say all kinds of evil against you falsely, on account of Me. Rejoice, and be glad, for your reward in heaven is great, for so they persecuted the prophets who were before you." What is remarkable about these verses is that Jesus says that you can not only *endure* the mistreatment of the enemy, *but rejoice in it.* This seems even more beyond our reach. If I could do this—if I could rejoice in being persecuted, then it would be possible to love my persecutors. If the miracle of joy in the midst of the horror of injustice and pain and loss could happen, then the miracle of love for the perpetrators could happen too.

Jesus gives the key to joy in these verses. He says, "Rejoice, and be glad, *for your reward in heaven is great."* The key to joy is future grace—"your reward in heaven is great." I believe this joy is the freeing power to love our enemies when they persecute us. If that is true, then the command to love is a command to set our minds on things that are above, not on things that are on the earth (Colossians 3:2). The command to love our enemy is a command to find our hope and our satisfaction in God and his great reward—his future grace. The key to radical love is faith in future grace. We must be persuaded in the midst of our agony that the love of God is "better than life" (Psalm 63:3). Loving your enemy doesn't earn you the reward of heaven. Treasuring the reward of heaven empowers you to love your enemy.

Consider carefully when you hear someone say that Christians would be more practically useful in the world if they were not so concerned about the future. It may be that some Christians are sidetracked in life by excessive fascination about prophetic teaching. But Jesus made it very clear that the key to our joy and our love in the midst of hard times is the deep, unshakable confidence that every loss on this earth in the service of love for the sake of the kingdom will be abundantly restored, "pressed down, shaken together, running over" (Luke 6:38; Mark 10:29–30). The mandate is clear: let us devote ourselves to cultivating stronger faith in the "great reward" of future grace. This is the power to love.

There are many more examples of how the New Testament teaches that obedience to God is by *faith in future grace*. Consider briefly four additional illustrations.

FAITH IN THE FUTURE GRACE OF THE JOY SET BEFORE US

First, when Hebrews 11 describes the obedience of the Old Testament saints as happening "by faith"—that is, by "the assurance of things hoped for" (v. 1)—it is not out of mere historical interest. The point is that Christians today are to obey in the same way.

We know this because Hebrews calls for the same kind of obedience in other texts. For example, it gives Jesus as an example of living by faith in future grace: "For the joy set before Him [he] endured the cross" (Hebrews 12:2). In other words, Jesus is in that great train of saints who *"by faith…* were tortured, not accepting their release, in order that they might obtain a better resurrection" (11:33, 35). We are to "[fix] our eyes on Jesus, the author and perfecter of faith" (12:2). Therefore Jesus links all the future-oriented believers of the Old Testament with us, by continuing their example of living by faith in future grace. He was strengthened to endure the high cost of love by banking his hope on "the joy set before Him." (See also Hebrews 10:32-34; 13:5–7.)

"WORK OF FAITH"

Second, the apostle Paul refers two times to the practical obedience of Christians as a "work of faith." The first time he wrote to the Thessalonians he said, "[We bear] in mind your *work of faith* and labor of love and stead-fastness of hope in our Lord Jesus Christ" (1 Thessalonians 1:3). The second time he wrote to them he said, "To this end also we pray for you always that our God may count you worthy of your calling, and fulfill every desire for goodness and the *work of faith* with power; in order that the name of our Lord Jesus may be glorified in you, and you in Him, according to the grace of our God and the Lord Jesus Christ" (2 Thessalonians 1:11-12).

The term "work of faith" refers to the practical acts of love and good-ness that Christians do. And the point is that these acts are done *by faith*. When Paul prays (in 2 Thessalonians 1:11) that God would "fulfill...the *work of faith* with [his] power," he shows that *faith* is the conduit God uses to transmit his power into obedience. And when he adds at the end of verse 12 that this work of faith glorifies the Lord Jesus "according to the *grace* of our God," he shows that the faith in view is faith in future grace. When we fix our faith on future grace, the power of God flows through that faith, and we are empowered to do the "work of faith and labor of love" which brings glory to God, not us, which is what grace is all about. We get the help, God gets the glory.

SPURGEON'S WORK OF FAITH FOR THE GLORY OF GOD

Charles Spurgeon, the great London preacher, loved to glorify God by ask-ing much from God. He cited Psalm 50:15 where God says, "Call upon Me in the day of trouble; I shall rescue you, and you will honor Me." We call for the help of future grace. God answers with delivering power. The result is that he is honored. "Here is a delightful partnership: we obtain that which we so greatly need, and all that God getteth is the glory which is due unto his name."[5]

Spurgeon believed that the way to get "much grace" from God was by faith in future grace. For example, he counseled young preachers to believe that the Word of God would not be preached in vain.

> *Beloved, have genuine faith in the Word of God, and in its power to save.*
> *Do not go up into the pulpit preaching the truth and saying, 'I hope some*
> *good will come of it;' but confidently believe that it will not return void,*

but must work the eternal purpose of God. Do not speak as if the gospel might have some power, or might have none. God sends you to be a miracle-worker; therefore, say to the spiritually lame, 'In the name of Jesus Christ of Nazareth, rise up and walk,' and men will rise up and walk; but if you say, 'I hope, dear man, that Jesus Christ may be able to make you rise up and walk,' your Lord will frown upon your dishonoring words. You have lowered Him, you have brought Him down to the level of your unbelief; and He cannot do many mighty works by you. Speak boldly; for if you speak by the Holy Spirit, you cannot speak in vain.[6]

FULFILLING THE LAW BY FAITH IN FUTURE GRACE, TODAY

Third, we saw in the last chapter from Romans 9:32 that the reason Israel as a whole did not fulfill the law was that "they did not pursue it by faith, but as though it were by works." This was not just a word about the past; it was a signpost for the future. We too are to fulfill what the law requires, not by works, but by faith.

Paul said that the reason God "[sent] His own Son in the likeness of sinful flesh and as an offering for sin [and] condemned sin in the flesh, [was] *in order that the requirement of the Law might be fulfilled in us, who do not walk according to the flesh, but according to the Spirit*" (Romans 8:3-4). The reference to our "walking according to the Spirit" shows that the fulfilling of the law is a real experiential fulfillment in our behavior. It is not a reference to the perfect obedience of Christ which he imputes to us. That is a great truth, but it is not what Paul is talking about here. As C.E.B. Cranfield says:

God's purpose in "condemning" sin was that His law's requirement might be fulfilled in us, that is, that His law might be established in the sense of at last being truly and sincerely obeyed—the fulfillment of the promise of Jeremiah 31:33 and Ezekiel 36:26f... [True Christians] fulfill it in the sense that they do have a real faith in God (which is the law's basic demand), in the sense that their lives are definitely turned in the direction of obedience, that they do sincerely desire to obey and are earnestly striving to advance ever nearer to perfection.[7]

Paul does not mention fulfilling the law *by faith* here. But he does say that the fulfillment is by those who "walk according to the Spirit." And we know from elsewhere that he believes the Spirit is supplied not by works, but *by faith.* "Does He then, who *provides you with the Spirit* and works miracles among you, do it by the works of the Law, or *by hearing with faith?* (Galatians 3:5). Answer: by hearing with faith. The Spirit empowers obedience; and the channel by which he comes, and moves, is faith. "Sanctification [is] by the *Spirit* and *faith* in the truth" (2 Thessalonians 2:13). Therefore Romans 8:4 fits perfectly with Romans 9:32 in teaching that the law is to be pursued not by works but by faith.

FULFILLING THE LAW THROUGH LOVE, BY FAITH IN FUTURE GRACE

Another beautiful confirmation of this comes from reflecting on what the fulfillment of the law really involves. Paul says "Love does no wrong to a neighbor; *love therefore is the fulfillment of the law*" (Romans 13:10). Then, in at least two places, he teaches that love comes from faith, which confirms that the fulfillment of the law is by faith. "For in Christ Jesus neither circumcision nor uncircumcision means anything, but *faith working through love*" (Galatians 5:6). "The goal of our instruction is *love from* a pure heart and a good conscience and *a sincere faith*" (1 Timothy 1:5; see also Colossians 1:4-5). We may conclude then that God meant for his commandments to be fulfilled in both the Old and New Testaments in essentially the same way—by *faith in future grace.*

DEAD FAITH CAN PRODUCE NO WORKS

Fourth, James gives us an unmistakable message: true saving faith is effective in producing practical obedience to God. "What use is it, my brethren, if a man says he has faith, but he has no works? Can that faith save him? (2:14) "Even so, faith, if it has no works, is dead, being by itself (2:17). "But are you willing to recognize, you foolish fellow, that faith without works is useless? (2:20). "Just as the body without the spirit is dead, so also faith without works is dead" (2:26).

The point here is not merely that saving faith is always accompanied by good works. The point is that the faith *produces* the works. That's why it is called "dead" if there are no works—because the life of faith is manifest through the works which this life generates. The kind of faith James has in mind is probably indicated by its use in James 1:6, and this use points to faith in future grace. If a man needs wisdom, James says, he should ask God for it, "but let him ask *in faith* [in God's *future grace* to give it] without any doubting" for the one who doubts is...a "double-minded man, unstable in all his ways" (1:5-6, 8). He would be double-minded because part of him has faith in the future grace of God to supply his need, and part of him does not. Therefore the faith that will receive the wisdom, and be enabled to live in obedience, is faith in future grace. This is the faith that is not dead but will produce obedience to God.

"WHO KEEP THE COMMANDMENTS OF GOD AND FAITH IN JESUS"

I conclude that the New Testament teaches us to obey the commandments of God *by faith in future grace.* The commandments of God are not negligible because we are under grace. They are *doable* because we are under grace. The new covenant gift of the Spirit is the power to obey the revealed will of God; but the path along which the Spirit comes and works is faith in future grace. In the first century, amid terrible persecution, Christians were known by simple and forceful names. One of them was "saints who keep the commandments of God and their faith in Jesus" (Revelation 14:12). The point of this chapter has been that those two things are not merely parallel. *Faith in Jesus* to care for us with future grace gave them the courage to *keep the commandments* of God even in the face of death.

That kind of confidence, in spite of staggering disappointments, yields a life of remarkable patience. We would do well to meditate for a few moments in the next chapter on how prizing God's gracious wisdom, and treasuring his sovereign reign over our circumstances, purifies us from the sin of impatience.

Judge not the Lord by feeble sense,

But trust him for his grace,

Behind a frowning providence

He hides a smiling face.

WILLIAM COWPER

Be patient, therefore, brethren, until the coming of the Lord...

As an example, brethren, of suffering and patience,

take the prophets who spoke in the name of the Lord.

Behold, we count those blessed who endured.

You have heard of the endurance of Job

and have seen the outcome of the Lord's dealings,

that the Lord is full of compassion and is merciful.

JAMES 5:7-11

The Lord is good to those who wait for Him.

LAMENTATIONS 3:25

Applying the Purifying Power

Faith in Future Grace
vs.
Impatience

IN GOD'S PLACE, AT GOD'S PACE, BY FUTURE GRACE

I mpatience is a form of unbelief. It's what we begin to feel when we start to doubt the wisdom of God's timing or the goodness of God's guidance. It springs up in our hearts when our plan is interrupted or shattered. It may be prompted by a long wait in a checkout line or a sudden blow that knocks out half our dreams. The opposite of impatience is not a glib denial of loss. It's a deepening, ripening, peaceful willingness to wait for God in the unplanned place of obedience, and to walk with God at the unplanned pace of obedience—to wait in his place, and go at his pace. And the key is faith in future grace.

MARIE DURANT'S UNBENDING COMMITMENT

In his book, *Passion*, Karl Olsson tells a story of incredible patience among the early French Protestants called Huguenots.

In the late Seventeenth Century in…southern France, a girl named Marie Durant was brought before the authorities, charged with the

*Huguenot heresy. She was fourteen years old, bright, attractive, mar-
riageable. She was asked to abjure the Huguenot faith. She was not
asked to commit an immoral act, to become a criminal, or even to
change the day-to-day quality of her behavior. She was only asked to say,
"J'abjure". No more, no less. She did not comply. Together with thirty
other Huguenot women she was put into a tower by the sea... For
thirty-eight years she continued... And instead of the hated word J'abjure she, together with her fellow martyrs, scratched on the wall of the
prison tower the single word* Resistez, resist!

*The word is still seen and gaped at by tourists on the stone wall at
Aigues-Mortes... We do not understand the terrifying simplicity of a
religious commitment which asks nothing of time and gets nothing from
time. We can understand a religion which enhances time... But we cannot understand a faith which is not nourished by the temporal hope that
tomorrow things will be better. To sit in a prison room with thirty others
and to see the day change into night and summer into autumn, to feel
the slow systemic changes within one's flesh: the drying and wrinkling of
the skin, the loss of muscle tone, the stiffening of the joints, the slow stu-
pefaction of the senses—to feel all this and still to persevere seems almost
idiotic to a generation which has no capacity to wait and to endure.*[1]

Patience is the capacity to "wait and to endure" without murmuring
and disillusionment—to wait in the unplanned place, and endure the
unplanned pace. Karl Olsson uses one key adjective that points to the
power behind patience. He said, "We cannot understand a faith which is
not nourished by the *temporal* hope that tomorrow things will be better." I
wonder if we can understand such patience. Surely we cannot, if "temporal" hope is the only kind we have. But if there is a hope beyond this
temporal life—if future grace extends into eternity—then there may be a
profound understanding of such patience in this life.

In fact it is precisely the hope of future grace beyond this life that carries the saints patiently through their afflictions. Paul made this crystal clear
in his own life: "We do not lose heart *[that is, we don't succumb to murmuring and impatience]*, but, though our outer man is decaying, yet our inner

man is being renewed day by day. For momentary, light affliction is producing for us an eternal weight of glory far beyond all comparison, while we look not at the things which are seen, but at the things which are not seen; for the things which are seen are *temporal,* but the things which are not seen are *eternal"* (2 Corinthians 4:16-18). I do not doubt that it was just this faith in future grace—beyond the temporal—that sustained the patience of Marie Durant and gave her the strength for thirty-eight years to write *Resistez* on the wall of her cell.

THE INNER STRENGTH OF PATIENCE

Strength is the right word. The apostle Paul prayed for the church at Colossae, that they would be *"strengthened* with all power, according to His glorious might, for the attaining of all *steadfastness and patience"* (Colossians 1:11). Patience is the evidence of an inner strength. Impatient people are weak, and therefore dependent on external supports—like schedules that go just right and circumstances that support their fragile hearts. Their outbursts of oaths and threats and harsh criticisms of the culprits who crossed their plans do not *sound* weak. But that noise is all a camouflage of weakness. Patience demands tremendous inner strength.

For the Christian, this strength comes from God. That is why Paul is *praying* for the Colossians. He is asking God to empower them for the patient endurance that the Christian life requires. But when he says that the strength of patience is "according to [God's] glorious might" he doesn't just mean that it takes divine power to make a person patient. He means that *faith* in this glorious might is the channel through which the power for patience comes. Patience is indeed a fruit of the Holy Spirit (Galatians 5:22) but, as we will see in Chapter Seventeen, the Holy Spirit empowers (with all his fruit) through "hearing with faith" (Galatians 3:5). Therefore Paul is praying that God would connect us with the "glorious might" that empowers patience. And that connection is faith.

TRUSTING GOD TO MAKE ALL BARRIERS BLESSINGS

Specifically the glorious might of God that we need to see and trust is the power of God to turn all our detours and obstacles into glorious outcomes.

If we believed that our hold-up at the long red light was God's keeping us back from an accident about to happen, we would be patient and happy. If we believed that our broken leg was God's way of revealing early cancer in the x-ray so that we would survive, we would not murmur at the inconvenience. If we believed that the middle-of-the-night phone call was God's way of waking us to smell smoke in the basement, we would not grumble at the loss of sleep. The key to patience is faith in the future grace of God's "glorious might" to transform all our interruptions into rewards.

In other words, the strength of patience hangs on our capacity to believe that God is up to something good for us in all our delays and detours. This requires great faith in future grace, because the evidence is seldom evident. There is a legend told by Richard Wurmbrand which illustrates the necessity of believing God for good, unseen purposes, when all we can see is evil and frustration.

> *A legend says that Moses once sat near a well in meditation. A wayfarer stopped to drink from the well and when he did so his purse fell from his girdle into the sand. The man departed. Shortly afterwards another man passed near the well, saw the purse and picked it up. Later a third man stopped to assuage his thirst and went to sleep in the shadow of the well. Meanwhile, the first man had discovered that his purse was missing and assuming that he must have lost it at the well, returned, awoke the sleeper (who of course knew nothing) and demanded his money back. An argument followed, and irate, the first man slew the latter. Where upon Moses said to God, "You see, therefore men do not believe you. There is too much evil and injustice in the world. Why should the first man have lost his purse and then become a murderer? Why should the second have gotten a purse full of gold without having worked for it? The third was completely innocent. Why was he slain?"*

> *God answered, "For once and only once, I will give you an explanation. I cannot do it at every step. The first man was a thief's son. The purse contained money stolen by his father from the father of the second man, who finding the purse only found what was due him. The third was a*

murderer whose crime had never been revealed and who received from the first the punishment he deserved. In the future believe that there is sense and righteousness in what transpires even when you do not understand."[2]

Moses' impatience with God in this story would surely be overcome if he had more faith in God's power and wisdom to turn all things for the good of his people. God has promised again and again in the Bible to do just that (2 Chronicles 16:9; Psalm 23:6; 84:11; Jeremiah 32:40–41; Isaiah 64:4; Romans 8:28, 32; 1 Corinthians 3:22–23). In fact, the only thing misleading in this legend is the comment put in the mouth of God that, "For once and only once, I will give you an explanation." The fact is, God has given us explanations like this repeatedly in the Bible with enough illustrations to fill a book.[3]

KEY TO PATIENCE: "GOD MEANT IT FOR GOOD"

For example, the story of Joseph in Genesis 37-50 is a great lesson in why we should have faith in the sovereign future grace of God. Joseph is sold into slavery by his brothers, which must have tested his patience tremendously. But he is given a good job in Potiphar's household. Then, when he is acting uprightly in the unplanned place of obedience, Potiphar's wife lies about his integrity and has him thrown into prison—another great trial to his patience. But again things turn for the better and the prison-keeper gives him responsibility and respect. But just when he thinks he is about to get a reprieve from the Pharaoh's cupbearer, whose dream he interpreted, the cupbearer forgets him for two more years. Finally, the meaning of all these detours and delays becomes clear. Joseph says to his long-estranged brothers, "God sent me before you to preserve for you a remnant in the earth, and to keep you alive by a great deliverance... And as for you, you meant evil against me, but God meant it for good, in order to bring about this present result, to preserve many people alive" (Genesis 45:7; 50:20).

What would have been the key to patience for Joseph during all those long years of exile and abuse? The answer is: faith in future grace—the sovereign grace of God to turn the unplanned place and the unplanned pace into the happiest ending imaginable.

A HONEYMOON TRAGEDY

Not everybody's story turns out so well in this life. Benjamin B. Warfield was a world-renowned theologian who taught at Princeton Seminary for almost 34 years until his death on February 16, 1921. Many people are aware of his famous books, like *The Inspiration and Authority of the Bible.* But what most people don't know is that in 1876, at the age of twenty-five, he married Annie Pierce Kinkead and took a honeymoon to Germany. During a fierce storm Annie was struck by lightning and permanently paralyzed. After caring for her for thirty-nine years Warfield laid her to rest in 1915. Because of her extraordinary needs, Warfield seldom left his home for more than two hours at a time during all those years of marriage.[4]

Now here was a shattered dream. I recall saying to my wife the week before we married, "If we have a car accident on our honeymoon, and you are disfigured or paralyzed, I will keep my vows, 'for better or for worse.'" But for Warfield it actually happened. She was never healed. There was no kingship in Egypt at the end of the story—only the spectacular, patience and faithfulness of one man to one woman through thirty-eight years of what was never planned—at least, not planned by man. But when Warfield came to write his thoughts on Romans 8:28, he said, "The fundamental thought is the universal government of God. All that comes to you is under His controlling hand. The secondary thought is the favour of God to those that love Him. If He governs all, then nothing but good can befall those to whom He would do good...Though we are too weak to help ourselves and too blind to ask for what we need, and can only groan in unformed longings, He is the author in us of these very longings...and He will so govern all things that we shall reap only good from all that befalls us."[5]

NOT EVEN DEATH IS A DECISIVE INTERRUPTION

This is true even in the case of death. Some saints die in prison (Revelation 2:10). But even death becomes the servant of God's children. This is what Paul meant when he said, "All things belong to you whether...the world or life or *death*...all things belong to you, and you belong to Christ; and Christ belongs to God" (1 Corinthians 3:22-23). As our possession, death serves us; it exists for our benefit. Another way of saying this is that death cannot separate us from the love of God, but that in it—as in "distress, or persecution, or famine, or nakedness, or peril, or sword—…we overwhelmingly conquer through Him who loved us" (Romans 8:35–37). Even if we die we conquer. And death ends up serving our best interest. (See Chapter Twenty-Nine.)

So the lesson of Joseph—and the whole Bible—stands: when delays and detours and frustrations and opposition ruin our plans and bode ill for us, faith in future grace lays hold on the sovereign purpose of God to bring something magnificent to pass. That is the key to patience.

THE PATH OF FAITHFUL PATIENCE IS NOT A STRAIGHT LINE

Another great lesson in how the sovereignty of God's grace leads to patience is the story of how the temple was rebuilt after the Babylonian exile. The way God turns things around is so amazing he must have been smiling. Israel had been in exile for decades. Now the time had come, in God's planning, for their restoration to the promised land. How could this happen? That was, no doubt, the question in many Jewish minds as they struggled to be patient with God's timing. The answer is that God is sovereign over emperors' wills. Ezra tells us that "in the first year of Cyrus king of Persia, in order to fulfill the word of the Lord by the mouth of Jeremiah, the Lord stirred up the spirit of Cyrus king of Persia…to build Him a house in Jerusalem" (Ezra 1:1-2). This is absolutely astonishing. Out of the blue, God moves the heart of Cyrus to pay attention to this little people called Jews, and send them off to Jerusalem to rebuild their temple. Who would have dreamed it could happen this way? Perhaps those who have faith in future grace. But the best is yet to come.

Over 42,000 Jewish refugees return and start building the temple in Jerusalem. Imagine the joy. But beware. The path of faithfulness is seldom a straight line to glory. Their enemies in Judah oppose them and discourage them. "Then the people of the land discouraged the people of Judah, and frightened them from building, and hired counselors against them to frustrate their purpose, all the days of Cyrus king of Persia, even until the reign of Darius king of Persia" (Ezra 4:4-5). Imagine the frustration and impatience of the people. God had seemingly opened the door to rebuild the temple, and now there was paralyzing opposition.

But God had a different plan. O, for people with faith in future grace to see what mere physical eyes cannot see! Yes, the people of the land had stopped the building. But can we not trust God that the same sovereignty that moved Cyrus also prevails over the local opponents? We are so slow to learn the lesson of God's sovereign grace! In Ezra 5:1 God sends two prophets, Haggai and Zechariah, to inspire the people to begin building again. Of course, the enemies are still there. They try again to stop the building of the temple. They write a letter to Darius, the new emperor. But it backfires entirely, and now we see why God had allowed the building to cease temporarily.

Instead of agreeing with the letter and stopping the temple-building, Darius searches the archives, and finds the original decree from Cyrus which authorized the building of the temple. The result is stunning. He writes back the news—beyond what they could ask or think. He says to the enemies in Judah, "Leave this work on the house of God alone...Moreover, I issue a decree concerning what you are to do for these elders of Judah in the rebuilding of this house of God: *the full cost is to be paid to these people from the royal treasury* out of the taxes of the provinces beyond the River, and that without delay" (Ezra 6:7-8). In other words, God ordained a setback for a season, so that the temple would not only be built but *paid for* under Darius! If faith could apprehend this kind of future grace, would not impatience be conquered?

And lest we doubt that this was really all a plan of God, Ezra 6:22 states the great fact plainly: "the Lord had turned the heart of the king of Assyria toward them to encourage them in the work of the house of God, the God of Israel." If William Cowper (1731-1800) had already written his great hymn, "God Moves in a Mysterious Way," I think the people of Israel would have been singing it.

Judge not the Lord by feeble sense,
But trust him for his grace,
Behind a frowning providence
He hides a smiling face.

Living by faith in future grace means believing that "the king's heart is like streams of water in the hand of the Lord; he turns it wherever he wills" (Proverbs 21:1). God did it to Cyrus (Ezra 1:1); he did it to Darius (Ezra 6:22) and he did it later to Artaxerxes: "Blessed be the Lord, the God of our fathers, who *put such a thing as this into the heart of the king,* to adorn the house of the Lord" (Ezra 7:27). God is ruling the world. He is ruling history. And it is all for the good of his people and the glory of his name. "From of old they have not heard nor perceived by ear, neither has the eye seen a God besides Thee, who *acts in behalf of the one who waits for Him*" (Isaiah 64:4). The power of patience flows through faith in the future, sovereign grace of God.

THE LORD IS FULL OF COMPASSION AND MERCY

We have stressed that this grace is "sovereign". We also need to stress that it is grace. It is merciful and full of good will toward us. This is what James stresses about Job's experience of suffering, and his struggle with impatience. James commands us to be patient and gives us the key:

> *Be patient, therefore, brethren, until the coming of the Lord. Behold, the farmer waits for the precious produce of the soil, being patient about it, until it gets the early and late rains. You too be patient; strengthen your hearts, for the coming of the Lord is at hand. Do not complain, brethren, against one another, that you yourselves may not be judged; behold, the Judge is standing right at the door. As an example, brethren, of suffering and patience, take the prophets who spoke in the name of the Lord. Behold, we count those blessed who endured. You have heard of the endurance of Job and have seen* the outcome of the Lord's dealings, that the Lord is full of compassion and is merciful. (James 5:7-11)

James wants us to see the outcome of Job's suffering. The word for "outcome" is *telos* and means "goal" not just result. It was God's goal in all his dealings with Job to be merciful, and fit him for a greater blessing. This is what Job had missed and why he repented from his murmuring the way he did: "Therefore I retract, and I repent in dust and ashes" (Job 42:6). The power of patience flows from faith in this truth: in all his dealings with us his goal "is full of compassion and is merciful." Faith in future grace is faith in grace that is sovereign, and sovereignty that is gracious.

THROUGH FAITH AND PATIENCE WE INHERIT THE PROMISES

Patience is sustained by faith in the promise of future grace. In every unplanned frustration on the path of obedience God's Word holds true: "I will not turn away from them, to do them good...and I will rejoice over them to do them good...with all My heart and with all My soul" (Jeremiah 32:40-41). He is pursuing us with goodness and mercy all our days (Psalm 23:6). Impatient complaining is therefore a form of unbelief.

Which is why the command to be patient takes on such immense significance. Jesus said, "By your [patient] *endurance* you will gain your lives" (Luke 21:19). And the writer to the Hebrews said, "[Be] imitators of those who through faith and patience inherit the promises" (Hebrews 6:12). We come into our inheritance on the path of patience, not because patience is a work of the flesh that earns salvation, but because patience is a fruit of faith in future grace.

Charles Simeon was in the Church of England from 1782 to 1836 at Trinity Church in Cambridge. He was appointed to his church by a bishop against the will of the people. They opposed him, not because he was a bad preacher, but because he was an evangelical—he believed the Bible and called for conversion and holiness and world evangelization.

For twelve years the people refused to let him give the Sunday afternoon sermon. And during that time they boycotted the Sunday morning service and locked their pews so that no one could sit in them. He preached to people in the aisles for twelve years! The average stay of a pastor in America is about four years, under average circumstances. Simeon began with twelve years of intense opposition—and lasted fifty-four years. How did he endure in such patience?

In this state of things I saw no remedy but faith and patience [Note: the linking of faith and patience!]. *The passage of Scripture which subdued and controlled my mind was this, "The servant of the Lord must not strive."* [Note: The weapon in the fight for faith and patience was the Word!] *It was painful indeed to see the church, with the exception of the aisles, almost forsaken; but I thought that if God would only give a double blessing to the congregation that did attend, there would on the whole be as much good done as if the congregation were doubled and the blessing limited to only half the amount. This comforted me many, many times, when without such a reflection, I should have sunk under my burden.*[6]

Where did he get the assurance that if he followed the way of patience there would be a blessing on his work that would make up for the frustrations of having all the pews locked? He got it from texts that promised future grace—texts like Isaiah 30:18, "Blessed are all those who wait for [the Lord]" (RSV). The Word conquered unbelief, and faith in future grace conquered impatience.

Fifty-four years later he was dying. It was October, 1836. The weeks dragged on, as they have for many dying saints. I've learned, beside many dying believers, that the battle with impatience can be very intense on the death bed. On October 21 those by his bed heard him say these words slowly and with long pauses:

Infinite wisdom has arranged the whole with infinite love; and infinite power enables me—to rest upon that love. I am in a dear Father's hands—all is secure. When I look to Him, I see nothing but faithfulness—and immutability—and truth; and I have the sweetest peace—I cannot have more peace.[7]

The reason Simeon could die like that is because he had trained himself for fifty-four years to go to Scripture and to take hold of the promises of future grace and use them to conquer the unbelief of impatience. He had learned to use the sword of the Spirit to fight the fight of faith in future grace. By faith in future grace he had learned to wait with God in the unplanned *place* of obedience, and to walk with God at the unplanned *pace* of obedience. With the psalmist he said, "I *wait* for the Lord, my soul does *wait,* and *in His word do I hope*" (Psalm 130:5). In his living and dying Charles Simeon makes plain and powerful the promise, "The Lord is good to those who wait for him" (Lamentations 3:25).

———

PART V

THE NATURE
OF FAITH IN
FUTURE GRACE

With respect to the promise of God,
he did not waver in unbelief,
but grew strong in faith,
giving glory to God.

ROMANS 4:20

God has chosen you from the beginning for salvation
through sanctification by the Spirit and faith in the truth.

2 THESSALONIANS 2:13

Faith is the God-appointed means of justification and sanctification because,
better than any other act,
it fits with the grace of God
and magnifies the glory of God.

CHAPTER FOURTEEN

What Guards the Glory of God's Sovereign Grace

FUTURE GRACE, THE POWER FOR ALL OBEDIENCE

All future obedience to God will be by the power of future grace.[1] Whatever work or ministry we may do, we should say with the apostle Paul, "I labored...yet not I, but the *grace of God* with me" (1 Corinthians 15:10)." Or, as he says in Romans 15:18, "I will not presume to speak of anything except what *Christ has accomplished through me.*" All our acts that please the Lord will be acts which the Lord has worked through us, as Hebrews 13:21 says, "[It is God who] equips you in every good thing to do his will, *working in us that which is pleasing in His sight.*" Which is also what Paul said in Philippians 2:13, "It is God who is at work in you both to will and to work for his good pleasure." If we find in ourselves any spiritual earnestness, we should thank God (not ourselves). That's what Paul did: he saw earnestness in the heart of Titus and said, "Thanks be to God who *puts the same earnestness on your behalf in the heart of Titus*" (2 Corinthians 8:16). All future obedience comes by the power of future grace.

DOES THE POWER OF GRACE MAKE US PASSIVE?

What then are we to do? Should I be passive because all obedience is by future grace? What act of mine will connect and fit with this future grace? What will highlight the glory of this future grace rather than compete with it? If God has reserved the right for himself to transform us by his future grace, then he must want the credit and the glory for all the goodness that results from his grace. As the apostle Paul says, God is doing everything for us "to the praise of the glory of His grace" (Ephesians 1:6, 12, 14). So it's very important that we find out what our role is in reflecting, rather than resisting, God's aim to glorify his grace in our transformation.

Any kind of response or act on our part that will highlight our self-sufficiency or obscure the freedom of God's future grace in making us holy will not fit with grace, but nullify it. What then is the act of our soul that avoids this contradiction? The biblical answer is that *faith* fits with grace and channels[2] it to obedience so that we boast not in our resources but in God's grace. That's why this book is subtitled *The Purifying Power of Living by Faith in Future Grace*.

WHAT MAGNIFIES RATHER THAN NULLIFIES GRACE?

The New Testament correlates faith and grace to make sure that we do not boast in what grace alone achieves. One of the most familiar examples goes like this: "For by *grace* you have been saved through *faith*" (Ephesians 2:8). By *grace,* through *faith.* There's the correlation that guards the freedom of grace. Faith is the act of our soul that turns away from our own insufficiency to the free and all-sufficient resources of God. Faith focuses on the freedom of God to dispense grace to the unworthy. It banks on the bounty of God.

Therefore faith, by its very nature, nullifies boasting and fits with grace. Wherever faith looks, it sees grace behind every praiseworthy act. So it cannot boast, except in the Lord. So Paul, after saying that salvation is by grace through faith, says, "...and that not of yourselves, it is the gift of God; not as a result of works, *that no one should boast*" (Ephesians 2:8-9). Faith cannot boast in human goodness or competence or wisdom, because faith focuses on the free, all-supplying grace of God. Whatever goodness faith sees, it sees as the fruit of grace. When it looks at our "wisdom and righteousness and sanctification and redemption," it says, "Let him who boasts boast in the Lord" (1 Corinthians 1:30-31).

When I lost my footing as a little boy in the undertow at Daytona Beach, I felt as if I were going to be dragged to the middle of the ocean in an instant. It was a terrifying thing. I tried to get my bearings and figure out which way was up. But I couldn't get my feet on the ground and the current was too strong to swim. I wasn't a good swimmer any way. In my panic I thought of only one thing: Could someone help me? But I couldn't even call out from under the water. When I felt my father's hand take hold of my upper arm like a mighty vice grip, it was the sweetest feeling in the world. I yielded entirely to being overpowered by his strength. I reveled in being picked up at his will. I did not resist. The thought did not enter my mind that I should try to show that things aren't so bad; or that I should add my strength to my Dad's arm. All I thought was, Yes! I need you! I thank you! I love your strength! I love your initiative! I love your grip! You are great! In that spirit of yielded affection one cannot boast. I call that yielded affection "faith." And my father was the embodiment of the future grace that I craved under the water. This is the faith that magnifies grace.

As we ponder how to live the Christian life, the uppermost thought should be: How can I magnify rather than nullify the grace of God? Paul answers this question in Galatians 2:20-21, "I have been crucified with Christ; and it is no longer I who live, but Christ lives in me; and the life which I now live in the flesh *I live by faith in the Son of God, who loved me, and delivered Himself up for me. I do not nullify the grace of God.*" Why does his life not nullify the grace of God? Because he lives by faith in the Son of God. Faith calls all attention to grace and magnifies it, rather than nullifying it.

CHRIST'S FUTURE WORK FOR US

When Paul says, "It is no longer I who live, but *Christ who lives in me,*" he pictures an ongoing work of the living Christ day by day and moment by moment working in him. This is the future grace that he banks on when he says, "I live by faith in the Son of God." As Paul contemplates the next moment or the next month or the next year of his life, what he sees is the living Christ ready and able to work in him what is pleasing in God's sight and to work all things together for his good. So Paul trusts him. And in this way future grace works its good work in Paul's life and ministry.

Very little in our culture encourages us to live by faith every hour of the day. On the contrary billboards, radio, television, newspapers and magazines mount a relentless appeal for us to look away from Jesus as the source of our hourly strength and guidance. We are told that cars will work for us and food will work for us and clothes will work for us. They will supply not just transportation and nourishment and covering, but more importantly, they promise that they will also meet the longings of the heart for attention and power and excitement and esteem.

If you and I are to live by faith in the hourly fellowship and performance of Jesus on our behalf, we need to set our minds steadfastly— starting now—to consciously think of him and look to him and trust his promise: "I will never desert you, nor will I ever forsake you…I am with you always, even to the end of the age…I will strengthen you, surely I will help you, surely I will uphold you with my righteous right hand…[I will work in you] that which is pleasing in [God's] sight" (Hebrews 13:5; Matthew 28:20; Isaiah 41:10; Hebrews 13:21). I encourage you to join me in forming spiritual habits of hourly looking to Jesus for the fulfillment of promises like this.

"THE LORD STOOD WITH ME"

In the last letter he wrote, probably not long before he was beheaded in the Neronean persecution, Paul bore witness to the way the Lord Jesus worked for him moment by moment. In 2 Timothy 4:16-18 he said:

> At my first defense no one supported me, but all deserted me; may it not be counted against them. But the Lord stood with me, and strengthened me, in order that through me the proclamation might be fully accomplished, and that all the Gentiles might hear; and I was delivered out of the lion's mouth. The Lord will deliver me from every evil deed, and will bring me safely to His heavenly kingdom; to Him be the glory forever and ever. Amen.

This is a sad and beautiful testimony. Others had deserted him. But not the Lord. The Lord was with him. The Lord strengthened him. The Lord delivered him out of the lion's mouth (Satan? 1 Peter 5:8).[3] And with the encouragement of this recent experience of past grace, Paul continues to walk by faith in future grace: "The Lord *will deliver me* from every evil deed, and bring me safely to His heavenly kingdom." This doesn't mean that future grace guarantees freedom from suffering and death. In fact, death is not an impediment, but a passage to the heavenly kingdom. The "evil deed" that would keep Paul out of the kingdom is apostasy—making shipwreck of his faith, and proving in the end that he was not really born of God (1 John 2:19). So what Paul probably means is that the Lord will preserve his faith and keep him from giving in to bitterness and unbelief, as friends forsake him and eventually he is martyred. This is the promise of future grace—Christ living in him, with him and for him.

The thought is the same as in 1 Corinthians 15:10, where he says, "I labored...yet not I but the grace of God with me." In Galatians 2:20 he says, "Not I, but Christ." In 1 Corinthians, "Not I, but grace." That is why, in this book, I sometimes say, "Faith in future grace" and sometimes, "Faith in Christ."

THE FAITH OF ABRAHAM A MODEL OF FAITH IN FUTURE GRACE

The apostle Paul is tremendously concerned that we not nullify future grace by putting our efforts in place of it, or by trying to receive it in the wrong way. He faces this problem again in Romans 4:14-16. He is arguing that all the descendants of Abraham are heirs of the breathtaking promise that believers will inherit the world (v. 13). I say "believers" because his point is that all who have the faith of Abraham (whether Jew or Gentile) are, in reality, descendants of Abraham and heirs of the promise. That would include all true Christians. His argument is rooted in the nature of God's future grace and how it correlates to faith.

He says, "If those who are of the Law are heirs, *faith* is made void and the *promise* is nullified" (v. 14). In other words, the "promise" of God's grace was meant to be received by "faith," not earned by what he calls, "being of the Law"—a phrase that probably implies relying on our religious culture or morality rather than on God's grace.

Then Paul says, "For this reason, it is by *faith*, that it might be in accordance with *grace*, in order that the promise may be certain to *all* the descendants" (v. 16). Here he makes explicit the correlation between faith and grace. *Grace* guarantees the promise to Jews and Gentiles alike. And *faith* is the indispensable link with the soul that guards the freedom of grace, so that it can be valid for those who do not have the Jewish distinctives. Faith in God's promise—faith in future grace—is the act which God has ordained to receive the power of grace and reflect the preciousness of grace.

Paul has in mind a special reason why faith glorifies God's future grace. Simply put, the reason is that this God-glorifying faith is a future-oriented confidence in God's integrity and power and wisdom to follow through on all his promises. Paul illustrates this faith with Abraham's response to the promise of God: that he would be the father of many nations (Romans 4:18). "In hope against hope *he believed*," that is, he had faith in the future grace of God's promise. "And without becoming weak *in faith* he contemplated his own body, now as good as dead since he was about a hundred years old, and the deadness of Sarah's womb; yet, with respect to the promise of God, *he did not waver in unbelief, but grew strong in faith, giving glory to God, and being fully assured that what He had promised, He was able also to perform*" (Romans 4:18-21).

The faith of Abraham was a faith in the promise of God to make him the father of many nations. This faith glorified God because it called attention to all the resources of God that would be required to fulfill it. Abraham was too old to have children, and Sarah was barren. Not only that: how do you turn a son or two into "many nations" which God said Abraham would be the father of? It all seemed totally impossible. Therefore Abraham's faith glorified God by being fully assured that he could and would do the impossible.

Here we can see, too, why Abraham's faith is held up as the model of the kind of faith we Christians must have in order to be justified and sanctified. Justifying faith and sanctifying faith are the kind of faith that Abraham had. Paul said that we become heirs of the promise of Abraham by having "the faith of Abraham" (Romans 4:16). Then he described his faith in detail as future-oriented, promise-trusting faith (vv. 18-21). Then he said that this faith "was reckoned to [Abraham] as righteousness" (v. 22). That is, this promise-trusting faith was justifying faith.[4]

This means that the faith that justifies—the faith of Abraham—is future-oriented, promise-trusting confidence in God. Paul confirms this in the next verses: "Now not for [Abraham's] sake only was it written, that it was reckoned to him [as righteousness], but *for our sake also,* to whom it will be reckoned, as those who believe in Him who raised Jesus our Lord from the dead" (Romans 4:23-24). In other words, we too will be justified—reckoned righteous—by the same kind of faith Abraham had. The difference now is that our future-oriented faith has a fuller revelation of God to trust.

Since Good Friday and Easter, we know God as the God who raised Jesus from the dead. But this is not essentially different from Abraham's faith, because when Paul wanted to describe Abraham's faith in God's promise back in verse 17, he said that it was a faith in "God who gives life to the dead, and calls into being that which does not exist." In other words, Abraham's faith and our faith are essentially the same in that they involve confidence in God's ability to do the impossible, like making barren women pregnant and raising the dead.

Therefore the faith which magnifies grace, instead of nullifying it, is future-oriented confidence in the wisdom and power and trustworthiness of God to do what he has promised. And this faith in future grace is the faith through which we are justified. It stands on the great achievements of past grace in the cross and resurrection (which we saw in Chapters Seven-Nine), but it does not remain in a past-oriented posture. It looks forward to all the inexhaustible future grace that those past achievements obtained and guaranteed.

"YOU NEVER ASK FOR MONEY?"

One of the most powerful testimonies to the all-sufficiency of future grace is the "faith principle" that has governed the lives of so many missionaries, notably those of Overseas Missionary Fellowship. Without condemning those who follow a different pattern, it has been the practice of those who follow in the steps of Hudson Taylor to move the hearts of people to give by talking to God and not people. Dr. James H. Taylor, the great-grandson of the founder, explains how this faith in future grace, rooted in demonstrations of bygone grace, honors God.

> *We…begin from a position of faith. We believe God does exist. We have become convinced of this in a variety of ways, but all of us have experienced the grace of God in bringing us to know Himself through Jesus Christ and through rebirth by His Spirit. We believe we have good grounds of believing in Him through the historical fact of the resurrection of Jesus Christ from the dead: we believe that someone who said He would die and rise again, and did it, is credible in every other way.* Therefore we are prepared to trust Him, not only for the eternal salvation of our souls, but also for the practical provision of our daily bread and financial support.[5]

OMF publishes testimonies of God's amazing faithfulness to demonstrate the glory of his all-supplying future grace. "We want to demonstrate that God can be trusted to do all that He says He will do, by sharing how He has provided for such mundane needs as plane tickets, meals, medical expenses, and the regular support of a whole group of Christian people for well over a hundred years."[6] What OMF is devoted to is glorifying the dependability of God—in their message and in their method. Hudson Taylor put it this way: "There is a living God. He has spoken in the Bible. He means what He says and will do all that He has promised."[7] Lives of faith are the great mirror of the dependability of God.

This witness to the all-sufficiency of God's future grace has changed lives. One woman in her early thirties came to an OMF prayer conference somewhat "by accident." She had recently been a member of a radical organization working to overthrow a corrupt and unjust government. She had now been converted and was in love with the Lord Jesus, but was still bitterly critical of the smug selfishness of the established church, as she saw it. When she heard that OMF does not appeal for funds, she was incredulous. OMF missionary, Linnet Hinton, explained to her, "The Fellowship is supported by God."

The conversation went on into the evening as Linnet answered the woman's questions—"How does it work? What about pensions? Etc." Finally the woman's resistance broke and she said,

> Then it's true. By God it's true! This is the reality I've been looking for all my life. When I became a Christian, I gave up my job because it was the sort of job a Christian can't do. I am now unemployed and the only thing I own is the car in which I came to this conference. I've been anxious and afraid. I've been disillusioned with the church and have despised the hypocrisy of many Christians who are so materialistic and complacent in spite of the poverty of others. But you have shown me that the life of faith works and that God can be trusted, and so, I too, from this day on, want to depend upon Him alone for all my needs."[8]

JUSTIFYING FAITH IS SANCTIFYING FAITH

Faith is a perfect fit with future grace. It corresponds to the freedom and all-sufficiency of grace. And it calls attention to the glorious trustworthiness of God. One of the important implications of this conclusion is that the faith that justifies and the faith that sanctifies are not two different kinds of faith. "Sanctify" simply means to make holy, or to transform into Christlikeness. This is what I was describing in the first paragraph of this chapter. It is all by grace.[9] Therefore, as we have seen, it must also be through faith. For faith is the act of the soul that connects with grace, and receives it, and channels it as the power of obedience, and guards it from being nullified through human boasting.

Paul makes this connection between faith and sanctification explicit, not only in Galatians 2:20 as we saw above ("I *live* by faith"), but also in 2 Thessalonians 2:13: "God has chosen you from the beginning for salvation through *sanctification by the Spirit and faith in the truth.*" Sanctification is by the *Spirit* and by *faith.* Which is another way of saying that it is by grace and by faith. The Spirit is "the Spirit of grace" (Hebrews 10:29). God's making us holy is the work of his Spirit; but the Spirit works through faith. And we will see, again and again in this book, that this sanctifying faith is the future-oriented, promise-trusting faith of Abraham.

The simple reason why the faith which justifies is also the faith which sanctifies is that both justification and sanctification are the work of sovereign grace. They are not the same kind of work,[10] but they are both works of grace. Sanctification and justification are "grace upon grace." We have seen in this chapter that the corollary of free grace is faith. If both justification and sanctification are works of grace it is natural that they would both be by faith.

Not only that, we also know from Scripture that the reason God justifies and sanctifies by grace is so that the glorious, self-sustaining all-sufficiency of his own fullness would be displayed and marveled at in the world.[11] Romans 15:9 (RSV) says Christ entered history on his great errand of grace *"in order that"* the Gentiles would "glorify God for his *mercy.*" And Ephesians 1:6 says that the whole great plan of redemption was designed by God to bring about "the praise of the glory of his *grace.*" God has determined that we will receive all by grace so that he will get all the glory. Charles Spurgeon put it like this: "One thing is past all question: we shall bring our Lord most glory if we get from Him much grace. If I have much faith, so that I can take God at His Word…I shall greatly honor my Lord and King."[12]

Which confirms why the grace of justification and the grace of sanctification are both by faith—because faith is the one response to grace that guards all the glory for God. Faith does not contaminate grace with human self-sufficiency. Therefore faith prevents boasting. "Where, then, is boasting?" Paul asks. And answers, "It is excluded. By what kind of law? Of works? No, but by a law of faith" (Romans 3:27). Faith excludes boasting and exalts the glory of grace. So faith not only fits with the freeness of grace, it also fits with the design of grace to bring all glory to God. "[Abraham] grew strong in faith, *giving glory to God"* (Romans 4:20). That means that Abraham's confidence in God's power and wisdom and trustworthiness displayed God's glory. Faith is the God-appointed means of justification and sanctification because, better than any other act, it fits with the grace of God and magnifies the glory of God.

The effect this truth should have on our hearts is expressed by the psalmist: "The Lord gives *grace* and glory…O Lord of hosts, how blessed is the man who *trusts* in Thee!" (Psalm 84:11-12). He exults in the blessed-ness of the person who trusts in the God of all grace. We need to let it sink in that grace is not only gotten by faith, but glorified by faith. This doubles our blessing in being people who trust in God. On the one hand, we long for the blessings of God's future grace, and they come to us by faith. But on the other hand, we long for God's grace to be glorified in our lives, and this too comes by faith. Faith receives the goodness of future grace, and faith reflects the glory of future grace. It is a double wonder. These two things are not at odds—our receiving the joy and God getting the glory. O, how this should set our hearts on a passionate quest to trust God hour by hour for all we need—for God's sake! Every moment of faith is a tribute to his grace.

Men don't know that they are godly,

by believing that they are godly.

SOLOMON STODDARD

In all the acts of saving faith the Holy Spirit enables us

not just to perceive and affirm factual truth,

but also to apprehend and embrace spiritual beauty.

It is the embracing of spiritual beauty that is the essential

core of saving faith.

This is what I mean by being satisfied with all that God is for us in Jesus.

Spiritual beauty is the beauty of God diffused in all his works and words.

Embracing this, or delighting in it, or being satisfied with it,

is the heart of saving—and sanctifying—faith.

CHAPTER FIFTEEN

A Taste of Spiritual Beauty

LOST "BELIEVERS"?

O ne of the reasons this book has so many chapters is that the longer I thought about faith in future grace, the more questions there were to answer. For example, is it possible to believe the promises of God about the security of the saints, and yet be lost? If faith in future grace means believing the promises of God, how is it that those promises could be believed and yet the "believer" not be saved?

This possibility is implied in Matthew 7:21-23: "Not everyone who says to me, 'Lord, Lord,' will enter the kingdom of heaven; but he who does the will of my Father who is in heaven. Many will say to me on that day, 'Lord, Lord, did we not prophesy in Your name, and in Your name cast out demons, and in Your name perform many miracles?' And then I will declare to them, 'I never knew you; depart from Me, you who practice lawlessness.'" These folks believed that they were secure. Otherwise they would not have been so stunned at Jesus' rejection. They knew Christian teaching. And when they read promises like, "I will never leave you or forsake you" (Hebrews 13:5), they *believed* them, or so it seems. At least they thought the promises were true for them and gave them security. They were shocked to hear that the Lord did not know them and that they were going to be cast out of his presence.

The breezy, light-hearted religious atmosphere of recent generations does not support the kind of seriousness and urgency needed to deal with such warnings. But there have been times and teachers who have dealt profoundly with them. Not many pastors and theologians have struggled more deeply with the frightening reality of deluded hypocrisy than Jonathan Edwards, during the days of the First Great Awakening in New England. His book, *Treatise Concerning the Religious Affections* (1746), probes the labyrinthine habitations of human affections. He was not alone. All the heirs of the Puritans cared deeply that religious experience be spiritual and gracious, not merely natural and counterfeit. Men like Thomas Shepard (1605-1649) and John Flavel (1630-1691) led the way for Edwards in his thinking about the subtlety of human sin and self-deception.

Edwards cites Shepard's reference to "presumptuous peace" in some professing believers.[1] He quotes Flavel's observation that "so strong may this false assurance be, that they dare boldly venture to go to the judgment seat of God, and there defend it."[2] He quotes his grandfather, Solomon Stoddard, "Men don't know that they are godly, by believing that they are godly."[3] Edwards develops his own extended thoughts under this thesis: "It is no sufficient reason to determine that men are saints, and their affections gracious, because the affections they have are attended *with an exceeding confidence* that their state is good."[4] In other words, Edwards was deeply concerned, especially in the fervor of revival, that the biblical nature of saving faith be grasped, lest people be deceived by their own experiences.

In this Edwards was following the apostle Paul who was concerned, for example, that some in the church at Corinth were deluded in their enthusiasm. "You are already filled, you have already become rich, you have become kings without us; and I would indeed that you had become kings so that we also might reign with you" (1 Corinthians 4:8). They thought they were much farther along in their spiritual life than they were. Some might not even be Christians. To such ones he cautioned, "Test yourselves to see if you are in the faith; examine yourselves! Or do you not recognize this about yourselves, that Jesus Christ is in you—unless indeed you fail the test?" (2 Corinthians 13:5).

WHAT WAS WRONG WITH WONDER-WORKING FAITH?

So, if we can believe the promises of God and still be lost, what does it take to make this believing real? In Matthew 7:23 Jesus called the deceived, "[people] who practice lawlessness." So their resistance to the "will" of God (v. 21) and their giving in to "lawlessness" (v. 23) betrayed the true condition of their heart, and the absence of authentic faith. We must not simply say, "What they needed was works alongside their faith." No, the faith was defective. We know this because Jesus said three verses earlier, "A good tree cannot produce bad fruit, nor can a bad tree produce good fruit" (Matthew 7:18). Which means that the fruit of obedience does *not* come in alongside a tree and make it good, but the authentic health of the tree is what produces the fruit of obedience.

The question then, is, What's wrong with the faith of these very religious people? Why did their faith (which could prophesy and exorcise and do miracles!) not produce the good fruit which Jesus calls "the will of my Father who is in heaven" (v. 21)? What would turn the "faith" that they thought they had, into sanctifying, and thus saving, faith? What is the essence of faith in future grace?

LISTENING TO THE WISDOM OF CHARLES HODGE

One way to get at the answer is to ponder something that a great old Christian teacher wrote over a century and a half ago. Charles Hodge was born in 1797. He became a profound theologian and professor at Princeton Seminary for over 50 years. Mark Noll calls him "the greatest representative of conservative Calvinism in the nation's last two hundred years."[5] But he was far more than an academic theologian. He was a deeply spiritual person. His lifelong friend, Henry Boardman wrote, "Christ was not only the ground of his hope, but the acknowledged sovereign of his intellect, the soul of his theology, the unfailing spring of his joy, the one all-pervading, all-glorifying theme and end of his life."[6]

It's not surprising, then, that in 1841 Hodge wrote a book on the Christian life for ordinary Christians. It was called *The Way of Life,* and contains a chapter on faith that has helped me clarify my understanding of the essence of faith in future grace. He shows in this chapter that the Bible uses the word "faith" for all sorts of different states of mind including "deadness" "For just as the body without the spirit is dead, so also faith without works is dead" (James. 2:19). "Faith" can also refer to faith that demons have: "You believe that God is one. You do well; the demons also *believe,* and shudder" (James. 2:26).

THE BASIS OF BELIEVING DETERMINES
THE EXPERIENCE OF BELIEVING

He points out that acts of believing may differ from each other as the *basis* of the believing differs from case to case. For example, believing something because you have heard a reliable testimony (as in John 4:42), is not necessarily the same mental and spiritual experience as believing something because you have tasted or apprehended its spiritual beauty.

When you believe merely on the basis of a testimony you might assent to the truth without delighting in it or seeing it as spiritually beautiful. But when you believe because you have had a spiritual "taste" or "apprehension" of spiritual beauty, then the faith itself is permeated by this taste of spiritual beauty. Hodge says, "We may believe on the testimony of those in whose veracity and judgment we confide, that a man of whom we know nothing has great moral excellence. But if we see for ourselves the exhibition of his excellence, we believe for other reasons, and *in a different way.*"[7]

This is where Hodge helps us with our question: What turns believing into saving faith? He says that when we see spiritual excellence for ourselves, we believe "in a different way." This "different way" is what makes believing into saving faith. Don't misunderstand here. There is nothing wrong with believing Christ or believing his promises on the basis of the testimony of others. In fact, that is how all of us came to faith. We came to rely on the testimony of the apostles in the Bible. But being persuaded that Christ and his promises are factual is not *by itself* saving faith. That is why some professing Christians will be shocked at the last day, when they hear him say, "I never knew you," even though they protest that he is "Lord, Lord." Believing that Christ and his promises are true, based on a testimony, is a necessary *part* of faith. But it is not sufficient to turn faith into saving faith.

What makes faith saving faith is this "different way" of believing that comes from a different (not alternative, or contradictory) way of apprehending or tasting the reality behind the testimony we affirm. This different way is what Hodge calls a "spiritual apprehension of the truth." He says, "It is a faith which rests upon the manifestation by the Holy Spirit of the excellence, beauty, and suitableness of the truth... It arises from a spiritual apprehension of the truth, or from the testimony of the Spirit with and by the truth in our hearts."[8]

To illustrate this kind of spiritual apprehension Hodge cites Luke 10:21, "At that very time [Jesus] rejoiced greatly in the Holy Spirit, and said, 'I praise Thee, O Father, Lord of heaven and earth, that Thou didst hide these things from the wise and intelligent and *didst reveal them to babes*. Yes, Father, for thus it was well-pleasing in Thy sight.'" In other words, the truth about Jesus and his ministry and the kingdom of God was seen externally by some; but to "the babes" God *revealed* it. This revelation enabled that spiritual apprehension and taste which moves the heart to embrace and *savor* the reality, not just *think* that it is true.

Hodge cited in a similar way Matthew 16:16-17. Jesus asked the disciples who he was, and Peter "answered and said, 'Thou art the Christ, the Son of the living God.' And Jesus answered and said to him, 'Blessed are you, Simon Barjona, because *flesh and blood did not reveal this to you, but My Father who is in heaven.*'" There were evidences for the truth of Jesus' messiahship. Peter saw these. He was persuaded by them. But Jesus told Peter that the decisive thing in his faith was that God, not flesh and blood, had revealed Christ to him. In other words, a spiritual work had been done to enable Peter to go beyond what human reason can do and taste the spiritual reality of Christ's worth and embrace it.

One other text that Hodge cited to illustrate this "different way" of coming to true faith was 2 Corinthians 4:6. "God, who said, 'Light shall shine out of darkness,' is the One who has shone in our hearts to give the light of the knowledge of the glory of God in the face of Christ." When the gospel of Christ is preached, some may affirm the testimony of the preacher for various reasons—perhaps he is logically compelling, or a charismatic speaker, or an admired leader, or a parent. There are many reasons—some reasonable and some not—for affirming a testimony to Christ. That affirmation is a necessary part of coming to faith in Christ (Romans 10:17).

But Paul says *a special work of God* is necessary too. God must do something in us like he did on the first day of creation when he said, "Let there be light." He must shine in our hearts to give us a spiritual apprehension of the glory of Christ. That is, we must have a spiritual "taste" that he is gloriously precious beyond all competing values and treasures. When this happens we not only affirm Christ as the true object of someone else's testimony; we also "embrace" him as the spiritually excellent treasure of our souls. This is the essence of saving faith.[9]

UNDERSTANDING AND EMBRACING

Therefore, two things are necessary for saving faith to emerge. One is to use our perception and our mind to hear and see and understand and validate a testimony to the truth of Christ. The other is that we must apprehend and embrace the spiritual beauty and worth of Christ through the illumination of the Holy Spirit. Without this compelling spiritual taste of Christ's captivating excellence, a person's conviction about a testimony may be no more than the devil's useless assurance *that* Jesus is the Way, the Truth and the Life. He "believes" it, but he does not apprehend it as beautiful and precious and wonderfully suited to accomplish good and holy purposes. He assents in one way, but not with a hearty, or, as the Puritans say, "cordial" assent. He does not taste Christ as compellingly attractive. His "faith" is dead because it is not animated by the essential thing: spiritual apprehension of spiritual beauty.

EMBRACING PROMISES

What then does this mean for my repeated claim in this book *that believing the promises of God is the essential thing in saving, life-changing faith?* My claim is that justifying and sanctifying faith are one, and that the heart of this faith is future-oriented, promise-trusting confidence in God. What then does this insight from Hodge imply for my claim?

It implies that I must say more about this act of believing the promises. I must say now that it includes a spiritual apprehension of the beauty of God in and behind the promises. I must draw attention to the element of faith that embraces or apprehends or tastes the glory of God which we will enjoy as the essence of these promises. In other words, saving faith in the promises of God must include spiritual delight in the God of the promises. I don't want to overstate this. I say that saving faith must "include" delight. Delight in the glory of God is not the whole of what faith is. But I think that without it, faith is dead.

DAVID BRAINERD'S MOST AGREEABLE CONVERSATION

David Brainerd, the young missionary to the Indians whose *Journal* was published by Jonathan Edwards in 1749, saw these things more clearly in his day than most of us do today. Three months before Brainerd died at the age of thirty in October, 1747, he was in Boston discussing the nature of saving faith. He had seen a wonderful awakening among the Indians in Crossweeksung, New Jersey, and so knew these things not just from study, but also from experience. It appears that there was a dispute between him and a certain unnamed man in Boston who argued that "the essence of saving faith lies in believing that Christ died for me in particular, and that this is the first act of faith in a true believer's closing with Christ."[10]

Brainerd, like Edwards, disagreed with this. As Edwards explained in his note in Brainerd's *Journal*, "The essence of saving faith was wholly left out of that definition of saving faith...the faith which he had defined *had nothing of God in it*, nothing above nature, nor indeed above the power of the devils."[11] In other words, the devils are fully capable of wanting to escape hell and believe that someone died to make a way for them. But they are not capable of believing this out of delight in the holiness and mercy of God that brought about this redemption. That is what Edwards meant by saying that saving faith must "have God in it."

A year earlier, July 7, 1746, Brainerd illustrated how he lived in the essence of saving faith, in spite of all his struggles with depression. He wrote, "My spirits were considerably refreshed and raised in the morning. There is no comfort, I find, in any enjoyment without *enjoying God* and being engaged in his service. In the evening, had the most agreeable conversation that ever I remember in all my life, upon God's being 'all in all' [1 Corinthians 15:28], and all enjoyments being just that to us which God makes them, and no more. *'Tis good to begin and end with God.*"[12]

SAFETY FROM HELL AND SATISFACTION IN GOD

That man in Boston had half the answer. He knew that true faith must be a resting of soul. There must be a sense of safety and security. But, as far as we can tell, the nature of this "resting" was not God-centered. We must clarify the spiritual nature of this "resting" in order to distinguish it from the deluded resting of Matthew 7:22, where hypocrites have a kind of "resting" in God's security. What we must say about resting is that to be a saving resting it must be a repose, not merely of safety from hell, but also a repose of satisfaction in the beauties of God (Psalm 16:11).

This is missing from the hearts of the hypocrites of Matthew 7:22. If it were there they would have delighted on earth in the very divine virtues that they were supposedly anticipating and resting in. But, instead, they were "evildoers" (RSV). It is not merely the *security* of the promises that frees us from motives to sin; but also the *sweetness* of the beauty of God in the promises. It is *the spiritual nature* of the things promised. When we apprehend the spiritual beauty or sweetness of what is promised, and delight in it, not only are we freed from the insecurity of greed and fear that motivate so much sin, but we are also shaped in our values by what we cherish in the promise (see 1 John 3:3). If we cherish the beauty of Christ in the gospel we will cherish behavior—even painful sacrificial behavior—that reflects that beauty.

HOW DO YOU BELIEVE A THREAT?

What does this view of saving faith imply for believing negative promises— that is, threats? Do we cherish the spiritual beauty of biblical threats like, "I forewarn you…that those who practice such things shall not inherit the kingdom of God" (Galatians 5:21; see 1 Corinthians 6:10)? In a sense we do. Hodge puts it like this: "Faith in his threatenings, founded upon a perception of their justice, their harmony with his perfections, and the ill-desert of sin, must produce fear and trembling."[13]

What Hodge is saying is that in order for faith in threatenings to be spiritually significant, the faith must be based on the apprehension of spiritual beauty in the threatenings: harmony, justice, and the moral repugnance of sin. It is not enough simply to believe that terrible things are going to happen to you. This has scared many a person into a "decision" for Christ that proved, over time, not to be saving faith. Rather we must perceive and embrace and approve, from the heart, the spiritual fitness (that is, the dark beauty) of God's threatening.

What all this implies is that faith gets an essential element of its reality from the way it perceives the reality believed. If faith perceives the spiritual beauty of divine *threatenings,* an essential element of faith is a sense of revulsion at the ugliness of sin and a withdrawal from the danger of sinning, and a pressing toward God and holiness. If faith perceives the spiritual beauty of divine *promises,* an essential element of faith is delight in the goodness of God, attraction to him and confidence in him. Hodge explains it like this: "Faith in his promises, founded upon the apprehension of his faithfulness and power, and their harmony with all his revealed purposes, [and] their suitableness to our nature and necessities, must produce confidence, joy and hope."[14]

THERE IS A JOY IN FAITH AND FROM FAITH

But I want to say a bit more than Hodge does. I don't want to say merely that faith in promises produces, "confidence, joy and hope," but that *an essential element* in the faith itself *is* confidence and joy and hope. It is not false to say that faith *produces* these things. But that does not contradict the other truth: that confidence and joy and hope are part of the warp and woof of faith. One kind of joy and hope can beget other kinds; and joy can follow upon joy. But I want to preserve what we have seen, namely, that the essence of saving faith is a spiritual apprehension or tasting of spiritual beauty, which **is** delight. Yes, it is true, that faith *yields* delights. *But if we do not taste the beauty of Christ in his promises as delightful, or as satisfying, we do* *not yet believe in a saving, transforming way.*

Is this not one of the reasons why so many professions of faith miscarry? Sometimes we call for decisions for Christ, and bring people to crisis without contemplation. The only conversion that endures is based on a "beholding as in a mirror the glory of the Lord" (2 Corinthians 3:18). Unless we see the Lord as glorious, we will not be "transformed into the same image from glory to glory." When affliction comes, we will fall away. What holds us is prizing the surpassing value of Jesus (Philippians 3:8).

SATISFIED WITH ALL THAT GOD IS FOR US IN JESUS

What then is the common essential element in all saving faith? What is it that makes believing in promises a saving act, rather than a deluded one like the experience of the hypocrites in Matthew 7:22? I have been putting it like this for some years: the essence of faith is "being satisfied with all that God is for us in Jesus."[15] I think this is as close as I know how to get, because it gets at this idea of "delighting in" or "cherishing" or "consenting to" or "embracing" spiritual beauty.[16]

Another way to say it would be that, in all the acts of saving faith, the Holy Spirit enables us not just to perceive and affirm factual truth, but also to apprehend and embrace spiritual beauty. It is the "embracing of spiritual beauty" that is the essential core of saving faith. This is what I mean by "being satisfied with all that God is for us in Jesus." Spiritual beauty is the beauty of God diffused in all his works and words. Embracing this, or delighting in it, or being satisfied with it, is the heart of saving faith.

OR BETTER: SATISFIED WITH ALL GOD WILL BE FOR US

Nothing I have said here diminishes the burden of this book to press home vigorously the future-oriented aspect of faith. I stand shoulder to shoulder with Daniel Fuller and the conviction of his book, *Unity of the Bible,* that

> *a faith that only looks back to Christ's death and resurrection is not sufficient... Forgiveness for the Christian also depends on having, like Abraham, a futuristic faith in God's promises. Thus we cannot regard justifying faith as sufficient if it honors only the past fact of Christ's death*

and resurrection but does not honor the future promises of God, thus mocking his character and integrity.[17]

Putting it all together, then, I would say that the spiritual beauty we need to embrace is the beauty of God that will be there for us in the future, certified for us by the glorious grace of the past. We need to taste the spiritual beauty of God in all his promises. Our confidence and trust must be in all that God himself *will be* for us in the next moment, and in the next month, and in the endless ages of eternity. It is HE and HE alone who will satisfy the soul *in the future*. And it is the future that has to be secured and satisfied with spiritual riches of glory, if we are to live the radical Christian life which Christ calls us to live here and now.

My prayer is that these reflections on the essence of faith will help us avoid superficial, over-simplified statements about believing the promises of God. It is a deep and wonderful thing. You do not have to be a theologian to experience it. God grants the experience to millions who cannot articulate all that is happening in their hearts. But we remain weak if we stay in the unthinking state of that beginning experience. We need to go deeper, and become stronger by understanding biblically what God has wrought in us. I join the apostle Paul in praying that the eyes of our hearts would be enlightened so that we might know the surpassing greatness of his power in us who believe (Ephesians 1:18-19). That power has awakened in us, not just a desire for God to give us a happy future, but for God himself to be the essence of our happy future. It has produced in us, not just a delight in the promises of God, but in the God of the promises. Faith embraces God in all his promises.

Jesus said to them,
"I am the bread of life;
he who comes to Me shall not hunger,
and he who believes in Me shall never thirst."

JOHN 6:35

Saving faith implies in its nature divine love...
Our love to God enables us to overcome
the difficulties that attend keeping God's commands;
which shows that love is the main thing in saving faith,
the life and power of it by which it produces great effects.

JONATHAN EDWARDS

CHAPTER SIXTEEN

Satisfied with All That God Is for Us in Jesus

I f we go wrong on the nature of faith, everything in the Christian life will go wrong. If all authentic obedience comes from faith in future grace, as this book maintains, then all obedience will be imperiled by misunderstanding and mis-experiencing what faith is. The essence of faith in future grace that we discovered in the previous chapter is so crucial we must now test it more thoroughly.

THE GREAT GOSPEL OF BELIEF

A good place to test our understanding of faith is the gospel of John. It has been called *The Gospel of Belief.*[1] The verb "believe" occurs in John's Gospel over 90 times, compared to eleven times in Matthew, twelve in Mark and nine in Luke. John says explicitly that the purpose of his gospel is "that you may *believe* that Jesus is the Christ, the Son of God; and that *believing* you may have life in His name" (20:31).

This theme of believing on Christ for the sake of eternal life runs through the whole gospel. We see it, for example, in John 3:16, "For God so loved the world, that He gave His only begotten Son, that whoever *believes* in Him should not perish, but have *eternal life.*" And John 5:24, "Truly, truly, I say to you, he who hears My word, and *believes* Him who sent

Me, has *eternal life.*" And in John 11:25, "I am the resurrection and the life; he who *believes* in Me shall *live* even if he dies." So it is clear that saving faith is a dominant concern of the apostle John. Believing on Christ is more frequently and consistently mentioned in this book than in any other book in the New Testament.

INCENTIVE FROM OSCAR CULLMANN

Will our understanding of faith's essence (as being satisfied with all that God is for us in Jesus) hold up in this Gospel? One of the reasons I believe it will is that it was John's Gospel that put me onto this understanding in the first place. In 1974 I was a new professor of Biblical Studies at Bethel College in St. Paul. It was my first semester of teaching after graduate school, and I was to teach the Introduction to the New Testament. When I came to the Gospel of John, I devoted my energy to pondering what John meant by faith. I had been inspired to take this angle because of having just sat under Oscar Cullmann at the University of Munich as he lectured on the Gospel of John. Cullmann's painstaking interpretation had opened my eyes afresh to the depth and complexity of John's thought beneath his apparently simple language.

BELIEVING THAT DOES NOT SAVE

First, I noticed that in John's Gospel "believing" can be a false or deficient act that does not save. For example, John says that "when [Jesus] was in Jerusalem at the Passover, during the feast, *many believed* in His name, beholding His signs which He was doing" (2:23). There is a warning here that this "believing" may not be saving faith. It is based on "beholding His signs." That is not bad in itself, especially since Jesus said, "Believe Me that I am in the Father, and the Father in Me; otherwise *believe on account of the works themselves*" (John 14:11). True faith can come through seeing the miracles of Jesus. But the danger is that some people were being carried away by the mere power of Jesus and its potential for overthrowing the Romans. Jesus rejected this kind of enthusiasm: "Jesus therefore perceiving that they were intending to come and take Him by force, to make Him king, withdrew again to the mountain by Himself alone" (John 6:15). And John himself said that Jesus' brothers, who believed in the miracle-working power of Jesus (John 7:3-4), and probably in his claim to be the Messiah, nevertheless were *"not* believing in Him" (John 7:5).

So when John says that "many believed in His name" (2:23) because they saw the signs he was doing, we are alerted to the fact that this "believing" may be a persuasion based on his power that does not go to the heart of who he is. This is, in fact, what seems to be the case with these "believers." For the next verse says, "But Jesus, on His part, was not entrusting Himself to them, for He knew all men" (John 2:24). In other words, what was on the inside did not correspond to what was professed on the outside. Their "faith" was, as C. K. Barrett says, "the appearance of faith."[2] Or, as Leon Morris says, "It is no more than a beginning."[3] Yet it is loosely called "believing."

The same deficiency of faith is found in John 8:31-37. This section begins with the words, "Jesus therefore was saying to those Jews who had believed Him…" (John 8:31). But before the section is concluded, Jesus says to these very Jews, "I know that you are Abraham's offspring; yet *you seek to kill Me, because My word has no place in you"* (John 8:37). The ones who "had believed Him" were trying to kill him. This causes one commentator to say, "Either John is writing very carelessly or he means that the faith of these Jews was very deficient."[4] John is anything but a careless craftsman. Therefore it is right to follow the second option. In the words of Leon Morris, "John is speaking of men who had made an outward profession, but that in this particular case it did not go very deep."[5]

Nevertheless John uses the word "believed" to describe this deficient and inadequate response to Jesus. What this points to is that "believing," in John's Gospel, is not something that lies on the face of the terms used, but is derived from the context of the Gospel. So we must try to get at the deeper content of *"believing"* in John's Gospel. What is the essence of it that makes it a saving sort of believing, rather than a sham?

A LOVE AFFAIR WITH THE PRAISE OF MEN
MAKES FAITH IMPOSSIBLE

One of the reasons that the miracles of Jesus might or might not lead to genuine faith was that they could so easily bolster the love of power and prestige that permeates the sinful heart and makes true faith impossible. Jesus addresses this problem in John 5:41-44.

"I do not receive glory from men; (42) but I know you, that you do not have the love of God in yourselves. (43) I have come in My Father's name, and you do not receive Me; if another shall come in his own name, you will receive him. (44) How can you believe, when you receive glory from one another, and you do not seek the glory that is from the one and only God?

In verse 44, John says that it is impossible to believe in Christ with true saving faith while the heart is carrying on a love affair with the praise of men. In other words, true faith involves a spiritual renovation of the heart. Faith cannot coexist with self-exaltation. It is inherently humble and God-exalting. It looks away from itself to God and delights not in the praises of men, but in the glory of God.

Verse 43 connects this principle with Jesus. He has come not in his own name, but in the name of his Father. This means that he embodies the kind of humble, God-exalting frame of heart that faith loves. But they will not receive him. Why not? Because he threatens their pride. If he came in his own name, Jesus says, they would receive him. Why? Because he would fit with the way they are: desiring that *their* own names be praised by men. The bottom line is that they do not love God (v. 42). That is, they don't delight in *his* exaltation, but their own. This disposition cannot believe. Faith is impossible for a person who is in love with the praise of men.

We may infer then that true faith in John's Gospel is of such a nature that it excludes the bondage to applause. It includes a love for God—a savoring or relishing of God—that makes the praise of men pale by comparison with the treasure that God is. This is what we saw about saving faith in the previous chapter.

LOVING THE LIGHT IS THE ROOT OF FAITH

Another passage that helps us get at the positive essence of saving faith in John's Gospel is John 3:19-21.

And this is the judgment, that the light is come into the world, and men loved the darkness rather than the light; *for their deeds were evil. (20) For everyone who does evil* hates the light, *and does* not come *to the light, lest his deeds should be exposed. (21) But he who practices the truth* comes to the light, *that his deeds may be manifested as having been wrought in God.*

John is saying here that, before you will come to Christ, you must *love* the light rather than hate it. "Coming to the Christ" is one expression John uses to describe saving faith in Christ. You can see this, for example, in John 5:40, "You are unwilling to *come* to Me, that you may have life." And John 6:37, "All that the Father gives Me shall *come* to Me, and the one who *comes* to Me I will certainly not cast out." And John 6:44, "No one can *come* to Me, unless the Father who sent Me draws him; and I will raise him up on the last day." Therefore John is saying that saving faith, or coming to Christ, must be preceded by some measure of transformation in the heart to take away the inborn hatred of spiritual light.

This means that saving faith in John's Gospel is the act of a quickened, or renewed, heart that loves the light. Saving faith is not the mental assent of an old heart that loves the darkness. Love is implicit in John's view of saving faith. This "love" is what we called, in the previous chapter, a "spiritual taste" for the beauty of Christ. Faith is not the mere affirmation that Christ is infinitely precious; faith is embracing Christ as precious because the light of Christ is loved and not hated.

BELIEVING IS COMING TO JESUS FOR SATISFACTION OF THIRST

I said in the previous chapter that the essence of saving faith is *being satisfied with all that God is for us in Jesus.* Another text in John that leads me to this conviction is John 6:35, "I am the Bread of Life; he who *comes* to Me shall not hunger, and he who *believes* in Me shall never thirst." This text points to the fact that believing in Jesus is a feeding and drinking from all that Jesus is. It goes so far as to say that our soul-thirst is satisfied with Jesus, so that we don't thirst anymore. He is the end of our quest for satisfaction. When we trust Jesus the way John intends for us to, the presence and promise of Jesus is so satisfying that we are not dominated by the alluring pleasures of sin (cf. Romans 6:14). This accounts for why such faith in Jesus nullifies the power of sin and enables obedience.

John 4:14 points in the same direction: "Whoever drinks of the water that I *shall give him will never thirst;* but the water that I shall give him shall become in him a spring of water springing up to eternal life." In accord with John 6:35, saving faith is spoken of here as a drinking of water that satisfies the deepest longings of the soul. It's the same in John 7:37-38: "Jesus stood and cried out, saying, 'If any man is thirsty, let him *come to Me and drink.* He who *believes* in Me, as the Scripture said, From his innermost being shall flow rivers of living water.'" Through faith, Christ becomes in us an inexhaustible fountain of satisfying life that lasts forever and leads us to heaven. This he does by sending us his Spirit (see John 7:38-39). This fits with what we saw in Chapter Twelve concerning the sanctifying work of the Holy Spirit which happens in us *by faith.*

FAITH IS A GIFT OF GRACE

This implies that saving faith in John is not a mere human work, but a free gift of God. John makes this plain is several ways. For example, in John 8:45-47 he shows that not believing is ultimately owing to not being born of God.

> But, because I tell you the Truth you do not believe Me. Which of you convicts Me of sin? If I speak the Truth, why do you not believe Me? He who is of God hears the words of God; for this reason you do not hear them, because you are not of God.

According to this text you cannot even hear the Word of God (in a compliant way) if you are not "of God," that is, not born anew by the free-blowing Spirit of God (John 3:8; 1:12-13). Therefore faith is not a self-wrought work, but a fruit of God's work in the soul. It grows out of a heart that has been begotten from above and drawn to Christ. This is what Jesus means in John 6:44 when he says, "No one can come to me unless the Father who sent me draws him." The drawing enables the "coming," which we have seen above is the same as faith.[6] The drawing corresponds to being "of God" in John 8:47.

WHAT DOES IT MEAN TO BE JESUS' SHEEP?

This being drawn to Christ by God also corresponds to being Jesus' sheep in John 10:27. In John 10:25-28, Jesus says,

> I told you, and you do not believe. *The works that I do in my Father's name, they bear witness to Me; but* you do not believe, because you are not of My sheep. *My sheep hear My voice, and I know them and they follow Me.*

The most amazing statement here is that we do not *become* sheep by believing; rather we believe only because we *are* sheep. This is the same as saying, "The reason you do not hear [my words] is that you are not *of God.*" Being "of God" and being a "sheep" are the same, and they are not the result of what we do in believing, but rather the result of what God does to us so that we can believe.

FAITH IS SO RADICAL IT CANNOT BE SELF-GENERATED

The point here is simply to say that this sovereign work of God's initiative in creating faith corresponds with the radical thing that faith is. It is so contrary to proud, self-exalting, unspiritual, world-loving hearts that there is no way it could be self-generated. If we are to come to Jesus the way Jesus teaches us to come, we will have to be drawn by God. Our hate for the light will have to be overcome by God. Our distaste for the bread of heaven and the water of life will have to be transformed by God. Our love affair with the praises of men will have to be shattered by God. Our only hope is free and sovereign grace.

Saving faith apprehends this grace as our only hope, tastes its beauty with spiritual discernment, and embraces it as the greatest treasure in the universe. Faith receives the gift of God's transforming grace as it beholds in Jesus his compelling worth. All that God is for us in Jesus—past, present and future—becomes the satisfaction of the believing soul. And the rest of life is lived not under the control of worldly desires, but in the powerful freedom of faith in future grace.

Another word for these "worldly desires" is *covetousness.* This sin stands about as close to the center of evil as you can get. Conquering it demands a relentless—but also thrilling—battle. Freedom from covetousness is one of the most satisfying works of God in the human soul. We turn in the next chapter to ponder the way prizing the promises of Jesus purifies us from the persistent assaults of covetousness.

Keep your life free from love of money,
and be content with what you have;
for He has said, "I will never fail you nor forsake you."
Hence we can confidently say,
"The Lord is my helper,
I will not be afraid; what can man do to me?"

HEBREWS 13:5-6 (RSV)

I have learned to be content in whatever circumstances I am.
I know how to get along with humble means,
and I also know how to live in prosperity;
in any and every circumstance
I have learned the secret of being filled and going hungry,
both of having abundance and suffering need.
I can do all things through Him who strengthens me.

PHILIPPIANS 4:11-13

There is great gain in godliness with contentment.

1 TIMOTHY 6:6 (RSV)

CHAPTER SEVENTEEN

Applying the Purifying Power

Faith in Future Grace vs. Covetousness

THE BIG PICTURE

L et's keep the big, strategic picture clear as we focus in these application chapters on the various tactical battles of the Christian life. The aim of this book is to fix in our minds this truth: the way to fight sin in our lives is to battle our bent toward unbelief. Or to put it more positively: the way to pursue righteousness and love is to fight for faith in future grace.

WHY FIGHT FOR FAITH IN FUTURE GRACE?

There is a practical holiness without which we will not see the Lord. "Strive for peace with all men and for the holiness without which no one will see the Lord" (Hebrews 12:14, RSV). Many live as if this were not so. There are professing Christians who live such unholy lives that they will hear Jesus' dreadful words, "I never knew you; depart from me, you who practice lawlessness" (Matthew 7:23). There are church-attending people who believe they are saved because they once prayed to receive Jesus, not realizing that the genuineness of that experience is proved by endurance: "He who *endures to the end* will be saved" (Matthew 24:13). Paul says to professing believers, "If you live according to the flesh you must die" (Romans 8:13). So there is a holiness without which no one will see the Lord. And learning to fight for holiness by faith in future grace is supremely important.

A second reason for stressing this particular strategy in fighting our sin is that there is another way to pursue holiness that backfires and leads to death. What a tragedy, that I might persuade you from Scripture that there is a holiness without which we will not see the Lord—only to have you start fighting for it in a way that is denounced in Scripture and doomed to failure!

Recall that Romans 9:31-32 says, "Israel, pursuing a law of righteousness, did not arrive at that law. Why? Because they did not pursue it *by faith, but as though it were by works.*" Which it isn't! Practical, daily righteousness is attained when the law of righteousness is pursued *by faith,* not by works. The term "works" refers to the warfare of righteousness unempowered by faith in the satisfying, liberating promises of future grace. I am writing this book because I am so eager that we learn to fight for holiness *by faith* and not by works.

A third reason for this focus on fighting for faith in future grace is that I long for God to be glorified in our pursuit of holiness and love. But God is not glorified unless our pursuit is empowered by faith in his promises. God is honored when we are humbled for our feebleness and failure, and when he is trusted for future grace (Romans 4:20). So unless we learn how to live by faith in future grace, we may perform remarkable religious rigors, but not for God's glory. He is glorified when the power to be holy comes from humble faith in future grace. Martin Luther said, "[Faith] honors him whom it trusts with the most reverent and highest regard, since it considers him truthful and trustworthy.[1] The trusted Giver gets the glory.

My great desire is that we learn how to live for God's honor. And that means living by faith in future grace, which, in turn, means battling unbelief in all the ways it rears its head, including covetousness.

WHAT IS COVETOUSNESS?

Amazingly, of all sins, covetousness ranks high enough—or low enough—to be explicitly forbidden in the Ten Commandments: "Thou shalt not covet" (Exodus 20:17, KJV). There's a good clue to its meaning in 1 Timothy 6:5-6. It speaks of "men of depraved mind and deprived of the truth, who suppose that godliness is a means of gain. But godliness *actually* is a means of great gain, when accompanied by contentment." The word "covetousness" isn't used here but the reality is what this text is all about. When verse 5 says that some are treating "godliness as a means of gain," Paul responds in verse 6 that "there is great gain in godliness *with contentment.*" This gives us the key to the definition of covetousness. *Covetousness is desiring something so much that you lose your contentment in God.*

The opposite of covetousness is contentment in God. When contentment in God decreases, covetousness for gain increases. That's why Paul says in Colossians 3:5 (RSV) that covetousness is idolatry. "Put to death what is earthly in you: fornication, impurity, passion, evil desire, and *covetousness, which is idolatry.*" It's idolatry because the contentment that the heart should be getting from God, it starts to get from something else.

So covetousness is desiring something so much that you lose your contentment in God. Or: losing your contentment in God so that you start to seek it elsewhere.

Have you ever considered that the Ten Commandments begin and end with virtually the same commandment—"You shall have no other gods before me" (Exodus 20:3) and "You shall not covet" (Exodus 20:17)? These are almost equivalent commands. Coveting is desiring anything other than God in a way that betrays a loss of contentment and satisfaction in Him. Covetousness is a heart divided between two gods. So Paul calls it idolatry.

FLEE COVETOUSNESS, FIGHT FOR FAITH

In 1 Timothy 6:6-12 Paul is trying to persuade and empower people not to be covetous. But let's be sure that we see how Paul understands this battle against covetousness. He gives reasons for not being covetous in verses 6-10 (which we will come back to). Then, in verse 11 he tells Timothy to flee the love of money and the desire to be rich. "Flee from these things, you man of God." Instead of giving in to covetousness, he continues, "Pursue righteousness, godliness, *faith*, love, perseverance, gentleness." Then out of that list he picks "faith" for special attention, and says in verse 12, "Fight the good fight of the faith." In essence, then, he says, "Flee covetousness...fight the good fight of faith."

In other words, the fight against covetousness is nothing other than the fight of faith in future grace. This is one of the clearest proofs that the way to obey the Ten Commandments (one of which is "Thou shalt not covet!") is by faith (as we saw in Romans 9:32). It is also additional evidence that covetousness is a form of unbelief in future grace.

THE FIGHT FOR CONTENTMENT, THAT IS,
FAITH IN FUTURE GRACE

When you stop and think about it, that's just what the definition of covetousness implies. I said that covetousness is desiring something so much that you lose your contentment in God. Or: it's losing your contentment in God so that you start to seek contentment elsewhere. But this contentment in God is just what faith is.

Recall from Chapter Sixteen how Jesus said in John 6:35, "I am the bread of life; he who comes to Me shall not hunger, and he who *believes* on Me shall never thirst." In other words, what it means to believe in Jesus is to experience him as the satisfaction of my soul's thirst and my heart's hunger. Faith is the experience of contentment in Jesus. The fight of faith is the fight to keep your heart contented in Christ—to really believe, and keep on believing, that he will meet every need and satisfy every longing.

GRATITUDE FOR GIFTS YOU ARE CONTENT WITHOUT

Paul said that this was not only a fight to be fought (1 Timothy 6:12), but a secret that had to be learned. "*I have learned* to be content in whatever circumstances I am... In any and every circumstance *I have learned the secret* of being filled and going hungry, both of having abundance and suffering need" (Philippians 4:11-12). The force of Paul's testimony here comes out more clearly if we see why he wrote it to the Philippians. He is writing this fourth chapter of Philippians to thank the church for their financial generosity to him. But Paul had been blistered with criticism more than once for having ulterior motives in his ministry—that he really wanted people's money, not their salvation (see 1 Corinthians 9:4-18; 2 Corinthians

11:7–12; 12:14–18; 1 Thessalonians 2:5,9; Acts 20:33). So he is skittish about giving any impression that he is eager to get their money.

How does he parry that suspicion? Twice he says, "Thanks, but…" In Philippians 4:10-11 he says, "I rejoiced in the Lord greatly, that now at last you have revived your [financial] concern for me…Not that I speak from want." In other words, my joy in your giving is not because I have lost my contentment. On the contrary, "I have learned to be content in whatever circumstances I am. I know how to get along with humble means, and I also know how to live in prosperity." To deflect the criticism that he is covetous for their gifts, he says that his gratitude for their gifts does not come from discontent.

He does the very same thing in the next paragraph (Philippians 4:15-17). He praises them for being the only church that has repeatedly sent him support. "You yourselves also know, Philippians, that…no church shared with me in the matter of giving and receiving but you alone…Not that I seek the gift itself, but I seek for the profit which increases to your account." Here again: "Thanks, but…" He deflects the accusation of covetousness. "I am glad you support me, but…don't misunderstand. If it sounds like I am seeking your gifts, that's a mistake.

Only this time, instead of saying that he has learned to be content without their gifts (vv. 11-12), he says that the cause of his joy is *their* benefit, not his. "I seek for the profit which increases to your account." *They* are the richer for their generosity, not just Paul. As Jesus said, they have been laying up for themselves treasures in heaven by being generous to the needy (Luke 12:33).

So, after his first expression of thanks he says, "Don't misunderstand, I'm not discontent" (see Philippians 4:11). And after his second expression of thanks he says, "Don't misunderstand, what I really seek is that you be blessed" (see Philippians 4:17). This shows that love is the flip side of contentment. Love "seeks not its own" (1 Corinthians 13:5, KJV). It seeks the good of the neighbor (1 Corinthians 10:24). This is what Paul was doing. "Not that I seek the gift itself, but I seek for the profit which increases to your account." Where did this impulse of love come from? It came from contentment. "I have learned to be content in whatever circumstances I am." *Therefore* what I seek is not the gift that comes to me in receiving, but the benefit that comes to you in giving. Contentment is the cause of love.

I CAN DO ALL THINGS THROUGH CHRIST, INCLUDING HUNGER

And whence this contentment? Verse 13 gives the answer: "I can do all things through Him who strengthens me." God's provision of day-by-day future grace enables Paul to be filled or to be hungry, to prosper or suffer, to have abundance or go wanting. "I can do *all things*" really means "all things," not just easy things. "All things" means, "Through Christ I can hunger and suffer and be in want." This puts the stunning promise of verse 19 in its proper light: "My God shall supply all your needs according to His riches in glory in Christ Jesus." What does "all your needs" mean in view of Philippians 4:14? It means "all that you need for God-glorifying contentment." Paul's love for the Philippians flowed from his contentment in God, and his contentment flowed from his faith in the future grace of God's infallible provision.

It's obvious then that covetousness is exactly the opposite of faith. It's the loss of contentment in Christ so that we start to crave other things to satisfy the longings of our heart. And there's no mistaking that the battle against covetousness is a battle against unbelief and a battle for faith in future grace. Whenever we sense the slightest rise of covetousness in our hearts we must turn on it and fight it with all our might using the weapons of faith.

WE MUST BELIEVE THE WARNINGS TOO

Paul saw clearly that the main fuel for faith is the Word of God—promises such as, "My God will supply..." So when covetousness begins to raise its greedy head, what we must do is begin to preach the Word of God to ourselves. We need to hear what God says. We need to hear his warnings about what becomes of the covetous and how serious it is to covet. And we need to hear his promises of future grace that give great contentment to the soul, and free us to love.

Consider some warnings against covetousness. Let them send you running to the covetousness-destroying promises.

1. COVETOUSNESS NEVER BRINGS SATISFACTION.

"He who loves money will not be satisfied with money; nor he who loves abundance with its income: this also is vanity" (Ecclesiastes 5:10). God's Word on money is that it does not satisfy those who love it. If we believe him, we will turn away from the love of money. It is a dead-end street.

Jesus put it like this in Luke 12:15, (RSV) "Beware of all covetousness; for a man's life does not consist in the abundance of his possessions." If the Word of the Lord needed confirming, there are enough miserable rich people in the world to prove that a satisfied life does not come from having things. Just as many people commit suicide by jumping off the Coronado Bridge in San Diego (in spite of wealth), as off the Brooklyn Bridge in New York (because of poverty).

2. COVETOUSNESS CHOKES OFF SPIRITUAL LIFE.

When Jesus told the parable of the soils (Mark 4:1-20), he said that some seed "fell among thorns, and the thorns came up and choked it." Then he interpreted the parable and said that the seed is the Word of God. The thorns choking the seed are: "the worries of the world, and the deceitfulness of riches, and the *desires for other things*" (v. 19). Covetousness is the "desire for other things" in competition with the Word of God.

A real battle rages when the Word of God is preached. "The desire for other things," can be so strong that the beginnings of spiritual life can be choked out altogether. This is such a frightful warning that we should all be on our guard every time we hear the Word to receive it with faith and not choke it with covetousness. This is the conclusion of Jesus after telling that parable: "Therefore take care how you listen" (Luke 8:18).

3. COVETOUSNESS SPAWNS MANY OTHER SINS.

When Paul says, "The love of money is the root of all evils" (1 Timothy 6:10, RSV), he means that the kind of heart that finds contentment in money and not in God is the kind of heart that produces all other kinds of evils. James gives an example, "You covet and cannot obtain so you fight and wage war" (James 4:2, my translation). In other words, if we were content, like Paul, in hard times and easy times, we would not be driven to fight and wage war like this. Covetousness is a breeding ground for a thousand other sins. And that heightens the warning to flee from it and fight for contentment in God with all our might.

4. COVETOUSNESS LETS YOU DOWN WHEN YOU NEED HELP MOST.

It lets you down in the hour of death. In 1 Timothy 6:7 (RSV) Paul says, "We brought nothing into the world and we cannot take anything out of the world." At the greatest crisis of your life, when you need contentment and hope and security more than any other time, your money and all your possessions take wings and fly away. They let you down. They are fair-weather friends at best. And you enter eternity with nothing but the measure of contentment that you had in God.

If you dropped dead right now, would you take with you a payload of pleasure in God or would you stand before him with a spiritual cavity where covetousness used to be? Covetousness lets you down just when you need help most.

5. IN THE END COVETOUSNESS DESTROYS THE SOUL.

In 1 Timothy 6:9 (RSV) Paul says again, "Those who desire to be rich fall into temptation, into a snare, into many senseless and hurtful *desires that plunge men into ruin and destruction.*" In the end covetousness can destroy the soul in hell. The reason I am sure that this destruction is not some temporary financial fiasco, but final destruction in hell, is what Paul says in verse 12 (RSV). He says that covetousness is to be resisted with the fight of faith; then adds, "*Take hold of the eternal life* to which you were called when you made the good confession." What's at stake in fleeing covetousness and fighting for contentment in future grace is eternal life.

So when Paul says in 1 Timothy 6:9 that the desire to be rich plunges people into ruin, he isn't saying that greed can mess up your marriage or your business (which it certainly can!). He is saying that covetousness can mess up your eternity. Or, as verse 10 says at the end, "By longing for it [some] have wandered away from the faith, and pierced themselves with many a pang" (literally: "impaled themselves with many pains").

God has gone the extra mile in the Bible to warn us mercifully that the idolatry of covetousness is a no-win situation. It's a dead-end street in the worst sense of the word. It's a trick and a trap. So my word to you is the word of 1 Timothy 6:11: Flee from it. When you see it coming (in a TV ad or a Christmas catalog or a neighbor's purchase), run from it the way you would run from a roaring, starving lion escaped from the zoo. *But where do you run?*

THE SWORD THAT PUTS COVETOUSNESS TO DEATH

You run to the arsenal of faith and quickly take the mantle of prayer from Psalm 119:36 and throw it around yourself: "[O Lord], *incline my heart* to Thy testimonies and not to dishonest gain." In other words, "Grant me the future grace of strong influences on my heart to give me an appetite for your truth that breaks the power of my appetite for things." Without the future grace of God, our hearts will pursue money. We must pray that he will incline our hearts to his Word, where the triumph over covetousness is promised.

After putting on this mantle of prayer, we must then quickly take down two cutlasses from the armory of God's Word: a short one and a long one, specially made by the Holy Spirit to slay covetousness. And we must stand our ground at the door. When the lion of covetousness shows his deadly face we show him the shorter cutlass, namely, 1 Timothy 6:6 (RSV), "There is great gain in godliness with contentment."

We preach it to our souls and thrust it at the attacking greed. "GREAT GAIN! Great gain in godliness with contentment! Stay where you are, lion of covetousness. I have great gain when I rest contented in God. He is my treasure now, and he will be to the end. This is my faith in future grace. Be gone!"

Then, if the lion persists, you take the longer cutlass (Hebrews 13:5-6), "Let your character be *free from the love of money, being content* with what you have; for He Himself has said, 'I will never desert you, nor will I ever forsake you,' so that we confidently say, 'The Lord is my helper, I will not be afraid. What shall man do to me?'" Trusting this all-satisfying promise of future grace, you drive it into the chest of the lion of greed. You do exactly what Paul says in Colossians 3:5, "Put covetousness to death."

Brothers and sisters, all covetousness is unbelief in future grace. Learn with me, O learn with me how to use the sword of the Spirit to fight the good fight of faith, and lay hold on the future grace of eternal life!

PART VI

UNMERITED, CONDITIONAL FUTURE GRACE

The two conditions of Romans 8:28 are simply clarifications
of what it really means to trust God for this great promise of future grace.
Trusting him for this promise is not merely
believing that he will work for your good.
You can believe that and be wrong.
It means looking through the promise to the one who promises,
and by grace—that is, by his sovereign call—
apprehending in him the spiritual worth and beauty
that will go on satisfying your heart forever;
and then embracing that beauty as your chief treasure
above all that the world can give.
This is the meaning of loving God,
and this is the essence of faith in future grace.
When you have this faith—
when you fulfill this condition by God's gracious call—
God works all things together for your good.

CHAPTER EIGHTEEN

How to Trust Conditional Promises

Our discussion in Chapters Fourteen through Sixteen, on the nature of saving faith, is tremendously important for understanding the *conditionality*[1] of future grace. I know that for many people the very term "conditional grace" sounds like a contradiction—like "dry water," or "short skyscraper." This is not entirely bad, because, in fact, not all grace is conditional. And not all that is conditional is conditional in the same way. Stay with me for a few minutes and I think the Scriptures will bring some wonderful clarity to this puzzle.

A PANORAMA OF CONDITIONAL GRACE

Take, for example, the precious promise of Romans 8:28 that we considered in Chapter Nine. It contains an all-encompassing promise of future grace, namely, that God will work all things together for your good. But this magnificent promise that has carried millions of believers through the darkest times, is *doubly* conditional. "We know that God causes all things to work together for good, *to those who love God, to those who are called according to his purpose.*" The first condition is that we must love God; the second condition is that we must be called according to God's purpose. A vast, eternal panorama of future grace is summed up in the promise that God will work all things for our good. And all this future grace is conditional.

With all our hearts we want that promise to be true for us. We want to *believe* it and put our *trust* and *hope* in it. But how do you believe a *conditional* promise? I mean, how do you believe it in a way that truly, rather than delusively, comforts your soul? I assume that the promise is not true for people who do not love God and are not called according to his purpose. If such people believed that God would work all things together for their good, they would be mistaken—like the people in Matthew 7:22-23 (see Chapter Fifteen).

Before I try to answer the question how to believe a conditional promise like Romans 8:28, I think we need to make sure that the magnitude of this issue is plainly before us. So first let me try to show from Scripture what magnificent works of grace are *not* conditional, and then what equally magnificent works of grace *are* conditional—and how they are.

Electing Grace Is Unconditional

It is an unspeakably precious grace that God has chosen for himself before the foundation of the world: a people to be saved from their sins and who will glorify and enjoy him forever. This choosing was absolutely *unconditional*. "He chose us in Him before the foundation of the world, that we should be holy and blameless before Him. In love He predestined us to adoption as sons through Jesus Christ to Himself, according to the kind intention of His will" (Ephesians 1:4-5).[2] Paul illustrates the unconditionality of God's choice in the case of Jacob. He says that God chose Jacob over Esau when they "were not yet born, and had not done anything good or bad, in order that God's purpose according to His choice might stand, not because of works, but because of Him who calls" (Romans 9:11)[3]

Notice in that last line that Paul does not contrast "works" with "faith." He does *not* say, "The choice stands not because of works, but because of faith." That would make faith a condition of election. But it isn't. Nothing is a condition of election except the grace and wisdom of God. That's why Paul says: "The choice stands not because of works, but because of—God, the one who calls."

REGENERATING GRACE IS UNCONDITIONAL

Which brings us to the second work of grace that is absolutely unconditional—the calling of God. The calling I have in mind here is not the
outward call that happens whenever the gospel is preached,[4] but the inward
work of God, when his call wakens a sinner from death, overcomes all resistance, and makes the glory of Christ irresistibly compelling. When this
happens, faith is created and a person believes in Christ freely from a new
heart (1 Corinthians 1:23-24; 2 Corinthians 4:4-6; Acts 16:14; Romans
8:30; Ezekiel 36:26).[5] This calling of God is not based on faith or works. It
precedes and enables both. Paul says, God has "*called* us with a holy calling, not according to our works, but according to His own purpose and
grace which was granted us in Christ Jesus from all eternity" (2 Timothy
1:9). Again, notice, just as with election, the ground of our calling is not
works and not faith, but "the purpose and grace" of God determined "from
all eternity."

This calling is also referred to as new birth (1 Peter 1:3) or regeneration
(Titus 3:5). It is unconditional because before this "call" or "new birth" we
were spiritually dead (Ephesians 2:1, 5), and unable to respond positively
to God (Romans 8:7–8; 1 Corinthians 2:14). This calling is the gracious act
by which God grants repentance (2 Timothy 2:25; Acts 5:31; 11:18) and
brings about faith (Ephesians 2:8-9; Philippians 1:29).

UNCONDITIONAL COMMON GRACES

Besides these two unconditional works of grace (election and calling), God
also unconditionally showers the world with common graces that no one
deserves. Jesus said, "[God] causes His sun to rise on the evil and the good,
and sends rain on the righteous and the unrighteous" (Matthew 5:45). And
Paul said the same thing to the Gentiles in Lystra who had never known the
true God: "[God] did not leave Himself without witness, in that He did
good and gave you rains from heaven and fruitful seasons, satisfying your
hearts with food and gladness" (Acts 14:17). The psalmist summed it up
like this: "The Lord is good to all, and His mercies are over all His works"
(Psalm 145:9). God lavishes his common graces on a world that in most

cases is not fulfilling any of the conditions of faith or righteousness that God calls for from all people.

Therefore, I conclude that, at least in these three instances, grace is unconditional—the saving grace of election and calling, and the many forms of common grace that sustain the world and keep it from reeling into chaos and anarchy.

THREE GREAT GRACES THAT ARE CONDITIONAL

But there are cherished parts of our salvation that *are* conditional. The condition of *justification* is faith. "A man is justified *by faith* apart from works of the Law" (Romans 3:28; 5:1; Galatians 2:16; 3:24). The condition of *sanctification* is also faith. "God has chosen you from the beginning for salvation through *sanctification by...faith in the truth*" (2 Thessalonians 2:13). The condition of final *glorification* is persevering in this same faith and hope. "[God will] present you before Him holy and blameless and beyond reproach—*if indeed you continue in the faith* firmly established and steadfast, and *not moved away from the hope of the gospel*" (Colossians 1:22-23).

Some great works of grace are unconditional and some are conditional. Election and new birth are not conditional on any human act. God does them freely without reference to our works or our faith. Justification, sanctification and final glorification, however, are all conditional upon faith. These are still acts of great grace. But God has ordained to make this grace a response to faith, whereas the grace of election and new birth precede and produce faith.

CONDITIONAL BUT NOT MERITED

It should be plain from this, that fulfilling conditions does not imply earning anything or meriting anything. Grace is still free, even when it is conditional. There is such a thing as unmerited, conditional grace. Do not equate meeting conditions of grace with earning or meriting grace. "Earning grace" would indeed be a contradiction in terms, like "hot snow" or "verdant desert."

Suppose I say, "If you are on the plane, you will fly to Chicago." That is a genuine condition that has to be met. But, it does not tell you who will buy your ticket or even if you will be carried, helpless, onto the plane. If someone else buys your ticket, and carries you onto the plane, then you have fulfilled the condition of getting to Chicago, but you have not necessarily earned or merited the ride. It is crucial that we keep this distinction in mind. Not all conditions are means of meriting. In fact, some conditions are means of renouncing merit. That is what I have in mind when I speak of conditional grace.

There are at least two reasons that conditional grace is free and unmerited. We have seen them already in Chapter Five. First, conditional grace is free and unmerited because the nature of the condition—faith—is such that it calls attention to God's free bounty and our helpless need. Faith doesn't earn. Faith banks on gifts of future grace. Second, conditional grace is free and unmerited because ultimately the condition of faith is a gift of grace. God graciously enables the conditions that he requires. St. Augustine (396-430) expressed this most forcibly in connection with his own struggles with lust and incontinence. He was converted from a life of debauchery and discovered that his only hope for purity was the transforming grace of God enabling him to meet what God required. In his *Confessions* he wrote, "O love that ever burnest and art never quenched! O Charity, my God, enkindle me! Thou commandest continence. Grant what thou commandest and command what thou wilt."[6] This is the very meaning of the new covenant, as we saw in Chapters Eleven and Twelve. "God will circumcise your heart...to love the Lord your God" (Deuteronomy 30:6).

HOW TO BELIEVE A CONDITIONAL PROMISE

There are other conditions for future grace. What they are and how they relate to faith and the freedom of grace we will discuss in the next chapter. But here I want to return to the question we asked at the beginning about Romans 8:28, namely, how do you believe such a doubly conditional promise? "We know that God causes all things to work together for good, *to those who love God, to those who are called according to His purpose.*" Two conditions: 1) love God; 2) be called. How do you believe this promise without mistakenly thinking that it applies to you when it doesn't?

FIRST CONDITION: LOVE GOD

In order to believe a conditional promise without delusion, you must be assured that the condition is true in your case. What would that mean for Romans 8:28? It would mean being sure that you are one who "loves God." Is that a different condition than the condition of faith? Here is where our discussion in Chapters Fifteen and Sixteen on the essence of faith becomes crucial. What emerged in those chapters is that the essence of saving and sanctifying faith is our *being satisfied with all that God is for us in Jesus.* We also saw that another way of describing this essence is to speak in terms of loving God, that is, delighting in him, or savoring him or cherishing him. We agreed with Jonathan Edwards who said, "Love is the main thing in saving faith, the life and power of it, by which it produces great effects."[7]

Therefore the condition of the promise in Romans 8:28 is not contrary to the condition of faith, but is in fact another way of saying that we must have genuine faith, not just intellectual assent. God does not work all things together for the good of those who merely believe that he will. He works all things together for the good of those who love him, that is, who are satisfied with all that he is in Jesus. The experience of being sure that you love God is the same as experiencing delight in all that God is for you in Jesus. When you walk in that experience, you are loving God. And in that experience you have the essential element of saving faith.

What this means is that the conditions given by God with the promise of Romans 8:28 are meant to make clear the true nature of faith in the promise of God. You cannot savingly believe the promises of God without spiritually apprehending and embracing God's worth and beauty. This apprehension and embracing is the essence of faith.

SECOND CONDITION: BEING CALLED

It is also the root evidence of your being called by God. That's the second condition given in Romans 8:28. "We know that God causes all things to work together for good, to those who love God, *to those who are called according to his purpose.*" I made a case earlier in this chapter and in Chapter Nine that being called by God in this context is a gracious act of God by which he wakens a sinner from death and gives him a new heart. It is the fulfillment of the new covenant promise of Deuteronomy 30:6, "God will circumcise your heart…*to love the Lord your God."*

In other words, the two conditions of the future grace in Romans 8:28 are two sides of the same coin. On the underside is the work of God "calling" into being the new heart of love to God. And on the upper side is the experience of that divine work—love to God. The way you know you are called is by whether your heart opens to the grace of God and is drawn out to God with a satisfaction that overcomes the competing allurements of the world and frees you for a life of love.

IN SUM, THE CONDITION OF FUTURE GRACE IS FAITH

Therefore the two conditions of Romans 8:28 are simply clarifications of what it really means to trust God for this great promise of future grace. Trusting him for this promise is not merely believing that he will work for your good. You can believe that and be wrong. It means looking through the promise to the one who promises, and by grace—that is, by his sovereign call—apprehending in him the spiritual worth and beauty that will go on satisfying your heart forever; and then embracing that beauty as your chief treasure above all that the world can give. This is the meaning of loving God, and this is the essence of faith in future grace. When you have this faith—when you fulfill this condition by God's gracious call—God works all things together for your good.

The promise of future grace is conditional. But it is not earned. And it is not merited. It is believed, trusted, hoped in. And the essence of this belief and trust and hope is that we are satisfied with all that God is for us in Jesus. With that satisfaction comes the confidence that this staggering promise is true for us. And with that confidence comes a radical, free lifestyle of sacrificial obedience that I call living by faith in future grace.

Turn to me and be gracious to me,
after Thy manner with those who love Thy name.

PSALM 119:132

Grace be with those
who love our Lord Jesus Christ
with love incorruptible.

EPHESIANS 6:24

The lovingkindness of the Lord is from everlasting to everlasting...
to those who keep his covenant.

PSALM 103:17-18

Even though we sin every day in various ways,
there is a profound difference between
sinners who keep God's covenant,
and sinners who don't.

CHAPTER NINETEEN

How Many Conditions Are There?

I n little things and big things it makes a difference when you don't know whether you are a beneficiary. Suppose you're a poor student, and your well-to-do uncle invites you and some of your friends to go with him to a world-class amusement park. But you don't know if he means to pay. As you approach the ticket window you look awkwardly toward him and see no clear sign that you will be the beneficiary of his wealth. So you order the cheapest set of tickets, to fit your budget. But all your friends order the "supreme value" set. As it turns out your uncle pays for them all. You had somehow missed the promise that you were included in the generosity.

Or suppose a donor of a healthy liver and pancreas had just died, and you, in your critical condition, knew that you were the beneficiary—would not your life be deeply affected? Your hope would be rekindled, and your planning for the future would awaken. The same is true—even more true—concerning issues of eternity.

One of the hindrances to living by faith in future grace is the uncertainty whether we qualify for the promises of God. Most of the promises of future grace in the Bible come with qualifying conditions attached. And this is not an issue of law versus grace. The Old and New Testaments are united in this pattern. The apostles of the new covenant of grace, as well as Moses and the prophets of the old covenant, give promises of future grace, not to all people without distinction, but to those who...

How is this sentence finished in the Bible? We have looked at the conditions of Romans 8:28 in Chapter Eighteen. But now we will cast our net much wider. What are the conditions of the promises of future grace? And how are they related to each other, and to saving faith? Everything hangs on this when the wee hours of the morning bring the heart-wrenching questions of whether we are really included in the redeemed. We know that we are sinners. We cannot qualify before a holy God. Yet the Bible offers promises to those who meet certain conditions. Can we be encouraged to believe in these promises if we are imperfect sinners? That's what we will deal with in this chapter and the next.

Those who love and meditate on the Bible day after day are probably aware how many and diverse are the conditions of the promises of future grace. But it will help us to put some of this diversity before us so that we can think carefully about what is really being required of us in order to enjoy God's future grace in our lives.[1]

THOSE WHO LOVE GOD AND HIS SON

Besides Romans 8:28, there are numerous promises of future grace made only to those who love God and his Son Jesus. In Ephesians 6:24 Paul says, "*Grace* be with all those *who love our Lord Jesus Christ* with a love incorruptible." Notice the correlation of future grace and genuine love for Jesus. He does not pray this same grace on all. There is a condition for this future grace—loving Jesus with genuine heartfelt, durable love. Paul also states the condition in a severe form of warning, "If anyone does *not love the Lord* let him be accursed." (1 Corinthians 16:22). A future curse rather than future grace comes on those who do not love Christ.

Jesus spoke in a similar way. He said, "He who loves Me shall be loved by My Father, and I will love him, and will disclose Myself to him" (John 14:21). The grace of being loved by the Father and the grace of knowing Jesus intimately is for those who love Jesus (see Matthew 10:37). So is the grace of receiving from him the crown of righteousness at the last day: "In the future there is laid up for me the crown of righteousness, which the

Lord, the righteous Judge, will award to me on that day, and not only to me, but also to *all who have loved His appearing*" (2 Timothy 4:8).

Similarly, in the Old Testament grace was offered on the condition that we love God. For example, in Psalm 119:132 the psalmist prays, "Turn to me and *be gracious* to me, after Thy manner with *those who love Thy name.*" The future grace we long for comes to us if we love God. This was the promise at the very heart of the Ten Commandments. In the second commandment about not making any likenesses of God, the Lord says, "I, the Lord your God, am a jealous God, *visiting the iniquity* of the fathers on the children, on the third and the fourth generations of *those who hate Me,* but *showing lovingkindness* to thousands, to *those who love Me* and keep My commandments" (Exodus 20:5-6). Don't make the mistake here of thinking that, because God's saving help under the old covenant of the law was conditional, it was therefore *not* grace. It *was* conditional, and it *was* grace; or, as Exodus 20:6 says, it was "lovingkindness" (KJV: "mercy," RSV: "steadfast love"). You will see in what follows that again and again it is *grace* that is conditional in both Old and New Testaments.

Paul links the Old and New Testaments in this regard by quoting Isaiah 64:4. He says "As it is written, 'Things which eye has not seen, and ear has not heard, and which have not entered the heart of man, all that God has prepared *for those who love Him;* For to us God has revealed them through the Spirit." (1 Corinthians 2:9-10). The unimaginable greatness of future grace is prepared for those who love God. The book of James drives this home in two clear promises of future grace. "Blessed is the man who perseveres under trial, for, once he has been approved, he will receive the crown of life, which the LORD has *promised to those who love Him*" (James. 1:12). "Did not God choose the poor of this world to be rich in faith and heirs of the Kingdom which He *promised to those who love Him?*" (James. 2:5).

THOSE WHO ARE HUMBLE

Grace is multiplied to the humble. "[God] gives a greater grace. Therefore it says, 'God is opposed to the proud, but *gives grace to the humble*'" (James. 4:6). There is future grace upon future grace. And the condition for this multiplied, greater future grace is a spirit of lowliness. "Clothe yourselves with humility toward one another, for God is opposed to the proud, but *gives grace to the humble"* (1 Peter 5:5).

THOSE WHO DRAW NEAR TO GOD

The future grace of God's increased intimacy with us, and his willingness to return to us in power and blessing after times of backsliding, is treasured by all who fall short of God's will. James says that this grace is conditional upon our drawing near to God: "Draw near to God and He will draw near to you. Cleanse your hands, you sinners; and purify your hearts, you double-minded" (James 4:8). The Old Testament puts it like this: "The Lord your God is gracious and compassionate, and will not turn His face away from you *if you return to Him"* (2 Chronicles 30:9). He is "gracious and compassionate." But his grace is conditional: he will look upon us "if we return to him." The flip side of the promise is the warning: If we do not return, we will forfeit grace: "I tell you, no; but unless you repent you will all likewise perish" (Luke 13:3).

THOSE WHO CRY TO GOD FOR GRACE

There is future grace that comes only if we cry to God for it. "Be *gracious* to me, O Lord, for to *Thee I cry* all day long" (Psalm 86:3). The psalmist makes his appeal for grace on the basis of his cry for help: be gracious because I cry to you. Isaiah makes a promise of future grace on this same condition: "He will surely *be gracious to you at the sound of your cry; when He hears it,* He will answer you" (Isaiah 30:19).

THOSE WHO FEAR GOD

Fearing God is not a negative experience for those who love God. It is the kind of deeply satisfying trembling, and sweet humility and submission that rises in the presence of the absolute power and holiness of God. Nehemiah spoke of the servants of the Lord as those "who *delight* to fear [his] name" (RSV Nehemiah 1:11; see Isaiah 11:3). And the psalmist said, "There is *forgiveness* with Thee, that Thou mayest be feared" (Psalm 130:4). God wins our fear through his forgiveness! There is a fear that is slavish and drives us away from God, and there is a fear that is sweet and draws us to God. Moses warned against the one and called for the other in the very same verse, Exodus 20:20: "Moses said to the people, *'Do not be afraid; for God has come in order to test you, and in order that the fear of Him may remain with you,* so that you may not sin.'"

The clearest illustration I have ever seen of this kind of fear was the time one of my sons looked a German shepherd in the eye. We were visiting a family from our church. My son Karsten was about seven years old. They had a huge dog that stood eye to eye with a seven-year-old. He was friendly and Karsten had no problem making friends. But when we sent Karsten back to the car to get something we had forgotten, he started to run, and the dog galloped up behind him with a low growl. Of course, this frightened Karsten. But the owner said, "Karsten, why don't you just walk. The dog doesn't like it when people run away from him." If Karsten hugged the dog, he was friendly and would even lick his face. But if he ran from the dog, the dog would growl and fill Karsten with fear.

Now that is a picture of what it means to fear the Lord. God means for his power and holiness to kindle fear in us, not to drive us from him, but to drive us to him. His anger is against those who forsake him and love other things more. The safest place in the universe is with our arms around the neck of God. And the most dangerous place is any path where we flee from his presence.

This fear of God is the "beginning of wisdom" (Psalm 111:10). Without it all else is built on sand. Therefore it's not surprising to find many promises of future grace given on this condition. Here are a few:

[God] will fulfill the desire of those who fear Him. (Psalm 145:19)

For as high as the heavens are above the earth, so great is His lovingkindness toward those who fear Him. (Psalm 103:11)

The eye of the Lord is on those who fear Him. (Psalm 33:18)

How great is Thy goodness, which Thou hast stored up for those who fear Thee. (Psalm 31:19)

The angel of the Lord encamps around those who fear Him, and rescues them. (Psalm 34:7)

To those who fear Him, there is no want. (Psalm 34:9)

Thou hast given me the inheritance of those who fear Thy name. (Psalm 61:5)

His salvation is near to those who fear Him. (Psalm 85:9)

Just as a father has compassion on his children, so the Lord has compassion on those who fear Him. (Psalm 103:13)

He will bless those who fear the Lord. (Psalm 115:13)

The Lord favors those who fear Him. (Psalm 147:11)

His mercy is upon generation after generation toward those who fear Him. (Luke 1:50)

Mercy, favor, blessing, compassion, salvation, lovingkindness, inheritance, angelic protection, goodness, watch-care, fulfilled desires—this is the future grace promised to those who fear God. It is all conditional and it is all free and unmerited grace.

THOSE WHO DELIGHT IN GOD

Remarkably, the promise that God will satisfy the desires of our heart is given not only on the condition that we fear him (Psalm 145:19), but also on the condition that we delight ourselves in him. "Delight yourself in the Lord; and He will give you the desires of your heart" (Psalm 37:4). But perhaps this should not seem odd since saints "delight to fear the Lord" (Nehemiah 1:11, RSV).

THOSE WHO HOPE IN GOD

The grace and kindness of the Lord comes to us in accord with our hope in him: "Let Thy lovingkindness, O Lord, be upon us, according as we have hoped in Thee" (Psalm 33:22). We are told, "Be strong, and let your heart take courage, all you who hope in the Lord" (Psalm 31:24). The reason those who hope in the Lord can take courage is that they are the beneficiaries of the promise of future grace: "The eye of the Lord is on...those who hope for His lovingkindness" (Psalm 33:18). The radical lifestyle of strength and courage in the cause of righteousness flows from hope in God's lovingkindness, that is, from faith in future grace.

THOSE WHO TAKE REFUGE IN GOD

The experience of future grace often hangs on whether we will take refuge in God, or whether we doubt his care and run for cover to other shelters. For those who take refuge in God the promises of future grace are many and rich.

O God, be gracious to me, For my soul takes refuge in Thee. (Psalm 57:1)

Preserve me, O God, for I take refuge in Thee. (Psalm 16:1)

How great is Thy goodness...which Thou hast wrought for those who take refuge in Thee! (Psalm 31:19)

And none of those who take refuge in Him will be condemned. (Psalm 34:22)

He delivers them from the wicked, and saves them, because they take refuge in Him. (Psalm 37:39)

He is a shield to all who take refuge in Him. (2 Samuel 22:31)

How blessed are all who take refuge in Him! (Psalm 2:12)

The Lord is good, a stronghold in the day of trouble, and He knows those who take refuge in Him. (Nahum 1:7)

We do not earn or merit anything by taking refuge in God. Hiding in something makes no contribution to the hiding place. All it does is show that we regard ourselves as helpless and the hiding place as a place of rescue. The condition we must meet to have this grace is not a meritorious one; it is the condition of desperation and acknowledged weakness and need. Destitution does not demand or deserve; it pleads for mercy and looks for grace.

THOSE WHO WAIT FOR GOD

Future grace comes in God's time. We must wait for it. And when the Bible speaks of waiting for the Lord it does not mean with impatience and distrust. It means that we trust him enough that even when he delays we do not turn away to other help. Waiting for the Lord is the condition that obtains much grace.

None of those who wait for Thee will be ashamed. (Psalm 25:3)

Those who wait for the Lord, they will inherit the land. (Psalm 37:9)

The Lord favors those…who wait for His lovingkindness. (Psalm 147:11)

The Lord is good to those who wait for Him. (Lamentations 3:25)

THOSE WHO TRUST GOD

God loves to be trusted. He cannot honor his own name and bless indefinitely those who do not trust him. Therefore trusting God is an indispensable condition for the blessings of future grace. And serious warnings are given concerning unbelief: "The Lord was full of wrath…because they did not believe in God, and did not trust in His salvation" (Psalm 78:22). But far more numerous are the positive promises with the condition of believing or trusting God.

He who trusts in the Lord, lovingkindness shall surround him. (Psalm 32:10)

If you will not believe, you surely shall not last. (Isaiah 7:9)

He who believes in [the cornerstone] will not be disturbed. (Isaiah 28:16)

The sons of Judah conquered because they trusted in the Lord. (2 Chronicles 13:18)

Help us, O Lord our God, for we trust in Thee. (2 Chronicles 14:11)

Put your trust in the Lord your God, and you will be established. Put your trust in His prophets and succeed. (2 Chronicles 20:20)

In Thee our fathers trusted; They trusted, and Thou didst deliver them. (Psalm 22:4)

Commit your way to the Lord, Trust also in Him, and He will do it. (Psalm 37:5)

Save Thy servant who trusts in Thee. (Psalm 86:2)

Trust in the Lord with all your heart...and He will make your paths straight. (Proverbs 3:5-6)

O Lord of hosts, How blessed is the man who trusts in Thee! (Psalm 84:12)

THOSE WHO KEEP HIS COVENANT

Keeping the covenant of God did not mean living perfectly. It meant a life of habitual devotion and trust and love to the Lord, that turned from evil and followed him in his ways. When there was a shortcoming, a covenant-keeping person remembered the words of the covenant on Mt. Sinai ("The Lord [is] merciful and gracious…forgiving iniquity, and transgression and sin," Exodus 34:6-7) and repented and offered a sacrifice and received forgiveness and restoration.

When the Old Testament says that covenant-keeping is the condition for receiving God's lovingkindness, that's what it meant. It did not imply perfection. "The lovingkindness of the Lord is from everlasting to everlasting…to those who keep His covenant" (Psalm 103:17–18). "All the paths of the Lord are lovingkindness and truth to those who keep His covenant and His testimonies" (Psalm 25:10). All the covenants of God are conditional covenants of grace—both the old covenant and the new covenant. They offer all-sufficient future grace for those who keep the covenant.

This covenant-keeping condition of future grace does not mean we lose security or assurance, for God has pledged himself to complete the work he began in the elect (Philippians 1:6). He is at work within us to will and to do his good pleasure (Philippians 2:12-13). He works in us what is pleasing in his sight (Hebrews 13:21). He fulfills the conditions of the covenant through us (Ezekiel 36:27). Our security is as secure as God is faithful.

But what it does mean is that almost[2] all future blessings of the Christian life are conditional on our covenant-keeping. One of the best places to see that this covenant-keeping is not impossible or onerous is Psalm 25. As you read the following section of the psalm, notice that the italicized words express God's gracious acts, which cannot be earned; and the words in **bold type** express conditions the psalmist meets in order to enjoy these blessings of grace.

(8) Good and upright is the Lord; therefore *He instructs sinners in the way.* (9) *He leads the* **humble** *in justice, and He teaches the* **humble** *His way.* (10) All the paths of the Lord are *lovingkindness* and truth to those who **keep His covenant** and His testimonies.

(11) For Thy name's sake, O Lord, *pardon my iniquity, for it is great.* (12) Who is the man who **fears the Lord?** He will *instruct him* in the way he should choose… (16) Turn to me and *be gracious to me,* for I am lonely and afflicted… (18) Look upon my affliction and my trouble, and *forgive all my sins*… (20) *Guard my soul and deliver me;* do not let me be ashamed, for I **take refuge in Thee**… (21) Let **integrity** and **uprightness** preserve me, for I **wait for Thee.**

Notice that there are conditions we meet in order to receive God's guidance (v. 9), God's lovingkindness (v. 10), God's instruction (v. 12), and God's protection (v. 20). But all this condition-keeping is done by "sinners" (vv. 8, 11). And notice that these *covenant-keeping sinners* who receive God's guidance and protection are being preserved by their "integrity and uprightness" (v. 21)!

In other words, even though we sin every day in various ways,[3] there is a profound difference between sinners who keep God's covenant (v. 10), and sinners who don't. The issue facing us in the light of this psalm is whether we "wait for the Lord" (v. 21) and "take refuge in him" (v. 20) and "fear" him (v. 12) and are "humble" before him (v. 9) and, in this way, "keep his covenant" (v. 10). These are the sinners whom God will guide and protect.

I am hard pressed to imagine something more important for our lives than fulfilling the covenant that God has made with us for our final salvation. The New Testament warning that some in the church "shall not inherit the kingdom of God" (Galatians 5:21; 1 Corinthians 6:9) is stunning. It is astonishing to me how many Christians are blasé about this matter. It's as though salvation were a casual and obvious thing. It's as though grace were a catch-all for every kind of divine-tolerance that anyone can imagine. I hope that the little we have seen sobers you out of those illusions. And I pray, even as I write, that you will press on with the next chapter where we ask how all these diverse conditions relate to each other. Are they really diverse? How do they relate to each other and to faith? Is there a unifying element that will help us bring solid focus to our lives, without anxiety and without carelessness? I think there is. I invite you to seek it with me.

We are not required to love others
before we become people who trust in God.
But trusting in God means trusting in his future grace.
So it is possible—indeed necessary—to bank on the promises of future grace
before we are transformed into the kind of people who love others.
We do not have to perform, before faith,
what faith is meant to perform.

CHAPTER TWENTY

What Faith
Alone
Can Perform

A LURKING PROBLEM

For those who have been called[1] into the fellowship of Christ, the ocean of future grace is free, inexhaustible, unmerited, unearned— and conditional. This is not a contradiction. It is pervasively biblical, as the previous two chapters show. And it is not contrary to the central theme of this book: that sanctification is *by faith* apart from meritorious works. But there is a problem lurking behind the conditionality of future grace. On the one hand I am arguing that faith in future grace is the means by which we become free from the deceptive promises of sin and gain strength and courage to live the radical, risk-taking, Christian life. On the other hand, the conditions of future grace seem to say that, before I can know the promises apply to me, I must already be living a life which the promises alone can empower.

In other words: do the promises enable me to be good; or must I be good to qualify for the promises?

I hope to show in this chapter that this is not a real dilemma. We are not required to perform, before faith, what faith alone can perform. But to see this we need to make clear that the conditions of future grace outlined in the previous chapter are all of a certain kind. The ten conditions were: loving God, being humble, drawing near to God, crying out to God from the heart, fearing God, delighting in God, hoping in God, taking refuge in God, waiting for God, and trusting God. The eleventh condition was keeping covenant with God, which I believe is a way of summarizing all the others.

THE INNER ACTS OF THE SOUL OF FAITH

What all these conditions have in common is that they are inner spiritual acts of the soul toward God. They are not outward acts of relationships with other people. Therefore what all these conditions represent is a certain kind of heart. They describe the heart that receives grace. These are not meritorious performances of the heart that call attention to our worth, so that God will be indebted to our value. They are acts of turning away from self and our emptiness to all that God is for us.

For example, loving God and delighting in God and drawing near to God mean looking to God as beautiful and worthy and precious. Waiting for God and taking refuge in God and hoping in God and crying out to God mean looking to him as a valiant rescuer. Trusting God means counting on his trustworthiness to meet every need. And fearing God means standing in awe at the infinite chasm between his holiness and power on the one hand, and my sin and weakness on the other. Having a heart like this is the inner condition of keeping covenant with God.

In fact, as you meditate on these ten conditions they begin to look less and less like separate and distinct requirements, and more and more like different ways of describing the heart of faith. This is, in fact, what I think is the case. The heart that is satisfied with all that God is for us in Jesus is characterized by all these things. All these acts of the heart are overlapping realities with saving faith. Faith is not identical with any of them, nor they with faith. But elements of each are woven into what faith is.

By its nature, saving faith loves God and delights in God as the sum of all that could ever satisfy the soul. Saving faith is humble because by nature it despairs of self and looks to God. Saving faith draws near to God and cries out to God and waits for God and takes refuge in God and trusts in God and hopes in God, because the essence of faith is to see and embrace God, and God alone, as the sum of all it will ever need. And saving faith trembles at the thought of offending such a great God through disbelief in his promises. All the conditions of future grace that we have looked at are not additions to faith, but expressions of faith.

OUTWARD CONDITIONS OF FUTURE GRACE THAT ARE NOT FAITH

Yet, the dilemma mentioned above is not so easily removed. What we did not look at in the previous chapter are the conditions of future grace that involve outward actions toward other people, as well as inner acts of the soul toward God. These conditions are not part of faith's essence. How do they fit in? Here are a few of them—conditions of future grace that are not faith, but come from faith.

Jesus said that "an hour is coming, in which all who are in the tombs shall…come forth; those who did the *good deeds* to a resurrection of life, those who committed the *evil deeds* to a resurrection of judgment" (John 5:28-29). So the future grace of resurrection to life is given to those who have done good deeds. On the flip side of this promise is the warning about doing evil deeds: "Those who practice such things shall not inherit the kingdom of God" (Galatians 5:21). The future grace of inheriting the kingdom is contingent on not practicing the works of the flesh.

John gives a similar warning in regard to the specific behavior of love: "We know that we have passed out of death into life, because *we love the brethren.* He who does not love abides in death" (1 John 3:14). We cannot count on the future grace of eternal life if we do not love. "The one who does not love does not know God, for God is love" (1 John 4:8).

Jesus takes a specific expression of love and makes it the condition of the future grace of God's ongoing forgiveness of us: "*If you forgive* men for their transgressions, your heavenly Father will also forgive you. But if you do not forgive men, then your Father will not forgive your transgressions" (Matthew 6:14-15). And the writer of Hebrews sums up the conditionality of future grace with the term "holiness" or "sanctification:" "Pursue peace with all men, and the *sanctification* without which no one will see the Lord" (Hebrews 12:14).

These added conditions of future grace are different from the ten that we saw in the previous chapter. They are actions or attitudes toward other people, not just inner acts of the heart toward God. Now the dilemma that we posed earlier is felt more keenly. Must we meet these conditions before we can know the promises of final future grace are ours, or is the confidence that they are ours the means by which we meet these conditions?

LOVE IS A FULFILLING OF THE LAW

First, notice that all the conditions are summed up in love. Paul said, concerning doing good and obeying God's commandments, that this is precisely what love does. "Love does no wrong to a neighbor; therefore love is the fulfillment of the law" (Romans 13:10). Forgiveness is clearly an expression of love (1 Corinthians 13:5). Paul also says that love is the essence of holiness or sanctification: "May the Lord cause you to increase and abound in love...so that he may establish your hearts...in holiness" (1 Thessalonians 3:12-13). In other words, all the behavior that is required of a Christian may be summed up in love. "Let all that you do be done in love" (1 Corinthians 16:14).

What we have seen, then, is that the ten conditions of future grace discussed in the previous chapter are all summed up in *faith*. And the behavioral conditions we have just discussed are all summed up in *love*. Which means we may now say that the conditions a Christian must meet, to go on enjoying the blessings of future grace, are faith and love.

There is remarkable confirmation that we are on the right track in this summary. Paul said that the whole law is to be pursued by faith (Romans 9:32), and he says that the law is fulfilled in one word: Love your neighbor as yourself (Romans 13:9). These two, faith and love, come to the fore in the Bible as the summation of all that God requires of his people.

John put it in a striking way in his first letter: "This is His commandment, that we *believe* in the name of His Son Jesus Christ, and *love* one another" (1 John 3:23). What is surprising here is that the word "commandment" is singular, even though he mentions two. This is the singular commandment: believe and love. For John they are a singular, inseparable, almost indistinguishable commandment—and the love in his mind is to "one another," while the faith is toward Christ.

You find in the writings of Paul that faith and love occur together again and again as a kind of sum, it seems, of what he expected from his churches. "[I] heard of the *faith* in the Lord Jesus which exists among you, and your *love* for all the saints" (Ephesians 1:15). "I hear of your *love,* and of the *faith* which you have toward the Lord Jesus" (Philemon 5). "We heard of your *faith* in Christ Jesus and the *love* which you have for all the saints" (Colossians 1:4). "Your *faith* is greatly enlarged, and the *love* of each one of you toward one another grows ever greater" (2 Thessalonians 1:3). "Timothy has come to us from you, and has brought us good news of your *faith* and *love*" (1 Thessalonians 3:6). "The grace of our Lord was more than abundant, with the *faith* and *love* which are found in Christ Jesus" (1 Timothy 1:14). "Retain the standard of sound words which you have heard from me, in the *faith* and *love* which are in Christ Jesus" (2 Timothy 1:13).

I conclude from this that it is not an accident that one set of conditions for future grace is summed up by faith and the other is summed up by love. This seems to be the way the apostles saw it.

HOW ARE FAITH AND LOVE CONDITIONS OF FUTURE GRACE?

Now we are in a position to ask again about our dilemma. Does the condition of loving others mean that before we can claim a promise of future grace, we must already be what the promise is designed to help us become—namely, a radical, risk-taking person of love? Must we perform, *before* faith, what faith is meant to perform?

The answer is no.

The reason is that faith toward God and love toward man are not coordinate conditions; they do not arise side by side in the heart. Faith arises first and begets love. This is clear from Galatians 5:6: "In Christ Jesus neither circumcision nor uncircumcision means anything, but *faith working through love.*" Faith produces all that God requires, and does it through love.[2] Similarly Paul says in 1 Timothy 1:5, "The goal of our instruction is *love* from a pure heart and a good conscience and a *sincere faith.*" Love is the goal and faith is the source.

What this means is that love is not expected of us before faith. For faith is the root and source of love. Don't get confused here because of our earlier statements that love is part of the essence of faith. That was a reference to love *for God*. Here we are talking about love for *other people*. We are not required to *love others* before we become people who trust in God. But trusting in God means trusting in his future grace. So it is possible—indeed necessary—to bank on the promises of future grace *before* we are transformed into the kind of people who love others. We do not have to perform, before faith, what faith is meant to perform.

What faith performs is sometimes unspeakably hard. In his book *Miracle on the River Kwai*, Ernest Gordon tells the true story of a group of POW's working on the Burma Railway during World War II.

> *At the end of each day the tools were collected from the work party. On one occasion a Japanese guard shouted that a shovel was missing and demanded to know which man had taken it. He began to rant and rave, working himself up into a paranoid fury and ordered whoever was guilty to step forward. No one moved. "All die! All die!" he shrieked, cocking and aiming his rifle at the prisoners. At that moment one man stepped forward and the guard clubbed him to death with his rifle while he stood silently to attention. When they returned to the camp, the tools were counted again and no shovel was missing.*[3]

What can sustain the will to die for others, when you are innocent? The answer is given in Hebrews 12:2. *"For the joy set before* Him [Jesus] endured the cross, despising the shame, and has sat down at the right hand of the throne of God."* Jesus was carried and sustained in his love for us by "the joy set before him." That means his love was sustained by faith in future grace.[4] As a man, modeling for us how to take up our cross and follow him on the Calvary road of love, Jesus entrusted himself to his Father (1 Peter 2:23) and banked his hope on the resurrection and all the joys of reunion with his Father and the redemption of his people. Faith in his Father worked itself out through love.

HOW IS LOVE A CONDITION OF FUTURE GRACE?

When the Bible mentions the behavior of love—or some form of it—as a condition of future grace, we need to remember two things. One is this: loving others does not spring forth already in full bloom from the soil of faith. It grows and increases (1 Thessalonians 3:12; Philippians 1:9). The condition of future grace is not perfect love, but real love. The Puritans used to speak of a new "principle" of love in the heart. This new principle is there in the heart as soon as we are born again. The *behaviors* of love are the outworkings of this principle of love, rooted in the soil of faith. Therefore we must not think that the more immediate blessings of future grace must wait till our love has a long time to prove itself. God can see the heart and he knows what is emerging.

There is a second thing we need to remember when the Bible mentions loving others as a condition of future grace. We must keep in mind that love relates to faith as evidence to origin.[5] Love is the necessary evidence of faith. Faith apprehends and embraces the spiritual beauty and worth of all that God is for us in the promises of future grace. This spiritual awakening to the glory of God in the promises is the means by which God unites us to Christ and to the Spirit's flow of future grace. But this kind of faith inevitably "works through love" (Galatians 5:6), so that love confirms the authenticity of faith. This is what Peter has in mind when he exhorts us in 2 Peter 1:10 to confirm our calling and election (as the connection with v. 7 shows) through love. It is also what John has in mind when he says, "We know that we have passed out of death into life, because we love the brethren" (1 John 3:14).

So the Bible sometimes makes love the condition of the ongoing and final experience of future grace. It does not mean that love must precede faith in the promise. On the contrary, it means that faith in the promise must be so real that the love which it produces proves the reality of the faith. Thus love for others is a condition of future grace in the sense that it confirms that the primary condition, faith, is genuine. We could call love for others a secondary condition, that confirms the authenticity of the primary condition of faith.

Consider an analogy. Suppose that you live in a village where electricity is supplied by a generator on a nearby hill. Each evening the owner of the generator regulates which houses receive the power. He gives two conditions for receiving power for the lamps in your house. First, he says, "If you plug the cord into the socket firmly you will tap into the power of the electricity for your light." And second, he says, "If I see light in the house I will keep the power flowing to your house, but if I do not see any light for a while, I will assume you are not home and turn off the power to your house."

In this analogy, plugging into the power is the condition of believing in the promises of God. It connects you with the power of future grace. That's the primary condition of future grace. But there is another condition. If you do not plug in the lamps and there is no light, the power source will be cut off. This light in the house is the secondary condition of loving others. You don't have light first in order to get power. Your light proves that the lamp is plugged in. And your love proves that your faith is genuine—that you are really connected to God as one who is satisfied with all that he is for you in Jesus. The light and the love are both conditions of future grace. If God sees that you don't have them, he will know that you are not plugging into the power of future grace by faith; and he will tell you that such lightlessness and lovelessness will not be given the benefits of future grace.[6]

Thus faith and love are conditions of future grace, but not in the same way. Faith perceives the glory of God in the promises of future grace, and embraces all that the promises reveal of what God is for us in Jesus. This spiritual apprehension and delight in God is the self-authenticating evidence that God has called us to be a beneficiary of his grace. This evidence frees us to bank on the promise as our own. And this banking on the promise empowers us to love. Which in turn confirms that our faith is real.

The world is desperate for a faith that combines two things: awe-struck apprehension of unshakable divine Truth, and utterly practical, round-the-clock power to make a liberating difference in life. That is what I want too. Which is why I am a Christian. There is a great God of grace who magnifies his own infinite self-sufficiency by fulfilling promises to helpless people who trust him. And there is a power that comes from prizing this God which leaves no nook and cranny of life untouched. It empowers us to love in the most practical ways. One of the ways this faith releases love is by overcoming the impulse to avenge ourselves for wrongs done to us. In the next chapter we meditate on how this works. How does prizing all that God promises to be for us purify us from the terrible power of bitterness and vengeance?

Never take your own revenge, beloved,

but leave room for the wrath of God,

for it is written,

"Vengeance is Mine, I will repay,"

says the Lord.

ROMANS 12:19

We cannot ignore inconsiderate acts in others;

yet we cannot execute the penalty of law.

We have no right to complete the moral cycle…

Although we sense no spiritual inhibition against

crying out against injustice,

the purity of our moral life deteriorates the moment

we attempt to administer justice.

EDWARD JOHN CARNELL

The dark-valley breath of bitterness

cannot survive the high paths of faith in future grace.

Grudges demand the valley-vapors of self-pity and fear and emptiness.

They cannot survive the contentment and confidence

and fullness of joy that come from satisfaction in

the forgiving God of future grace.

Applying the Purifying Power

Faith in Future Grace vs. Bitterness

WHAT ABOUT FAITH IN FUTURE JUSTICE?

I s the judgment of God on our enemies an act of future grace toward us? This is a crucial question because the point of this book is to help people live by faith in future grace. But what I find in the New Testament is that one powerful way of overcoming bitterness and revenge is to have faith in the promise that God will settle accounts with our offenders so that we don't have to. The New Testament teaches that we are freed from vengeance by believing that God will take vengeance for us, if he must. So my question is this: Is believing in God's vengeance an example of faith in future *grace,* or is it only faith in future *justice?* My answer is that faith in God's judgment is another form of faith in future grace. Therefore living by faith in future grace involves overcoming vengeance and bitterness by trusting God to settle all our accounts justly.

Ponder with me for a moment God's promise of future justice. In Revelation 18 there is a description of God's judgment on the anti-Christian powers of the world. These powers are sometimes called "Babylon," to signify their animosity toward the people of God, and sometimes called "the great harlot," to signify their immorality. Here is a great temptation for Christian

261

bitterness and anger. These enemies flout the laws of God in immorality and they shed the blood of Christians. Moreover, they are impenitent to the end. In the book of Revelation, John says, "In [Babylon] was found the blood of prophets and of saints." She is "the great harlot who [corrupts] the earth with her immorality" (Revelation 18:24; 19:2). How should Christians respond to this immorality and persecution?

The command of Jesus in this world is, "Love your enemies, and pray for those who persecute you" (Matthew 5:44). The reason Jesus gives this command is "that you may be sons of your Father who is in heaven, for he causes his sun to rise on the evil and the good" (Matthew 5:45). While life endures in this age God gives many blessings to those who are immoral and cruel. Paul said to the Gentiles who had never heard of the true God, "[God] did good and gave you rains from heaven and fruitful seasons, satisfying your hearts with food and gladness" (Acts 14:17). In all of this, God is showing undeserved "kindness and forbearance and patience" that should lead the nations to repentance (Romans 2:4). Jesus commands us to imitate our Father in these things: "Love your enemies, and do good, and lend, expecting nothing in return; and your reward will be great, and you will be sons of the Most High; for He Himself is kind to ungrateful and evil men. Be merciful, just as your Father is merciful" (Luke 6:35-36).

Indeed, while there is hope for their conversion, we should feel with the apostle Paul, "My heart's desire and my prayer to God for them is for their salvation" (Romans 10:1). If we are persecuted as Christians we are to turn the other cheek (Matthew 5:39), and bless those who curse us (Luke 6:28), and not return evil for evil (1 Thessalonians 5:15; 1 Peter 3:9), but, if possible, to live in peace with all (Romans 12:17-18).

FUTURE JUDGMENT IS ALSO FUTURE GRACE

But there will come a time when the patience of God is over. When God has seen his people suffer for the allotted time and the appointed number of martyrs is complete (Revelation 6:11), then vengeance will come from heaven. Paul describes it like this: "It is only just for God to repay with affliction those who afflict you, and to give relief to you who are afflicted...when the Lord Jesus shall be revealed from heaven with His mighty angels in flaming fire, dealing out retribution to those who do not know God and to those who do not obey the gospel of our Lord Jesus" (2 Thessalonians 1:6–8). Notice that God's vengeance on our offenders is experienced by us as "relief." In other words, the judgment on "those who afflict" us is a form of *grace* toward us.

Jesus taught a similar truth in the parable of the unjust judge. He told the story of a widow who "kept coming to [the judge], saying, 'Give me legal protection from my opponent'" (Luke 18:3). Finally the judge relented and gave her what she needed. Jesus interprets the story: "Shall not God bring about justice for His elect, who cry to Him day and night, and will He delay long over them? I tell you that He will bring about justice for them speedily" (Luke 18:7-8). So again God's future justice for the opponents of his people is pictured as relief—like the relief of a widow in distress. Future justice for God's enemies is pictured as *future grace* for God's people.

Perhaps the most remarkable picture of judgment as grace is the picture of Babylon's destruction in Revelation 18. At her destruction, a great voice from heaven cries, *"Rejoice over her,* O heaven, and you saints and apostles and prophets, because God has pronounced judgment for you against her" (Revelation 18:20). Then a great multitude is heard saying, *"Hallelujah!* Salvation and glory and power belong to our God; because His judgments are true and righteous; for He has judged the great harlot who was corrupting the earth with her immorality, and He has avenged the blood of His bond-servants on her" (Revelation 19:1-2).

When God's patience has run its long-suffering course, and this age is over, and judgment comes on the enemies of God's people, the saints will not disapprove of God's justice. They will not cry out against him. On the contrary, the apostle John calls on them to "rejoice" and to shout "hallelujah!" This means that the final destruction of the unrepentant will not be experienced as a misery for God's people. The unwillingness of others to repent will not hold the affections of the saints hostage. Hell will not be able to blackmail heaven into misery. God's judgment will be approved and the saints will experience the vindication of truth as a great grace.

Two hundred fifty years ago Jonathan Edwards commented on Revelation 18:20 with these words: "Indeed [the saints] are not called upon to rejoice in having their revenge glutted, but in seeing justice executed, and in seeing the love and tenderness of God towards them, manifested in his severity towards their enemies."[1] This is what is stressed in Revelation 19:2, "His judgments are true and righteous." Thus Edwards' answer to our question is that God's final judgment is indeed a *future grace* to the people of God. He says, "It is often mentioned in Scripture, as an instance of the great love of God to his people, that his wrath is so awakened, when they are wronged and injured. Thus Christ hath promised…'if any man offend one of his little ones, it were better for him that a millstone were hanged about his neck, and that he were drowned in the depth of the sea'" (Matthew 18:6).[2]

PROMISE: VENGEANCE IS MINE I WILL REPAY

This future grace of God's judgment is promised to us as a means of helping us overcome a spirit of revenge and bitterness. For example, in Romans 12:19 Paul says, "Never take your own revenge, beloved, but leave room for the wrath of God, for it is written, 'Vengeance is Mine, I will repay,' says the Lord. But if your enemy is hungry, feed him, and if he is thirsty, give him a drink; for in so doing you will heap burning coals upon his head."

Paul's argument is that we should not take vengeance, because vengeance belongs to the Lord. And to motivate us to lay down our vengeful desires he gives us a promise—which we now know is a promise of future grace—"'I will repay,' says the Lord." The promise that frees us from an unforgiving, bitter, vengeful spirit is the promise that God will settle our accounts. He will do it more justly and more thoroughly than we ever could. Therefore we can back off and "leave room for God" to work.

IS IT WRONG TO WANT JUSTICE DONE?

Why is this such a crucial promise in overcoming our bent toward bitterness and revenge? The reason is that this promise answers to one of the most powerful impulses behind anger—an impulse that is not entirely wrong.

I can illustrate with an experience I had during my seminary days. I was in a small group for couples that began to relate at a fairly deep personal level. One evening we were discussing forgiveness and anger. One of the young wives said that she could not and would not forgive her mother for something she had done to her as a young girl. We talked about some of the biblical commands and warnings concerning an unforgiving spirit. "Be kind to one another, tenderhearted, forgiving each other, just as God in Christ also has forgiven you" (Ephesians 4:32). "If you do not forgive men, then your Father will not forgive your transgressions" (Matthew 6:15; see also 18:34-35; Mark 11:25; Luke 17:4; 2 Corinthians 2:7). But she would not budge. I warned her that her very soul was in danger if she kept on with such an attitude of unforgiving bitterness. But she was adamant that she would not forgive her mother.

What gives so much force to the impulse of anger in such cases is the overwhelming sense that the offender does not *deserve* forgiveness. That is, the grievance is so deep and so justifiable that not only does self-righteousness strengthen our indignation, but so does a legitimate sense of moral outrage. It's the deep sense of legitimacy that gives our bitterness its unbending compulsion. We feel that a great crime would be committed if the magnitude of the evil we've experienced were just dropped and we let bygones be bygones. We are torn: our moral sense says this evil cannot be ignored, and the Word of God says we must forgive.

IF YOU HOLD A GRUDGE, YOU DOUBT THE JUDGE

In his penetrating book, *Christian Commitment*, Edward John Carnell described this conflict between moral outrage and forgiveness as the "judicial predicament." He said, "We cannot ignore inconsiderate acts in others; yet we cannot execute the penalty of law. We have no right to complete the moral cycle…Although we sense no spiritual inhibition against crying out against injustice, the purity of our moral life deteriorates the moment we attempt to administer justice."[3] Nevertheless the indignation we feel usually gets the upper hand and holds onto the offense, because it would be morally repugnant to make light of the wrong.

Now we can see why the biblical promise of God's judgment is so crucial in helping overcome this craving for revenge. It gives us a way out of the "judicial predicament." God intervenes as the avenger so that we can acknowledge the crime; but also so that we don't have to be the judge. God's promised vengeance removes the moral legitimacy of our personal craving for retaliation. God's promise says, "Yes, an outrage has been committed against you. Yes, it deserves to be severely punished. Yes, the person has not yet experienced that punishment. But, No, you may not be the one to punish, and you may not go on relishing personal retribution. Why? Because God will see to it that justice is done. God will repay. You cannot improve on his justice. He sees every angle of the evil done against you—far better than you can see it. His justice will be more thorough than any justice you could administer." If you hold a grudge, you doubt the Judge.

That's what the promise of Romans 12:19 says. And the question for the angry, offended person now becomes, "Do you believe this promise?" In other words, the issue of releasing grudges is an issue of *faith* in God's promises of future grace—the future grace of judgment on the offender. If we believe God's promise, "Vengeance is mine, I will repay," then we will not belittle God with our inferior efforts to improve upon his justice. We will leave the matter with him and live in the freedom of love toward our enemy—whether the enemy repents or not. And if he does not repent? What then? Three hundred years ago Thomas Watson said it well: "We are not bound to trust an enemy; but we are bound to forgive him."[4] We are not responsible to make reconciliation happen. We are responsible to seek it. *"So far as it depends on you,* live at peace with all men" (Romans 12:18).

HOW JESUS SOLVED THE "JUDICIAL PREDICAMENT"

The apostle Peter shows that Jesus himself handled the "judicial predicament" in this same way. No one was more grievously sinned against than Jesus. Every ounce of animosity against him was fully undeserved. No one has ever lived who was more worthy of honor than Jesus; and no one has been dishonored more. If anyone had a right to get angry and be bitter and vengeful, it was Jesus. How did he control himself when scoundrels, whose very lives he sustained, spit in his face?

Peter gives the answer in these words: "[Jesus] committed no sin, nor was any deceit found in His mouth; and while being reviled, He did not revile in return; while suffering, He uttered no threats, but *kept entrust-*

ing[5]...*to Him who judges righteously*" (1 Peter 2:22-23). What this means is that Jesus had faith in the future grace of God's righteous judgment. He did not need to avenge himself for all the indignities he suffered, because he entrusted his cause to God. He left vengeance in God's hands and prayed for his enemies' repentance (Luke 23:34).

Peter gives this glimpse into Jesus' faith so that we would learn how to live this way ourselves. He said, "You have been called [to endure harsh treatment patiently]...since Christ also suffered for you, *leaving you an example for you to follow in his steps*" (1 Peter 2:21). If Christ conquered bitterness and vengeance by faith in future grace, how much more should we, since we have far less right to murmur for being mistreated than he did.

THE BASIS OF FORGIVING OTHER CHRISTIANS

But now another crucial question emerges. If God's promise of judgment is the basis for not holding grudges against unrepentant enemies, what is the basis of our not holding grudges against Christian brothers and sisters who do repent? Our moral indignation at a terrible offense does not evaporate just because the offender is a Christian. In fact we may feel even more betrayed. And a simple, "I'm sorry," will often seem utterly disproportionate to the painfulness and ugliness of the offense.

But in this case we are dealing with fellow Christians and the promise of God's wrath does not apply because there is "no condemnation to those who are in Christ Jesus" (Romans 8:1). "God has not destined [Christians] for wrath, but for obtaining salvation through our Lord Jesus Christ" (1 Thessalonians 5:9). So now where do we look, to escape from the "judicial predicament"? Where shall we turn to assure ourselves that justice will be done—that Christianity is not a mockery of the seriousness of sin?

The answer is that we look to the cross of Christ. All the wrongs that have been done against us by *believers* were avenged in the death of Jesus. This is implied in the simple, but staggering fact that *all* the sins of all God's people were laid on Jesus (Isaiah 53:6; 1 Corinthians 15:3; Galatians 1:4; 1 John 2:2; 4:10; 1 Peter 2:24; 3:18). The suffering of Christ was the recompense of God on every hurt I have ever received from a fellow Christian (Romans 4:25; 8:3; 2 Corinthians 5:21; Galatians 3:13). Therefore,

Christianity does not make light of sin. It does not add insult to our injury. On the contrary it takes the sins against us so seriously that, to make them right, God gave his own Son to suffer more than we could ever make anyone suffer for what they have done to us.

Therefore when God says, "Vengeance is mine," the meaning is more than we may have thought. God undertakes vengeance against sin not only by means of hell, but also by means of the cross. All sin will be avenged— severely and thoroughly and justly. Either in hell, or at the cross. The sins of the unrepentant will be avenged in hell; the sins of the repentant were avenged on the cross.

What this means is that we have no need or right to harbor bitterness toward believers or unbelievers. The judicial predicament is broken. God has intervened to deliver us from the moral demand to recompense the wrongs we've endured. He has done this, in great measure, by promising, "Vengeance is mine, I will repay." If we believe him, we will not presume to take vengeance into our own hands. Rather we will glorify the all-sufficiency of the cross and the terrible justice of hell by living in the assurance that God, and not we, will set all wrongs right. Ours is to love. God's is to settle accounts justly. And faith in future grace is the key to freedom and forgiveness.

BYGONE GRACE: NECESSARY, BUT NOT ENOUGH

The cross is in the past. And I am eager to affirm that the backward look to Calvary is utterly crucial for maintaining our faith in future grace. If my wife hurts me with an unkind word, I do not need to have the last word. I don't need to get even, because her sin was laid on Jesus, and he has suffered horribly to bear it for her—and for me. Jesus has taken that offense against himself and against me so seriously that he died to expose its evil and remove my wife's guilt. If this is to free me from holding a grudge, I must look back and believe that this is what happened on the cross. The backward glance is essential. The point of this book—living by faith in future grace—does not nullify that.

But the backward look is not enough. What Jesus accomplished on the cross lasts forever. I must be assured of that. The grace of Calvary that consumed the sins done against me, is also the future grace that keeps me and my wife in Christ, so that the cross is effectual for us. It is future grace that promises me and my wife that if we confess our sins, God is faithful and just to forgive our sins (1 John 1:9). In other words, the past grace of the atoning cross will have to be appropriated repeatedly by future confession. And that is assured only by future grace.

THE POWER OF GOD'S FORGIVENESS

Of course, for any who knows me and my wife, it is more likely that I will be the one needing her forgiveness more often than she needs mine. I am the one with the quick, unguarded tongue. This is why the Bible not only speaks of God's being the avenger of sins done against us, but also speaks of God's being the forgiver of sins that we do against others. This too is crucial for breaking the bondage of bitterness and freeing us to forgive.

Paul says, "Be kind to one another, tenderhearted, *forgiving each other, just as God in Christ also has forgiven you.* Therefore be imitators of God, as beloved children; and walk in love, just as Christ also loved you, and gave Himself up for us" (Ephesians 4:32–5:2). Here the power to forgive is flowing not from how God deals with the sins done against me, but from how God deals with the sins I do against others.

The battle against bitterness is fought not only by trusting the promise of God to avenge wrongs done against us, it is also fought by cherishing the experience of being forgiven by God. How does being forgiven make us forgiving people? I answer: by *faith* in our being forgiven. By *believing* that we are forgiven. But there is something perplexing here. That woman who was in the small group with me back in my seminary days would not forgive her mother, but she believed adamantly that she was forgiven. She would not let the sin of her grudge shake her security. Does faith in being forgiven then really liberate us from grudges?

What's wrong here? What's wrong is that she was apparently missing the essence of true saving faith—I say it with trembling. Saving faith is not merely believing *that* you are forgiven. Saving faith means tasting this forgiveness as part of the way God is and experiencing it (and him!) as precious and magnificent. Saving faith looks at the horror of sin, and then looks at the holiness of God, and apprehends spiritually that God's forgiveness is unspeakably glorious. Faith in God's forgiveness does not merely mean a persuasion that I am off the hook. It means savoring the truth that a forgiving God is the most precious reality in the universe. That's why I used the word "cherish." Saving faith cherishes being forgiven by God, and from there rises to cherishing the God who forgives—and all that he is for us in Jesus.

Again we see that the backward look is insufficient. The great act of forgiveness is past—the cross of Christ. By this backward look we learn of the grace in which we will ever stand (Romans 5:2). We learn that we are now and always will be loved and accepted. We learn that the living God is a forgiving God. But the great experience of being forgiven is all future. Fellowship with the great God who forgives is all future. Freedom for forgiveness flowing from this all-satisfying fellowship with the forgiving God is all future.

I have learned that it is possible to go on holding a grudge if your faith simply means you have looked back to the cross and concluded that you are off the hook. I have been forced to go deeper into what true faith is. It is being satisfied with all that God is for us in Jesus. It looks back not merely to discover that it is off the hook, but to see and savor the kind of God who offers us a future of endless reconciled tomorrows in fellowship with him.

It may be that, as you read this, no long-term grudges come to mind. Perhaps God has remarkably freed you from old hurts and disappointments and given you the grace to lay them down. But be sure to test yourself about short-term anger as well. Are there repeated *present* frustrations that may not have the character of long-term bitterness, but are like chronic reappearances of the same short-term anger? Are there traits of your children or your spouse or your church or your boss that week after week provoke you so deeply that you grit your teeth and rehearse in your head all the reasons why this is intolerable and should not go on? My experience has been that there is as much struggle with unbelief in these short-term, recurrent frustrations as there is in the long-term bitterness for some great abuse or betrayal. Here too we need to trust God's promises in a practical, day-by-day way.

The dark-valley breath of bitterness—short-term or long-term—cannot survive the high paths of faith in future grace. Grudges demand the valley-vapors of self-pity and fear and emptiness. They cannot survive the contentment and confidence and fullness of joy that come from satisfaction in the forgiving God of future grace.

PART VII

THE SANCTIFYING POWER OF FAITH IN FUTURE GRACE

*In Christ Jesus neither circumcision nor uncircumcision
means anything, but faith working through love.*

GALATIANS 5 : 6

*Faith, thus receiving and resting on Christ and his righteousness,
is the alone instrument of justification;
yet is it not alone in the person justified,
but is ever accompanied with all the saving graces,
and is no dead faith, but worketh by love.*

WESTMINSTER CONFESSION OF FAITH

Creating Love in a Desire Factory

The times that I have felt love welling up in my heart most powerfully have been the times when I have been blessed in the midst of my sin. I recall one morning about 20 years ago when this truth hit me clearly for the first time. My wife Noël and I had just had an argument—I can't even remember what it was about. But I was angry. So I took the garbage can out the door as an excuse to go outside and get some space. Looking back, it is clear that my emotions were way out of proportion to the issue, whatever it was.

As I walked down the driveway toward the street where we set the garbage for the pickup, the sun broke through the morning clouds. To this day, the profoundness of that moment grips me. Here I was huffing and puffing with my hurt feelings and desires for vindication and anger at my most valuable treasure on earth, and God, who had every right to strike me dead for my sin, opened the window of heaven and covered me with pleasure. I recall stopping and letting it soak in. The morning breeze was cool and the sun was warm. The leaves of the trees were an almost translucent yellow-green. It felt like paradise—garbage in hand.

The effect on me was not to feel vindicated, but to feel broken. I thought, *God has a thousand times more reason to frown on me than I have to frown on my wife. Yet here I am being lavished with delights in the very moment of my sin.* This brought tears to my eyes. But far more important than tears, it brought powers of love and forgiveness and reconciliation. So I set the garbage down (in more ways than one), and went back to Noël and apologized.

There is a spiritual dynamic here that I now call *living by faith in future grace*. God smiled on me and opened a morning to me that seemed full of joy and hope. That's what the sunshine and the breeze and the trees all spoke—this is the day that the Lord had made for you and you may rejoice and be glad in it. There is hope. There is kindness. There is forgiveness. And as that hope settled on me, something broke inside of me. New perspective on my sin was given. New power was granted to lay down my perceived "rights." And fresh love was kindled. It has happened again and again in my life.

FAITH IN FUTURE GRACE FILLS THE LIFE WITH LOVE

Why is it that living by faith in future grace must always be a life of love? What is it about faith in future grace that inevitably "works through love"? Galatians 5:6 says, "In Christ Jesus neither circumcision nor uncircumcision means anything, but *faith working through love.*" Texts like this have caused the church to teach that faith alone justifies, but the faith that justifies is never alone. That is, it is always accompanied by the works of love.

For example, the 1647 *Westminster Confession of Faith* says,

> *Faith, thus receiving and resting on Christ and his righteousness, is the alone instrument of justification; yet is it not alone in the person justified, but is ever accompanied with all the saving graces, and is no dead faith, but worketh by love.*[1]

One hundred years before the *Westminster Confession*, John Calvin commented on Galatians 5:6 like this: "It is not our doctrine that the faith which justifies is alone. We maintain that it is always joined with good works."[2] For over five hundred years this has been the common Protestant way of speaking about the relationship between faith and love.

WHY IS THIS CONNECTION SO SELDOM PROBED?

But it is remarkable how seldom the effort is made to dig into the experiential dynamics of *how* faith gives rise to love. It surprises me that in Calvin's commentary on the phrase, "faith works through love," he does not analyze the dynamics of *how* or *why* faith works through love. This neglect seems to continue into our own day, even though experience teaches that *understanding* our sanctification actually advances it. When we finally grasp the biblical, God-ordained means of transformation, then our minds and hearts are more engaged with it and can make more progress in the way of love. What is the reason for this neglect?

Could one reason be that the key that unlocks the experiential connection between faith and love is the nature of faith as a future-oriented satisfaction in all that God is for us in Jesus? Is it the failure to deal adequately with the true nature of faith that hinders the recognition of its power to sever the root of sin and energize works of love? Failing to give due attention to the future-oriented, promise-trusting essence of faith that is satisfied with all that God is for us in Jesus, limits our understanding of how this faith sanctifies the heart (Acts 15:9) and serves others with love (Galatians 5:6). What I have found in my reading is that to the degree that a writer probes the nature of faith's power to *satisfy the heart* with all God promises to be for us, to that degree is the writer able to render an account of *how* "faith works through love;" but to the degree that this aspect of faith is omitted, to that degree is faith's role in sanctification truncated, and appeal is usually made to the fruit-bearing work of the Holy Spirit without the corresponding explanation of the experiential dynamics which are so crucial in our lives.

So in this chapter I want to probe into why faith in future grace "works through love." *The key to faith's power is that it embraces the future grace promised by God, and is more satisfied with this than with the pleasures promised by sin—even if it costs us our lives.*

THE HEART IS A DESIRE FACTORY

The human heart produces desires as fire produces heat. As surely as the sparks fly upward, the heart pumps out desire after desire for a happier future. The condition of the heart is appraised by the kinds of desires that hold sway. Or, to put it another way, the state of the heart is shown by the things that satisfy its desires. If it is satisfied with mean and ugly things, it is a mean and ugly heart. If it is satisfied with God, it is a godly heart. As Henry Skougal put it, "The worth and excellency of a soul is to be measured by the object of its desire."[3]

THE HEART OF "WORKS"

Consider the difference between a heart of "faith" and a heart of "works." The heart of works gets satisfaction from the ego-boost of accomplishing something in its own power. It might be a religious thing or a worldly thing. What matters is that the heart feels it has achieved something to boast in. The heart set on works will attempt to scale a vertical rock face, or take on extra responsibilities at work, or risk life in a combat zone, or agonize through a marathon, or perform religious fasting for weeks—all for the satisfaction of conquering a challenge by the force of its own will and the stamina of its own body.

The heart with a works-orientation may also express its love of independence and self-direction and self-achievement by rebelling against courtesy and decency and morality (cf. Galatians 5:19-21). But it's the same self-determining, self-exalting works-orientation that also gets disgusted with boorish behavior and sets out to prove its superiority through self-denial, courage and personal greatness. In all of this the basic satisfaction of the works-orientation is the savor of being an assertive, autonomous and, if possible, triumphant self.

THE HEART OF FAITH

The heart of faith is radically different. Its desires are no less strong as it looks to the future. But what it desires is the fullest satisfaction of experiencing all that God is for us in Jesus. If "works" wants the satisfaction of feeling *itself* overcome an obstacle, "faith" savors the satisfaction of feeling *God* overcome an obstacle. Works longs for the joy of being glorified as capable, strong and smart. Faith longs for the joy of seeing God glorified for his capability, strength and wisdom. In its religious form, works accepts the challenge of morality, conquers its obstacles through great exertion, and offers the victory to God as a payment for his approval and recompense. Faith, too, accepts the challenge of morality, but only as an occasion to become the instrument of God's power. And when the victory comes, faith rejoices that all the glory and thanks belong to God.

Therefore, as faith contemplates its own power to work through love, it recognizes that only God can produce love. Any "love" that we might achieve without God would not be true love because you cannot do lasting good for anyone without God. All the benefits of the world, minus God, would mean misery in the end. Moreover, achievements of compassion without God only feed the self-exalting ego; they are anathema to faith. Faith loves to experience all that God can do, not all that self can do.

FAITH WILL NOT MAKE A MOVE WITHOUT THE HOLY SPIRIT

What this means is that faith will not attempt to "work through love" without the Holy Spirit. Faith knows from Galatians 5:22 that "The fruit of the Spirit is love." Love is generated in Christians by the Holy Spirit. It is not a "work" of the flesh. When it comes, it gives no ground for boasting. Faith delights in this. This is what faith loves—to experience all that *God* is for us in Jesus, including the power to love.

But the Holy Spirit will not bring forth the fruit of love apart from faith. This is clear from Galatians 3:2-5. Paul is criticizing some of the Galatians for failing to continue in the Christian life the way they began it, namely, by faith in future grace. He points out to them that the way they began the Christian life was by receiving the Spirit; not by works but by faith: "Did you receive the Spirit by the works of the Law, or by hearing with faith?" (v. 2). The answer is, by hearing with faith. When they first heard the Word of God with its promises of forgiveness and help and eternal life, they put their faith in Christ and his future grace. They took heart that Christ's death and resurrection was sufficient to give them such a future.

That was the way they began the Christian life—by receiving the Holy Spirit through faith in future grace (founded on past grace). But then they started to drift toward a works-orientation. They started to think that the Christian life is *begun* by faith in the power of the Spirit, but is completed or perfected by the efforts of the "flesh." "Are you so foolish? Having begun by the Spirit, are you now being perfected by the flesh?" (v. 3). They were falling into the trap that ensnares many today, thinking that the event of justification is by faith, but the process of sanctification is by works.

But Paul says this is "foolish." "If we live by the Spirit, let us also walk by the Spirit" (Galatians 5:25). The Spirit came, the first time, by faith in the blood-bought promises of God. And the Spirit keeps on coming, and keeps on working, by this same means. So Paul asks, rhetorically, "Does He then, who provides you with the Spirit and works miracles among you, do it by the works of the Law, or by hearing with faith?" (Galatians 3:5). Answer: "by hearing with faith." Therefore, the Spirit came the first time, and the Spirit keeps on being supplied, through the channel of faith. What he accomplishes in us is through faith.

If you are like me, you may have strong longings from time to time for the mighty working of the Holy Spirit in your life. Perhaps you do cry out to God for the outpouring of the Spirit in your life or in your family or church or city. Such cries are right and good. Jesus said, "How much more shall your heavenly Father give the Holy Spirit to those who ask Him" (Luke 11:13). But what I have found most often in my own life is the failure to open myself to the full measure of the Spirit's work by believing the promises of God. I don't mean merely the promise that the Spirit will come when we ask. I mean all the other precious promises that are not *directly* about the Spirit but, perhaps, about God's provision for my future—for example, "My God shall supply all your needs" (Philippians 4:19). This is what is missing in the experience of so many Christians as they seek the power of the Spirit in their lives. The Spirit is supplied to us "by hearing with faith" (Galatians 3:5)—not just faith in one or two promises about the Spirit himself, but about all the soul-satisfying presence of God in our future.

WHY DOES THE SPIRIT BIND HIMSELF TO FAITH?

The fruit of love is worked in us through the Spirit "by hearing with faith." The Spirit will not bear his fruit in us apart from our faith. Why is this? Why does the Spirit unite himself to faith as a way of bringing about the works of love?

The answer seems to be that the Holy Spirit loves to glorify the all-satisfying dependability of Christ and his Word (John 16:14). If the Holy Spirit simply caused acts of love in the human heart without any clear, on-going causal connection between love, on the one hand, and faith in Christ's promises, on the other hand, then it would not be plain that Christ's all-satisfying dependability is honored through love. But the Spirit is utterly committed to getting glory for Jesus. Therefore, he keeps himself quietly beneath the surface, as it were, and puts forward "hearing with faith" as the conscious cause of love.

"Hearing with faith" (Galatians 3:2, 5) means hearing the Word of God, or the Word of Christ, and embracing it with deep satisfaction. The Word we hear is largely promises. Galatians 3:29 sums up the Word of the gospel like this: "If you belong to Christ, then you are Abraham's offspring, *heirs according to promise.*" The promise that we are "heirs of God" (Romans 8:17) embraces virtually all of future grace. Romans 4:13 says that Abraham, along with his descendants, is an "heir of *the world.*" In other words, God will give us *all things* with Christ (Romans 8:32)—whether "the world or life or death or things present or things to come; all things belong to you; and you belong to Christ; and Christ belongs to God" (1 Corinthians 3:22-23).

The Holy Spirit conceals himself and ascribes the conscious cause of love to "faith working through love." He does this because the focus of faith is the dependability of Christ and his word concerning the inexhaustibility of future grace. The Spirit loves to exalt Christ; and nothing exalts Christ like being trusted and treasured above all other future fortunes.

CHRIST IS HONORED BY THE CONNECTION: FAITH IN FUTURE GRACE AND LOVE

Therefore we strive against the Holy Spirit if we do not make much of the Christ-exalting capacity of faith to "work through love." It does not accord with the will of the Spirit to simply say: justifying faith is always accompanied by the Spirit of holiness. The Spirit wills for us to highlight the dependability of Christ as the focus of faith, and then to show why this faith works through love. Be assured that he will be the decisive "fruit-bearer" of love. And be assured that faith will always rejoice that it was the power of the Spirit at work beneath and through faith. Nevertheless, Christ and his boundless resources of all-satisfying future grace will not get their proper due if we do not trace love to faith in future grace.

What is at stake is the praise of the glory of God's grace (Ephesians 1:6), most of which is future, and stretches from now to the endless ages of eternity. The glory of this future grace will shine with its proper praise and honor only in the mirror of faith. Abraham "grew strong in faith, giving glory to God…fully assured that what he had promised, he was able also to perform" (Romans 4:20-21). The satisfying dependability of God is glorified when we entrust our future to him. We honor the Christ of future grace by putting faith in future grace, and by living in the freedom of love that this faith gives.

The glory of God's future grace is magnified when we define saving faith as being satisfied with all that God is for us in Jesus. We have devoted Chapters Fifteen and Sixteen to developing this understanding of faith. What we need to do now is show that this understanding is the key to why faith inevitably engenders love. It is not complicated: If the heart is satisfied with all that God is for us in Jesus, the power of sin to lure us away from the will of Christ is broken, and the beauty of God's path of love is compelling.

HOW FAITH EXPELS ANTI-LOVE FORCES

Faith in future grace expels from the heart the sinful powers that hinder love. For example, guilt and fear and greed stand in the way of love. If we feel *guilty,* we tend to wallow in self-centered depression and self-pity, unable to see, let alone care, about anyone else's need. Or we play the hypocrite to cover our guilt, and so destroy all sincerity in relationships. Or we talk about other people's faults to minimize the guilt of our own. And so, in every case, guilt hinders love.

It's the same with *fear.* If we feel fearful, we tend not to approach a stranger at church who might need a word of welcome and encouragement. Or we may reject frontier missions for our lives, because it sounds too dangerous. Or we may waste money on excessive insurance, or get swallowed up in all manner of little phobias that make us preoccupied with ourselves and blind us to the needs of others. And so fear hinders love.

If we are *greedy* we may spend money on luxuries—money that ought to go to the spread of the gospel. We don't undertake anything risky, lest our precious possessions and our financial future be jeopardized. We focus on things instead of people, or see people as resources for our material advantage. And so greed hinders love.

Faith in future grace produces love by pushing guilt and fear and greed out of the heart. It pushes out *guilt* because it holds fast to the hope that the death of Christ is sufficient to secure acquittal and righteousness now and forever (Hebrews 10:14). It pushes out *fear* because it banks on the promise, "Do not fear, for I am with you...I will strengthen you, surely I will help you, surely I will uphold you with my righteous right hand" (Isaiah 41:10). And it pushes out greed because it is confident that Christ is greater wealth than all the world can offer (Matthew 13:44; Philippians 3:8; Hebrews 11:26). In every case the glory of Christ is magnified when we are more satisfied with his future grace than we are with the promises of sin.

HOW FAITH IMPELS THE SACRIFICES OF LOVE

Faith in future grace produces love not only by what it pushes out of the heart, but also by the strong desires it brings to the heart. Faith has an insatiable appetite for experiencing as much of God's grace as possible. Therefore, faith presses toward the river where God's grace flows most freely, namely, the river of love. When all guilt and fear and greed have been removed by the power of faith in future grace, what force will move us out of our contented living rooms to take upon ourselves the inconveniences and suffering that love requires?

What will propel us to greet strangers when we feel shy, to go to an enemy and plead for reconciliation when we feel indignant, to tithe when we've never tried it, to speak to our colleagues about Christ, to invite new neighbors to a Bible study, to cross cultures with the gospel, to create a new ministry for alcoholics, to spend an evening driving a van, or a morning praying for renewal? None of these costly acts of love just happens. They are impelled by a new appetite—the appetite of faith for the fullest experience of God's grace. Faith loves to rely on God and see him work miracles in us. Therefore, faith pushes us into the current where the power of God's future grace flows most freely—the current of love. I think this is what Paul meant when he said that we should "sow to the Spirit" (Galatians 6:8). By faith, we should put the seeds of our energy in the furrows where we know the Spirit is at work to bear fruit—the furrows of love.

GOD-SATISFIED FAITH SEVERS THE ROOT OF LOVELESSNESS

In summary, love is a fruit of the Holy Spirit. But it is also a "work of faith" (Galatians 5:6, 22). The Spirit and faith are linked because God supplies the Spirit to us "by hearing with faith" (Galatians 3:5). But if that is all we said about the way faith begets love, the glory of God's future grace would not be magnified the way it should be. The glory of future grace is magnified in the mirror of faith. Therefore to honor the unending stream of future grace, God has ordained that the conscious cause of love be the experience of faith in future grace. Faith magnifies the all-satisfying greatness of all that God is for us in Jesus.

This God-satisfied faith severs the root of guilt and fear and greed. Therefore, it frees us from the love-destroying power of those conditions. This faith also fills us with a passion to experience as much of God's grace as we can. Thus it impels us toward the stream where God, the Spirit, is flowing in power, namely, the stream of love. O, that God would pour out his Spirit on us in extraordinary measure! May he open our eyes to see the irresistibly attractive and overwhelmingly satisfying beauty of all that God promises to be for us in Jesus. And thus may we live by faith in future grace, and love the way we have been loved!

And God is able to make all grace abound to you,

that always having all sufficiency in everything,

you may have an abundance for every good deed.

2 CORINTHIANS 9:8

By the grace of God I am what I am,

and His grace toward me did not prove vain;

but I labored even more than all of them,

yet not I, but the grace of God with me.

1 CORINTHIANS 15:10

I will not presume to speak of anything

except what Christ has accomplished through me,

resulting in the obedience of the Gentiles by word and deed.

ROMANS 15:18

CHAPTER TWENTY-THREE

Loving Ministry
More
Than Life

MINISTRY IS MORE IMPORTANT THAN LIFE

Accarding to the New Testament, "ministry" is what all Christians do. Pastors have the job of equipping the saints for the work of ministry (Ephesians 4:12). But ordinary Christians *do* the ministry. What ministry looks like is as varied as Christians are varied. It's not an office; it's a lifestyle devoted to advancing other people's faith and holiness. In this sense the only life that counts for anything is a life of ministry—whether you're a banker or a bricklayer. Fulfilling your ministry is more important than staying alive.

This conviction is what makes the lives of radically devoted people so inspiring to watch. Most of them speak the way Paul did about his ministry: "I do not consider my life of any account as dear to myself, in order that I may finish my course, and the *ministry* which I received from the Lord Jesus" (Acts 20:24). Doing the ministry that God gives us to do is more important than life.

You may think you need to save your life in order to do your ministry. On the contrary, how you lose your life may be the capstone of your ministry. It certainly was for Jesus, at age 33. We need not fret about keeping ourselves alive in order to finish our ministry. God alone knows the appointed time of our service. Henry Martyn was right when he said, "If [God] has work for me to do, I cannot die."[1] In other words, I am immortal until my work is done. Therefore, ministry is more important than life.

THEY LOVED NOT THEIR LIVES ABOVE MINISTRY

O, how many examples could be multiplied from the glorious history of God's faithful saints! William Carey sailed to India from England in 1793. He lost his five-year-old son, his wife became mentally ill, he labored seven years for his first convert, and he lost years' worth of precious translation work in a fire. But still he pressed on—for forty years without a furlough. Because ministry is more important than life. Adoniram Judson, "America's first foreign missionary," went to Burma in 1814. He lost a six-month-old baby boy, spent a year and a half in a "death prison," lost his wife from fever, suffered a mental breakdown, and waited five years for his first convert. But he kept on, because ministry is more important than life. Robert Morrison, the first Protestant missionary to go to China (in 1807), lost his young wife and worked seven years for his first convert. But he kept on, because ministry is more important than life.[2]

NO MIRROR FOR THE LAST TWENTY YEARS

Evelyn Harris Brand, the mother of Paul Brand, the world-renowned hand surgeon and leprosy specialist, grew up in a well-to-do English family. She had studied at the London Conservatory of Art and dressed in the finest silks. But she went with her husband to minister as missionaries in the Kolli Malai range of India. After about ten years her husband died at age 44 and she came home "a broken woman, beaten down by pain and grief." But after a year's recuperation, and against all advice, she returned to India. Her soul was restored and she poured her life into the hill people, "nursing the sick, teaching farming, lecturing about guinea worms, rearing orphans, clearing jungle land, pulling teeth, establishing schools, preaching the gospel." She lived in a portable hut, eight feet square, that could be taken down, moved and erected again.

At age 67 she fell and broke her hip. Her son, Paul, had just come to

India as a surgeon. He encouraged her to retire. She had already suffered a broken arm, several cracked vertebrae and recurrent malaria. Paul mounted as many arguments as he could think of to persuade her that sixty-seven years was a good investment in ministry, and now it was time to retire. Her response? "Paul, you know these mountains. If I leave, who will help the village people? Who will treat their wounds and pull their teeth and teach them about Jesus? When someone comes to take my place, then and only then will I retire. In any case, why preserve this old body if it's not going to be used where God needs me?" That was her final answer. So she worked on.

At the age of 95 she died. Following her instructions, villagers buried her in a simple cotton sheet so that her body would return to the soil and nourish new life. "Her spirit, too, lives on, in a church, a clinic, several schools, and in the faces of thousands of villagers across five mountain ranges of South India." Her son commented that "with wrinkles as deep and extensive as any I have ever seen on a human face...she was a beautiful woman." But it was not the beauty of the silk and heirlooms of London high society. For the last twenty years of her life she refused to have a mirror in her house! She was consumed with ministry, not mirrors. A coworker once remarked that Granny Brand was more alive than any person he had ever met. "By giving away life, she found it."[3] This is what happens, paradoxically, when ministry is more important than life.

DOING MINISTRY AND DYING WELL
BY FAITH IN FUTURE GRACE

I stress this radical orientation on ministry simply to double the impact of the importance of future grace. For no one fulfills any spiritual ministry without relying on future grace. This is the unmistakable witness of the New Testament. And it makes future grace central and indispensable in doing ministry and dying well.

In 2 Corinthians 9:8 Paul said, "God is able to make all grace abound to you, that always having all sufficiency in everything, you may have an abundance for every good deed." The immediate context relates to financial liberality. But the principle is stated more broadly than that. God is able to make all grace—all the *future grace* you need—abound to you so that you will (literally) "abound unto every good work." Future grace is the means God supplies "for every good work"—not "every good work" imaginable, but "every good work" appointed by God along your unique path of ministry. The power for every one of them is future grace.

The church at Antioch gives us an example how this promise is to be trusted. When God called Paul and Barnabas to be missionaries, the church saw it as a summons to faith in future grace. They prayed, and then sent Paul and Barnabas on the first missionary journey with the confidence that future grace would go before them and give them success. We know this because when they got back, the book of Acts describes their arrival in relation to this work of grace: "They sailed [back] to Antioch, from which *they had been commended to the grace of God* for the work that they had accomplished" (Acts 14:26).

The connection here between future grace and ministry is clear. Literally it says, "they were handed over to the grace of God *for the work* which they fulfilled." This was how the Christians in Antioch trusted the promise of 2 Corinthians 9:8. The promise said that God will make all *grace* abound to you "for every good work." So by faith in future grace the church "handed Paul and Barnabas over to the grace of God *for the work.*" Future grace was like an armed guard, and a supply of goods, and a team of physicians, and a spiritual force from heaven. It was strategically positioned in the future just out from the port of Antioch. And by faith the church entrusted the missionaries to God's great provision called future grace (see Acts 15:40).

GRACE IS THE GREAT DOER IN PAUL'S MINISTRY

Paul confirmed with his own words the absolute necessity of future grace for ministry. He said, "By the grace of God I am what I am, and His grace toward me did not prove vain; but I labored even more than all of them, yet not I, but *the grace of God with me*" (1 Corinthians 15:10). Paul realized that the first part of this verse might be misunderstood. Someone might say, "See, he is telling us that God gave him grace in the past and now Paul is simply *responding* to that grace, out of gratitude, by working for God as hard as he can." That would be a partial, but distorted, truth. It is not the picture of Christian ministry Paul wants to leave in our minds. So he goes on to say, "Yet not I, but the grace of God with me."

This text does not say that Paul is obeying Christ out of gratitude for past grace. There is no doubt that Paul was filled with gratitude to God for multiplied bygone grace. And no doubt, as we saw in Chapter Two, this gratitude nourished his faith in future grace with happy reminders of the past. But this is *not* what the text says. It says that, at every moment, the *future* grace of God enabled Paul's work. Does it really say that? Doesn't it just say that the grace of God [worked] *with Paul?* No, it says more. We have to come to terms with the words, "Yet not I." Paul wants to exalt the moment-by-moment grace of God in such a way that it is clear that he himself is not the decisive doer of this work. "Yet not I."

Nevertheless, he *is* a doer of this work: "I worked harder than any of them." He worked. But he said, it was the grace of God "with me." If we let all the parts of this verse stand, the end result is this: grace is the decisive doer in Paul's work. Since Paul is also a doer of his work, the way grace becomes the decisive doer is by becoming the enabling power of Paul's work.

I take this to mean that, as Paul faced each day's ministry burden, he bowed his head and confessed that unless future grace was given for that day's work, he would not be able to do it. He recalled the words of Jesus, "Apart from Me you can do nothing" (John 15:5). So he prayed for future grace for the day, and he trusted in the promise that it would come with power. "My God shall supply all your needs according to His riches in glory in Christ Jesus" (Philippians 4:19). Then he acted with all his might. And when he came to the end of the day, he called *his* might the might of *grace* and gave God the glory. "Yet not I, but the grace of God with me." Or, with different words, "I can do all things through Him who strengthens me" (Philippians 4:13).

THE GRACE TO WILL AND TO DO

This is the way Paul saw all Christian ministry happening, not just his. That's why he wrote to the Philippians, "Work out your salvation with fear and trembling; for it is God who is at work in you, both to will and to work for His good pleasure" (Philippians 2:12-13). God is the decisive worker here. He wills and he works for his good pleasure. But believing this does not make Christians passive. It makes them hopeful and energetic and courageous. Each day there is a work to be done in our special ministry. Paul commands us to work at doing it. But he tells us how to do it in the power of future grace: believe the promise that in this day God will be at work in you to will and work for his good pleasure.

It is not the memory of past grace that "wills and works for God's good pleasure." It is God himself, graciously arriving each moment, that brings the future into the present. It is not the gratitude for past grace that Paul focuses on when explaining how he "works harder than any of them." It is fresh grace for every new conquest in his missionary labor. He does not say that the grace to do ministry comes from the past, as a memory, through the channel of gratitude; he says it comes from the future, as divine power, through the channel of faith.[4]

The power of future grace is the power of the living Christ—always there to work for us at every future moment that we enter. So when Paul describes the effect of the grace of God which was with him he says, "I will not presume to speak of anything except what *Christ* has accomplished through me, resulting in the obedience of the Gentiles by word and deed" (Romans 15:18). Therefore since he would not dare to speak of anything but what Christ accomplished through his ministry, and yet he did, in fact, speak of what grace accomplished through his ministry (1 Corinthians 15:10), this must mean that the power of grace is the power of Christ. Which means that the power we need for tomorrow's ministry is the future grace of the omnipotent Christ, who will always be there for us—ready to will and ready to work for his good pleasure.

ABUNDANT GRACE WAS ON THEM ALL—TO WITNESS

If our ministry is to witness to Christ tomorrow in some unsympathetic situation, the key will not be our brilliance; the key will be abundant future grace. Of all people, the apostles seemed to need least help to give a compelling witness to the risen Christ. They had been with him for three years. They had seen him die. They had seen him alive. In their witnessing arsenal they had "many convincing proofs" (Acts 1:3). You might think that, of all people, their ministry of witnessing, in those early days, would sustain itself on the strength of the past glories that were still so fresh.

But that is not what the book of Acts tells us. It says, "With great power the apostles were giving witness to the resurrection of the Lord Jesus, and *abundant grace was upon them all*" (Acts 4:33). The power to witness with faithfulness and effectiveness did not come mainly from memories of grace, or reservoirs of knowledge; it came from the new arrivals of "abundant grace." That's the way it was for the apostles and that's the way it will be for us in our ministry of witnessing.

Whatever added signs and wonders God may show to amplify our witness to Christ, they will come the same way they came for Stephen. "And Stephen, *full of grace and power,* was performing great wonders and signs among the people" (Acts 6:8). There is an extraordinary future grace and power that we may bank on in the crisis of special ministry need. It is a fresh act of power by which God "bears witness to the word of His grace" (Acts 14:3; Hebrews 2:4). The grace of power bears witness to the grace of truth. This is not the performance of gratitude for what is past; it is the performance of faith in what is future.

SPIRITUAL GIFTS: CHANNELS OF FUTURE GRACE

When we think of the ministry of ordinary Christians, we think not only of the ministry of witnessing to Christ, but also the use of spiritual gifts for the building up of the church. Here the crucial point is: no one can exercise a spiritual gift without future grace. In fact, ministering through spiritual gifts is defined by the apostle Peter as mediating grace from God to other people. "As each one has received a special gift, employ it in serving one another, as *good stewards of the manifold grace of God* (1 Peter 4:10).

Future grace is "manifold grace." It comes in many colors and shapes and sizes. This is one of the reasons spiritual gifts in the body are so diverse. The prism of your life will refract one of the colors of grace that would never come through my prism. There are as many future graces as there are needs in the body of Christ—and more. The purpose of spiritual gifts is to receive and dispense the future grace of God to those needs.

But someone may ask, "Why do you take Peter to refer to future grace?

Doesn't a steward manage a household store that is already on hand?" The main reason I take Peter to refer to future grace is because the next verse illustrates how this works, and the reference there is ongoing supplies of future grace. He says, "Whoever serves, let him do so as by *the strength which God supplies;* so that in all things God may be glorified through Jesus Christ" (1 Peter 4:11b).

When you fulfill your spiritual gift to serve someone tomorrow, you will be serving "in the strength that God supplies" *tomorrow.* The word is "supplies," not "supplied." God goes on, day-by-day, moment-by-moment, supplying the "strength" in which we minister. This means that spiritual gifts are fulfilled by the power of future grace, not merely in the power that we muster through thinking about past grace.

And when we rely on future grace in this way what happens is that our gifts do in fact become grace for others. We channel grace from God to others. Paul gives a beautiful example of this in Ephesians 4:29, "Let no unwholesome word proceed from your mouth, but only such a word as is good for edification, according to the need of the moment, *that it may give grace to those who hear.*" Before this day is done, there will be an occasion in your life which Paul calls "the need of the moment." Someone will be positioned to benefit from your words. This is the ministry that you will be called to at that moment: "edification according to the need of the moment." If you put your faith in future grace and serve in the strength that God supplies, you will become a channel of that grace. You will "give grace to those who hear." They do not have it now. It is future. But when it comes—to you and *through* you—the satisfaction is so deep, you will know why you were created and why you were called.

THE TIMING OF FUTURE GRACE

All ministry is in the future—a moment away, or a month, or a year, or a decade. We have ample time to fret about our inadequacy. When this happens, we must turn to prayer. Prayer is the form of faith that connects us today with the grace that will make us adequate for tomorrow's ministry. Timing is everything. What if grace comes too early or comes too late? The traditional translation of Hebrews 4:16 hides from us a very precious promise in this regard. We need a more literal rendering to see it. The more traditional wording goes like this: "Let us draw near with confidence to the *throne of grace,* that we may receive mercy and may find *grace to help in time of need.*" The Greek original behind the phrase "grace to help in time of need" would be translated literally, "grace for a well-timed help."[5]

The point is that prayer is the way to find future grace for a well-timed help. This grace always arrives from the "throne of grace" on time. The phrase, "throne of grace" means that future grace comes from the King of the Universe who sets the times by his own authority (Acts 1:8). His timing is perfect, but it is rarely ours: "For a thousand years in [his] sight are like yesterday when it passes by" (Psalm 90:4). At the global level, he sets the times for nations to rise and fall (Acts 17:26). And at the personal level, "My times are in [his] hands" (Psalm 31:15). When we wonder about the timing of future grace, we must think on the *"throne* of grace." Nothing can hinder God's plan to send grace when it will be best for us. Future grace is always well-timed.

Future grace is the constant plea of the praying psalmists. They pray for it again and again to meet every need. They leave every minister a model of daily dependence on future grace for every exigency. They cry out for future grace when they need help: "Hear, O Lord, and be *gracious* to me; O Lord, be Thou my helper" (Psalm 30:10). They cry out for future grace when they are weak: "Turn to me, and be *gracious* to me; O grant Thy strength to Thy servant" (Psalm 86:16). They cry out for future grace when they need healing: "Be *gracious* to me, O Lord, for I am pining away; heal me, O Lord" (Psalm 6:2). They cry out for future grace when they are afflicted by enemies: "Be *gracious* to me, O Lord; behold my affliction from those who hate me" (Psalm 9:13). They cry out for future grace when they are lonely: "Turn to me and be *gracious* to me, For I am lonely and afflicted" (Psalm 25:16). They cry out for future grace when they are grieving: "Be *gracious* to me, O Lord, for I am in distress; My eye is wasted away from grief" (Psalm 31:9). They cry out for future grace when they have sinned: "O Lord, be *gracious* to me; Heal my soul, for I have sinned against Thee" (Psalm 41:4). They cry out for future grace when they long for God's name to be exalted among the nations: "God be *gracious* to us and bless us...that Thy way may be known on the earth" (Psalm 67:1-2).

Unmistakably, prayer is the great link of faith between the soul of the saint and the promise of future grace. If ministry was meant by God to be sustained by prayer, then ministry was meant to be sustained by faith in future grace.

MINISTRY IS A GIFT OF GRACE, JUST LIKE SALVATION

I recall coming to the end of my graduate studies in Munich, Germany, back in 1974. I had no idea where to go. I was ready to enter any ministry the Lord would open for me. I sent my résumé to dozens of schools and missions and agencies. One of the most encouraging letters I received in those days was from my friend and former professor, Daniel Fuller. He knew I was struggling to trust God for a place of ministry. So he quoted a little-known verse, 2 Corinthians 4:1, "Since we have this ministry, as we received mercy, we do not lose heart." He pointed out the word "as" in the phrase "as we received mercy." Then he showed me the link between "having a ministry" and "receiving mercy." He said that ministry is given as freely and as sovereignly and as graciously as the first experience of mercy that we received in salvation. That is what I needed then. And that is what I need now, to press on in my ministry. The place of ministry, and the ongoing performance of ministry, are gifts of grace, just like my conversion was. Therefore, ministry means living by faith in future grace.

One of the great threats to persevering in ministry is the paralyzing effect of despondency. Therefore we must find a way to triumph over this crippling sense of oppression. In the next chapter we will ponder how prizing the promises of God can fight off the destructive effects of despondency.

The greatest need of the hour is a revived and joyful Church...
Unhappy Christians are, to say the least,
a poor recommendation of the Christian faith.

MARTYN LLOYD-JONES

Why are you in despair, O my soul?
And why have you become disturbed within me?
Hope in God,
for I shall again praise Him
For the help of His presence.

PSALM 42:5

His anger is but for a moment,
His favor is for a lifetime;
Weeping may last for the night,
But a shout of joy comes in the morning.

PSALM 30:5

Applying the Purifying Power

Faith in Future Grace vs. Despondency

A DOCTOR OF SOULS

I n 1954 one of my heroes, Martyn Lloyd-Jones, preached a series of sermons at Westminster Chapel, London, which he later published in a book called *Spiritual Depression*. His assessment of the church at the middle of the twentieth century is still valid, as far as I can see. He said, "I have no hesitation in asserting again that one of the reasons why the Christian Church counts for so little in the modern world is that so many Christians are in this condition [of spiritual depression]."[1] "The greatest need of the hour is a revived and joyful Church...Unhappy Christians are, to say the least, a poor recommendation of the Christian faith."[2]

Lloyd-Jones was an esteemed medical doctor before he became a preacher. This gives a special weight to his observations about the causes of despondent feelings that plague so many Christians. He is not naive about the complexity of what causes despondency. For example, he says, "There are certain people who are more prone to depression in a natural sense than others...Though we are converted and regenerated, our fundamental personality is not changed. The result is that the person who is more given to

299

depression than another person before conversion, will still have to fight that after conversion."[3]

A LINEAGE OF DEPRESSION

There are many painful examples of this in the history of the church. One of the most poignant is the story of David Brainerd, the young missionary to the Indians of New England in the eighteenth century. It seems that there was an unusual strain of weakness and depression in his family. Not only did the parents die early, but David's brother Nehemiah died at 32, his brother Israel died at 23, his sister Jerusha died at 34, and he died at 29. In 1865 a descendant, Thomas Brainerd, said, "In the whole Brainerd family for two hundred years there has been a tendency to a morbid depression, akin to hypochondria."[4]

So on top of having an austere father and suffering the loss of both parents as a sensitive child, he probably inherited some kind of tendency to depression. Whatever the cause, he suffered from the blackest dejection, off and on, throughout his short life. He says at the very beginning of his diary, "I was, I think, from my youth something sober and inclined rather to melancholy than the other extreme."[5]

Nevertheless he said that there was a difference between the depression he suffered before and after his conversion. After his conversion there seemed to be a rock of electing love under him that would catch him, so that in his darkest times he could still affirm the truth and goodness of God, even though he couldn't sense it for a season.[6]

THE BURDEN OF THE BODY

Not only is there the issue of hereditary temperament and personality, but there is also the issue of how physical conditions affect low moods. Lloyd-Jones says, "There are many, I find, who come to talk to me about these matters, in whose case it seems quite clear to me that the cause of the trouble is mainly physical. Into this group, speaking generally, you can put tiredness, overstrain, illness, any form of illness. You cannot isolate the spiritual from the physical for we are body, mind and spirit."[7] When the psalmist cried out, "My flesh and my heart may fail" (Psalm 73:26), he was showing us how interwoven the "heart" and the "flesh" are in the despondency he so often experienced.

Charles Haddon Spurgeon is a prime example of a great Christian and a great preacher whose recurrent despondency was almost surely owing in large measure to his painful disease of gout. It is not easy to imagine the omni-competent, eloquent, brilliant, full-of-energy Spurgeon weeping like a baby for no reason that he could think of. In 1858, at age 24, it happened for the first time. He said, "My spirits were sunken so low that I could weep by the hour like a child, and yet I knew not what I wept for."[8] As years went by the times of melancholy came again and again. At times he seemed ready to give up: "Causeless depression cannot be reasoned with, nor can David's harp charm it away by sweet discoursings. As well fight with the mist as with this shapeless, undefinable, yet all-beclouding hopelessness… The iron bolt which so mysteriously fastens the door of hope and holds our spirits in gloomy prison, needs a heavenly hand to push it back."[9]

Yet he did fight. He saw his depression as his "worst feature." "Despondency," he said, "is not a virtue; I believe it is a vice. I am heartily ashamed of myself for falling into it, but I am sure there is no remedy for it like a holy faith in God."[10]

Before we look at that remedy more closely, one more complicating cause should be mentioned. There is the whole area of family conditioning. One small example: if parents reward a child for whining, and give in to the manipulation of a child's moodiness, then that child will be trained that a good pout will get pity. And thirty years later the mastery of his moods will be twice as hard.

THE ROOT OF DESPONDENCY

What then is the root of despondency? Lloyd-Jones would agree that it is oversimplifying to say that the *single* root of despondency is unbelief. But it would be right to say, as Lloyd-Jones does say, "The *ultimate* cause of all spiritual depression is unbelief."[11] For example, where did the kind of parenting come from that sanctions pouting? Did it come from a strong *belief* in the Word of God as the best book on parenting? And why do so many people pursue nighttime activities that guarantee fatigue which leads to despondency and irritability and moral vulnerability? Is it owing to a strong *belief* in God's counsel to get good rest (Psalm 127:2) and a firm *trust* in his power to work for those who wait for him (Isaiah 64:4; Psalm 37:5)?

And could it be that brain research is in such infancy that even though we know a little bit about how chemicals can produce emotional states, we know almost nothing about the ways emotional and spiritual states may produce healing chemicals? Could anyone disprove the possibility that being satisfied with all that God is for us in Jesus has no physical effect on the body's production of natural antidepressants? Why should we not assume that the powerful affection of faith in future grace promotes even physical means of mental health? My own conviction is that when we get to heaven we will learn some astonishing things about the profound connection between sound faith and sound minds.

We may say, therefore, that the roots of despondency are not simple. They are complex. So my focus in this chapter is limited. Without denying the complexity of our emotions and their hereditary and physical and family dimensions, what I want to show is that unbelief in future grace is the root of *yielding* to despondency. Or to put it another way, unbelief is the root of not making war on despondency with the weapons of God. Unbelief lets despondency take its course without a spiritual fight.

Lloyd-Jones said that if we are converted with a bent toward despondency we "will still have to *fight* that after conversion." It's the *fight* we are talking about in this chapter, not the onslaught of melancholy that demands the fight. Let me illustrate this from the Psalms and then from the kind of despondency that Jesus had to deal with.

WHEN THE PSALMIST'S HEART FAILED

In Psalm 73:26 the psalmist says, "My flesh and my heart may fail." Literally the verb is simply, "My flesh and my heart *fail!*" I am despondent! I am discouraged! But then immediately he fires a broadside against his despondency: "But God is the strength of my heart and my portion forever." The psalmist does not yield. He battles unbelief with counterattack.

In essence, he says, "In myself I feel very weak and helpless and unable to cope. My body is shot and my heart is almost dead. But whatever the reason for this despondency, I will not yield. I will trust God and not myself. He is my strength and my portion."

The Bible is replete with instances of saints struggling with sunken spirits. Psalm 19:7 says, "The law of the Lord is perfect, *reviving the soul.*" This is a clear admission that the soul of the saint sometimes needs to be revived. And if it needs to be *revived,* in a sense it was "dead." David says the same thing in Psalm 23:2-3, "He leads me beside quiet waters; *he restores my soul.*" The soul of the "man after [God's] own heart" (1 Samuel 13:14) needs to be restored. It was dying of thirst and ready to fall exhausted, but God led the soul to water and gave it life again.

God has put these testimonies in the Bible so that we might use them to fight the unbelief of despondency. Wherever despondency might come from, Satan paints it with a lie. The lie says, "This is it. You will never be happy again. You will never be strong again. You will never have vigor and determination again. Your life will never again be purposeful. There is no morning after this night. No joy after weeping. All is gathering gloom, darker and darker. This is not a tunnel, it is a cave, an endless cave."

That is the color that Satan paints on our despondency. And God has woven his Word with strands of truth directly opposed to that lie. The law of God *does* revive (Psalm 19:7). God *does* lead to springs of water (Psalm 23:3). God *does* show us the path of life (Psalm 16:11). Joy *does* come with the morning (Psalm 30:5). So the psalms illustrate for us the truth that unbelief is the root of yielding to despondency; but faith in future grace takes the promises of God and throws them against despondency. "God is the strength of my heart and my portion forever!" (Psalm 73:26).

LEARNING TO PREACH TO OURSELVES

We must learn to fight despondency. The fight is a fight of faith in future grace. It is fought by preaching truth to ourselves about God and his promised future. This is what the psalmist does in Psalm 42. "My tears have been my food day and night, While they say to me all day long, 'Where is your God?'...Why are you in despair, O my soul? And why have you become disturbed within me? Hope in God, for I shall again praise Him For the help of His presence'" (Psalm 42:3, 5). The psalmist preaches to his troubled soul. He scolds himself and argues with himself. And his main argument is future grace: *"Hope* in God!—Trust in what God will be for you in the future. A day of praise is coming. The presence of the Lord will be all the help you need. And he has promised to be with us forever" (see Psalm 23:4, 6).

Lloyd-Jones believes this issue of preaching truth to ourselves about God's future grace is all-important in overcoming spiritual depression.

> *I say that we must talk to ourselves instead of allowing "ourselves" to talk to us! Do you realize what that means? I suggest that the main trouble in this whole matter of spiritual depression in a sense is this, that we allow our self to talk to us instead of talking to our self. Am I just trying to be deliberately paradoxical? Have you realized that most of your unhappiness in life is due to the fact that you are listening to yourself instead of talking to yourself? Take those thoughts that come to you the moment you wake up in the morning. You have not originated them, but they start talking to you, they bring back the problems of yesterday, etc. Somebody is talking. Who is talking to you? Your self is talking to you. Now [the psalmist's] treatment was this; instead of allowing this self to talk to him, he starts talking to himself. "Why art thou cast down, O my soul?" he asks. His soul had been depressing him, crushing him. So he stands up and says: "Self, listen for a moment, I will speak to you. . . Why art thou cast down?—what business have you to be disquieted?. . .And then you must go on to remind yourself of God, Who he is, and what God is and what God has done, and what God has pledged Himself to do. Then having done that, end on this great note: defy yourself, and defy other people, and defy the devil and the whole world, and say with this man: "I shall yet praise Him for the help of His countenance."[12]*

The battle against despondency is a battle to believe the promises of God. And that belief in God's future grace comes by hearing the Word. And so preaching to ourselves is at the heart of the battle. But I stress again that the issue in this chapter is not mainly how to avoid meeting despondency, but how to fight it when it comes. If we go to the example of Jesus we will see that even the sinless Son of God met and wrestled with this enemy.

WHEN JESUS MET THE ENEMY OF DESPONDENCY

The night Jesus was betrayed he fought some deep spiritual battles. What was happening that night on the eve of our everlasting redemption was an awful spiritual war. Satan and all his strongest hosts were gathered to fight against the Son of God. And whatever Paul means (in Ephesians 6:16) by the "fiery darts of the evil one" you can be sure they were flying in volleys against the heart of Jesus in Gethsemane that night.

We get a glimpse of the battle in Matthew 26:36-38:

Then Jesus came with them to a place called Gethsemane, and said to His disciples, "Sit here while I go over there and pray." And He took with Him Peter and the two sons of Zebedee, and began to be grieved and distressed. Then He said to them, "My soul is deeply grieved, to the point of death; remain here and keep watch with Me."

What is going on here? What is Jesus distressed about? John 12:27 says, "Now My soul has become *troubled*; and what shall I say, 'Father, save Me from this hour'? But for this purpose I came to this hour.'" In other words, the *distressing, troubling* temptation was to despair and fail to carry out his mission. The flaming darts coming against him were thoughts—thoughts like, "It's not worth it. It won't work." Or perhaps just a volley of hideous distractions. And the effect of these assaults on Jesus was a tremendous emotional upheaval. What Satan wanted to produce in Jesus was a spirit of despondency that would sink, unopposed, in resignation and prompt Jesus not to carry out what his Father had given him to do.

Now think about this for a minute. Jesus was a sinless man (Hebrews 4:15; 2 Corinthians 5:21). This means that the emotional turmoil he was enduring that night was a proper and fitting response to the kind of extraordinary testing he was experiencing. The demonic thought that Calvary would be a meaningless black hole is so horrendous it *ought* to make the soul of Christ shudder. This is the first shockwave of the blast of despondency. But it is not sin. Not yet.

But here is something surprising. The Gospel of John says that Jesus was troubled (John 12:27; 13:21). The first shockwaves of despondency broke the tranquillity of his soul. But in this same Gospel it also says that the disciples should *not* be troubled. In John 14:1 Jesus says, "Let not your hearts be *troubled* (same word as in 12:27 and 13:21); believe in God, believe also in me." And in John 14:27 Jesus says, "Peace I leave with you; my peace I give to you; not as the world gives to you. Let not your hearts be *troubled.*"

In both cases Jesus is dealing with the danger of despondency. The disciples were beginning to feel disheartened and hopeless because their Leader and their Friend was going away. Instead of getting brighter, things were getting darker. In both cases he said, Don't feel troubled and despondent like that.

Now, is this a contradiction? When Satan dangles the thought in front of Jesus and his disciples that their future is hopeless, is it right for Jesus to feel despondent, but not the disciples?

LET NOT YOUR HEARTS BE TROUBLED

I don't think there's a contradiction. Here's how they fit together. Jesus was warning the disciples against *giving in* to despondency, *yielding* to it unopposed. Letting it fester and spread. And so he says, Fight back: Believe God, believe also in me (John 14:1). The first shockwaves of the blast of despondency are not the sin. The sin is in not turning on the air-raid siren, and not heading for the bomb shelters, and not deploying the antiaircraft weapons. If Satan drops a bomb on your peace, and you don't make ready for war, people are going to wonder whose side you're on.

It's just the same with Jesus. The first shockwaves of despondency that he feels because of the assaults of temptation are not sin. But no one knew better than Jesus how quickly they can become sin, if they are not counterattacked immediately. You cannot read Matthew 26:36-39 and come away saying, "Despondency's not so bad, because Jesus had it in Gethsemane and he's sinless." Instead, what you come away with is an impression of how earnestly he fought off the unbelief of despondency. How much more should we!

HOW JESUS FOUGHT IN THE DARK HOUR

There were several tactics in Jesus' strategic battle against despondency. First, *he chose some close friends to be with him.* "He took with Him Peter and the two sons of Zebedee" (Matthew 26:37). Second, *he opened his soul to them.* He said to them, "My soul is deeply grieved, to the point of death" (v. 38). Third, *he asked for their intercession and partnership* in the battle. "Remain here and keep watch with Me" (v. 39). Fourth, *he poured out his heart to his Father in prayer.* "My Father, if it is possible, let this cup pass from Me." (v. 39). Fifth, *he rested his soul in the sovereign wisdom of God.* "Yet not as I will, but as Thou wilt" (v. 39). Sixth, *he fixed his eye on the glorious future grace that awaited him on the other side of the cross.* "For the joy set before Him [He] endured the cross, despising the shame, and has sat down at the right hand of the throne of God" (Hebrews 12:2).

When something drops into your life that seems to threaten your future, remember this: the first shockwaves of the bomb are not sin. The real danger is yielding to them. Giving in. Putting up no spiritual fight. And the root of that surrender is unbelief—a failure to fight for faith in future grace. A failure to cherish all that God promises to be for us in Jesus.

Jesus shows us another way. Not painless, and not passive. Follow him. Find your trusted spiritual friends. Open your soul to them. Ask them to watch with you and pray. Pour out your soul to the Father. Rest in the sovereign wisdom of God. And fix your eyes on the joy set before you in the precious and magnificent promises of God.

DON'T SIT DOWN IN THE DARK

Preach to yourself that even the great apostle Paul was "afflicted in every way, but not crushed; perplexed, but not despairing" (2 Corinthians 4:8); that David discovered in the darkness that "[God's] anger is but for a moment, His favor is for a lifetime; weeping may last for the night, but a shout of joy comes in the morning" (Psalm 30:5). Preach to yourself what David learned in his battle with despair—that even when he says despairingly, "Surely the darkness will overwhelm me, and the light around me will be night," nevertheless there is a greater truth: "Even the darkness is not dark to Thee, and the night is as bright as the day. Darkness and light are alike to Thee" (Psalm 139:11-12).

The final lesson of Gethsemane and Calvary and the book of the Psalms is that all the dark caves of despondency are really tunnels leading to the fields of joy—for those who don't sit down in the dark and blow out the candle of *faith in future grace*.

PART VIII

BATTLING AGAINST
UNBELIEF IN
FUTURE GRACE

The time of my departure has come.
I have fought the good fight,
I have finished the course,
I have kept the faith;
in the future there is laid up for me
the crown of righteousness.

2 TIMOTHY 4:6-8

Was so overwhelmed with dejection that I knew not how to live:
I longed for death exceedingly: My soul was "sunk in deep waters,"
and "the floods" were ready to "drown me":
I was so much oppressed that my soul was in a kind of horror.

DAVID BRAINERD

Fight the good fight of faith.

1 TIMOTHY 6:12

CHAPTER TWENTY-FIVE

The Struggle Is as Easy as Dropping a Nut

A YEARLY REHEARSAL FOR DYING

For me, the end of a year is like the end of my life. The last hours of New Year's Eve are like the ticking away of the final minutes of my time on earth. The 365 days leading to the year's end are like a miniature lifetime. It's like a rehearsal for the real thing. I imagine meeting Christ on New Year's morning, and I ask, Will he look back over this year's life and say, "Well done, good and faithful servant"?

It's a great advantage to have a trial run at my own dying every year. If you come to the end of the rehearsal and find that the year wasn't lived well, you usually have another go at it, with a brand new beginning the next morning. The great thing about rehearsals is that they show you where your weaknesses are. They leave time for you to improve before the opening night.

But to judge the past year—or lifetime—you need a good biblical measuring stick. The one I have used, and the one that carries this book a crucial step forward, is the one Paul used at the end of his life. Second Timothy was probably the last letter he wrote. It has the flavor of finality about it. Near the end he gives Timothy a strong exhortation, "...Endure hardship...fulfill your ministry" (2 Timothy 4:5). Then, to inspire Timothy, he mentions his own endurance to the end and how he measured his life. "The time of my departure has come. I have fought the good fight, I have finished the course, I have kept the faith; in the future there is laid up for me the crown of righteousness" (2 Timothy 4:6-8).

The criterion of success that Paul used to measure his life was whether he had "kept the faith." The criterion applies to us. Will we be able to say at the end of our lives, "I have kept the faith"? Not just, Have I held fast to a body of doctrines. That is not all that Paul meant. But more: have we lived by faith in future grace? Not just for a moment, or a year, or a decade, but all the way to the end?

Paul uses two other phrases to describe keeping the faith: "I have fought the good fight," and, "I have finished the race." These are pictures that Paul uses to show what is involved in keeping the faith. In 1 Timothy 6:12 he says, "Fight the good fight *of faith.*" So we know he sees "fighting the good fight" and "keeping the faith" as the same. It is the "good fight of [keeping the] faith."

These two images—the fight and the race—teach us what is involved in a lifetime of living by faith in future grace. The first thing we can say is that enduring in faith for a lifetime must be hard. There must be some sort of stress and strain and discomfort involved. Boxers get hit in the face; and runners push themselves to the limit of tolerance. And both of them train for long, monotonous hours. Therefore keeping the faith must involve some kind of strenuous effort like this.

THE STRUGGLE IS AS EASY AS DROPPING A NUT

Jesus put it like this: "The gate is wide, and the way is broad that leads to destruction, and many are those who enter by it. For the gate is small, and the way is narrow that leads to life, and few are those who find it" (Matthew 7:13-14). The small gate and the narrow way imply that the way to life is not easy. This is why Jesus said, "Strive to enter by the narrow door" (Luke 13:24). The word "strive" is *agōnizomai* and means "struggle," or "contend for victory like an athlete."

Both Paul and Jesus speak of keeping the faith as a rigorous struggle like running a marathon and boxing with fists. How can this square with other images of the Christian life, like the following one from Matthew 11:28-30, where Jesus says,

> Come to Me, all who are weary and heavy-laden, and I will give you rest. Take My yoke upon you, and learn from Me, for I am gentle and humble in heart; and you shall find rest for your souls. For My yoke is easy, and My load is light.

Here the life of faith in future grace is pictured as a light burden and an easy yoke. Can it be both hard and easy?

Yes. Faith in future grace is intrinsically easy. What could be easier than trusting God to work for you (Isaiah 64:4), and take care of you (1 Peter 5:7), and give you all you need (Philippians 4:19; Hebrews 13:6), and strengthen you for every challenge (Isaiah 41:10). In one sense, faith is the opposite of straining. It is ceasing from the effort to earn God's approval or demonstrate your worth or merit. It is resting in the gracious promises of God to pursue us with goodness and mercy all our days. Faith is intrinsically easy.

But this ease of faith assumes that our hearts are humble enough to renounce all self-reliance and self-direction and self-exaltation. It assumes a heart that is spiritual enough to taste and delight in the beauty and worth of God. It assumes that the world and the devil have lost their power to lure us away from satisfaction in God. If these assumptions are not true, then living by faith in future grace will not be as easy as we might have thought, but will involve a lifetime of struggle.

It's like the monkey with his hand caught in the jar. It would be easy for him to slip his hand out of the opening except that he has his fist clenched around a nut. If he loves the nut more than he loves freedom from the jar, then getting his hand out of the jar will be hard, even impossible (as Jesus said in Mark 10:27 about the young man who had his fist clenched around his wealth). But what could be easier than dropping a nut? The battle that Paul and Jesus are talking about is the battle to love the freedom of faith more than the nut of sin.

So the first thing we can say about a lifetime of keeping the faith is that it is like a race and a fight. It involves relentless warfare and vigilance.

FAITH IN FUTURE GRACE FINISHES THE COURSE

The second thing we can say is that we must endure to the end in faith. The crown of righteousness is given to the saint who "finishes the course." You can run for five miles or ten miles or fifteen miles in a marathon; but if you don't go the full 26 miles and 385 yards, you don't get the crown.

The necessity to continue in faith to the end is taught in many places in the New Testament. One of the clearest is Colossians 1:22-23, "[God will] present you before Him holy and blameless and beyond reproach—*if indeed you continue in the faith* firmly established and steadfast, and not moved away from the hope of the gospel." We must fight the fight and "keep the faith" to the end. Paul says that the gospel saves you *"if you hold fast the word* which I preached to you, unless you believed in vain" (1 Corinthians 15:2).

Jesus said, "The one who *endures* to the end, he shall be saved" (Matthew 24:13). The race must be run to the end. Again, in the Revelation, Jesus said to the suffering church, "Do not fear what you are about to suffer...*Be faithful until death,* and I will give you the crown of life" (Revelation 2:10). All the way to the finish line, and you will receive the crown.

A CALL FOR ENDURANCE

The writer to the Hebrews stressed this message of endurance more than anyone. It was he who said, "We have become partakers of Christ, *if we hold fast the beginning of our assurance firm until the end"* (Hebrews 3:14). And: "We desire that each one of you show the same diligence so as to realize *the full assurance of hope until the end"* (Hebrews 6:11). And: "Do not throw away your confidence, which has great reward. For you have need of *endurance,* so that when you have done the will of God, you may receive what is promised" (Hebrews 10:35-36). Keeping the faith is a lifelong battle. It calls for relentless vigilance. *"If we endure,* we shall also reign with Him" (2 Timothy 2:12).

THE DANGER OF NOT KNOWING THE KIND OF BATTLE IT IS

Sometimes it is hard for us to accept that a lifetime of vigilance and running and fighting is compatible with the joy and peace that the New Testament says we can enjoy here and now. I have known people who gave up on Christianity because they felt as if they were always swimming upstream. They felt like every day was a battle. My response to them depends on what I see going on inside of them.

It may be that they are not truly born of God and do not have the Spirit working in them. Then, indeed, they would be swimming in their own strength, trying to look like a Christian when they have no new heart and no power inside. In that case they need to stop the charade and let their hearts be broken and cleansed of self-reliance. They need to seek the Lord's face and look to him for the refreshing beauty and power that he offers to those who cherish him and rely on his future grace. In short, they need to find in God himself the all-satisfying treasure of their lives and turn away from the futile striving of the unsatisfied flesh.

But there is another possible explanation for why a person might grow weary of the battle and consider giving up on Christianity. They might be poorly taught about what the Christian life really is. They might think that things are going wrong, when they are going right. They might think that they are losing, when they are in fact winning. They may not know the biblical categories for understanding what God is really doing in their lives.

Theologian J. I. Packer tells the story of his early days as a young Christian, and how he was not at first well-taught about the struggle with sin in the Christian life. I've heard him tell the story of the crisis he came into soon after his conversion. He was in danger in his student days of despairing under a perfectionistic teaching that did not take indwelling sin seriously. The discovery of John Owen's balanced biblical teaching on the battle with sin brought him back to reality; and, in a real sense, saved his life. "Suffice it to say," Packer recalls, "that without Owen I might well have gone off my head or got bogged down in mystical fanaticism."[1]

THE FIGHT IS A FIGHT FOR JOY

In order to keep the fight and the marathon in proper perspective we need to remember several things. First, we need to keep in mind that it is not at odds with joy; it is a battle to maintain joy. The question is not: How can fighting be compatible with joy? The question is: Since the joy is so precious, what strategies of fighting will protect and preserve it amid all life's adversities?

Often the Christian must cry out with David, "Restore to me the joy of Thy salvation, and sustain me with a willing spirit" (Psalm 51:12). Often we must say with Psalm 23, "He restores my soul" (v. 3). If there were no fight for joy, there would be no need for the *re*-storing of our soul and our joy.

We have seen in Chapters Fifteen and Sixteen that at the heart of saving faith is a delight in who God is and a satisfaction in all that God is for us in Jesus. This means that "the good fight of faith" (1 Timothy 6:12) is at its root a fight for delight. It's a fight to maintain satisfaction in God against all the enticements of the world and all the deceptions of the devil. The fight for faith in future grace is a fight for joy. Knowing this will help us understand what is happening to us when the temptations come. Diminishing delight is a summons to war.

THE GREATEST HAVE STRUGGLED MOST

A second thing to keep in mind is that the greatest Christians have all fought this fight with us and some of them are still fighting it for us. David Brainerd, the young missionary to the American Indians from 250 years ago, struggled painfully and valiantly with the loss of joy. His journal is still encouraging people today.

> *Sunday, December 16, 1744. "Was so overwhelmed with dejection that I knew not how to live: I longed for death exceedingly: My soul was 'sunk in deep waters,' and 'the floods' were ready to 'drown me': I was so much oppressed that my soul was in a kind of horror."*[2]

But he never stopped fighting the fight. And again and again the joy was restored for his short life of 29 years.

> *April 17, 1747. "O I longed to fill the remaining moments all for God! Though my body was so feeble, and wearied with preaching and much private conversation, yet I wanted to sit up all night to do something for God. To God the giver of these refreshments, be glory forever and ever;*

Amen."³ February 21, 1746. "My soul was refreshed and comforted, and I could not but bless God, who had enabled me in some good measure to be faithful in the day past. Oh, how sweet it is to be spent and worn out for God!"⁴

"WORKERS WITH YOU FOR YOUR JOY"

The apostle Paul saw his whole ministry as a calling to help Christians fight for the joy of faith. In Philippians 1:25 he ponders whether he will live or die. He concludes, "I know that I shall abide and continue with you all *for your furtherance and joy of faith*" (KJV). And to the Corinthians he wrote, "Not that we lord it over your faith, but are *workers with you for your joy*" (2 Corinthians 1:24). His ministry then and now—through his writings—was a camaraderie in combat for the sake of our joy.

THE VICTORY IS ASSURED

One final thing to remember about the good fight of faith in future grace: the victory is assured. Our assurance is not destroyed by the demands for endurance. The key to assurance is not to eliminate the biblical commands for endurance, but rather to magnify grace as a future power to believe, as well as a past pardon for sin. Our assurance does not lie in looking back to a momentary decision we made for Christ, but in looking forward to the certainty of God's preserving grace, based on the all-sufficient atonement of his Son's death.

Jesus is still praying for us today (Romans 8:34) the way he did for Peter on earth. "Simon, Simon, behold, Satan has demanded permission to sift you like wheat; but *I have prayed for you that your faith may not fail*; and you, when once you have turned again, strengthen your brothers" (Luke 22:31-32). Though Peter failed miserably, the prayer of Jesus preserved him from utter ruin. He was brought to bitter weeping and restored to the joy and boldness of Pentecost. So Jesus is interceding for us today that our faith in future grace might not fail.

Jesus promised that his sheep would be preserved and never perish. "My sheep hear My voice, and I know them, and they follow Me; and I give eternal life to them, and they shall never perish, and no one shall snatch them out of My hand" (John 10:27-28). The reason for this is that God will work to preserve the faith of the sheep. "He who began a good work in you will perfect it until the day of Jesus Christ" (Philippians 1:6). We are not left to ourselves to fight the fight of faith. "It is God who is at work in you, both to will and to work for His good pleasure" (Philippians 2:13).

You have the assurance of God's Word that, if you are his child, he will "equip you in every good thing to do His will, working in us that which is pleasing in His sight, through Jesus Christ" (Hebrews 13:21). Our endurance in faith and joy is finally and decisively in the hands of God. Yes, we *must* fight. But this very fight is what God "works in us." And he most certainly will do it, for "whom He justified, these He also glorified" (Romans 8:30). He will lose none of those he has brought to faith and justified. "[He] shall also confirm you to the end, blameless in the day of our Lord Jesus Christ. God is faithful, by Whom you were called" (1 Corinthians 1:8-9). Our future is as secure as the faithfulness of God. "Faithful is He Who calls you, and He will bring it to pass" (1 Thessalonians 5:24).

With this assurance, we may turn now, in the next chapter, to a more specific focus on our living enemy in this fight, the devil. It is true, as Martin Luther says, "His doom is sure" and "One little word will fell him," but the fight is not a charade. We are not playing war games. The guns are loaded. The stakes are high. And our only hope is to live and fight not by our own strength, but by, and for, faith in future grace.

Simon, Simon, behold, Satan has demanded permission
to sift you like wheat,
but I have prayed for you that your faith may not fail.

LUKE 22:31-32

When I could endure it no longer,
I also sent to find out about your faith,
for fear that the tempter might have tempted you,
and our labor should be in vain.

1 THESSALONIANS 3:5

Your adversary, the devil, prowls about like a roaring lion,
seeking someone to devour.
But resist him, firm in your faith.

1 PETER 5:8-9

CHAPTER TWENTY-SIX

Sin Is Worse Than Satan

TWO GREAT ENEMIES OF OUR SOUL

The two great enemies of our soul are sin and Satan. And sin is the worst enemy, because the only way that Satan can destroy us is by getting us to sin. God may give him leash enough to rough us up, the way he did Job, or even to kill us, the way he did the saints in Smyrna (Revelation 2:10); but Satan cannot condemn us or rob us of eternal life. The only way he can do us ultimate harm is by influencing us to sin.

Which is exactly what he aims to do. All his other shenanigans—like sickness and lost visas and spooky sounds and green apparitions and various intimidations—all these things cannot do us ultimate harm, unless they lead us to sin. So Satan's main business is to advocate, promote, assist, titillate and confirm our bent to sinning. We see this in Ephesians 2:1-2. Paul says, "You were dead in your trespasses and sins, from NASB, in which you formerly walked. . .*according* to the prince of the power of the air." Sinning "accords" with Satan's power in the world. When he brings about moral evil, it is through sin. When we sin, we move in his sphere, and come into accord with him. When we sin, we "give place to the devil" (Ephesians 4:27, KJV).

The only thing that will condemn us at the judgment day is unforgiven sin—not sickness or afflictions or persecutions or intimidations or apparitions or nightmares. Satan knows this. Therefore his great focus is not primarily on how to scare Christians with weird phenomena (though there's plenty of that), but on how to corrupt Christians with worthless fads and evil thoughts.

WHAT SATAN KNOWS ABOUT THE SPRING OF SIN

But Satan also knows something else—far better, I think, than many Christians know it—namely, that all sin comes from failing to live by faith in future grace (see Romans 14:23). Which means that the number one aim of Satan is the destruction of faith. Faith in future grace is the spring of radical righteousness. It's the root of love and all Christ-exalting living. And its absence is the root of all sin. Satan knows this. Therefore he aims all his efforts, one way or the other, at the prevention or destruction of faith in future grace.

SATAN'S JAGGED SIEVE

You can see this in the way Jesus prayed for Simon Peter just before Peter's great temptation. He said, "Simon, Simon, behold, Satan has demanded permission to sift you like wheat; but I have prayed for you, that your faith may not fail; and you, when once you have turned again, strengthen your brothers" (Luke 22:31-32). Satan's aim was to sift Simon Peter. What does that mean? Jesus gives us the clue by saying, "I have prayed *that your faith not fail.*" This must mean that what Satan wanted to do was to sift the faith out of Peter. Satan has a sieve with a jagged mesh designed to sift the faith out of Christians. That's his main goal.

Paul implies the same thing in 1 Thessalonians 3:5. He is concerned about the new church he had just started in Thessalonica. So he sends Timothy to see how they are doing. Timothy comes back with a good report, and Paul writes this letter to explain what his deepest concern really was: "When I could endure it no longer, I also sent to find out *about your faith,* for fear that *the tempter* might have tempted you, and our labor should be in vain." Paul's greatest concern was that Satan would have attacked their faith and ruined the work he had begun.

Similarly, when Peter writes to the churches of Asia Minor, he warns that Satan is always prowling around trying to "devour someone." Then Peter adds, "Resist him, firm in your faith" (1 Peter 5:9). This implies that Satan wants to catch us at a time when our faith is not firm, when it is vulnerable. It makes sense that the very thing Satan wants to destroy would also be the means of our resisting his efforts. That's why Peter says, "Resist him, firm *in your faith.*" It is also why Paul says that the "shield of *faith*" can "extinguish all the flaming missiles of the evil one" (Ephesians 6:16). The way to thwart the devil is to strengthen the very thing he is trying most to destroy.

WITHOUT FAITH IN FUTURE GRACE WE WILL ONLY SIN

All true virtue comes from faith in future grace; and all sin comes from lack of faith in future grace. That is one of the reasons for writing this book. I've devoted a lot of space so far to the claim that faith works through love— that faith in future grace is the spring of all true obedience and holiness and love. But I have not said as much about the flip side of this truth—that failing to have faith in future grace, that is, failing to be satisfied with all that God is for us in Jesus, is the root of all sin. Satan knows this; and it shapes his whole strategy of how to get people to sin.

It's important that we see this as clearly as he does, so that it can affect our counter-strategy. All the sinful states of our hearts are owing to unbelief in God's super-abounding future grace. All our sin comes from failing to be satisfied with all that God is for us in Jesus. Misplaced shame, anxiety, despondency, covetousness, lust, bitterness, impatience, pride—these are all sprouts from the root of unbelief in the promises of God. Let me illustrate from a familiar text that seems to trace all sin back to a surprising source, the love of money.

THE HEART THAT LOVES MONEY

Paul said in 1 Timothy 6:10, "The love of money is the *root of all evils*" (literal translation). What did he mean? He couldn't have meant that money is always in your mind when you sin. A lot of sin happens when we are not thinking about money. My suggestion is this: he meant that all the evils in the world come from a certain kind of heart, namely, the kind of heart that loves money.

Now what does it mean to love money? It doesn't mean to admire the green paper or the copper coins or the silver shekels. To know what it means to love money, you have to ask, What is money? I would answer that question like this: Money is simply a symbol that stands for human resources. Money stands for what you can get from man instead of God. God deals in the currency of grace, not money: "Ho! Everyone who thirsts, come to the waters; and you who have *no money* come buy and eat!" (Isaiah 55:1). Money is the currency of *human* resources.

So the heart that loves money is a heart that pins its hopes, and pursues its pleasures, and puts its trust in what human resources can offer. So the *love* of money is virtually the same as *faith* in money—belief (trust, confidence, assurance) that money will meet your needs and make you happy. Love of money is the alternative to faith in future grace. It is faith in future human resources. Therefore the love of money, or trust in money, is the underside of unbelief in the promises of God. Jesus said in Matthew 6:24, "No one can serve two masters...You cannot serve God and mammon." You can't trust in God and in money at the same time. Belief in one is unbelief in the other. A heart that loves money—banks on money for happiness—is not banking on the future grace of God for satisfaction.

WHATEVER IS NOT FROM FAITH IS SIN

So when Paul says that the love of money is the root of all evils, he implies that unbelief in the promises of God is the taproot of every sinful attitude in our heart. He said it even more plainly in Romans 14:23, "whatever is not from faith is sin." The absence of faith gives rise only to sinful motives and acts. This may sound extreme. But it is simply a clear expression of Paul's radical God-centeredness. What does not come *from* satisfaction in God, and *through* the guidance of God, and *for* the glory of God, is God-less—it is sin. And no matter how philanthropic or esteemed or costly it may appear among men, it is deficient in the main thing: love for the glory of God.

There are numerous pointers in the Bible that putting our trust in anything but God causes sin. For example, there seems to be a connection between trusting money and the enticement into sin in Job's defense of his integrity: "If I have put my *confidence in gold*, and *called fine gold my trust*...and my heart became secretly enticed, and my hand threw a kiss from my mouth, that too would have been an iniquity calling for judgment, for I would have denied God above" (Job 31:24, 27-28). Confidence in gold and trust in fine gold leads to denying God and committing sin. Similarly, when the Proverb says, "He who *trusts in his riches* will fall" (Proverbs 11:28), it probably means that he will come to ruin through a life of sin.

Isaiah warns those who trust in human military resources that this false trust will lead to evil and sin, and eventually to destruction. "Woe to those who go down to Egypt for help, and *rely on horses*, and *trust in chariots*... But they do not look to the Holy One of Israel, nor seek the Lord!" (Isaiah 31:1). Then he describes the Lord's judgment in response to this reliance on human resources and rejection of future grace. Surprisingly he says that the judgment is upon evil and iniquity—the outcroppings of faith in human fortune. "[God] will arise against the house of *evildoers*, and against the help of the *workers of iniquity*" (Isaiah 32:2). The point is that unbelief in the future grace of God produced "evildoers" and "workers of iniquity" (see Hosea 10:13-14).

TRUSTING THE GIFT OF GOODNESS, NOT THE GIVER

One of the saddest instances of false hope occurs when people trust in what God has worked in them instead of trusting God himself. For example, God says, "When I say to the righteous he will surely live, and he *so trusts in his righteousness that he commits iniquity*, none of his righteous deeds will be remembered" (Ezekiel 33:13). It is possible to trust in your own goodness in such a way that it produces iniquity. Any trust, except in God, brings about sin. "You *trusted in your beauty* and played the harlot because of your fame" (Ezekiel 16:15). God had made Israel beautiful. But when she became satisfied with her beauty, instead of her Beautifier, the result was harlotries.

THE POWER OF SATAN IS THE POWER OF DECEIT

The point I am pressing is the one that Satan knows and uses: where faith in God fails, sin follows. For Satan, this means that the focus of his work is the subversion of faith. This fits with his fundamental character. Jesus said, "Whenever [Satan] speaks a lie, he speaks from his own nature; for he is a liar and the father of lies" (John 8:44). This is his primary means of subverting faith. Faith stands or falls on the truth that the future with God is more satisfying than the one promised by sin. Where this truth is embraced and God is cherished above all, the power of sin is broken. The power of sin is the power of deceit. Sin has power through promising a false future. In temptation sin comes to us and says: "The future with God on his narrow way is hard and unhappy; but the way I promise is pleasant and satisfying." The power of sin is in the power of this lie.

Satan's main strategy is to use a thousand devious ways to make this lie look appealing and persuasive. The beginning of all our misery came from Satan's first great success on the earth. It was not by means of scaring or harassing or possessing Adam and Eve. It was by deceiving them. And the deception was just this: God cannot be trusted to meet your needs and satisfy you. The serpent says only two things. One is a question that suggests God is stingy, "Has God said, 'You shall not eat from any tree of the garden?'" The other utterance is a murderous half-truth, "You surely shall not die!" (Genesis 3:1, 4).

In his penetrating study of the Pentateuch John Sailhamer sums up the scene like this:

> The snake speaks only twice, but that is enough to offset the balance of trust and obedience between the man and the woman and their Creator. The centerpiece of the story is the question of the knowledge of the "good." The snake implied by his questions that God was keeping this knowledge from the man and the woman (3:5), while the sense of the narratives in the first two chapters has been that God was keeping this knowledge for the man and the woman (e.g. 1:4, 10, 12, 18, 21, 25, 31; 2:18). In other words, the snake's statements were a direct challenge to the central theme of the narrative of chapters 1 and 2; God will provide

the "good" for human beings if they will only trust him and obey him.[1]

Satan began by calling God's goodness into question and that has been his primary strategy ever since. His aim is to subvert trust by influencing us to believe that the promise of sin is more satisfying than the promise of God.

PROMISE AGAINST PROMISE

The only actions Satan really cares about are future actions. The sins of the past are gone. He cannot change them. He can only deepen them, by influencing our future responses to them, or add to them, with more future sins. All the sins that can be committed are future sins. If Satan is going to bring us into sinful states of mind and into sinful actions, he will have to use promises. This is what he did with Adam and Eve. This is what he does with us. He holds out alternative promises to the promises of God. He subverts faith in future grace with promises of God-neglecting pleasure.

To do this he must blind the mind of unbelievers and distort the spiritual perception of believers. "The god of this world has blinded the minds of the unbelieving, that they might not see the light of the gospel of the glory of Christ, who is the image of God" (2 Corinthians 4:4). Satan's only hope of success is to hide the truth and beauty of Christ from the mind of man. It is the glory of Christ that compels the heart to embrace him in the promises of future grace. Satan makes every effort to obscure this compelling glory, so that we will *not* be satisfied with all that God is for us in Jesus.

What this means for living by faith in future grace is not only that it is a lifelong battle, but that it is specifically a battle *against sin* (which is the only condemning instrument Satan has), and a battle *for faith* (which Satan wants most to destroy).

In our day, and probably in every age before us, one of the most relentless temptations of Satan is lust. There is a deep interweaving of influences between our own thoughts and desires on the one hand and the insinuations of Satan's power on the other (Ephesians 2:2-3). In the next chapter we will consider the superior power of faith in future grace over the seemingly overwhelming power of sexual temptation.

He breaks the power of canceled sin.
He sets the prisoner free.

CHARLES WESLEY

If by the Spirit
you are putting to death the deeds of the body,
you will live.

ROMANS 8:13

He has granted to us His precious and magnificent promises,
in order that by them you might become partakers of the divine nature,
having escaped the corruption that is in the world by lust.

2 PETER 1:4

Applying the Purifying Power

Faith in Future Grace
vs.
Lust

WOULD YOU CUT OFF YOUR OWN LEG?

On July 20, 1993, Donald Wyman was clearing land near Punxsutawney, Pennsylvania, as part of his work for a mining company. In the process, a tree rolled onto his shin causing a severe break and pinning Wyman to the ground. He cried for help for an hour, but no one came. He concluded that the only way to save his life would be to cut off his leg. So he made a tourniquet out of his shoe string and tightened it with a wrench. Then he took his pocket knife and cut through the skin, muscle, and bone just below the knee and freed himself from the tree. He crawled thirty yards to a bulldozer, drove a quarter-mile to his truck, then maneuvered the standard transmission with his good leg and a hand until he reached a farmer's house one-and-a-half miles away, with his leg bleeding profusely. Farmer John Huber Jr. helped him get to a hospital where his life was spared.[1]

Jesus knew that humans love to live. So he appealed to this passion in order to show the importance of purity. Just as Donald Wyman cut off his leg to save his life, Jesus commanded that we gouge out our eye to escape the fatal effect of lust. "Everyone who looks on a woman to lust for her has committed adultery with her already in his heart. And if your right eye makes you stumble, tear it out, and throw it from you; for it is better for you that one of the parts of your body perish, than for your whole body to be thrown into hell" (Matthew 5:28-29). Of course, if you gouge out your "right eye," as Jesus says, you can still see the magazine with your left eye. So Jesus must have something even more radical in mind than literal mutilation.

PONDER THE DANGER OF LUST

A few years ago I spoke to a high school student body on how to fight lust. One of my points was called, "Ponder the eternal danger of lust." I quoted the words of Jesus—that it's better to go to heaven with one eye than to hell with two—and said to the students that their eternal destiny was at stake in what they did with their eyes and with the thoughts of their imagination.

I tried to counteract the prevalent notion that personal, sexual morality, including the life of the mind, is of minor moral significance. Idealistic students (and adults) often think that what they do with their bodies and their minds, on the personal level, is no big deal. If it's sin at all, it's sin with a little "s". "Shouldn't we just get on with the big issues like international peace, and global environmental strategies, and racial reconciliation, and social justice, and health-care initiatives, and the elimination of violence? Sleeping around is simply no big deal, if you are on the picket line for justice; and flipping through *Playboy* is utterly insignificant if you are on your way to peace talks in Geneva.

I stressed that Jesus sees things very differently. Those global issues are important. But the reason they are is because they all have to do with people—not just statistical aggregates, but real individual people. And the most important thing about people is that, unlike animals and trees, they live forever in heaven glorifying God, or in hell defying God. People are not important because they breathe. They're important because they have the capacity to honor God with their hearts and minds and bodies long after they stop breathing—forever.

What Jesus is saying, therefore, is that the consequences of lust are going to be worse than the consequences of war or environmental catastrophe. The ultimate scourge of war is that it can kill the body. But Jesus said, "do not be afraid of those who kill the body, and after that have no more that they can do. But I will warn you whom to fear: fear the One who after He has killed has authority to cast into hell; yes, I tell you, fear Him!" (Luke 12:4-5). In other words, God's final judgment is much more fearful than earthly annihilation.

LUST AND ETERNAL SECURITY

After my message in the high school auditorium, one of the students came up to me and asked, "Are you saying then that a person can lose his salvation?" In other words, If Jesus used the threat of hell to warn about the seriousness of lust, does that mean that a Christian can perish?

This is exactly the same response I got a few years ago when I confronted a man about the adultery he was living in. I tried to understand his situation and I pled with him to return to his wife. Then I said, "You know, Jesus says that if you don't fight this sin with the kind of seriousness that is willing to gouge out your own eye, you will go to hell and suffer there forever." As a professing Christian he looked at me in utter disbelief, as though he had never heard anything like this in his life, and said, "You mean you think a person can lose his salvation?"

So I have learned again and again from firsthand experience that there are many professing Christians who have a view of salvation that disconnects it from real life, and that nullifies the threats of the Bible, and puts the sinning person who claims to be a Christian beyond the reach of biblical warnings. I believe this view of the Christian life is comforting thousands who are on the broad way that leads to destruction (Matthew 7:13). Jesus said, if you don't fight lust, you won't go to heaven. Not that saints always succeed. The issue is that we resolve to fight, not that we succeed flawlessly.

The stakes are much higher than whether the world is blown up by a thousand bombs, or the ozone layer is depleted, or AIDS sweeps the nations. All these calamities can kill only the body. But if we don't fight lust we lose our soul. The apostle Peter said, "Abstain from fleshly lusts that *wage war against the soul* (1 Peter 2:11)." The stakes in *this* war are infinitely higher than in any threat of World War III. The apostle Paul listed "immorality, impurity, passion, evil desire, and greed," then said, "it is on account of *these* things that the wrath of God will come" (Colossians 3:6). And the wrath of God is immeasurably more fearful than the wrath of all the nations put together. In Galatians 5:19 Paul mentions immorality, impurity and sensuality and says, "Those who practice such things shall not inherit the kingdom of God" (Galatians 5:21).

JUSTIFYING FAITH IS LUST-FIGHTING FAITH

What then is the answer to this student and this man living in adultery? The answer has been given before in this book: we are justified by grace alone through faith alone (Romans 3:28; 4:5; 5:1; Ephesians 2:8f); and all those who are thus justified will be glorified (Romans 8:30)—that is, no justified person will ever be lost. Nevertheless those who give themselves up to impurity *will* be lost (Galatians 5:21), and those who forsake the fight against lust will perish (Matthew 5:30), and those who do not pursue holiness will not see the Lord (Hebrews 12:14), and those who surrender their lives to evil desires will succumb to the wrath of God (Colossians 3:6).

The reason these two groups of texts are not contradictory is that the faith that justifies is a faith that also sanctifies. And the test of whether our faith is the kind of faith that justifies is whether it is the kind of faith that sanctifies. Robert L. Dabney, the nineteenth century southern Presbyterian theologian, expressed it like this: "Is it by the instrumentality of faith we receive Christ as our justification, without the merit of any of our works? Well. But this same faith, if vital enough to embrace Christ, is also vital enough to 'work by love,' 'to purify our hearts.' This then is the virtue of the free gospel, as a ministry of sanctification, that the very faith which embraces the gift becomes an inevitable and a divinely powerful principle of obedience."[2]

Faith delivers from hell, and the faith that delivers from hell delivers from lust. Again I do not mean that our faith produces a *perfect flawlessness* in this life. I mean that it produces a *persevering fight*. The evidence of justifying faith is that it fights lust. Jesus didn't say that lust would entirely vanish. He said that the evidence of being heaven-bound is that we gouge out our eye rather than settle for a pattern of lust.

The main concern of this book is to show that the battle against sin is a battle against unbelief. Or: the fight for purity is a fight for faith in future grace. The great error that I am trying to explode is the error that says, "Faith in God is one thing and the fight for holiness is another thing. You get your justification by faith, and you get your sanctification by works. You start the Christian life in the power of the Spirit, you press on in the efforts of the flesh. The battle for obedience is optional because only faith is necessary for final salvation." Faith alone is necessary for justification, but the purity that confirms faith's reality is also necessary for *final* salvation. (See Chapters Eighteen-Twenty.)

FAITH IN FUTURE GRACE BREAKS THE POWER OF CANCELED SIN

The battle for obedience is absolutely necessary for our final salvation, because the battle for obedience **is** the fight of faith. The battle against lust is absolutely necessary for our final salvation, because that battle **is** the battle against unbelief. I hope you can see that this is a greater gospel than the other one. It's the gospel of God's *victory* over sin, not just his *tolerance* of sin. It is the gospel of Romans 6:14: "Sin shall not be master over you, for you are not under law but under grace." Almighty grace! Sovereign grace! The kind of grace that is the future power of God to defeat the temptations of lust.

> *He breaks the* power *of canceled sin,*
> *He sets the prisoner free;*
> *His blood can make the foulest clean,*
> *His blood availed for me.*

Charles Wesley's hymn ("O, For a Thousand Tongues to Sing!") is right: the blood of Christ obtained for us not only the cancellation of sin, but also the conquering of sin. This is the grace we live under—the sin-conquering, not just sin-canceling, grace of God. Triumph over the sin of lust is all of grace—past grace, canceling lust's guilt through the cross, and future grace, conquering lust's power through the Spirit. That's why the only fight we fight is the fight of faith. We fight to be so satisfied with all that God is for us in Jesus that temptation to sin loses its power over us.

HOW DO YOU PUT LUST TO DEATH?

One of the ways that Paul talks about this battle is to say, "If by the Spirit you are putting to death the deeds of the body, you will live" (Romans 8:13). This is close to Jesus' teaching that if we are willing to gouge out our eye rather than lust we will enter into life (Matthew 18:9). Paul agrees that eternal life is at stake in the battle against sin: "If you are living according to the flesh, you must die; but if by the Spirit you are putting to death the deeds of the body, you will live" (Romans 8:13). The fight against lust is mortal combat.

How then do we obey Romans 8:13—to put to death the deeds of the body, to kill lust? We have answered, "By faith in future grace." But practically, what does that involve?

Suppose I am tempted to lust. Some sexual image comes into my mind and beckons me to pursue it. The way this temptation gets its power is by persuading me to believe that I will be happier if I follow it. The power of all temptation is the prospect that it will make me happier. No one sins out of a sense of duty, when what they really want is to do what's right.

So what should I do? Some people would say, "Remember God's command to be holy (1 Peter 1:16), and exercise your will to obey because he is God!" But something crucial is missing from this advice, namely, faith in future grace. A lot of people strive for moral improvement who cannot say, "The life I live I live *by faith*" (Galatians 2:20). They strive for the purity of love but don't realize that such love is the fruit of faith in future grace: "In Christ Jesus neither circumcision nor uncircumcision means anything, but *faith working through love*" (Galatians 5:6).

How then do you fight lust by faith in future grace? When the temptation to lust comes, Romans 8:13 says, in effect, "If you kill it *by the Spirit, you will live.*" By the Spirit! What does that mean? Out of all the armor God gives us to fight Satan, only one piece is used for killing—the sword. It is called the *sword of the Spirit* (Ephesians 6:17). So when Paul says, "Kill sin by the Spirit," I take that to mean, Depend on the Spirit, especially his sword.

What is the sword of the Spirit? It's the Word of God (Ephesians 6:17). Here's where faith comes in. "Faith comes from hearing and hearing by the Word of Christ" (Romans 10:17). The Word of God cuts through the fog of Satan's lies and shows me where true and lasting happiness is to be found. And so the Word helps me stop trusting in the potential of sin to make me happy. Instead the Word entices me to trust in God's promises.

When faith has the upper hand in my heart I am satisfied with Christ and his promises. This is what Jesus meant when he said, "He who *believes* in Me shall *never thirst*" (John 6:35). When my thirst for joy and meaning and passion are satisfied by the presence and promises of Christ, the power of sin is broken. We do not yield to the offer of sandwich meat when we can smell the steak sizzling on the grill.

The fight of faith against lust is the fight to stay satisfied with God. "By faith Moses...[forsook] the fleeting pleasures of sin...he looked to the reward" (Hebrews 11:24-26, RSV). Faith is not content with "fleeting pleasures." It is ravenous for joy. And the Word of God says, "In Thy presence is fulness of joy; in Thy right hand there are pleasures forever" (Psalm 16:11). So faith will not be sidetracked into sin. It will not give up so easily in its quest for maximum joy.

The role of God's Word is to feed faith's appetite for God. And, in doing this, it weans my heart away from the deceptive taste of lust. At first, lust begins to trick me into feeling that I would really miss out on some great satisfaction if I followed the path of purity. But then I take up the sword of the Spirit and begin to fight. I read that it is better to gouge out my eye than to lust. I read that if I think about things that are pure and lovely and excellent, the peace of God will be with me (Philippians 4:8f). I read that setting the mind on the flesh brings death, but setting the mind on the Spirit brings life and peace (Romans 8:6). I read that lust wages war against my soul (1 Peter 2:11), and that the pleasures of this life choke out the life of the Spirit (Luke 8:14). But best of all, I read that God withholds no good thing from those who walk uprightly (Psalm 84:11), and that the pure in heart will see God (Matthew 5:8).

As I pray for my faith to be satisfied with God's life and peace, the sword of the Spirit carves the sugar coating off the poison of lust. I see it for what it is. And by the grace of God, its alluring power is broken. I wield the sword of the Spirit against the sin of lust by believing the promise of God more than I believe in the promise of lust. My faith is not just a backward-looking belief in the death of Jesus, but a forward-looking belief in the promises of Jesus. It's not just being sure of what he did do, but also being satisfied with what he will do.

It is this superior satisfaction in future grace that breaks the power of lust. With all eternity hanging in the balance, we fight the fight of faith. Our chief enemy is the lie that says *sin* will make our future happier. Our chief weapon is the Truth that says *God* will make our future happier. And faith is the victory that overcomes the lie, because faith is satisfied with God.

FIGHTING FIRE WITH FIRE

I have often told young people that they must fight fire with fire. The fire of lust's pleasures must be fought with the fire of God's pleasures. If we try to fight the fire of lust with prohibitions and threats alone—even the terrible warnings of Jesus—we will fail. We must fight it with a massive promise of superior happiness. We must swallow up the little flicker of lust's pleasure in the conflagration of holy satisfaction. When we "make a covenant with our eyes," like Job did (Job 31:1), our aim is not merely to avoid something erotic, but also to gain something excellent.

Peter described this powerful liberating process in 2 Peter 1:3-4. He said,

> [God's] divine power has granted to us everything pertaining to life and godliness, through the true knowledge of Him who called us by His own glory and excellence. For by these He has granted to us His precious and magnificent promises, in order that by them you might become partakers of the divine nature, having escaped the corruption that is in the world by lust.

How do we escape from the corruption that comes from lust? The answer is that God has given us a revelation of his "glory and excellence" expressed in "precious and magnificent promises." These have been given to us for this very purpose: that "by them" we might share God's character and be freed from the corruption of lust. The key is the power of promises. When we are entranced by the *preciousness* of them and the *magnificence* of them, the effect is liberation from the lusts, which are, in fact, not precious and not magnificent. Paul calls these enslaving lusts, "lusts of *deceit*" (Ephesians 4:22), and he says that the "lustful passion" of the Gentiles stems from the fact that they "do not know God" (1 Thessalonians 4:5). Similarly, Peter calls these lusts, "lusts which were yours *in ignorance*"—that is, ignorance of God's glory and his precious and magnificent promises (1 Peter 1:14). What Paul and Peter mean is that these lusts get their power by lying to us in order to deceive us. They prey upon our ignorance of the promises of God. They claim to offer precious pleasures and magnificent experiences. What can free us from them? Compelling, inspiring, enthralling Truth. The truth of God's precious and magnificent promises that expose the lie of lust in the light of God's all-surpassing glory.

THE PURE SHALL SEE GOD

In the fall of 1982, *Leadership* magazine carried an unsigned article by a pastor who confessed to years of bondage to pornography of the grossest kind. He tells the story of what finally released him. It is a resounding confirmation of what I am trying to say. The author ran across a book by Francois Mauriac, the Catholic French novelist, *What I Believe*. In it Mauriac admitted how the plague of guilt had not freed him from lust. He concludes that there is one powerful reason to seek purity, the one Christ gave in the Beatitudes: "Blessed are the pure in heart, for they shall see God" (Matthew 5:8). It is the "precious and magnificent" promise that the pure see God that empowers our escape from lust. The lust-bound pastor wrote,

> *The thought hit me like a bell rung in a dark, silent hall. So far, none of the scary, negative arguments against lust had succeeded in keeping me from it...But here was a description of what I was missing by continuing to harbor lust: I was limiting my own intimacy with God. The love he offers is so transcendent and possessing that it requires our faculties to be purified and cleansed before we can possibly contain it. Could he, in fact, substitute another thirst and another hunger for the one I had*

never filled? Would Living Water somehow quench lust? That was the gamble of faith.[3]

It was not a gamble. You can't lose when you turn to God. He discovered this in his own life, and the lesson he learned is absolutely right: The way to fight lust is to feed faith with the precious and magnificent promise that the pure in heart will see, face to face, the all-satisfying God of glory.

The challenge before us in our fight against lust is not merely to do what God says because He is God, but to desire what God says because he is glorious. The challenge is not merely to *pursue* righteousness, but to *prefer* righteousness. The challenge is to get up in the morning and prayerfully meditate on the Scriptures until we experience "joy and peace in believing" the "precious and magnificent promises" of God (Romans 15:13; 2 Peter 1:4). As faith in future grace satisfies us with the joy set before us, the biblical demand for purity of heart will not be burdensome (1 John 5:3), and the power of lust will be broken. Its deceitful compensation will appear too brief and too shallow to lure us in.

PART IX

THE FINALITY
OF
FUTURE GRACE

To you it has been granted
for Christ's sake
...to suffer.

PHILIPPIANS 1 : 2 9

Momentary, light affliction
is producing for us an eternal weight of glory
far beyond all comparison,
while we look not at the things which are seen,
but at the things which are not seen;
for the things which are seen are temporal,
but the things which are not seen are eternal.

2 CORINTHIANS 4 : 1 7 - 1 8

Horror spread everywhere through the congregations; and the number
of lapsi [the ones who renounced their faith when threatened]...
was enormous. There was no lack, however, of such as remained firm,
and suffered martyrdom rather than yielding;
and, as the persecution grew wider and more intense,
the enthusiasm of the Christians and their power of resistance
grew stronger and stronger.

ALBRECHT VOGEL

CHAPTER TWENTY-EIGHT

The Future Grace of Suffering

WE WILL SUFFER

The reason I focus on suffering in this chapter is not just my sense that the days are evil and the path of righteousness costly, but the promise of *the Bible* that God's people will suffer. For example, Psalm 34:19 says, "Many are the afflictions of the righteous; but the Lord delivers him out of them all." In Acts 14:22 Paul tells all his young churches, "Through many tribulations we must enter the kingdom of God." Jesus said to his disciples, "If they persecuted Me, they will also persecute you" (John 15:20). Peter said, "Beloved, do not be surprised at the fiery ordeal among you, which comes upon you for your testing, as though some strange thing were happening to you" (1 Peter 4:12). Suffering is not strange, it is to be expected. "Indeed, all who desire to live godly in Christ Jesus will be persecuted" (2 Timothy 3:12). Most amazingly, suffering is called a gracious gift: "To you it has been granted *[echaristhē* = graciously given] for Christ's sake, not only to believe in Him, but also *to suffer for His sake"* (Philippians 1:29).

In fact, the way of life that comes from living by faith in future grace will very likely involve *more* suffering, not *less*. When you know that your future is in the hands of an all-powerful, all-knowing, all-wise God who promises to work all things for your good, you are free to take any risk that love demands—no matter the cost. It is a biblical truth that the more earnest we become about being the salt of the earth and the light of the world, and the more devoted we become to reaching the unreached peoples of the world, and exposing the works of darkness, and loosing the bonds of sin and Satan, the more we will suffer.

This suffering always threatens to destroy our faith in future grace. But if we are well-taught in the Word, and if the truth of God has gone deep into our soul, we will not be shaken. Instead we will see the suffering itself not merely as a *consequence* of living by faith in future grace, but as another *gift* of future grace.

MARTYRS ARE MEANT TO BE

David Barrett, the missionary scholar who edited the Oxford *World Christian Encyclopedia,* publishes each year an update on the state of the Christian movement around the world.[1] Among his many statistics is the estimate of how many Christian martyrs there are each year. In 1980, for example, he estimated that there were 270,000 Christians who were killed, more or less directly, because of their faith. After the remarkable developments in the former U.S.S.R. at the end of the 1980s, the number dropped. In 1995 he estimated the number at 157,000. But his projections into the future remain in the hundreds of thousands.

Near the end of the New Testament period, the apostle John had a vision of heaven and saw under the altar the souls of those who had been martyred. They cried out and wondered how long until God would rise up in triumph and vindicate them. God's answer in Revelation 6:11 is stunning: "There was given to each of them a white robe; and they were told that they should rest for a little while longer, until the number of their fellow servants and their brethren who were to be killed even as they had been, should be completed also." In other words, there is a number of martyrs appointed by the Lord. That number must be fulfilled before the consummation comes. "Rest, says the Lord, until the number is completed who are to die as you have died."

For almost three hundred years Christianity grew in soil that was wet with the blood of the martyrs. Until the Emperor Trajan (about A.D. 98), persecution was permitted but not legal. From Trajan to Decius (about A.D. 250) persecution was legal, but mainly local. From Decius, who hated the Christians and feared their impact on his reforms, until the first edict of toleration in 311, the persecution was not only legal but widespread and general. One writer described the situation in this third period:

> *Horror spread everywhere through the congregations; and the number of lapsi [the ones who renounced their faith when threatened]... was enormous. There was no lack, however, of such as remained firm, and suffered martyrdom rather than yielding; and, as the persecution grew wider and more intense, the enthusiasm of the Christians and their power of resistance grew stronger and stronger.*[2]

So, for 300 years, to be a Christian was an act of immense risk to your life and possessions and family. It was a test of what you loved more. And at the extremity of that test was martyrdom. And above that martyrdom was a sovereign God who said, there is an appointed number. They have a special role to play in planting and empowering the church. They have a special role to play in shutting the mouth of Satan, who constantly says that the people of God serve him only because life goes better (Job 1:9-11).

Martyrdom is not something accidental. It is not taking God off guard. It is not unexpected. And it is emphatically not a strategic defeat for the cause of Christ. It may look like defeat. But it is part of a plan in heaven that no human strategist would ever conceive or could ever design. And it will triumph for all those who endure to the end by faith in future grace.

SHIFTING CRISES, STEADY SUFFERING

By the time you are reading this book, the crises of the world will have shifted, but it is unlikely that they will be gone. The suffering may be a Somalia where tens of thousands of Christians were intentionally isolated and starved to death by rival factions. It may be a Rwanda where the churches became the killing fields. It may be explosive tensions between Muslim and Christian populations in Nigeria. It may be the millions of Christians in China harassed and driven underground. It may be hostilities in Peru or Myanmar.

One journal in December, 1994, carried this notice:

In some parts of the world Christians are still being crucified, quite literally so. News agencies report that five Christians have been crucified since July in Sudan, one being an Anglican priest. The detail is supplied that the executioners used six-inch-long nails. In Wad Medani two Catholic converts have been sentenced by an Islamic law court to be crucified. Anglican Bishop Daniel Zindo reports that widows and orphans of slain Christian men are sold into slavery in north Sudan and Libya for $15 per slave.[3]

Another periodical reported in February, 1995:

A 14-year-old Christian and a 44-year-old man were found guilty of blasphemy by a Pakistani court and sentenced to hang. Witnesses claimed the pair wrote anti-Islamic slogans in chalk on a mosque wall in 1993, a charge the two denied. A third defendant was gunned down outside a courtroom in Lahore last April...Prime Minister Benazir Bhutto told reporters she will try to have the law amended.[4]

Another reported in February, 1995, about Iranian persecution of Christians:

One year after the murder of Iranian Assemblies of God superintendent Haik Hovsepian-Mehr, sources say the Protestant church continues to live in a mood of fear. According to Christians who recently fled the country because of safety concerns, most churches are taking extra security precautions at worship services.... Haik, an outspoken human-rights advocate, disappeared January 19, 1994, days after Assemblies of God pastor Mehdi Dibaj, a Muslim convert jailed for nine years on apostasy charges, had been freed—largely because of Haik's international crusade. Police produced photographs of Haik's stabbed corpse 11 days after his death.

In July, Dibaj and another Protestant leader, Tateos Michaelian, disappeared and subsequently were murdered. An Armenian evangelical Presbyterian pastor, Michaelian had become chair of the Council of

Protestant Ministers in Iran after Haik's death.[5]

The crises change. The suffering continues in a steady stream of pain. These reports will be old by the time you read this book. But you can be sure that, somewhere in the world, this very moment as you read, Christians are suffering for their faith. We do well to prepare to join them.

THE COST OF DISCIPLESHIP WILL INCREASE

In the United States, the secular society at large, especially many of the intellectual elite and media leaders, are increasingly hostile to the evangelical church. The biblical vision of faith and righteousness is not shared or admired in many segments of our society. The first amendment has been so twisted in the service of secular antagonists as to make it the warrant of harassment against Christians. The name of Jesus is openly despised and blasphemed by famous entertainers in a way that in previous decades would have made them reprehensible in the eyes of the public, but today is approved or passed over.

What all this amounts to is that being a Christian may cost more in the years to come. And finishing the Great Commission will probably cost some of us our lives—as it already has, and which it *always* will. Eighteen hundred years ago Tertullian said, "We [Christians] multiply whenever we are mown down by you; the blood of Christians is seed" (*Apologeticus,* 50). And 200 years later St. Jerome said, "The Church of Christ has been founded by shedding its own blood, not that of others; by enduring outrage, not by inflicting it. Persecutions have made it grow; martyrdoms have crowned it" (*Letter 82*).

ARE THERE "CLOSED COUNTRIES," OR FEARFUL HEARTS?

In regard to spreading the gospel today, we talk so much about "closed countries" that we have almost lost God's perspective on missions—as though he ever meant it to be safe. There are no closed countries to those who assume that persecution, imprisonment and death are the likely results of spreading the gospel. And Jesus said plainly that these *are* likely results. "They will deliver you up to tribulation, and put you to death; and you will be hated by all nations for My name's sake" (Matthew 24:9. RSV). Until we recover God's perspective on suffering and the spread of the gospel we will not rejoice in the triumphs of future grace that he plans for the church and the world.

Obedience in missions and social justice has always been costly, and always will be. In the village of Miango, Nigeria, there is an SIM guest house and a small church called Kirk Chapel. Behind the chapel is a small cemetery with 56 graves. Thirty-three of them hold the bodies of missionary children. Some of the stones read: "Ethyl Armold: September 1, 1928–September 2, 1928." "Barbara J. Swanson: 1946–1952." "Eileen Louise Whitmoyer: May 6, 1952–July 3, 1955." For many families this was the cost of taking the gospel to Nigeria. Charles White told his story about visiting this little graveyard and ended it with a tremendously powerful sentence. He said, "The only way we can understand the graveyard at Miango is to remember that God also buried his Son on the mission field."[6]

And when God raised him from the dead, he called the church to follow him into the same dangerous field called "all the world" (Mark 16:15). But are we willing to follow? In Ermelo, Holland, Brother Andrew told the story of sitting in Budapest, Hungary, with a dozen pastors of that city, teaching them from the Bible. In walked an old friend, a pastor from Romania who had recently been released from prison. Brother Andrew said that he stopped teaching and knew that it was time to listen.

After a long pause the Romanian pastor said, "Andrew, are there any pastors in prison in Holland?" "No," he replied. "Why not?" the pastor asked. Brother Andrew thought for a moment and said, "I think it must be because we do not take advantage of all the opportunities God gives us." Then came the most difficult question. "Andrew, what do you do with 2 Timothy 3:12?" Brother Andrew opened his Bible and turned to the text and read aloud, "All who desire to live a godly life in Christ Jesus will be persecuted." He closed the Bible slowly and said, "Brother, please forgive me. We do nothing with that verse."[7]

We have, I fear, domesticated the concept of *godliness* into such inoffensive, middle-class morality and law-keeping that 2 Timothy 3:12 has become unintelligible to us. I think many of us are not prepared to suffer for the gospel. We do not grasp the great truth that God has purposes of future grace that he intends to give his people through suffering. We can speak of *purposes* of suffering because it is clearly God's purpose that we at times suffer for righteousness' sake and for the sake of the gospel. For example, "Let those who suffer *according to the will of God* entrust their souls to a faithful Creator in doing what is right" (1 Peter 4:19; see also 3:17; Hebrews 12:4-11).

To live by faith in future grace we must see that the suffering of God's people is the instrument of grace in their lives.

SUFFERING SHAPES AN UNSHAKABLE FAITH

Strange as it may seem, one of the primary purposes of being shaken by suffering is to make our faith more unshakable. Faith in future grace is like muscle tissue: if you stress it to the limit, it gets stronger, not weaker. That's what James means when he says, "Consider it all joy, my brethren, when you encounter various trials, knowing that the testing of your faith produces endurance" (James 1:2-3). When your faith is threatened and tested and stretched to the breaking point, the result is greater capacity to endure.

God loves faith in future grace so much that he will test it to the breaking point so as to keep it pure and strong. For example, he did this to Paul according to 2 Corinthians 1:8-9, "We do not want you to be unaware, brethren, of our affliction which came to us in Asia, that we were burdened excessively, beyond our strength, so that we despaired even of life; indeed, we had the sentence of death within ourselves *in order that we should not trust in ourselves, but in God who raises the dead.*" The words "in order that" show that there was a purpose in this extreme suffering: it was "in order that" Paul would not rely on himself and his resources, but on God—specifically the future grace of God in raising the dead.

God so values our wholehearted faith in future grace that he will, graciously, take away everything else in the world that we might be tempted to rely on—even life itself. His aim is that we grow deeper and stronger in our confidence that he himself will be all we need. He wants us to be able to say with the psalmist, "Whom have I in heaven but Thee? And besides Thee, I desire nothing on earth. My flesh and my heart may fail, but God is the strength of my heart and my portion forever" (Psalm 73:25-26).

Not everyone responds to suffering this way. The faith of some is broken instead of built. Jesus knew this and described it in Mark 4:16-17. In the parable of the four soils he said that some people who hear the Word receive it at first with gladness but then suffering makes them fall away: "When they hear the Word, [they] immediately receive it with joy; and they have no firm root in themselves, but are only temporary; then, when affliction or persecution arises because of the Word, immediately they fall away." So we see that affliction does not always make faith stronger. Sometimes it crushes faith. And then come true the paradoxical words of Jesus, "Whoever does not have, even what he has shall be taken away from him" (Mark 4:25b).

This is a call for us to endure suffering with firm faith in future grace, so that our faith might grow stronger and not be proved vain (1 Corinthians 15:2). "Whoever has, to him will more be given" (Mark 4:25a). Knowing God's design in suffering is one of the main means of growing through suffering. If you think your suffering is pointless, or that God is not in control, or that he is whimsical or cruel, then your suffering will drive you *from* God, instead of driving you from everything *but* God—as it should. So it is crucial that faith in future grace includes faith in the grace of future suffering.

The grace of suffering is evident in Romans 5:2-4. In this text the apostle Paul says that Christians "exult in hope of the glory of God." That is, our faith revels in the future grace of seeing God. But then Paul adds immediately, "(3) And not only this, but we also exult in our tribulations, knowing that tribulation brings about perseverance; (4) and perseverance, proven character; and proven character, hope."

THREE EFFECTS OF AFFLICTION

There are three specific effects of affliction mentioned in verses 3 and 4. First, tribulations bring about perseverance, or patient endurance. For those who have the Spirit of Christ, who continually opens our eyes to grace, the effect of affliction is perseverance. Until hardship comes into our lives, especially hardship for the sake of Christ and his righteousness, we do not experience the extent and depth of our own faith. Until times get hard we do not taste and really know if we are fair-weather "Christians."

That leads to the second effect of affliction. "And [this] perseverance [brings about] proven character." Literally the word behind "proven character" (dokimēn) means "the experience of being tested and approved." We could say "approvedness" or "provenness." If, when tribulations come, you persevere with faith in future grace, then you come out of that experience with a stronger sense that your faith is real; you are *proven*, you are not a hypocrite. The tree of trust was bent and it didn't break. Your fidelity and loyalty were put to the test and they passed. Now they have a "proven character." The gold of your faith was put in the fire and it came out refined, not consumed. As George Keith expressed in "How Firm a Foundation,"

When through fiery trials thy pathway shall lie,
My grace, all sufficient, shall be thy supply;
The flame shall not hurt thee, I only design
Thy dross to consume and thy gold to refine.

That's the second effect of affliction in Romans 5:3-4. Perseverance in faith in future grace brings about the assurance of provenness. The third effect comes from this sense of being tested and approved and refined. Verse 4b: "And proven character [brings about] *hope.*" This takes us back to where we began in verse 2, "We exult in the *hope* of the glory of God." The Christian life begins with hope in the promises of God in the gospel, and moves painfully up through affliction to more and more hope—that is, more faith in future grace.

The reason that "approvedness" brings about more hope is because our hope grows when we experience the reality of our own authenticity through testing. We learn through pain that God is faithful and that our faith is real. The people who are most unwavering in their hope are those who have been tested most deeply. The people who look most earnestly and steadfastly and eagerly to the hope of glory are those who have had the comforts of this life stripped away through tribulations. These are the freest of all people. Their love cannot be daunted by threats or calamities.

SUFFERING MAGNIFIES THE WORTH OF CHRIST

Another of God's designs for suffering is that it magnify Christ's worth and power. This is grace, because the greatest joy of Christians is to see Christ magnified in our lives. When Paul was told by the Lord Jesus that his "thorn in the flesh" would not be taken away, he supported Paul's faith by explaining why. The Lord said, "My grace is sufficient for you, for power is perfected in weakness" (2 Corinthians 12:9). God ordains that Paul be weak, so that Christ might be seen as strong on Paul's behalf. If we feel and look self-sufficient, *we* will get the glory, not Christ. So Christ chooses the weak things of the world "so that no man should boast before God" (1 Corinthians 1:29). And sometimes he makes seemingly strong people weaker, so that the divine power will be the more evident. We know that Paul experienced this as grace because he rejoiced in it: "*Most gladly,* therefore, I will rather boast about my weaknesses, that the power of Christ may dwell in me. Therefore *I am well content* with weaknesses, with insults, with distresses, with persecutions, with difficulties, for Christ's sake; for when I am weak, then I am strong" (2 Corinthians 12:9-10).

Living by faith in future grace means being satisfied with all that God is for us in Jesus. Therefore faith in future grace will not shrink back from what reveals and magnifies all that God is for us in Jesus. That is what our own weakness and suffering does. "We have this treasure in earthen vessels, that the surpassing greatness of the power may be of God and not from ourselves" (2 Corinthians 4:7). Therefore faith in future grace is glad, with the apostle Paul, to see the "surpassing greatness of God" in our affliction.

SUFFERING HELPS US SEE THAT GOD IS EVERYTHING WE NEED

There are other purposes of God in our suffering.[8] But they relate so closely to the next two chapters, it will be better to deal with them there. Through suffering God is preparing for us an eternal weight of glory beyond death, and he is working out his infallible purposes to gather all the elect from the nations of the world and bring in the consummation of his kingdom. The critical point is this: the suffering that seems to threaten future grace is, in reality, grace upon grace. To know this, and to see how it can be so, will help you believe that when all around your soul gives way, the Lord is all your hope and stay.

For to me, to live is Christ,
and to die is gain.

PHILIPPIANS 1:21

We are of good courage, I say,
and prefer rather to be absent from the body
and to be at home with the Lord.

2 CORINTHIANS 5:8

Since therefore the children share in flesh and blood,
He Himself likewise partook of the same nature,
that through death He might destroy
him who has the power of death, that is, the devil,
and deliver all those who through fear of death
were subject to lifelong bondage.

HEBREWS 2:14-15 (RSV)

CHAPTER TWENTY-NINE

The Future Grace of Dying

I f you can make the leap of faith into the full-blown creed of evolution, then you will believe that what happens to you when you die is no more significant than what happens to a tree when it dies. It's over. You go out of existence. You feel nothing, know nothing, have no consciousness. And your opinion of this book would be that it has no real basis in objective historical facts, but represents the subjective religious feelings of some Christians. It may have a measure of life-changing significance for us, the way Santa Claus affects the behavior of a child, but its significance is not based on reality outside our own imagination. It has nothing to do with what is really going to happen after death.

But if you find, written on the tablet of your heart, the truth that there is a Creator, and that you are created to have a relationship with him, and that what separates you from whales and dolphins and chimpanzees is not mutations and chemicals, but personhood in the image of God, then you will probably lie awake at night and think about eternity. Because, as Ecclesiastes 3:11 says, "[God] has also set eternity in their heart." And if, like millions of others, you have met Jesus Christ—a real, historical and living person— in the pages of the Bible, and have been persuaded that he is worthy of your trust, then you do not have to be unsure about what is coming when you die. He has told us many things, to encourage us and free us from the emptiness of evolutionary creeds and from the slavery to the fear of death.

FREED FROM SLAVERY TO THE FEAR OF DEATH

The aim of this book is to liberate people from fears and desires that enslave the soul and hinder radical obedience to Jesus. The aim is that we be so free from enslaving sin that people see our good deeds and give glory to our Father in heaven (Matthew 5:16). Living by faith in future grace is the pathway of liberty—including liberty from slavery to the fear of death. The reason I speak of *slavery* to the fear of death is because the Bible does in Hebrews 2:14-15, "Since then the children share in flesh and blood, [Christ] Himself likewise also partook of the same, that through death He might render powerless him who had the power of death, that is, the devil; and might deliver those who *through fear of death were subject to slavery all their lives.*"

THE DISORDERS OF ILLUSORY DENIAL

Have you ever asked yourself how much addiction and personality dysfunction and disordered lifestyle may originate in the repressed fear of death? Very few people live their daily lives with the conscious fear of death in their minds. Yet this text says that Christ came to die for people "who *through fear of death* were subject to slavery all their lives." There is something profound here. The point is not that people are enslaved to a constant, conscious fear of dying, but that they are enslaved to a thousand ways of avoiding this fear. They are enslaved to "the denial of death."[1] "Let us eat and drink, for tomorrow we die" (1 Corinthians 15:32), is not an exultation of true freedom, but another form of benumbing denial. Death looms as the great enemy. And we become its slaves in the illusory flight of denial, until we face the enemy, and triumph by faith in future grace. That's what this chapter is about.

How does Christ deliver us from the fear of death and set us free to live with the kind of loving abandon that can "let goods and kindred go, this mortal life also"? Let's begin with this very text: Hebrews 2:14-15. Take it a phrase at a time.

"Since then the children share in flesh and blood..."

The term "children" is taken from the previous verse and refers to the spiritual offspring of Christ, the Messiah (see Isaiah, 8:18; 53:10). These are also the "children of God." In other words, in sending Christ, God has the salvation of his "children" especially in view. It is true that "God so loved the *world,* that he gave his only begotten Son" (John 3:16). But it is also true that, in sending his Son, he was *especially* gathering "the children of God who are scattered abroad" (John 11:52). God's design was to *offer* Christ to the world, and to *effect* the salvation of his "children" (see 1 Timothy 4:10).

"...He Himself likewise also partook of the same [flesh and blood]..."

The Son of God, who existed before the incarnation as the eternal Word (John 1:1; Colossians 2:9), took on flesh and blood and clothed his deity with humanity. He became fully man and remained fully God. It is a great mystery in many ways. But it is at the heart of our biblical faith.

"...that through death..."

The reason Christ became human was to die. As pre-incarnate God, he could not die for sinners. But united to flesh and blood, he could. His aim was to die. Therefore he had to be born a human. He was born to die.

"...He might render powerless him who had the power of death, that is, the devil..."

In dying, Christ defanged the devil. How? By covering all our sin (Hebrews 10:12). This means that Satan has no legitimate grounds to accuse us before God. "Who will bring a charge against God's elect? God is the one who justifies" (Romans 8:33). On what grounds does he justify? Through the blood of Jesus (Hebrews 9:14; Romans 5:9). Satan's ultimate weapon against us is our own sin. If the death of Jesus takes it away, the chief weapon the devil has is taken out of his hand. In that sense "he is rendered powerless." He cannot destroy those for whom Christ died. He cannot make a successful case for the death penalty, because the Judge has acquitted us by the death of his Son!

"...and might deliver those who through fear of death were subject to slavery all their lives."

So we are free from the fear of death. God has justified us. There is only future grace in front of us. Satan cannot overturn that decree. And God means for our *ultimate* safety to have an *immediate* effect on our lives. He means for the happy ending to take away the slavery and fear of the present. If we do not need to fear our last and greatest enemy, death, then we do not need to fear anything. We can be free. Free for joy. Free for others.

IS FREE-FALLING FREEDOM?

Picture two skydivers. They are both free-falling. Their speed is the same. They both seem to be free. They are not entangled in any cords. They are not restrained by any safety wires. They are as free as birds—it seems. But there is one crucial difference: only one of them has a parachute. Does this change the sense of freedom that they enjoy? Yes. Both are free to fall with gravity, but only one of them is free not to. The other is a slave to gravity, and gravity will kill him in the end. If he can somehow deny that he has no parachute he might be able to have an exhilarating experience. But if he realizes he is doomed, he will be enslaved through fear during his entire fall, and all the joy of this so-called freedom will vanish. He must either deny the reality (which will mean slavery to illusion), or succumb to fear (which will mean slavery to terror), or be rescued by someone with a parachute. So it is in this world. Apart from Christ, we are subject to slavery all our lives through fear of death.

It is astonishing how disinterested people are in the reality of dying. Few things are more certain and universal. The possibilities for joy and misery after you die are trillions of times greater than in the few years on this earth before you die. Yet people give almost all their energies to making this life secure, and almost none to the next. The Bible compares this life to a vapor that appears on a cold winter morning and then vanishes (James 4:14). That's about two seconds. But it describes the time after death as "ages of ages" (Revelation 14:11, literal translation)—not just one or two ages that last a thousand years, but ages of ages—thousands and thousands of ages.

It matters infinitely what happens to you after you die.

This question of what happens when we die has a sobering, wakening effect on our minds. It forces us to ask whether our faith is real, substantial, biblical. It forces us to deal with whether our faith is an objective, external reality *outside* ourselves, namely, in God, or whether our "faith" is a mere subjective experience of feelings and thoughts *inside* ourselves that function as an emotional cushion to soften the bumps of life and give us a network of friends. Facing eternity has an amazing effect of sobering us out of religious delusions. It helps keep God as the center of our lives by testing whether we are more in love with this world than we are with God himself. Does the thought of dying give us more pain at losing friends than it gives us joy at gaining Christ? Thinking of death helps us prove whether we are prizing God.

COURAGE TO LIVE AND DIE BY FAITH IN FUTURE GRACE

But when the future grace of dying in Christ takes hold of you, it frees from fear and gives courage to live the most radical, self-sacrificing life of love. The person who can truly say, with the apostle Paul, "To die is gain," will be able to say, like no one else, "To live is Christ" (Philippians 1:21). But if we can't say, "To die is gain—to die is future grace!" then we will probably say, in one degree or another, "Let us eat, drink and be merry." Which means we will be enslaved to our own private earthly comforts. That's all we will have to look forward to. So we will feel the compulsion to deny the truth of dying and to maximize the kind of pleasures we can get now without God. Therefore, being sure of what happens when we die as Christians is indispensable for a life of joyful, loving sacrifice, and for not losing heart through the pain and the diminishing health of this life.

Carl Lundquist was the president of Bethel College and Seminary in St. Paul, Minnesota, for 28 years. He retired in 1982. I worked under his leadership for six of those years, and then we served on a prayer commission together near the end of his life. He was a relentlessly gracious Christian leader. In 1988 the doctors told him he had a rare form of cancer called mycosis fungoides, a variant of cutaneous T-cell lymphoma that invades the skin over the entire body. He was 72 years old and in seemingly robust health. But on February 27, 1991, he died after a heartrending deterioration of his skin.

He wrote a final letter to his friends about the day he heard the news of his cancer.

That day in the hospital room, I picked up my Bible when the doctor had left. I turned to the joy verses of Philippians, thinking one might stand out. But what leaped from the page was Paul's testimony in chapter one, "I eagerly expect and hope that I will in no way be ashamed but will have sufficient courage so that now, as always, Christ will be exalted in my body, whether by life or by death. For to me to live is Christ and to die is gain." And I discovered that a verse I had lived by in good health also was a verse that I could live by in ill health. To live—Christ; to die—gain. But by life or by death, it's all right either way…So I simply trust that the Great Physician in His own way will carry out for me His will which I know alone is good and acceptable and perfect. By life or by death. Hallelujah!

That trust in the good will of the Great Physician is what I mean by faith in future grace. Carl Lundquist lived by it in those next three years of misery, and it freed him for remarkable service while his "outer nature was wasting away."

HOW PAUL COPED WITH WASTING AWAY

The apostle Paul wrestled as much as anybody with the temptation to lose heart because of the wasting away of his body. He strengthened his heart with truth about the future grace of dying. And he wrote it down so that we might follow him. In 2 Corinthians 4:16–5:10 Paul shows the Corinthians why he does not lose heart in spite of all his afflictions (4:8-12), and especially in view of the fact that he knows he is dying. "We do not lose heart, but though *our outer man is decaying,* yet our inner man is being renewed day by day" (4:16).

He can't see the way he used to (and there were no glasses). He can't hear the way he used to (and there were no hearing aids). He doesn't recover from beatings the way he used to (and there were no antibiotics).

His strength, walking from town to town, doesn't hold up the way it used to. He sees the wrinkles in his face and neck. His memory is not as good. His joints get stiff when he sits still. He knows that he, like everybody else, is dying. And he admits that this is a threat to his faith and joy and courage.

But he doesn't lose heart. Why?

The first part of his answer is in verse 16: "Therefore we do not lose heart, but though our outer man is decaying, yet *our inner man is being renewed day by day.*" He doesn't lose heart because his inner man is being renewed. How? The renewing of his heart comes from something very strange: it comes from looking at what he can't see. Verse 18: *"We look not at the things which are seen, but at the things which are not seen;* for the things which are seen are temporal, but the things which are not seen are eternal." This is Paul's way of not losing heart: looking at what you can't see. What did he see?

A few verses later in 2 Corinthians 5:7, he says, "We walk by faith, not by sight." This doesn't mean that he leaps into the dark without evidence of what's there. It means that the most precious and important realities in the world are beyond our physical senses. We "look" at these unseen things through the gospel. By the grace of God we see what Paul called "the light of the gospel of the glory of Christ who is the image of God" (2 Corinthians 4:4). We strengthen our hearts—we renew our courage—by fixing our gaze on the invisible, objective truth that we see in the testimony of those who saw Christ face to face.

AN ETERNAL WEIGHT OF GLORY

But what unseen reality does Paul look at to sustain his faith in future grace? A great summary statement of this reality is given in 2 Corinthians 4:17. He says that he is sustained in his deteriorating condition by this truth: "Momentary, light affliction is producing for us an eternal weight of glory far beyond all comparison." This means that the decaying of his body was not meaningless. The pain and pressure and frustration and affliction were not happening in vain. They were not vanishing into a black hole of pointless suffering. Instead this affliction was "producing for [him] an eternal weight of glory far beyond all comparison."

The unseen thing that Paul looked at to renew his inner man was the immense weight of glory that was being prepared for him not just *after,* but *through* and *by,* the wasting away of his body. There is a causal correlation between the present decay of Paul's body and the future display of Paul's glory. When he is hurting, he fixes his eyes not on how heavy the hurt is, but on how heavy the glory will be because of the hurt. In another place he said, "I consider that the sufferings of this present time are not worthy to be compared with the glory that is to be revealed to us" (Romans 8:18).

But what does he see, when he looks to this unseen glory? The answer is given in the first verses of 2 Corinthians 5. I'll quote verses 1-5 here with my explanations in brackets.

For we know that if the earthly tent which is our house is torn down [he's talking about his body which is decaying], *we have a building from God* [a building as opposed to a tent—that is, something more durable and lasting, namely, a new resurrection body], *a house not made with hands, eternal in the heavens. For indeed in this house* [our present body] *we groan, longing to be clothed with our dwelling from heaven* [that is, our resurrection body: he mixes metaphors here, shifting back and forth between being clothed and being housed]; *inasmuch as we, having put it on, shall not be found naked* [in other words, he does not prefer to put off his present body like a garment and become a disembodied soul—that's what nakedness means]. *For indeed while we are in this tent, we groan, being burdened, because we do not want to be unclothed* [we don't want to be mere bodiless souls, contrary to Greek thought that wanted this very much], *but to be clothed* [on top of our present clothes—he wants the Second Coming of Christ to happen so that he will not have to die and be without a body, but rather have his present body swallowed up in the glorious resurrection life of the new body], *in order that what is mortal may be swallowed up by life. Now He who prepared us for this very purpose is God, who gave to us the Spirit as a pledge.*

We will say more about the resurrection body in the next chapter. But the crucial point here is this: If Paul had his preference he would choose to experience the Second Coming of Christ over the experience of death. The reason he gives is that the experience of "nakedness"—that is, being stripped of his body by death—is not something as good as having his body swallowed up by life, in the twinkling of an eye at the Second Coming of Christ (1 Corinthians 15:52).

This means that the great, final hope of Christians is not to die and be freed from our bodies, but to be raised with new, glorious bodies, like Christ's resurrection body (Philippians 3:21); or, best of all, to be alive at the Second Coming so that we do not have to lose our bodies temporarily and be "naked" until the resurrection.

WHAT ABOUT THE MOMENT AFTER DEATH?

But what does this mean for our hope for the moments immediately after death? Is Paul discounting this? No. He puts things back in perspective in verses 6-8.

Therefore, being always of good courage, and knowing that while we are at home in the body we are absent from the Lord—for we walk by faith, not by sight—we are of good courage, I say, and prefer rather to be absent from the body and to be at home with the Lord.

Recall that, in verse 4, Paul said that he does not want "to be unclothed." It is not his first preference to be "absent from the body." He says this because he is comparing death with the glorious Second Coming, not because he is comparing it with his life on earth. His first preference would be to put on his new resurrection body immediately at the Second Coming, with no death intervening. But if that is not possible—if the choice is between more life here, on the one hand, and dying, on the other hand—he prefers that God would take him, even if it means nakedness, that is, *even if* it means that he must be stripped of his body. "[We] prefer rather to be absent from the body and at home with the Lord."

And the reason for this willingness to leave his body behind is not because the body *per se* is bad—O, how he wants the experience of the transformed resurrection body!—but because being "at home with the Lord" is so irresistibly attractive to Paul (v. 8).

So Paul renews his inner man by looking to unseen things. He looks at three possibilities and prefers them in descending order: First, he prefers that Christ would come and clothe his mortal body with immortality so that he would not have to die and be an incomplete, disembodied soul. But if God does not will that, Paul prefers to be absent from the body, rather than to live on here, because he loves Christ more than he loves anything else, and to be absent from the body will mean to be at home with the Lord. Death will bring a deeper intimacy and greater at-homeness with the Lord than anything we can know in this life. Finally, if God wills that it is not time for the Second Coming, or time for death, then Paul will continue to walk by faith in future grace, and not by sight.

And in that faith he will be of good courage; and, even though his body is decaying, his inner man will be renewed day by day through this faith in the unseen future grace called "the weight of glory" (2 Corinthians 4:17). Here we must test ourselves. Do we share Paul's priorities and values in life? Do we long mainly for the Second Coming of Christ and the glory of being swallowed up in life with Jesus? Or, short of that, do we long to be at home with Christ even if it costs us the surrender of our bodies? Or, short of that, are we committed to live by faith in future grace until he comes or until he calls?

IS THE FINAL JUDGMENT AN ACT OF FUTURE GRACE?

We need to tackle one more thing in this chapter. Someone might say, "My faith in future grace is strengthened when I hear these things about death; but I become fearful when I think about judgment after death; that too is in this chapter of Scripture." So let's ponder for a moment the judgment that believers face after death. Is this, too, a "future grace"?

The key statement comes two verses later: "For we must all appear before the judgment seat of Christ that each one may be recompensed for his deeds in the body, according to what he has done, whether good or bad" (2 Corinthians 5:10). Consider four simple and obvious observations about this judgment before we try to answer the question, why Christians will be judged, if in fact Christ has already been judged for us (Romans 5:8-9), and if there is now no condemnation for those who are in Christ Jesus (Romans 8:1).

First, all Christians will stand before Christ as judge. "We must *all* appear before the judgment seat of Christ." Not just unbelievers, but "we." And not some of us, but "all of us."

Second, our judge will be Christ. It is *God's* judgment too (Romans 14:10-12), "We must all stand before the judgment seat of *God,*" but God "gave [Christ] authority to execute judgment" (John 5:27). So God the Son and God the Father are one in their judgment, but the Son is the one who stands forth as the immediate Judge to deal with us.

Third, our judgment will be *after* we die. That's implied in the text, but Hebrews 9:27 makes it explicit: "It is appointed for men to die once and after this comes judgment." We don't need to be more specific than that, for that is what the historic confessions of the church have declared.[2] We need only say that before we enter the final state of glory with our resurrection bodies on the new earth, we will stand before Christ as Judge.

Fourth, when we stand before Christ we will be judged according to our deeds in this life. "For we must all appear before the judgment seat of Christ that each one may be recompensed *for his deeds in the body, according to what he has done,* whether good or bad" (2 Corinthians 5:10). This is not an isolated teaching in the New Testament. Jesus said in Matthew 16:27, "The Son of Man is going to come in the glory of His Father with His angels; and will then recompense every man according to his deeds." And in the very last chapter of the Bible, Jesus said, "Behold, I am coming quickly, and my reward is with me, to render to every man according to what he has done" (Revelation 22:12).

Now the more difficult question: why is this judgment important? Why are the "deeds done in the body" the evidence in this divine court-room? Is the aim of this judgment to declare who is lost and who is saved, according to the works done in the body? Or is the aim of this judgment to declare the measure of your reward in the age to come according to the works done in the body?

The answer of the New Testament, if you interpret carefully, is: both. Our deeds will reveal who enters the age to come, and our deeds will reveal the measure of our reward in the age to come. I will try to show you in a moment why I think this is so, but let me mention the biggest problem for many Christians in saying this. It sounds to many like a contradiction of salvation by grace through faith. Ephesians 2:8 says, "By grace you have been saved through faith; and that not of yourselves, it is the gift of God, not of works, that no one should boast." Salvation is not "of works." That is, works do not earn salvation. Works do not put God in our debt so that he must pay wages. That would contradict grace. "The *wages of sin* is death, but the *free gift of God* is eternal life in Christ Jesus our Lord" (Romans 6:23). Grace gives salvation as a free gift to be received by faith, not earned by works.

How then can I say that the judgment of believers will not only be the public declaration of our differing rewards in the kingdom of God, according to our deeds, but will also be the public declaration of our salvation— our *entering* the kingdom—according to our deeds?

The answer is that our deeds will be the public evidence brought forth in Christ's courtroom to demonstrate *that our faith is real.* And our deeds will be the public evidence brought forth to demonstrate *the varying measures of our obedience of faith.* In other words, salvation is by grace through faith, and rewards are by grace through faith, but the evidence of invisible faith in the judgment hall of Christ will be a transformed life. Our deeds are not the basis of our salvation, they are the evidence of our salvation. They are not foundation, they are demonstration. All our salvation will be by grace through faith—demonstrated by what this book calls "*living* by faith in future grace."

Now let me try to show you from Scripture why I think this.

Both Jesus and Paul teach that believers will receive differing rewards in accord with the degree that their faith expresses itself in acts of service and love and righteousness. For example, in 1 Corinthians 3:8 Paul says, "He who plants and he who waters are one; but each will receive his own reward according to his own labor." And in Ephesians 6:8 Paul says, "Whatever good thing each one does, this he will receive back from the Lord." These works are not "works of the law" in the pejorative sense of acts done to earn or merit God's payment of wages. They are, as this book has argued throughout, "works of faith" (1 Thessalonians 1:3; 2 Thessalonians 1:11). They are done by faith in future grace. Therefore the reward redounds to the grace of God at work in the life of the believer and not to human initiative.

The parable of the talents (or pounds) in Luke 19:12-27 teaches the same thing. Jesus refers to his going to heaven and returning, and compares it to a nobleman who went away and gave to ten of his servants one pound each with the command to trade with them, so that his estate would be advanced in his absence. When the nobleman returns, one of his servants had traded so as to turn his pound into ten. And the nobleman says that his reward will be authority over ten cities. Another servant had turned his pound into five. And the nobleman said that his reward would be authority over five cities. Another had just kept the pound and done nothing with it. To this one the nobleman said, "I will condemn you from your own mouth." And he took the one pound from him.

What this parable teaches is the same thing Paul taught, namely, that there are varying degrees of reward for the faithfulness of our lives. But it also moves beyond that and teaches that there is a loss not only of reward, but of heaven, for those who claim to be faithful but do nothing to show that they prize God's gifts and love the Giver. That's the point of the third servant who did nothing with his gift. He did not just lose his reward, he lost his life. Jesus says in Matthew 25:30, "Cast out the worthless slave into the outer darkness; in that place there shall be weeping and gnashing of teeth."

That leads us to the second purpose of the judgment. The first was that the judgment makes a public demonstration of the varying degrees of reward that Christians receive for living by faith in future grace. The second purpose of the judgment is to declare openly the authenticity of the faith of God's people *by the evidence of their deeds.* Salvation is *owned* by faith. Salvation is *shown* by deeds. So when Paul says (in 2 Corinthians 5:10) that each "[will] be recompensed…according to what he has done," he not only means that our *rewards* will accord with our deeds, but also our *salvation* will accord with our deeds.

Why do I think this?

There are numerous texts that point in this direction. For example, Paul refers to the "revelation of the righteous *judgment of God,*" and then says, "[God] will render to every man *according to his deeds:* to those who by perseverance in doing good seek for glory and honor and immortality [he will render] *eternal life;* but to those who…do not obey the truth…[he will render] wrath and indignation." In other words, the judgment is according to what a person has done. But here the issue is explicitly "eternal life" versus "wrath and indignation" (Romans 2:5-8).

Several times Paul listed certain kinds of deeds and said, "those who practice such things shall not inherit the kingdom of God" (Galatians 5:21; 1 Corinthians 6:9-10). In other words, when these deeds are exposed at the judgment as a person's way of life, they will be the evidence that their faith is dead and he will not be saved. As James said, "Faith without works is dead" (James 2:26). That is what will be shown at the judgment.

Jesus put it like this—and he used exactly the same words for good and evil deeds that we have here in 2 Corinthians 5:10. He said (in John 5:28-29), "An hour is coming, in which all who are in the tombs shall hear His voice, and shall come forth; those who *did the good deeds* to a resurrection of life, those who *committed the evil deeds* to a resurrection of judgment." In other words, the way one lived will be the evidence whether one passes through judgment to life or whether one experiences judgment as condemnation.

He says this, even though five verses earlier in John 5:24 he said, "Truly, truly I say to you, he who hears My word and *believes* Him who sent Me has eternal life." To hear and to *believe* is to have eternal life—it is by grace through faith. But when that faith is real—not dead—the life will change (that's what this book is written to explain and promote), so that Jesus can say, with no contradiction: the deeds of this life will be the public criteria of judgment at the resurrection. Because our works are the evidence of the reality of our faith. And it is faith in Christ that saves.

Perhaps an illustration will clarify how deeds will function in the final judgment. Recall the story of how two harlots brought a baby to King Solomon, each claiming that the baby was hers (1 Kings 3:16-27). They asked King Solomon to act as judge between them. In his extraordinary wisdom, he said that a sword should be brought, and that the baby should be divided, with half given to the one woman and half to the other. The true mother cried out, "O, my Lord, give her the living child, and by no means kill him." Solomon said, "give [this] woman the living child…she is his mother.

What was Solomon looking for? He was *not* looking for a deed that would earn the child, or would *create* a relationship that didn't already exist. He was looking for a deed that would *demonstrate* what was already true, namely, that the child was truly this woman's child by birth. That is the way God looks at our deeds on the judgment day. He is not looking for deeds that purchase our pardon in his judgment hall. He is looking for deeds that prove we are already enjoying the fruits of our pardon. He is looking for the practical evidences of our living by faith in future grace. The purchase of our salvation was the blood of Jesus, sufficient once for all to cover all our sins. We do not add to the worth of his righteousness imputed to us by God for our justification. But the means by which we receive this gift is faith—a being satisfied with all that God is for us in Jesus. And that kind of faith frees us from lifelong slavery to the fear of death, and works through love.

I conclude therefore that the dying of Christians—with all its pain and grief—may be anticipated as future grace. Not only will we be "at home with the Lord" which is far better than anything on earth, but even the judgment, at its appointed time, will fill us with wonder and gratitude and joy. *The Belgic Confession* of 1561 puts it like this:

> *The consideration of this judgment is justly terrible and dreadful to the wicked and ungodly, but most desirable and comfortable to the righteous and the elect; because then their full deliverance shall be perfected, and there they shall receive the fruits of their labor and trouble which they have borne. Their innocence shall be known to all... The faithful shall be crowned with glory and honor; and the Son of God will confess their names before God the Father, and his elect angels; all tears shall be wiped from their eyes; and their cause which is now condemned...will then be known to be the cause of the Son of God. And for a gracious reward, the Lord will cause them to possess such a glory as never entered into the heart of man to conceive.*

> *Therefore we expect that great day with a most ardent desire, to the end that we may fully enjoy the promises of God in Christ Jesus our Lord. Amen.*[3]

*[Christ] will transform the body of our humble state
into conformity with the body of His glory,
by the exertion of the power that He has
even to subject all things to Himself.*

PHILIPPIANS 3:21

*And I saw a new heaven and a new earth;
for the first heaven and the first earth passed away…
And I heard a loud voice from the throne, saying,
"Behold, the tabernacle of God is among men,
and He shall dwell among them,
and they shall be His people,
and God Himself shall be among them,
and He shall wipe away every tear from their eyes;
and there shall no longer be any death;
there shall no longer be any mourning, or crying, or pain;
the first things have passed away."*

REVELATION 21:1-4

*And the wolf will dwell with the lamb,
And the leopard will lie down with the kid,
And the calf and the young lion and the fatling together;
And a little boy will lead them.
Also the cow and the bear will graze;
Their young will lie down together;
And the lion will eat straw like the ox.
And the nursing child will play by the hole of the cobra,
And the weaned child will put his hand on the viper's den.
They will not hurt or destroy in all My holy mountain,
For the earth will be full of the knowledge of the Lord
As the waters cover the sea.*

ISAIAH 11:6-9

CHAPTER THIRTY

The Rebirth of Creation

WHY I THINK ABOUT WHAT COMES AFTER DEATH

The faith that grows in the ground of God's promises takes away fear and fills us instead with hope and confidence. And when fear goes, and hope in God overflows, we live differently. Our lives show that our treasure in God is more precious than the fleeting attractions of sin. When we rely on God who raises the dead (2 Corinthians 1:9), and revel in the hope of the glory of God (Romans 5:2), we don't yield to the sinful pleasures of the moment. We are not suckered in by advertising that says the one with the most toys wins. We don't devote our best energies to laying up treasures on earth. We don't dream our most exciting dreams about accomplishments and relationships that perish. We don't fret over what this life fails to give us (marriage, wealth, health, fame).

Instead we savor the wonder that the Owner and Ruler of the universe loves us, and has destined us for the enjoyment of his glory, and is working infallibly to bring us to his eternal kingdom. So we live to meet the needs of others, because God is living to meet our needs (Isaiah 64:4; 41:10; 2 Chronicles 16:9; Psalm 23:6). We love our enemies, and do good, and bless those who curse us and pray for those who despise us, because we are not enslaved to the fleeting, petty pleasures that come from returning evil for evil, and we know that our reward is great in heaven (Luke 6:35; Matthew 5:45; 1 Peter 3:9).

All this flows from a growing hope in future grace. When you know the truth about what happens to you after you die, and you believe it, and you are satisfied with all that God will be for you in the ages to come, that truth makes you free indeed. Free from the short, shallow, suicidal pleasures of sin, and free for the sacrifices of mission and ministry that cause people to give glory to our Father in heaven. That freedom, that love and that glory are the aim of this book.

To that end we take one more look (alas, through a glass darkly) into what God has prepared for those who love him—"Things which eye has not seen and ear has not heard, and which have not entered the heart of man," but have now been revealed, in part, through the Spirit, in the writings of the apostles (1 Corinthians 2:9-13). We look first at the resurrection of our bodies and then at the new earth in which we will live with Christ forever.

A MOMENT OF ILLUMINATION IN MUNICH

It is strange how God, from time to time, causes the preciousness and power of a biblical truth to penetrate the heart. I recall a moment about twenty-five years ago when I was a graduate student in Munich, Germany. As a kind of spiritual breather from my studies, I was reading a biography of the New Testament scholar, Julius Schniewind. The book was called *Charisma der Theologie* by Hans-Joachim Kraus. On page 35, Kraus was telling about the final weeks of Schniewind's life as he was being laid low by a kidney disease. Schniewind had just finished leading a lay Bible study, and, as he put on his coat to go home, he groaned aloud with the Greek phrase, *"soma tapeinōseōs, soma tapeinōseōs!"*

For me it was one of those rare moments of spiritual illumination. I knew where that phrase came from. It came from Philippians 3:21, where Paul says that we eagerly await a Savior from heaven "who will transform our *lowly body (soma tapeinōseōs)* into one like his glorious body, according to the exertion of his power to subdue all things to himself" (my translation). The fact that Julius Schniewind lived in such intimate awareness of this hope—so much so that in his final pains he groaned with the very words of the Greek New Testament—that fact awakened in me as never before the preciousness and power of this amazing promise of future grace. I saw the pain of Schniewind's dying body expressed in words of a triumphant promise of future grace. And the triumph seemed more real to me than ever before.

Our bodies here on this earth are "bodies of lowliness." They are fragile, disease-prone, wasting away, and mortal. But, O, how we love them! As Paul said, "No one ever hated his own flesh, but nourishes and cherishes it, just as Christ also does the church" (Ephesians 5:29). And they are indeed precious. They are the very "temple of the Holy Spirit" (1 Corinthians 6:19). They are the creation of God, for the glory of God (1 Corinthians 6:20). They are living and holy sacrifices acceptable to God in spiritual service (Romans 12:1). They are part of who we are—part of our identity as persons. Therefore, the promise that they will be raised from the dead is a precious promise. And the fact that Christ is committed to this mighty act of future grace, with all the omnipotent power that enables him to subdue all things to himself, gripped me that evening years ago in Munich as never before.

IF GOD IS YOUR GOD YOU MUST BE RAISED

Jesus said, "Regarding the resurrection of the dead, have you not read that which was spoken to you by God, saying, 'I am the God of Abraham, and the God of Isaac, and the God of Jacob'? He is not the God of the dead but of the living" (Matthew 22:31-32). The point here is that if God is your God, you must be *raised*. God is not the God of the dead! When he says, "I am your God," he means "I will always be your God. And your life with me and in me will not be a diminishing thing. It cannot be. I am God! Your life will be a growing and flourishing experience. For I am your God. I do not diminish what is mine. I make it better forever and ever."

WILL "FLESH AND BLOOD" INHERIT THE KINGDOM?

What does the apostle Paul mean in 1 Corinthians 15:50 when he says, "Flesh and blood cannot inherit the kingdom of God"? Is this statement a denial of the bodily resurrection? No. "Flesh and blood" simply mean "human nature as we know it"—mortal, perishable, sin-stained, decaying. Something so fragile and temporary as the body we now have will not be the stuff of the eternal, durable, unshakable, indestructible kingdom of God. But that doesn't mean there won't be bodies.

It means that our bodies will be greater. They will be *our* bodies, but they will be different and more wonderful. Two verses later Paul says, "We shall all be changed in a moment, in the twinkling of an eye, at the last trumpet; for the trumpet will sound, and the dead will be raised imperishable, and we shall be changed" (1 Corinthians 15:51-52). When he says "the dead will be raised" he means we—the dead—will be raised. If God meant to start all over with no continuity between the body I have now and the one I *will* have, why would Paul say, "the dead will be raised"? Why would he not say, "The dead will not be raised (since they are decomposed and their molecules are scattered into plants and animals for a thousand miles) and so God will start from scratch"? He did not say that, because it is not true.

He said two things: the dead will be *raised* (that teaches continuity); and the dead will be *changed* (they will be made imperishable and immortal). The old body will become a new body. But it will still be your body. There will be continuity. God is able to do what we cannot imagine. The resurrection is not described in terms of a totally new creation but in terms of a *change* of the old creation. "We shall all be changed in a moment, in the twinkling of an eye."

Paul compares the resurrection to what happens to a seed when it goes into the ground. "That which you sow, you do not sow the body which is to be, but a bare grain, perhaps of wheat or of something else. But God gives it a body just as He wished, and to each of the seeds a body of its own" (1 Corinthians 15:37-38). The point is that there is connection and continuity between the simple seed and the full-grown plant. If you plant a seed of wheat, you don't get a stalk of barley. But, on the other hand, there is a difference. A plant is more beautiful than a seed.

Then Paul applies the analogy to the resurrection body: "So also is the resurrection of the dead. It is sown a perishable body, it is raised an imperishable body; it is sown in dishonor, it is raised in glory; it is sown in weakness, it is raised in power; it is sown a natural body, it is raised a spiritual body" (1 Corinthians 15:42-44). I can hear someone say, "Why bother? Let it go. Who needs it? All that matters is the spiritual reality of love and joy and peace and righteousness and goodness and truth. Why the big fuss over arms and legs and hands and feet and hair and eyes and ears and tongues? It seems so earthly."

GOD DID NOT CREATE MATTER TO THROW IT AWAY

Paul's answer will ultimately take us to the reality of the new earth and the purpose of God to fill the universe with material manifestation of his glory. God did not create the physical-material universe willy-nilly. He had a purpose, namely, to add to the ways his glory is externalized and made manifest. "The heavens are telling of the glory of God; and their expanse is declaring the work of His hands" (Psalm 19:1). Our bodies fit into that same category of physical things that God created for this reason. He is not going to back out on his plan to glorify himself through human beings and human bodies. So in 1 Corinthians 6:19-20 Paul says, "Do you not know that your *body* is a temple of the Holy Spirit who is in you, whom you have from God, and that you are not your own? For you have been bought with a price: therefore *glorify God in your body.*"

Why does God go to all the trouble to dirty his hands, as it were, with our decaying, sin-stained flesh, in order to reestablish it as a resurrection body and clothe it with immortality? Answer: Because his Son paid the price of death so that the Father's purpose for the material universe would be fulfilled, namely, that he would be glorified in it, including in our bodies forever and ever. That's what the text says: "You have been bought with a price [the death of his Son]: therefore glorify God in your body." God will not disregard or dishonor the work of his Son. God will honor the work of his Son by raising our bodies from the dead, and we will use our bodies to glorify him forever and ever. That is why you have a body now. And that is why it will be raised to be like Christ's glorious body.

A WORD FROM MY FAVORITE PASTOR

Jonathan Edwards, the great pastor and theologian from 250 years ago, wrote a profound essay on "The End for Which God Created the World." Few works have had a deeper influence on my thinking. His answer to the question of why God created the world was "that there might be a glorious and abundant emanation of his infinite fullness of Good *ad extra,* or without himself; and that the disposition to communicate himself, or diffuse his own fullness, was what moved him to create the world…The diffusive disposition that excited God to give creatures existence, was…a disposition in the fullness of the divinity to flow out and diffuse itself."[1] This is what God says, in effect, in Isaiah 43:7 when he refers to "everyone who is called by My name, and whom I have *created for My glory.*" God created the universe and all that is in it as an emanation or manifestation of the fullness of his glory.

We have no reason to think that God has ever changed his mind in this regard. There is no reason to think that God would now prefer that there be no created universe. Christianity is not a platonic religion that regards material things as mere shadows of reality, which will be sloughed off as soon as possible. Not the mere immortality of the soul, but rather the resurrection of the body and the renewal of all creation is the hope of the Christian faith.[2] Just as our bodies will be raised imperishable for the glory of God, so the earth itself will be made new and fit for the habitation of risen and glorified persons.

WILL THE FIRST HEAVEN AND FIRST EARTH PASS AWAY?

One of the most alluring visions of that future grace is found in Revelation 21:1-4. John says that there will be a new earth and that heaven will come down, and God will make his eternal dwelling among men on the new earth.

> *And I saw a new heaven and a new earth; for the first heaven and the first earth passed away, and there is no longer any sea. And I saw the holy city, new Jerusalem, coming down out of heaven from God, made ready as a bride adorned for her husband. And I heard a loud voice from*

the throne, saying, "Behold, the tabernacle of God is among men, and He shall dwell among them, and they shall be His people, and God Himself shall be among them, and He shall wipe away every tear from their eyes; and there shall no longer be any death; there shall no longer be any mourning, or crying, or pain; the first things have passed away.

This is a beautiful picture of what is coming: a new earth, the people of God living there with no death, no pain, no tears. And best of all, God will not be far away, but will pitch his tent, as it were, in our midst, and dwell among us forever.

But a critical question is raised here: When John says in verse 1, "The first heaven and the first earth passed away," does he mean that the earth we live on and the sky over our head will be totally done away with, and that God will start over with a totally new creation? This is a question like the one raised above concerning our resurrection bodies: will God raise us up or will he start over with a totally new creation of different bodies? I have tried to show that there will be continuity between our bodies now and our bodies in the resurrection. That is also what needs to be shown concerning the new earth.

BURNED, BUT NOT ANNIHILATED

But what does John mean, when he says, "The first heaven and the first earth passed away"? Peter, in his second letter says something similar, but even more graphically. He describes how the present earth and heaven will "pass away."

But the day of the Lord will come like a thief, in which the heavens will pass away with a roar and the elements will be destroyed with intense heat, and the earth and its works will be burned up. Since all these things are to be destroyed in this way, what sort of people ought you to be in holy conduct and godliness, looking for and hastening the coming of the day of God, on account of which the heavens will be destroyed by burning, and the elements will melt with intense heat! But according to His promise we are looking for new heavens and a new earth, in which righteousness dwells. (2 Peter 3:10-13)

Peter's vision of our great hope for eternity is "new heavens and a new earth in which righteousness dwells"—the same as John's vision in Revelation 21. He also speaks of the heavens passing away (v. 10). He goes even farther, and says three times that there will be a destruction of the present world. Verse 10: "the elements will be destroyed with intense heat." Verse 11: "these things are to be destroyed." Verse 12: "the heavens will be destroyed by burning, and the elements will melt with intense heat." The question then is: Does this mean that the earth we live on, and the heavens we live under, will be totally done away with? And will God start over with a totally new creation?

First, I would say that when Revelation 21:1 and 2 Peter 3:10 say that the present earth and heavens will "pass away," it does not have to mean that they go out of existence, but may mean that there will be such a change in them that their present condition passes away. We might say, "The caterpillar passes away, and the butterfly emerges." There is a real passing away, and there is a real continuity, a real connection.

And when Peter says that this heaven and earth will be "destroyed" it does not have to mean entirely "put out of existence." We might say, "The flood destroyed many farms." But we don't mean that they vanished out of existence. We might say that on May 18, 1980, the immediate surroundings of Mt. St. Helens in Washington were destroyed by a blast 500 times more powerful than the Hiroshima atomic bomb. But anyone who goes there now and sees the new growth would know that "destroy" did not mean "put out of existence."

And so what Peter may well mean is that at the end of this age there will be cataclysmic events that bring this world to an end *as we know it*— not putting it out of existence, but wiping out all that is evil and cleansing it by fire and fitting it for an age of glory and righteousness and peace that will never end.

Yes, it may mean that. But does it really mean that?

PAUL'S GRAND HOPE FOR THE MATERIAL WORLD, AND US

The apostle Paul gives a strong confirmation of this interpretation in Romans 8:18-25. There are at least four reasons in these verses for thinking that the creation we know and the earth we live on will not be annihilated, but will be renewed as our eternal home.

First of all, in Romans 8:19-20 Paul says, "The anxious longing of the creation waits eagerly for the revealing of the sons of God. For the creation was subjected to futility, not of its own will, but because of Him who subjected it, in hope." He pictures the creation—the heavens and the earth—as having longings and eager expectation. Something is coming that makes creation, as it were, stand on tiptoe. He says that the reason for this eager expectation of creation is the very "futility" in which she finds herself— decay, disaster, disease, pain. Why does this produce hope and expectation in the creation? The reason is that the "subjection to futility" is a temporary curse that God himself put on creation with a view to removing it some day. This is what Paul means when he says that the creation was subjected to futility "in hope." Satan didn't do that. Satan does not do anything for the hope of the world's redemption. God did it. God's curse on the creation in Genesis 3 is not his final word. He did it *"in hope."* Therefore creation is not appointed for annihilation, but for restoration. He subjected it *in hope.*

The second reason Paul gives for why we should not expect creation to be annihilated is found in verse 21 (the content of the hope). "The creation itself also will be set free from its slavery to corruption into the freedom of the glory of the children of God." The creation is not destined for annihilation. It is destined for liberation. It will be set free from the "slavery to corruption"—the futility that God subjected it to *in hope.* This is the clearest statement that the earth and the heavens will not "pass away" or be "destroyed" *in the sense of going out of existence.* Paul says plainly, *they will be set free from corruption.* The futility will be destroyed. The bondage to corruption will be consumed in the purifying, liberating fire of God's judgment. But the earth will remain. And there will be no more corruption. No more futility. No more sin or pain or death or crying.

The third argument Paul gives against the annihilation of the present creation is found in Romans 8:22: "We know that the whole creation groans and suffers the pains of childbirth together until now." In other words, the upheavals of creation are like labor pains during the last stages of pregnancy. Something is about to be brought forth *from* creation, not *in place of* creation.

Creation is not going to be annihilated and recreated with no continuity. The earth is going to bring forth like a mother in labor (through the upheavals of fire and earthquake and volcanoes and pestilence and famine) a new earth.

Jesus used the same imagery of labor pains when he said, "Nation will rise against nation, and kingdom against kingdom, and in various places there will be *famines* and *earthquakes*. But all these things are merely the beginning of *birth pangs*" (Matthew 24:7-8). This earth is like a mother about to give birth to a new earth where righteousness dwells and where God reigns in the midst of his people.

Finally, Paul gives one last argument against the annihilation of the earth: "And not only this [not only does the natural world groan], but also we ourselves, having the firstfruits of the Spirit, even we ourselves groan within ourselves, waiting eagerly for our adoption as sons, the redemption of our body" (Romans 8:23). The reason this is so crucial is that he connects the redemption of our bodies—that is, the resurrection and restoration of our bodies after a lifetime of groaning—with the restoration of the creation. Our bodies are part of this present creation. What happens to our bodies and what happens to the creation go together. And what happens to our bodies is not annihilation but redemption: "We await the redemption of our bodies." Our bodies will be redeemed, restored, made new, not thrown away. And so it is with the heavens and the earth.

THE REBIRTH OF CREATION

Jesus calls this great work of universal renewal "the *regeneration* when the Son of Man will sit on his glorious throne" (Matthew 19:28). Creation will be "regenerated" or "born again." In Acts 3:21, Peter calls it "the period of *restoration of all things* about which God spoke by the mouth of his holy prophets."

GOD WILL BE ALL IN ALL

And what did the prophets say about the new earth? Isaiah 11:6-9 gives us an example.

And the wolf will dwell with the lamb, and the leopard will lie down with the kid, And the calf and the young lion and the fatling together; and a little boy will lead them. Also the cow and the bear will graze; their young will lie down together; and the lion will eat straw like the ox. And the nursing child will play by the hole of the cobra, and the weaned child will put his hand on the viper's den. They will not hurt or destroy in all my holy mountain, for the earth will be full of the knowledge of the Lord as the waters cover the sea. (See also Numbers 14:21; Isaiah 65:25; Micah 4:3; Habakkuk 2:14)

So history as we know it will come to an end with God at the center. His glory will be so bright as to make a moon out of the sun (Revelation 21:23). And on the earth there will be a great sea of knowledge reflecting the glory of the Lord back to him. And just as the rejection of that knowledge brought a curse on the creation, so the restoration of that knowledge will bring blessing to the creation, and the animals themselves with be free from the curse and reflect the beauty of the Lord.

Thus the purpose of God in creation will be fulfilled: the exhibition of his glory for the enjoyment of his people in the never-ending increase of infinite future grace. Jonathan Edwards soars as he thinks about it:

In the creature's knowing, esteeming, loving, rejoicing in, and praising God, the glory of God is both exhibited and acknowledged; his fullness is received and returned. Here is both emanation and remanation. The refulgence shines upon and into the creature, and is reflected back to the luminary. The beams of glory come from God, and are something of God, and are refunded back again to their original. So that the whole is of God, and in God, and to God, and God is the beginning, middle and end in this affair.[3]

Some visions of future grace plead for more than prose. Several years ago the vision of resurrection into a new earth of glory with Christ drew out from me this poem. For now, I can't do better than to end with it.

JUSTIFIED FOR EVERMORE
As far as any eye could see
There was no green. But every tree
Was cinder black, and all the ground
Was gray with ash. The only sound
Was arid wind, like spirits' ghosts,
Gasping for some living hosts
In which to dwell, as in the days
Of evil men, before the blaze
Of unimaginable fire
Had made the earth a flaming pyre
For God's omnipotent display
Of holy rage.

        The dreadful Day
Of God had come. The moon had turned
To blood. The sun no longer burned
Above, but, blazing with desire,
Had flowed into a lake of fire.
The seas and oceans were no more,
And in their place a desert floor
Fell deep to meet the brazen skies,
And silence conquered distant cries.

The Lord stood still above the air.
His mighty arms were moist and bare.
They hung, as weary, by his side,
Until the human blood had dried
Upon the sword in his right hand.
He stared across the blackened land
That he had made, and where he died.
His lips were tight, and deep inside,
The mystery of sovereign will
Gave leave, and it began to spill
In tears upon his bloody sword
For one last time.

        And then the Lord
Wiped every tear away, and turned

To see his bride. Her heart had yearned
Four thousand years for this: His face
Shone like the sun, and every trace
Of wrath was gone. And in her bliss
She heard the Master say, "Watch this:
Come forth, all goodness from the ground,
Come forth, and let the earth redound
With joy."

        And as he spoke, the throne
Of God came down to earth and shone
Like golden crystal full of light,
And banished, once for all, the night.
And from the throne a stream began
To flow and laugh, and as it ran,
It made a river and a lake,
And everywhere it flowed, a wake
Of grass broke on the banks and spread
Like resurrection from the dead.

And in the twinkling of an eye
The saints descended from the sky.

And as I knelt beside the brook
To drink eternal life, I took
A glance across the golden grass,
And saw my dog, old Blackie, fast
As she could come. She leaped the stream —
Almost—and what a happy gleam
Was in her eye. I knelt to drink,
And knew that I was on the brink
Of endless joy. And everywhere
I turned I saw a wonder there.
A big man running on the lawn:
That's old John Younge with both legs on.
The blind can see a bird on wing,
The dumb can lift their voice and sing.
The diabetic eats at will,
The coronary runs uphill.

The lame can walk, the deaf can hear,
The cancer-ridden bone is clear.
Arthritic joints are lithe and free,
And every pain has ceased to be.
And every sorrow deep within,
And every trace of lingering sin
Is gone. And all that's left is joy,
And endless ages to employ
The mind and heart, and understand,
And love the sovereign Lord who planned
That it should take eternity
To lavish all his grace on me.

O, God of wonder, God of might,
Grant us some elevated sight,
Of endless days. And let us see
The joy of what is yet to be.
And may your future make us free,
And guard us by the hope that we,
Through grace on lands that you restore,
Are justified for evermore.

PART X

LONGING FOR GOD
AND
LIVING BY FAITH

God is most glorified in us,
when we are most satisfied in him.

God is glorified not only
by His glory's being seen,
but by its being rejoiced in.
When those that see it delight in it,
God is more glorified than if they only see it.
His glory is then received by the whole soul,
both by the understanding and by the heart.
God made the world that He might communicate,
and the creature receive, His glory;
and that it might [be] received both by the mind and heart.
He that testifies his idea of God's glory
[doesn't] glorify God so much as
he that testifies also his approbation of it
and his delight in it.

JONATHAN EDWARDS

Prizing
is the essence of
praising.

CHAPTER THIRTY-ONE

The Debt I Owe to Jonathan Edwards

GOD IS MOST GLORIFIED IN US WHEN WE ARE MOST SATISFIED IN HIM

The burden of this book has been to promote living by faith in future grace to the glory of God. I have argued that the faith which justifies also sanctifies, because the nature[1] of faith is *to be satisfied with all that God is for us in Jesus.*[2] I hope to show that I am in the tradition of Jonathan Edwards who wrote, "The sum of that eternal life which Christ purchased is holiness; it is a holy happiness. And there is in faith *a liking of the happiness that Christ has procured and offers.*"[3] This "liking of the happiness Christ offers" is what I mean by "being satisfied with all that God is for us in Jesus." I have stressed the future orientation of faith, because the future is where God promises to satisfy the hearts of those who wait for him. Bygone grace is of infinite value, especially the death and resurrection of Jesus; but only because of what it secured for the future—a fellowship with God that satisfies us and glorifies him forever. Not to have faith in the future grace, which was secured by past grace, is to make the cross of Christ of no effect.[4]

Therefore, living by faith in future grace glorifies God for *all* his grace, both past and future. It honors past grace by banking fearlessly on the future which the past was designed to purchase. It honors future grace by breaking the power of sin through the superior happiness[5] of being satisfied with all that God promises to be for us from now to eternity. There is a deep conviction beneath this argument, namely, that *God is most glorified in us when we are most satisfied in him.*

I HAVE CALLED IT CHRISTIAN HEDONISM

This conviction comes as close as anything to summing up my entire theology. Elsewhere I have called it *Christian hedonism.*[6] Here at the end we may reflect on whether the message of this book is in concert with that earlier vision of God and life. Consider some of the implications of what has been said. If the nature of faith is *to be satisfied with all that God is for us in Jesus,* then the universal biblical mandate to believe is a radical and pervasive call to pursue our own happiness in God. To say that you are indifferent to your own happiness would amount to saying that you are indifferent to the nature of faith. But that would be sin. The call of this book is that we stop sinning like that, and seek, with all our might, the greatest possible satisfaction in God. Therefore living by faith in future grace is Christian hedonism—the mandate to pursue our happiness in all that God is for us in Jesus—even if it costs us our life. For the steadfast love of the Lord is better than life (Psalm 63:3).

Moreover, I have argued that the key to fighting sin is to battle unbelief, and keep the fire of faith in God's promises red hot.[7] The power of sin is the *false* promise that it will bring more happiness than holiness will bring. Nobody sins out of duty. Therefore, what breaks the power of sin is faith in the true promise that the pleasures of sin are passing and poisonous, but at God's right hand are pleasures for evermore (Psalm 16:11). This way of fighting sin with the hope of superior satisfaction, is called, in Hebrews 11:24-26, living "by faith": "*By faith* Moses...[chose] to endure ill-treatment with the people of God, [rather] than to enjoy the passing pleasures of sin...for he was looking to the reward." Therefore the cry of this book, to fight sin, is a cry to pursue a joy superior to anything sin could offer. It is the cry of Christian Hedonism.

Most important, this book is based on the conviction that living by faith in future grace will display more of the glory of God than any other way of life. At the heart of the book is the belief that radical, free obedience to Jesus Christ comes only through the channel of faith in future grace. And that channel is the embracing and cherishing and trusting and enjoying of all that God promises to be for us in Jesus. So someone may well ask whether a book that advocates the pursuit of human happiness so vigorously—even if it is a happiness in God—can really be a book devoted to the *glory of God*. Does not *living by faith in future grace,* alias *Christian hedonism,* make a god out of pleasure? I answer, No, we make a god out of what we take most pleasure in. My aim, in all my life and writing, is to make God God. The biblical truth by which I endeavor to do that is: *God is most glorified in us when we are most satisfied in him.* The breadth and depth of our pursuit of joy in God is the measure of his worth in our life.

THE DEBT I OWE TO JONATHAN EDWARDS

Good counsel tells me to alert the reader that what is coming may be heavy sledding. We are not used to reading material that is two centuries old, from a thought-world foreign to our day. Yet, as I said before: raking is easy, but you get only leaves; digging is hard, but you might find diamonds. That is what I found in a great eighteenth century pastor and theologian.

It is no secret, from what I have written elsewhere, that I am deeply indebted to Jonathan Edwards in the development of my understanding of God and life. J. I. Packer said of my book, *Desiring God: Meditations of a Christian Hedonist,* "Jonathan Edwards, whose ghost walks through most of Piper's pages, would be delighted with his disciple." That was a very generous tribute. I hope it is true of this book as well. I write with Edwards looking over my shoulder.

So in this final chapter I would like to show that living by faith in future grace and Christian hedonism stand in faithful continuity with the thinking of Jonathan Edwards. I do not claim that Edwards would have chosen my way of bringing biblical truth to bear on the modern church. Nor do I assume it is the only or even the best way. But I do want to claim that it is biblical, and that it is in the Reformed tradition of Jonathan Edwards, and that, if properly understood and applied, it leads to a God-centered life of joyful and sacrificial love.

There are at least two features of Edwards' thought that appear at first glance to be at odds with Christian hedonism. One is his treatment of "self-love." He shows that its branches don't reach high enough and its roots don't go deep enough. How will this criticism of self-love fit with our stress on faith as *being satisfied with all that God is for us in Jesus?* Christian hedonism sounds like self-love. Is it? The other feature of Edwards' thought that seems contrary to Christian hedonism is his use of the term "disinterested." Genuine love to God must be *disinterested,* he would say, which of course does not sound like the language of hedonism. Or is it?

THE PLACE OF SELF-LOVE IN THE THOUGHT OF EDWARDS

"Self-love" was a burning topic in Edwards' day. He had a love-hate relationship with the term, because it carried so much potential truth and so much potential error. He once wrote, "O, how is the world darkened, clouded, distracted, and torn to pieces by those dreadful enemies of mankind called words!"[8]

HIS PEJORATIVE USE OF SELF-LOVE

Edwards knew that some moralists in his day used the term self-love to refer simply to man's love for his own happiness, which was not a pejorative use.[9] But his preference was to use the term in its more narrow and negative sense. He says in *The Nature of True Virtue,* "Self-love, as the phrase is used in common speech, most commonly signifies a man's regard to his confined private self, or love to himself with respect to his private interest."[10] In other words, self-love was ordinarily used with the negative connotation of narrowness. It was virtually synonymous with selfishness. What makes a selfish person happy is not when others are benefited but when his own private happiness increases without consideration for others. That is the usual meaning of self-love as Edwards treats it.

In 1738 he preached a series of expositions on 1 Corinthians 13, later published under the title, *Charity and its Fruits.* One of his sermons is based on the phrase in verse 5, "Charity...seeketh not her own." The title of the sermon is "The Spirit of Charity, the Opposite of a Selfish Spirit." In it he describes the fall of man into sin like this:

The ruin that the fall brought upon the soul of man consists very much in his losing the nobler and more benevolent principles of his nature, and falling wholly under the power and government of self-love…Sin like some powerful astringent, contracted his soul to the very small dimensions of selfishness; and God was forsaken, and fellow creatures forsaken, and man retired within himself, and became totally governed by narrow and selfish principles and feelings. Self-love became absolute master of his soul, and the more noble and spiritual principles of his being took wings and flew away.[11]

So self-love in this sense is the same as the vice of selfishness. People who are governed by self-love "place [their] happiness in good things that are confined or limited to themselves, to the exclusion of others. And this is selfishness. This is the thing most clearly and directly intended by that self-love which the Scripture condemns."[12] So self-love is a trait that man has after the fall, and its evil, as we will see, is not its desire for happiness, but its finding that happiness in narrow, merely private interests.

Edwards knew quite well that even benevolence for others could be rooted in a confined and narrow self-love. Much benevolence simply rises out of natural affinity groups that unite others to ourselves—groups like family and community and nationality. Edwards called this benevolence on the basis of self-love "compounded self-love" and did not recognize it as true virtue.

But Edwards did raise the question, When can the breadth of the benevolent effects of self-love be broad enough, so that it can be called true virtue? In 1755, 17 years after he preached the sermons on 1 Corinthians 13, Edwards gave an extremely radical answer. He said, Only when it embraces the good of the whole universe of being. Or more simply, Only when it embraces God. For until then, self-love embraces "an infinitely small part of universal existence" because it does not embrace God.

If there could be a cause [like self-love] determining a person to benevolence towards the whole world of mankind, or even all created sensible natures throughout the universe, exclusive of union of heart to

general existence and of love to God—not derived from that temper of
mind which disposes to a supreme regard to him, nor subordinate to such
divine love—it cannot be of the nature of true virtue.[13]

Norman Fiering said of this statement, "We may admire the audacity of
such a statement… But it is also open to obvious criticism."[14] Then he pro-
ceeds to critique Edwards in a way that seems to ignore the aim and
achievement of Edwards in the *Nature of True Virtue*. What Edwards aims
to do is show that God is central and indispensable in the definition of true
virtue—to keep God at the center of all moral considerations, to stem the
secularizing forces of ethical thinking in his day. Edwards could not conceive of calling any act truly virtuous that did not have in it a supreme
regard to God. This is why Edwards seems to me so utterly relevant to our
day, and why he is a model of God-centered thinking.

So what Edwards was trying to do by focusing on the negative, narrow,
confined sense of self-love was to show in the end that *all* love is a narrow,
merely natural kind of love unless it has a supreme regard to God. The inadequacy of self-love is that its branches do not reach up to God. They might
embrace great causes and make great sacrifices, but if love does not embrace
God, it is infinitely parochial. In other words, Edwards' treatment of self-
love, like everything else he wrote, was aimed at defending the centrality
and indispensability of God. And that is precisely the aim of "living by faith
in future grace" as I have unfolded it in this book, and the aim of Christian
hedonism as I developed it in *Desiring God* and *The Pleasures of God*.

EDWARD'S POSITIVE TREATMENT OF SELF-LOVE

But we have not yet shown that Edwards' view of self-love can encompass
the mandate of Christian hedonism to pursue joy in God as an essential element of all true virtue and satisfaction in God as an essential element of all
true faith. So we turn now to another approach Edwards took to self-love,
one that at first is remarkably positive, but then turns up its inadequacy
because its roots don't go deep enough. My contention is that what
Edwards does here is strip away from hedonism everything that obscures
its radical God-centeredness. What is left is what I (not Edwards) call Christian hedonism.

In *Charity and Its Fruits* Edwards says,

It is not contrary to Christianity that a man should love himself, or, which is the same thing, should love his own happiness. If Christianity did indeed tend to destroy a man's love to himself, and to his own happiness, it would therein tend to destroy the very spirit of humanity… That a man should love his own happiness, is as necessary to his nature as the faculty of the will is, and it is impossible that such a love should be destroyed in any other way than by destroying his being.[15]

Edwards took all this for granted the way he took the very existence of human will for granted. But my experience is that it hits people today as though it were a new religion—which I think shows just how far we have come (fallen) from the biblical vision of Jonathan Edwards.

I suppose it may be a slight overstatement to say that Edwards took all this for granted, because he does undertake to argue for it somewhat. For example, he says,

That to love ourselves is not unlawful, is evident also from the fact, that the law of God makes self-love a rule and measure by which our love to others should be regulated. Thus Christ commands (Matthew 19:19), "Thou shalt love thy neighbor as thyself," which certainly supposes that we may, and must love ourselves… And the same appears also from the fact, that the Scriptures, from one end of the Bible to the other, are full of motives that are set forth for the very purpose of working on the principle of self-love. Such are all the promises and threatenings of the Word of God, its calls and invitations, its counsels to seek our own good, and its warnings to beware of misery.[16]

But now how does all this relate to our supreme regard for God, which Edwards argues is so indispensable to true virtue? For many thoughtful Christians, the quest for happiness seems self-centered, not God-centered. But, in fact, Edwards can help us see that the attempt to abandon that quest produces a worse self-centeredness. He clears away a lot of fog when he poses the question, "Whether or no a man ought to love God more than himself?" He answers like this:

Self-love, taken in the most extensive sense, and love to God are not things properly capable of being compared one with another; for they are not opposites or things entirely distinct, but one enters into the nature of the other… Self-love is only a capacity of enjoying or taking delight in anything. Now surely 'tis improper to say that our love to God is superior to our general capacity of delighting in anything.[17]

You can never play off self-love against love to God when self-love is treated as our love for happiness. Rather love to God is the form that self-love takes when God is discovered as the all-satisfying fountain of joy. Norman Fiering catches the sense here perfectly when he sums up Edwards' position like this: "Disinterested love to God is impossible because the desire for happiness is intrinsic to all willing or loving whatsoever, and God is the necessary end of the search for happiness. Logically one cannot be disinterested about the source or basis of all interest.[18]

DOES "DISINTERESTED" REALLY MEAN DISINTERESTED?

This is very important, because Edwards does in fact use the word "disinterested" when he talks about love to God.[19] And this is one of the features of Edwards' thought that I said earlier looks contrary to Christian hedonism, but in fact isn't. Rather, the same ambiguity exists in the term "disinterested" as with the term "self-love." When Edwards speaks of a *disinterested* love to God he means a love that is grounded not in a desire for God's gifts, but in a desire for God himself. This is absolutely crucial for understanding Edwards' relation to Christian hedonism and living by faith in future grace.

"Disinterestedness" is *not* an anti-hedonistic word as Edwards uses it. It is simply his way (common in the eighteenth century) of stressing that we must seek our joy in God himself and not in the health, wealth and prosperity he gives. It is a word designed to safeguard the God-centeredness of joy, not to oppose the pursuit of it.

You know immediately that you are in the realm of Christian hedonism when you read Edwards describing the seemingly paradoxical phrase, *disinterested delight!* This shows how careful we must be not to jump to conclusions when we see apparently non-hedonistic terms in Edwards (and

other older writers). The following crucial insights come from Edwards'
mature work on the *Religious Affections:*

> As it is with the love of the saints, so it is with their joy, and spiritual
> delight and pleasure: *the first foundation of it, is not any consideration
> or conception of their interest in* [understand: material benefit from]
> *divine things; but it primarily consists in the* sweet entertainment *their
> minds have in the view or contemplation of the divine and holy beauty
> of these things, as they are in themselves. And this is indeed the very
> main difference between the joy of the hypocrite, and the joy of the true
> saint. The former rejoices in himself; self is the first foundation of his joy:
> the latter* rejoices in God…*True saints have their minds, in the first
> place,* inexpressibly pleased and delighted *with the sweet ideas of the
> glorious and amiable nature of the things of God. And this is the spring
> of all their delights, and* the cream of all their pleasures…*But the
> dependence of the affections of hypocrites is in a contrary order: they first
> rejoice…that they are made so much of by God; and then on that
> ground, he seems in a sort, lovely to them.*[20]

A paragraph like this puts an end, once and for all, to the thought that
the term "disinterested" in Edwards means that we should not pursue our
deepest and highest pleasures in God. On the contrary! He is "the cream of
all [our] pleasures," and contemplating him is "sweet entertainment." We
should be driven on by longing for satisfaction in God himself, never content with the mere gifts of God, which are but tributaries flowing from the
Fountain himself. It is a radically hedonistic paragraph, and a profound call
to live by faith in future grace.

SHOULD WE BE WILLING TO BE DAMNED FOR THE GLORY OF GOD?

Perhaps the best proof that supreme love for God can never be played off
against the pursuit of satisfaction in God is Edwards' answer to the question, whether we should be willing to be damned for the glory of God.

> 'Tis impossible for any person to be willing to be perfectly and finally
> miserable for God's sake, for this supposes love to God is superior to

*self-love in the most general and extensive sense of self-love, which
enters into the nature of love to God... If a man is willing to be perfectly
miserable for God's sake...then he must be willing to be deprived [not
only of his own natural benefits, but also] of that which is indirectly his
own, viz., God's good, which supposition is inconsistent with itself; for to
be willing to be deprived of this latter sort of good is opposite to that principle of love to God itself, from whence such a willingness is supposed to
arise. Love to God, if it be superior to any other principle, will make a
man forever unwilling, utterly and finally, to be deprived of that part of
his happiness which he has in God's being blessed and glorified, and the
more he loves Him, the more unwilling he will be. So that this supposition, that a man can be willing to be perfectly and utterly miserable out
of love to God, is inconsistent with itself...The more a man loves God,
the more unwilling will he be to be deprived of this happiness [in God's
glory].[21]*

Phrases like, "happiness in God's being glorified," are complex. On the
one hand, they speak of God's being blessed through being glorified. Our
desire for this could almost sound altruistic toward God: he is blessed by
what happens to us. But, on the other hand, the phrase speaks of our *"happiness in God's being glorified."* Thus it becomes obvious that we are the
beneficiaries here. In fact, as I have come to see and say, God is most glorified in us when we are most satisfied in him. These two great goals are not
at odds: my joy and God's glory. The more I delight in God's being glorified,
the more valuable that glory appears.[22] To try to abandon the pursuit of one
will nullify the other.

So there is no such thing in the thought of Edwards as the ultimate
abandonment of the quest for happiness. *Disinterestedness* is affirmed only
to preserve the centrality of God himself as the object of our satisfaction.
And *self-love* is rejected only when it is conceived as a narrow love for happiness that does not have God as its supreme focus. In the words of Norman
Fiering, "The type of self-love that is overcome in finding union with God
is specifically selfishness, not the self-love that seeks the consummation of
happiness.[23]

BUT EVEN GOOD SELF-LOVE IS MERELY NATURAL

Let us press deeper with Edwards. Is there then any reason to speak of the inadequacy of self-love when it is used in this broad sense of our love for happiness that reaches all the way up to embrace God? Yes, there is. And it appears when we ask, "Why do some people put their happiness in God and others don't?" Edwards' answer was the miracle of *regeneration*. And the reason he gave this answer was the reason he did everything he did: to put God not only at the top but also at the bottom of true virtue and true faith—to make him the ground as well as the goal.

His battle was against the secularizing tendencies that he saw in the ethical theories of his day—theories that reduced all virtue into powers that man has by nature. Edwards saw this as a naive estimation of man's corruption and as an assault on the centrality of God in the moral life of the soul. How then do people come to have God as their true happiness? (Which is the same as asking, How is a Christian Hedonist created? Or: How does one come to live by faith in future grace?) Edwards observed that a love to God that arises solely from self-love "cannot be a truly gracious and spiritual love...for self-love is a principle entirely natural, and as much in the hearts of devils as angels; and therefore surely nothing that is the mere result of it can be supernatural and divine."[24]

So he goes on to insist that those who say that all love to God arises solely from self-love

> ought to consider a little further, and inquire how the man came to place his happiness in God's being glorified, and in contemplating and enjoying God's perfections... How came these things to be so agreeable to him, that he esteems it his highest happiness to glorify God?... If after a man loves God, and has his heart so united to him, as to look upon God as his chief good...it will be a consequence and fruit of this, that even self-love, or love to his own happiness, will cause him to desire the glorifying and enjoying of God; it will not thence follow, that this very exercise of self-love, went before his love to God, and that his love to God was a consequence and fruit of that. Something else, entirely distinct from self-love might be the cause of this, viz. a change made in the views of his

mind, and relish of his heart whereby he apprehends a beauty, glory, and supreme good, in God's nature, as it is in itself.[25]

So Edwards says that self-love alone can't account for the existence of spiritual love to God because, prior to the soul's pursuing happiness in God, the soul has to perceive the excellency of God and be given a relish for it. This is what happens in regeneration.

Divine love...may be thus described. 'Tis the soul's relish of the supreme excellency of the Divine nature, inclining the heart to God as the chief good. The first thing in Divine love, and that from which everything that appertains to it arises, is a relish of the excellency of the Divine nature; which the soul of man by nature has nothing of... When once the soul is brought to relish the excellency of the Divine nature, then it will naturally, and of course, incline to God every way. It will incline to be with Him and to enjoy Him. It will have benevolence to God. It will be glad that He is happy. It will incline that He should be glorified, and that His will should be done in all things. So that the first effect of the power of God in the heart in REGENERATION, is to give the heart a Divine taste or sense; to cause it to have a relish of the loveliness and sweetness of the supreme excellency of the Divine nature; and indeed this is all the immediate effect of the Divine power that there is; this is all the Spirit of God needs to do, in order to a production of all good effects in the soul.[26]

Very simply, what he is saying is this: a capacity to taste a thing must precede our desire for its sweetness. That is, regeneration must precede love's pursuit of happiness in God. So Edwards speaks of the natural power of self-love being "regulated" by this supernatural taste for God:

The change that takes place in a man, when he is converted and sanctified, is not that his love for happiness is diminished, but only that it is regulated with respect to its exercises and influence, and the courses and objects it leads to...When God brings a soul out of a miserable state and condition into a happy state, by conversion, he gives him happiness that before he had not [namely, in God], but he does not at the same time take away any of his love of happiness.[27]

So the problem with our love for happiness is never that its intensity is too great. The main problem is that it flows in the wrong channels toward the wrong objects,[28] because our nature is corrupt and in desperate need of renovation by the Holy Spirit.[29] And lest we think that, in speaking of love to God, we have moved afield from our concern with living by *faith* in future grace, recall from an earlier discussion[30] that, for Edwards, "love is the main thing in saving faith, the life and power of it, by which it produces great effects."[31]

HOW THEN SHALL WE LIVE?

This leads us finally to the duties that flow from Edwards' teaching, and its relation to living by faith in future grace and Christian hedonism. Once the renovation of our hearts happens through the supernatural work of regeneration, the pursuit of the enjoyment of the glory of God becomes more and more clearly the all-satisfying duty of the Christian. And indifference to this pursuit, as though it were a bad thing, appears as an increasingly great evil.

The heart is more and more gripped with the truth that God created the world for his own glory and that this glory echoes most clearly in the enjoyments of the saints. Listen as Edwards unfolds for us the deepest roots of Christian hedonism in the very nature of the Godhead. And notice how God's passion to be glorified and our passion to be satisfied unite into one experience.

> *God is glorified within Himself these two ways: 1. By appearing…to Himself in His own perfect idea* [of Himself], *or in His Son, who is the brightness of His glory. 2. By enjoying and delighting in Himself, by flowing forth in infinite love and delight towards Himself, or in his Holy Spirit… So God glorifies Himself toward the creatures also in two ways: 1. By appearing to…their understanding. 2. In communicating Himself to their hearts, and in their rejoicing and delighting in, and enjoying, the manifestations which He makes of Himself… God is glorified not only by His glory's being seen, but by its being rejoiced in. When those that see it delight in it, God is more glorified than if they only see it. His glory is then received by the whole soul, both by the understanding and*

by the heart. God made the world that He might communicate, and the creature receive, His glory; and that it might [be] received both by the mind and heart. He that testifies his idea of God's glory [doesn't] glorify God so much as he that testifies also his approbation of it and his delight in it.[32]

In other words, the chief end of man is to glorify God *by enjoying him forever*—which is the essence of Christian hedonism, and of living by faith in future grace. There is no final conflict between God's passion to be glorified and man's passion to be satisfied. God is most glorified in us when we are most satisfied in him.

As Edwards put it,

Because [God] infinitely values his own glory, consisting in the knowledge of himself, love to himself, and complacence and joy in himself; he therefore valued the image, communication or participation of these, in the creature. And it is because he values himself, that he delights in the knowledge, and love, and joy of the creature; as being himself the object of this knowledge, love and complacence... [Thus] God's respect to the creature's good, and his respect to himself, is not a divided respect; but both are united in one, as the happiness of the creature aimed at, is happiness in union with himself.[33]

MAXIMIZE SPIRITUAL SATISFACTION; MANIFEST THE SPLENDOR OF GOD

It follows from all this that it is impossible that anyone can pursue happiness with too much passion and zeal and intensity.[34] This pursuit is not sin. Sin is pursuing happiness where it cannot be lastingly found (Jeremiah 2:12f.), or pursuing it in the right direction, but with lukewarm, halfhearted affections (Revelation 3:16). Virtue, on the other hand, is to do what we do with all our might[35] in pursuit of the enjoyment of all that God is for us in Jesus. Therefore the cultivation of spiritual appetite is a great duty for all the saints. "Men...ought to indulge those appetites. To obtain as much of those spiritual satisfactions as lies in their power."[36]

398

The aim of this book has been to root ever more deeply in Scripture the vision of God and life called "living by faith in future grace." I take subordinate pleasure in rooting it in the thought of one of the greatest theologians in the history of the church. I put little stock in whether anybody calls this vision of God and life "Christian hedonism." That is a term that will pass away like vapor. But my prayer is that the truth in it will run and triumph. Another pastor will say it differently, and probably better, for another generation. I am called to serve mine. My passion is to assert the supremacy of God in every area of life. My discovery is that God is supreme not where he is simply served with duty but where he is savored with delight. "Delight yourself in the Lord" (Psalm 37:4) is not a secondary suggestion. It is a radical call to pursue your fullest satisfaction in all that God promises to be for you in Jesus. It is a call to live in the joyful freedom and sacrificial love that comes from faith in future grace. Then will come to pass the purpose of God who chose us in Christ to live "to the praise of his glory."

THE END

A Note on Resources

DESIRING GOD MINISTRIES

The reader who wants to ponder further the vision of God and life presented in this book may be interested in the resources provided by Desiring God Ministries (DGM)—an extension of Bethlehem Baptist Church in Minneapolis, Minnesota. DGM exists to spread a passion for the supremacy of God in all things for the joy of all peoples by:

1. producing and distributing resources for the wider Christian church that promote the vision that *God is most glorified in us when we are most satisfied in him;* and
2. appealing to non-Christians to hope in God and be satisfied with all that he is for them in Jesus.

We make all of John Piper's books available at a significant discount, and we are continually producing new audio tape, article, and manuscript collections from our archives, containing over twenty years of Dr. Piper's preaching and writing ministry. At your request we would be happy to send you a free resource catalog. We are equipped to accept VISA and MasterCard if you would like to place your order over the phone.

WHATEVER YOU CAN AFFORD!

Our goal at DGM is not to make money. Our goal is to make the treasure of the gospel as accessible to you as possible. The suggested prices in our catalog help to cover our costs, but we offer all of our resources on a whatever-you-can-afford basis. We won't allow money to be a barrier to those who wish to receive biblical teaching for their personal use. Don't be afraid to use this policy!

FOR MORE INFORMATION

Toll Free: 1-888-346-4700
On the Web: www.DesiringGod.org
E-Mail: DGMinistry@aol.com

Write: Desiring God Ministries
           Bethlehem Baptist Church
           720 13th Avenue South
           Minneapolis, Minnesota 55415-1793
           1-612-338-7653

Other Books by the Author

Love Your Enemies: Jesus' Love Command in the Synoptic Gospels and the Early Christian Paraenesis (Baker Book House, 1991, orig. 1979).

The Justification of God: An Exegetical and Theological Study of Romans 9:1-23; 2nd Edition (Baker Book House, 1993, orig. 1983).

Desiring God: Meditations of a Christian Hedonist (Multnomah Press, 1986).

The Supremacy of God in Preaching (Baker Book House, 1990).

The Pleasures of God: Meditations on God's Delight in Being God (Multnomah Press, 1991).

Recovering Biblical Manhood and Womanhood: A Response to Evangelical Feminism (edited with Wayne Grudem,Crossway Books, 1991).

Let the Nations Be Glad: The Supremacy of God in Missions (Baker Book House, 1993).

A Hunger For God: Desiring God Through Fasting and Prayer (Crossway Books, 1997).

A Godward Life: Savoring the Supremacy of God in All of Life (Multnomah Publishers, 1997).

ENDNOTES

INTRODUCTION ONE (PAGES 9-20)

1. Alister McGrath, *Spirituality in An Age of Change: Rediscovering the Spirit of the Reformers* (Grand Rapids: Zondervan Publishing House, 1994), p. 9.

2. Ibid., pp. 9, 12.

3. Ibid., p. 12.

4. Thomas Chalmers, "The Expulsive Power of a New Affection," in *The Protestant Pulpit*, ed. by Andrew Watterson Blackwood, (Grand Rapids: Baker Book House, 1947), p. 50; emphasis added.

5. J. C. Ryle, *Holiness: Its Nature, Hindrances, Difficulties, and Roots* (Grand Rapids: Baker Book House, 1979, orig., 1883), p. 382.

6. Andrew Murray, *Abide in Me* (New York: Grosset and Dunlap, n. d.), pp. vi-vii.

7. Ed. by William Goold, *The Works of John Owen*, Vol. 10, (Edinburgh: The Banner of Truth Trust, 1965, orig. 1850-53), p. 149.

INTRODUCTION TWO (PAGES 21-29)

1. The reason I do not say "alone" in this half of the sentence is that it is not precisely true, if it means "alone" in *exactly the same sense* that justification is by faith alone. Justification is by faith alone in the sense that no other acts of the soul or the body function as the God-given channel or agency of pardon. Whatever preparations the Holy Spirit may have performed in advance of faith to bring the heart to believe, and whatever accompanying acts of Bible-reading or praying or sermon-listening or weeping may have accompanied the moment of believing, or followed as a result, they are not acts that unite the soul with the justifying grace of God. Moreover, justification is an event that happens at a point in time, and is not an ongoing act of God as sanctification is. Not only that, justification is not an act that comes in varying degrees, but one that is a once-for-all and total reckoning of righteousness to us for Christ's sake. It is not mediated to us in varying measures as sanctification is. However, when it comes to sanctification, while faith is always the essential element in appropriating the power of transforming grace, there are other acts of the soul that the Word of God prescribes as a means of experiencing the ongoing empowerment of sanctifying grace, though I would say that all of these "means of grace" are exercised "from faith" (ek pisteōs) and not "from works" (ex ergōn), as Romans 9:32 says. Thus faith is the decisive human agency that connects with the sanctifying grace of God.

2. Quoted from Philip Schaff, ed., *The Creeds of Christendom,* Vol. 3, (Grand Rapids: Baker Book House, 1977, orig. 1877), pp. 10-11, 24-25.

3. Ibid., p. 218, my own translation from the original German.

4. Ibid., p. 494.

5. Ibid., p. 626; emphasis added.

6. See a more extended list of witnesses in Robert L. Dabney, "The Moral Effects of a Free Justification," in *Discussions: Evangelical and Theological,* Vol. 1, (London: The Banner of Truth Trust, 1967, orig. 1890), pp. 73-106.

7. James Buchanan, *The Doctrine of Justification* (Edinburgh: The Banner of Truth Trust, 1961, orig. 1867), p. 357.

8. Keep in mind that, in this book, this phrase "justifying faith" is always shorthand for "faith through which alone grace justifies."

9. Jonathan Edwards, "Concerning the Perseverance of the Saints," in *The Works of Jonathan Edwards,* Vol. 2, (Edinburgh: The Banner of Truth Trust, 1976, orig., 1834), p. 596.

10. John Calvin, *Sermons on Ephesians* (Edinburgh: The Banner of Truth Trust, 1973, orig., 1562), p. 290, emphasis added.

11. Ernest Reisinger, *Lord and Christ* (Phillipsburg, NJ: P&R Publishing Co., 1994), p. 45.

CHAPTER 1 (PAGES 31-39)

1. See Chapters Twelve, Sixteen, and Twenty.

2. See Chapters Fourteen and Fifteen for an extended discussion of how faith in future grace relates to "fearing God" and "hoping in God" and "taking refuge in God" and "waiting for God" and "keeping his covenant".

3. I tell the whole story later in Chapter Three.

4. This does not contradict the warnings of James (5:12) and Jesus (Matthew 5:33-37) where the warning is given not to take oaths. Oaths, in these verses are attempts to buttress the truth of your own word by calling on some reality beyond your control to bear witness to your truthfulness. A vow is simply a promise to keep your word.

CHAPTER 2 (PAGES 41-49)

1. Evelyn Miranda-Feliciano, *Filipino Values and Our Christian Faith,* (Manila: OMF Lit. 1990), p. 70.

2. Ibid., p. 70.

3. Ibid., p. 72.

4. Blanchard, Michael Kelly, "Be Ye Glad," Copyright 1980 Paragon Music Corporation (ASCAP) ARR. UBP Of Benson Music Group, Inc. (365 Great Circle Road, Nashville, TN). Diadem Sky/Gotz Music (Admin. By Diadem Music, Inc. Nashville, TN).

5. Andrew Murray, *Abide in Christ* (New York: Grosset and Dunlap, n. d.), pp. 17-18; emphasis added.

6. Ibid., p. 34.

CHAPTER 3 (PAGES 51-63)

1. I gladly give tribute to Daniel Fuller for the conception of each of these "Applying the Purifying Power" chapters. In his powerful book, *Unity of the Bible* (Grand Rapids: Zondervan Publishing House, 1992) he has a section titled "Fighting Ten Specific Attitudes of Unbelief." The conception of the Christian life behind that section was the inspiration for my own treatment of how we battle the sins that come from lack of faith in future grace.

CHAPTER 4 (PAGES 65-73)

1. Rom. 1:7; 16:20; 1 Cor. 1:3; 16:23; 2 Cor. 1:2; 13:14; Gal. 1:3; 6:18; Eph. 1:2; 6:24; Phil. 1:2; 4:23; Col. 1:2; 4:18; 1Thess. 1:1; 5:28; 2 Thess. 1:2; 3:18; 1 Tim. 1:2; 6:21; 2 Tim. 1:2; 4:22; Titus 1:4; 3:15; Philem. 3, 25.

2. Disconnected from the blessing of grace, Paul expresses the longing that the "God of peace" will be with his readers (Rom. 15:33; 2 Cor. 13:11; Phil. 4:9; 2 Thess. 3:16). Eph. 6:23 is a blessing with peace separate from the blessing with grace. But it remains noteworthy that all the blessings of grace at the end of the letters do not include peace as they did at the beginning.

3. All my observations are based on the original Greek of Paul's letters. But you can confirm this in a good literal translation like the New American Standard Bible. I put the verb "be" in brackets because in the original there is no verb. It simply says "Grace to you," and "Grace with you."

CHAPTER 5 (PAGES 75-83)

1. These are common distinctions but I have taken them most directly from J. L. Dagg, *Manual of Theology and Church Order, Part One* (Harrisonburg, VA: Gano Books, Sprinkle Publications, 1982, orig. 1857), p. 76.

2. John Sailhamer, *The Pentateuch as Narrative* (Grand Rapids: Zondervan Publishing House, 1992), p. 101.

3. Ibid., p. 103.

4. Examples of mercy oriented toward misery are Matt. 9:27; 15:22; Mark 5:19; Luke 10:37; 16:24. Examples of grace oriented toward sin and the need for forgiveness are Rom. 5:20; 6:1; 11:6; Eph. 2:8; Titus 3:7.

5. For a fuller treatment of the issue of conditional, unmerited grace see Chapters Eighteen-Twenty.

6. John Calvin, *Institutes of the Christian Religion*, Vol. 1, (Philadelphia: The Westminster Press, 1960), p. 306.

7. For a detailed support of this interpretation see John Piper, *The Justification of God: An Exegetical and Theological Study of Romans 9:1-23* 2nd ed. (Grand Rapids: Baker Book House, 1993), pp. 75-89.

8. Ibid., pp. 88-89.

9. This is my literal translation. The NASB translates, "Now to the one who works, his wage is not reckoned as a favor, but as what is due."

CHAPTER 6 (PAGES 85-99)

1. Ralph Georgy, "If God Is Dead, Then the Late 20th Century Buried Him," Minneapolis *Star Tribune*, September 12, 1994.

2. Quoted from Stephen Charnock, in *A Puritan Golden Treasury* (Edinburgh: The Banner of Truth Trust, 1977), p. 223.

3. G. K. Chesterton, *Orthodoxy* (Garden City, NY: Image Books, Doubleday and Company, 1959, orig. 1924), p. 31.

4. A quote from *Mere Christianity* cited in *A Mind Awake: An Anthology of C. S. Lewis*, Clyde Kilby, ed.,(New York: Harcourt, Brace and World, Inc., 1968), p. 115.

5. C. S. Lewis, *Letters of C. S. Lewis*, ed., W. H. Lewis, (New York: Harcourt, Brace and World, Inc., 1966), p. 256.

6. John Piper, *Desiring God: Meditations of a Christian Hedonist* (Portland: Multnomah Press, 1986), p. 222.

7. On the meaning of Christian hedonism, see Chapter Thirty-One.

CHAPTER 8 (PAGES 111-119)

1. John Flavel, *The Works of John Flavel* (Edinburgh: Banner of Truth Trust, reprint, 1988) p. 418.

CHAPTER 9 (PAGES 121-129)

1. For a fuller discussion of this truth see John Piper, *The Pleasures of God* (Portland: Multnomah Press, 1991), Chapter Five, especially pp. 138-142.

2. See further evidence for this in Chapter Five where Paul explains the freedom of grace by showing that it raises the spiritually dead (Eph. 2:5).

3. See Rom. 11:1-2; Gen. 18:17-19; Hos. 13:4-5; Ps. 1:6; Matt. 7:23; 1 Cor. 8:3; Gal. 4:8-9; 2 Tim. 2:16-19. See Piper, *The Pleasures of God*, pp. 139-141.

CHAPTER 10 (PAGES 131-141)

1. I am aware that in common psychological parlance this has not been the definition. The common definition in psychotherapy has been this: "While guilt is a painful feeling of regret and responsibility for one's actions, shame is a painful feeling about oneself as a person." Quoted from *Facing Shame* by M. Fossum and M. Mason, in John Bradshaw, *Healing the Shame That Binds You*, (Deerfield Beach, Florida: Health Communications, Inc., 1988), p. 17. I do not embrace this definition, first, because it is not the definition used in Scripture. So the use of it makes understanding and applying Scripture more difficult. Secondly, I don't use it because it generally goes hand in hand with an assessment of the human

situation that minimizes the biblical doctrine of original sin (Bradshaw, p. 65), relativizes moral absolutes (Bradshaw, p. 199), rejects biblical conditions of love (Bradshaw, p. 120), and turns God into the spiritual embodiment of absolutely unconditional approval, which never says, "should," "ought" or "must."

2. Sometimes we speak of all our sins, past, present and future, as already forgiven in the past, since they were "condemned" in the death of Jesus (Rom. 8:3) and covered by the blood of Christ (Heb. 9:14; 10:12) and forgiven through his blood (Eph. 1:7). Other times we speak of God forgiving us in an ongoing way as we confess our sins (John 1:9) and ask for forgiveness (Matt. 6:12) on the basis of the once-for-all atonement that he made for us in Christ.

CHAPTER 11 (PAGES 143-155)

1. For my effort to explain God's sovereignty in light of sin and calamity see Piper, *The Pleasures of God*, Chapter Two, "God's Pleasure in All That He Does," (Portland: Multnomah Press, 1991), pp. 47-78.

2. As we just saw, Deuteronomy 30:6 mentioned "love" as a missing link in the heart of the people. We will see in Chapters Sixteen and Eighteen how loving God and trusting God are overlapping and interworven realities. We will define the heart of faith as being satisfied with all that God is for us in Jesus. But this means that love to God is woven into the heart of faith since love means delighting in who God is.

3. The translation of the NASB is awkward because the original Greek is difficult. It could mean that the unbelievers were not united to people like Moses and Caleb and Joshua in their faith. Or it might mean that the word of God was not united to them by faith. In either case one point is clear: the reason the word of God did not produce obedience was that faith was missing in those who heard. It is also clear that God's demand was that the Word meet with faith.

4. Gen. 15:6; see Chapter Fourteen, note 4.

5. See Chapter Fourteen, note 4.

6. In the context Isaiah 64:6 does not mean that all righteousness performed by God's people is unacceptable to God. Isaiah is referring to people whose righteousness is in fact hypocritical. It is no longer righteousness. But in the verse just before this Isaiah says that God approvingly meets "him who rejoices in doing righteousness" (v. 5).

7. "Good works, being the effects and evidences of faith, and, as such, the signs or tokens of Justification, they cannot form any part of the ground of which faith relies, or on which Justification depends." Buchanan, *The Doctrine of Justification*, p. 358.

CHAPTER 12 (PAGES 157-169)

1. The Greek word for commandment, *entole,* is used 67 times in the New Testament.

2. Jonathan Edwards, "Concerning Faith" in *The Works of Jonathan Edwards*, 2 (Edinburgh: The Banner of Truth Trust, 1974), p. 586. On page 588 he argues that "love belongs

to the essence of saving faith" because of the way Paul quotes Isa. 64:4 in 1 Cor. 2:9 where loving God replaces waiting on God, which is an Old Testament way of referring to "faith in God, or trusting in God."

3. See Chapters Fifteen and Sixteen.

4. Ernest Reisinger, *Lord and Christ: The Implications of Lordship for Faith and Life* (Phillipsburg, NJ: P&R Publishing, 1994), p. 45.

5. Charles Spurgeon, *Twelve Sermons on Prayer* (Grand Rapids: Baker Book House, 1971), p. 115.

6. Charles Spurgeon, *An All Round Ministry* (Edinburgh: Banner of Truth Trust, 1969, orig. 1900) p. 343.

7. C.E.B. Cranfield, *The Epistle to the Romans,* Vol. 1, (Edinburgh: T. & T. Clark Limited, 1975), p. 384

CHAPTER 13 (PAGES 171-183)

1. Karl Olsson, *Passion* (New York: Harper and Row Publishers, 1963), pp. 116-117.

2. Richard Wurmbrand, *One Hundred Prison Meditations* (Middlebury, IN: Living Sacrifice Books, 1982), pp. 6-7.

3. In fact I have a book in mind—Steve Halliday's, *No Night Too Dark: How God Turns Defeat into Glorious Triumph* (Sisters, OR: Multnomah Books, Questar Publishers, Inc., 1993).

4. See Roger Nicole, "B. B. Warfield and the Calvinist Revival," in John D. Woodbridge, ed., *Great Leaders of the Christian Church* (Chicago: Moody Press, 1988), p. 344.

5. B. B. Warfield, *Faith and Life* (Edinburgh: The Banner of Truth Trust, 1974, orig. 1914), p. 204.

6. H. C. G. Moule, *Charles Simeon* (London: The InterVarsity Fellowship, 1948, orig. 1892), p. 39.

7. Ibid., p. 172.

SEE CHAPTER 14 (PAGES 185-195)

1. See Chapter Four, note 1.

2. Over a hundred years ago James Buchanan spoke of the relation between faith and grace as a "channel." It may have connotations today that might mislead some. But it is not a new word in this connection. Buchanan was speaking in regard to justification and the imputed righteousness of Christ: "Faith is not itself the righteousness by which we are justified, but only the *channel* through which we receive another righteousness" (italics added). James Buchanan, *The Doctrine of Justification*, p. 375.

3. I think Henry Alford is right when he says, "How is the danger generally described? As [every evil work]: and it is implied that the falling into such a danger would preclude him from enduring to Christ's heavenly kingdom. It was then an [evil work] from which he was on this occasion delivered. What [evil work]? *The falling into the power of the tempter;*

the giving way, in his own weakness and the desertion of all, and betraying the Gospel for which he was sent as a witness. The *lion* then is the *devil.*" Henry Alford, *The Greek New Testament,* Vol. 3, (Chicago: Moody Press, 1958), p. 405.

4. The best brief discussion I know concerning the meaning of the phrase, "faith was reckoned to him as righteousness," is found in John Murray, *The Epistle to the Romans,* 1, Appendix A, (Grand Rapids: Wm. B. Eerdmans Pub. Co., 1959), pp. 353-359. Murray develops nine arguments why this phrase does not mean that faith itself is the ground of our being viewed as righteous before God. The righteousness reckoned to us for our righteous standing before a holy God is "the righteousness of God" (Rom. 10:3) which is "from faith" (Rom. 10:6). We believe "unto" this righteousness in the same way that we confess "unto" salvation (Rom. 10:10), however, confession does not constitute salvation, but leads to it, just as believing does not constitute our righteousness, but leads to it. In Romans 3:22, justification is explained as the revealing of the "righteousness of God through faith in Jesus Christ for all who believe." Again faith is the agency of receiving the justifying righteousness of God. 2 Corinthians 5:21 says that "[God] made [Christ] who knew no sin to be sin on our behalf, that we might become *the righteousness of God* in Him." In Philippians 3:9, Paul says that he was "found in [Christ] not having a righteousness of my own derived from the Law, but that which is *through faith* in Christ, the righteousness which comes from God *on the basis of faith.*" 1 Corinthians 1:30 says that Christ is to us righteousness. And Romans 5:19 speaks of God constituting us righteous through the obedience of Christ in a way similar to the way we were constituted sinners through the disobedience of Adam. Moreover the context of Romans 4:7-8 (referring to Ps. 32) suggests that the righteousness in view in Rom. 4:3 includes the complete covering of all the sins of the one who receives it. This would not fit well with saying that God simply treats our faith as our righteousness. The upshot of all these texts, as well as contextual considerations of Romans 4:3-8, is that *faith being reckoned for righteousness* probably means that God "counts" faith as the indispensable connection with the gift of righteousness that he gives—his own righteousness. For example, I might tell my son that he must clean his room, or he can't go to the ball game tonight. He plans wrong and leaves for school without doing it. I discover the messy room and clean it. He comes home and realizes what he has done and feels terrible. He apologizes and offers to accept the punishment. To which I say, "I will reckon your apology as a clean room." What I mean is not that the apology is a clean room. Nor that he really cleaned his room. I did. It was pure grace. All I mean is that, in my way of reckoning, faith connects him with the blessing given to the clean room. The clean room is his clean room. I reckon it to be so "by his apology." But it is a perfectly acceptable use of language to say, "I reckon your apology as a clean room."

5. James H. Taylor, "You Never Ask for Money?" in: *When God Provides* (Singapore: OMF Books, 1986), p. 6; emphasis added.

6. Ibid., p. 6.

7. Ibid., p. 7.

8. Ibid., p. 5.

9. See Chapter Four.

10. Some may prefer to be more precise and say that justification is an "act" of God, while sanctification is a "work" of God. A.A. Hodge, for example, says, "[Justification] is an act of God pronouncing that with respect to this person the law has no penal demands—that all its demands in the covenant of salvation have been satisfied...[But sanctification] is not an *act* but a *work* of God's grace, wherein he sustains and develops, perfects and continues, the work which he has commenced [in regeneration]." *Evangelical Theology* (Edinburgh: The Banner of Truth Trust, 1976, orig. 1890), pp. 295-296. Leonardus Riissenius gave the traditional Protestant distinction between justification and sanctification as follows: (1) justification is a forensic action; sanctification is physical and real; (2) justification takes place to a great extent outside a man in the word of God and in Christ; sanctification takes place in a man; (3) justification involves no more than a moral change and one of status; sanctification imports a real and new creation; (4) justification takes place perfectly once for all; sanctification is gradual." Quoted in Heinrich Heppe, *Reformed Dogmatics*, ed. Ernst Bizer, (Grand Rapids: Baker Book House, 1978, orig. 1861), p. 566.

11. See Piper, *The Pleasures of God*, Chapter Four, pp. 101-122; and *Desiring God*, Appendix One, pp. 227-235.

12. Charles Spurgeon, *An All-Round Minister* (Edinburgh: Banner of Truth Trust, 1960, orig., 1900), p. 233.

CHAPTER 15 (PAGES 197-207)

1. Quoted in *Treatise Concerning the Religious Affections*, in *The Works of Jonathan Edwards*, Vol. 2, (New Haven: Yale University Press, 1959), p. 174.

2. Ibid., p. 171.

3. Ibid., p. 177.

4. Ibid., p.170; italics added. For a contemporary assessment of what aspects of revival today are spiritual and what are not see John White, *When the Spirit Comes with Power*, (Downers Grove, IL: InterVarsity Press, 1988): "In itself, a given manifestation [of the Spirit] is no sign that something of spiritual value has been accomplished" (p. 82).

5. Charles Hodge, *The Way of Life*, ed. Mark Noll, (New York: Paulist Press, 1987), p. 31.

6. Ibid., p. 43.

7. Ibid., p. 154.

8. Ibid., p. 156.

9. A hundred years before Charles Hodge pondered these things, Jonathan Edwards was probing the depths of true faith as he wrestled with much inauthenticity of religious affection in the Great Awakening in New England. This text in 2 Corinthians 4:4-6 was also central for Edwards' understanding of saving faith. He said of this text, "Nothing can be more evident than that a saving belief of the gospel is here spoken of by the apostle as arising from the mind being enlightened to behold the divine glory of the things it exhibits." *Dissertation Concerning the Religious Affections*, in *The Works of Jonathan Edwards*, Vol. 1,

(Edinburgh: The Banner of Truth Trust, 1974), p. 290.

Edwards believed that saving faith must be reasonable and spiritual. "By a reasonable conviction I mean a conviction founded on *real evidence,* or upon that which is good reason, or just ground of conviction." Where does this evidence come from? "The gospel of the blessed God does not go abroad abegging for its evidence, so much as some think: it has its highest and most proper evidence in itself." Specifically "the mind ascends to the truth of the gospel by one step, and that is its *divine glory*... Unless men may come to a reasonably solid persuasion and conviction of the truth of the gospel...*by a sight of its glory,* it is impossible that those who are illiterate and unacquainted with history, should have any thorough and effectual conviction of it at all" (p. 292).

Thus, as in the view of Hodge, "It is requisite not only that the belief...should be *reasonable,* but also a *spiritual* belief or conviction." Not all reasonable conviction is genuine, saving conviction, for "some natural men yield a kind of assent of their judgments to the truth of the Christian religion from the rational proofs or arguments that are offered to evince it." He cites, for example, Judas and others who heard Jesus (John 2:23-25) and Simon the Sorcerer (Acts 8:13, 23). True faith must be spiritual as well as reasonable. "A *spiritual* conviction of the truth of the great things of the gospel, is such a conviction as arises from having a spiritual apprehension" (p. 290). This spiritual apprehension "consists in a *sense* and *taste* of the divine, supreme, and holy excellency and beauty of those things." "He that has perceived the sweet taste of honey, knows much more about it than he who has only looked upon it and felt it." Thus "spiritual understanding primarily consists in this sense of taste of the moral beauty of divine things" (p. 283).

10. Jonathan Edwards, *The Life of David Brainerd,* ed. Norman Pettit, *The Works of Jonathan Edwards,* Vol. 7, (New Haven: Yale University Press, 1985, orig. 1749), p. 456.

11. Ibid., p. 456; italics added.

12. Ibid., p. 412; italics added.

13. Ibid., p. 158.

14. Ibid., p. 158.

15. This definition was implicit in Piper, *Desiring God,* p. 53; and it became explicit in *The Pleasures of God,* pp. 254, 292. I am gratified to read the same definition commended by John MacArthur in his excellent book, *Faith Works* (Dallas: Word Publishing Co., 1993). He says, "Notice we have come full circle to the definition of faith suggested by the [Oxford] English dictionary: Faith is being satisfied with Christ." p. 48. See also pp. 30, 39, 52. He cites John 6:35 in support, which we will deal with in the next chapter. Similarly Ernest Reisinger makes the observation concerning saving faith: "There is, however, one thing common to all who possess true saving faith, namely, a heart-satisfaction with God's plan of salvation by Christ [including, of course, fellowship with Christ himself]. When one is pleased with God's method of satisfying His justice through Christ's person and work, and when the soul and heart embrace that plan, then one is believing unto salvation." *Lord and Christ: The Implications of Lordship for Faith and Life* (Phillipsburg, NJ: P&R Publishing, 1994), p. 46.

16. See the support for this from Jonathan Edwards and our interpretation of 1 John 5:1-5 in Chapter Twelve, note 2. Edwards argues that love "belongs to the essence of saving faith."

17. Daniel Fuller, *The Unity of the Bible* (Grand Rapids: Zondervan Publishing House, 1992), p. 272.

CHAPTER 16 (PAGES 209-217)

1. Merrill Tenney, *John: The Gospel of Belief* (Grand Rapids: William B. Eerdman's Publishing Co., 1948).

2. C.K. Barrett, *The Gospel According to John* (London: S.P.C.K., 1960), p. 168.

3. Leon Morris, *The Gospel According to John* (Grand Rapids: Wm. B. Eerdmans Pub. Co., 1971), p. 206.

4. Barrett, *The Gospel According to John*, p. 287.

5. Morris, *The Gospel According to John.*, p. 455.

6. Sometimes it is objected that the drawing is not effectual but only suggestive since, in John 12:32, Jesus says, "And I, if I be lifted up from the earth, will *draw all men* to Myself." If he draws "all men," they say, then the drawing can't really be the decisive thing in their coming, since many do not come. There are two problems with this objection. One is that "all men" is a loose translation of "all." There is no word for "men" in the verse. It simply says, "I will draw all to myself." It is likely that this "all" refers to "his own sheep" whom, as John 10:3 says, he calls and they follow him. In John 10:16 Jesus says, "I have other sheep, which are not of this fold; I *must bring* them also, and they shall hear My voice." The words "must bring them" correspond to "draw all" in John 12:32. The other problem with saying that the drawing of John 6:44 is not effectual is that the same drawing is referred to once more at the end of chapter 6 in reference to why Judas betrayed Jesus: John 6:64 "'But there are some of you who do not believe.' For Jesus knew from the beginning who they were who did not believe, and who it was that would betray Him. And He was saying, 'For this reason [that is, because Judas betrayed him] have I said to you, that no one can come to Me, unless it has been granted him from the Father.'" This means that the ultimate explanation for why Judas betrayed Jesus is that it was not granted him by the Father to come. God left him in his rebellion as the "son of perdition" (John 17:12). Therefore John does indeed intend for the "drawing" of John 6:44, 65 to be understood as decisive in begetting faith.

CHAPTER 17 (PAGES 219-229)

1. Martin Luther, *Freedom of a Christian*, in *Three Treatises* (Philadelphia: Fortress Press, 1960), p. 284.

CHAPTER 18 (PAGES 231-237)

1. In this book, the term "condition" carries the simple dictionary definition, "something essential to the appearance or occurrence of something else: prerequisite." *Webster's New*

Collegiate Dictionary (Springfield, Mass., G.&C. Merriam Co., 1977), p. 235. It does not imply "uncertainty" about whether the condition will be fulfilled. Such a claim will be determined by the context.

2. For a justification of this interpretation see Piper, *The Pleasures of God,* pp. 153-154, note 13.

3. For a fuller discussion of this text see Piper, *The Pleasures of God,* pp. 130-131; and *The Justification of God: An Exegetical and Theological Study of Romans 9:1-23,* 2nd edition, (Grand Rapids: Baker Book House, 1993), pp. 47-74.

4. This is the meaning of the word "called" in Matthew 22:14, "Many are called, but few are chosen," but not in the writings of the apostle Paul.

5. For an fuller explanation of the unconditional call of God see, Chapter Nine, pp. ** and Piper, *The Pleasures of God,* pp. 140, 155.

6. Quoted in Henry Bettenson, *Documents of the Christian Church* (London: Oxford University Press, 1967), p.54.

7. See Chapter Twelve, note 2.

CHAPTER 19 (PAGES 239-249)

1. A much fuller collection of texts relating to the conditionality of future grace is given in Piper, *The Pleasures of God* pp. 291-305.

2. I say "almost" because at the deepest root of our lives, the grace to keep us seeking God is an unconditional work of God causing us to endure to the end and be saved. When we are about to forsake the faith, the last decisive impulse that turns our hearts back to God is the ongoing keeping power of God. It is *conditional* in the sense that God is committed to do it only in those who are justified by faith. But it is *unconditional* in the sense that the ongoing pursuit of God depends ultimately on God's keeping power, not vice versa. God has committed himself to supply the elect with the grace to seek God in prayer, which brings down the additional grace to meet the condition of faith, that brings down the additional grace to meet the condition of holiness, that brings the additional grace of final glory.

3. A. A. Hodge explains why we must confess sin every day. "St. Augustine said fourteen hundred years ago—and the language has never been improved—'Every lesser good has an essential element of sin.' Now, for instance, suppose that you loved God, suppose that there is nothing in your heart but love to God. It does not follow that you do not sin. You say, 'I love God, and there is nothing in my heart but love to God. Is not love right?' Yes, if you love God with all your heart, with all your mind, and with all your strength, and with all your manhood. But if there be in this love any defect—if it come short in quality, if it come short in quantity—then it partakes of the nature of sin; for every lesser good, as well as every degree of good short of perfection, is of the essential nature of sin itself." *Evangelical Theology* (Edinburgh: The Banner of Truth Trust, 1976), pp. 300-301.

CHAPTER 20 (PAGES 251-259)

1. I say it like this because for those who are not yet called and are still in unbelief some future grace is indeed unconditional, namely, their calling out of darkness into light and their regeneration. See Chapter Nine.

2. See Chapter Twenty-Two for how this works out in real life.

3. This summary quote is taken from Nicky Gumbel, *Questions of Life* (Eastbourne, England: Kingsway Publications, 1993), pp. 47-48.

4. In saying that Jesus trusted in future "grace" I do not imply that he was deficient and needed to be forgiven. He is the one human being who perfectly fulfilled the expectations of God and was thus able to stand in our place as our flawless sacrificial substitute and our covenant representative before a holy God. Yet I am hesitant to call Jesus' obedience in life and death the fulfilment of a "covenant of works." This term generally implies that "works" stand over against "grace," and are not the fulfillment of faith in grace. Thus works implies a relationship with God that is more like an employer receiving earned wages than like a Son trusting a Father's generosity.

I have explained briefly in Chapter Five the way I see God's grace as the basis of his relationship with Adam and Eve before the fall. I see Christ, the Second Adam, fulfilling this covenant of grace (not works) perfectly by trusting his Father's provision at every moment and obeying all his commandments by faith. His relationship to the Father was one of constant trust. His obedience was the effect of this trust. "Grace" toward Jesus was not exactly the same as grace toward fallen sinners. He never sinned (Heb. 4:15). Yet, in his human life he was dependent on God similar to the way we are. Not only that, he took our sin on himself (Isa. 53:6). Thus God exerted a kind of "grace" in overcoming his curse on sin in order to exalt Jesus.

This may be why Paul, in Philippians 2:9 said that because Christ humbled himself like a servant even unto death on a cross, "therefore also God highly exalted Him and bestowed (*echarisatō*) on Him the name which is above every name." The word for "bestowed" is always used by Paul (12 times) to indicate free, gracious giving and forgiving by God or by Christians. It is not the word one would have expected if God were relating to Jesus as a "wage-earner" to a "wage-payer." On this text (Phil. 2:9) Peter O'Brien agrees with Paul Feinberg in saying, "[Jesus'] death upon the cross was offered 'through the eternal Spirit' (Heb. 9:14). Thus Feinberg concludes that 'while Jesus' actions were his and while they were the ground of God's action they were done through the Holy Spirit, and as such do not constitue a doctrine of merit or works.'" Peter T. O'Brien, *The Epistle to the Philippians,*(Grand Rapids: William B. Eerdmans Publishing Company, 1991), p. 234.

This does not nullify the substitutionary work of Christ nor does it make his obedience any less the ground of our justification and the vindication of the Father's righteousness. Rather it says that the obedience that Adam failed to perform by faith, Christ has perfectly performed by faith. In this way Christ is indeed a perfect example to us how we should live and love by faith in future grace, even if grace for him was Fatherly beneficence without having to overcome sinful deficiency—except in the sense of the Father's overcoming Christ's taking our sin upon him. See my chapter on "The Pleasure of God in Bruising the Son" in *The Pleasures of God*, (Portland: Multnomah Press, 1991), pp. 161-186.

5. James Buchanan expresses the classic Protestant view of how the works of love relate to saving faith. "[Good works] are the effects of faith, and, as such, the evidences both of faith, and of justification. That they are the effects of faith is clear; for 'whatsoever is not of faith is sin' [Rom. 14:23]; and 'without faith it is impossible to please God' [Heb. 11:6]; and 'the end of the commandment is charity, out of a pure heart, and of a good conscience, and of faith unfeigned' [1 Tim. 1:5]. It is equally clear that, being the effects, they are also the evidences, of a true and living faith; for 'a man may say, Thou hast faith, and I have works: show me thy faith without thy works, and I will show thee my faith by my works' [James 2:18]; and all the good works, which are ascribed to believers under the Old Testament, are traced to the operation of faith [Heb. 11:4, 7, 8, 17, 23, 32]." *The Doctrine of Justification* (Edinburgh: The Banner of Truth Trust, 1961, orig. 1867), p. 357.

6. Of course in the case of an unconverted person, I do not mean to say that the grace of regeneration, which, for him, is still future, is conditional upon faith and love. I have explained that in Chapter Eighteen. What I am referring to here are all the blessings of future grace promised to those who have been brought to faith. The ongoing experience of these blessings is conditional on a faith that loves others.

CHAPTER 21 (PAGES 261-273)

1. Jonathan Edwards, "The End of the Wicked Contemplated by the Righteous," in *The Works of Jonathan Edwards*, Vol. 2, (Edinburgh: Banner of Truth Trust, 1974), pp. 207-208. Edwards explains further "why the sufferings of the wicked will not cause grief to the righteous, but the contrary." He says, *"Negatively;* it will not be because the saints in heaven are the subjects of any ill disposition; but on the contrary, this rejoicing of theirs will be the fruit of an amiable and excellent disposition: it will be the fruit of a perfect holiness and conformity to Christ, the holy Lamb of God. The devil delights in the misery of men from cruelty, and from envy and revenge, and because he delights in misery, for its own sake, from a malicious disposition.

"But it will be from exceedingly different principles, and for quite other reasons, that the just damnation of the wicked will be an occasion of rejoicing to the saints in glory. It will not be because they delight in seeing the misery of others absolutely considered. The damned, suffering divine vengeance, will be no occasion of joy to the saints merely as it is the misery of others, or because it is pleasant to them to behold the misery of others merely for its own sake...It is not to be understood, that they are to rejoice in having their revenge glutted, but to rejoice in seeing the justice of God executed, and in seeing his love to them in executing it on his enemies.

"Positively; the sufferings of the damned will be no occasion of grief to the heavenly inhabitants, as they will have *no love nor pity* to the damned as such. It will be no argument

of want of a spirit of love in them, that they do not love the damned; for the heavenly inhabitants will know that it is not fit that they should love them, because they will know then, that God has no love to them, nor pity for them."

Edwards raises the objection that, since it is right and good that we grieve over the faithlessness and lostness of men now in this age (Rom. 9:1-3; Luke 19:41), surely it would be right to feel the same in the age to come. He answers, "It is now our duty to love all men, though they are wicked; but it will not be a duty to love wicked men hereafter. Christ, by many precepts in his word has made it our duty to love all men. We are commanded to love wicked men, and our enemies and persecutors, but this command doth not extend to the saints in glory, with respect to the damned in hell. Nor is there the same reason that it should. We ought now to love all and even wicked men; we know not but that God loves them. However wicked any man is, yet we know not but that he is one whom God loved from eternity; we know not but that Christ loved him with a dying love, had his name upon his heart before the world was, and had respect to him when he endured those bitter agonies on the cross. We know not but that he is to be our companion in glory to all eternity..."

"We ought now to seek and be concerned for the salvation of wicked men, because now they are capable subjects of it...It is yet a day of grace with them and they have the offers of salvation. Christ is as yet seeking their salvation; he is calling upon them inviting and wooing them; he stands at the door and knocks. He is using many means with them, is calling them, saying *Turn ye, turn ye, why will ye die?*... But it will not be so in another world: there wicked men will be no longer capable subjects of mercy. The saints will know, that it is the will of God the wicked should be miserable to all eternity. It will therefore cease to be their duty any more to seek their salvation, or to be concerned about their misery. On the other hand it will be their duty to rejoice in the will and glory of God. It is not our duty to be sorry that God hath executed just vengeance on the devils, concerning whom the will of God in their eternal state is already known to us" (pp. 208-210).

2. Edwards, "The End of the Wicked Contemplated by the Righteous," p. 210.

3. Edward John Carnell, *Christian Commitment* (New York: Macmillan Company, 1957), pp. 94-95.

4. Thomas Watson, *Body of Divinity* (Grand Rapids: Baker Book House, 1979, orig. 1692), p. 581. Watson's definition of forgiveness is very helpful, both for what it says and what it does not say. He asks, "When do we forgive others?" And he answers, "When we strive against all thoughts of revenge; when we will not do our enemies mischief, but wish well to them, grieve at their calamities, pray for them, seek reconciliation with them and show ourselves ready on all occasions to relieve them" (p. 581).

5. The NASB translates "entrusting himself to him who judges justly." But the word "himself" is not in the original Greek. It simply says "entrusting to him who judges justly."

CHAPTER 22 (PAGES 275-285)

1. Chapter 11, paragraph 2 on "Justification" Quoted from Schaff, *The Creeds of Christendom*, Vol. 3, (Grand Rapids: Baker Book House, 1977), p. 626.

2. John Calvin, *The Epistle of Paul to the Galatians*, trans. T.H.L. Parker, (Grand Rapids: Wm. B. Eerdmans Pub. Co., 1965), p. 96.

3. Henry Skougal, *The Life of God in the Soul of Man* (Harrisonburg, Va.: Sprinkle Publications, 1986, orig. 1677), p. 62.

CHAPTER 23 (PAGES 287-297)

1. Henry Martyn, *Journal and Letters of Henry Martyn* (New York: Protestant Episcopal Society for the Promotion of Evangelical Knowledge, 1851), p. 460.

2. I took these little summary vignettes from Clay Sterrett, "Hanging Tough," *Faith and Renewal*, Vol. 16, No. 4, January/February, 1992, p. 19.

3. The facts and quotes of this story of Evelyn Brand are taken from Paul Brand with Philip Yancy, "And God Created Pain," *Christianity Today*, January 10, 1994, pp. 22-23.

4. Again I stress that gratitude is a precious and indispensable response to God in the Christian heart. But, contrary to much of Christian thinking, the New Testament does not portray gratitude as the motive for ministry. See Chapters One and Two.

5. "While the throne of grace is open, and you yourselves not overwhelmed by the danger"—Henry Alford, *The Greek New Testament*, Vol. 4, (Chicago: Moody Press, 1958), p. 90. "At the divinely appointed time"—*Theological Dictionary of the New Testament*, Vol. 3., ed. G. Kittel, trans. G. Bromiley, (Grand Rapids: Wm. B. Eerdmans Pub. Co., 1965), p. 462.

CHAPTER 24 (PAGES 299-309)

1. Martyn Lloyd-Jones, *Spiritual Depression* (Grand Rapids: Wm. B. Eerdmans Pub. Co., 1965). p 37.

2. Ibid., p. 6.

3. Ibid., p. 109.

4. Edwards, *The Life of David Brainerd*, ed. Norman Pettit, in *The Works of Jonathan Edwards*, Vol. 7, (New Haven: Yale University Press, 1985), p. 64.

5. Ibid., p. 101.

6. Ibid., pp. 93, 141, 165, 278.

7. Ibid., pp. 18-19.

8. Darrel W. Amundsen, "The Anguish and Agonies of Charles Spurgeon" in *Christian History*, Issue 29 (Vol. 10, No. 1), p. 24.

9. Charles Spurgeon, *Lectures to My Students* (Grand Rapids: Zondervan Publishing House, 1972), p. 163.

10. Amundsen, "The Anguish and Agonies of Charles Spurgeon," p. 24.

11. Lloyd-Jones, *Spiritual Depression*, p. 20; italics added.
12. Ibid., pp. 20-21.

CHAPTER 25 (PAGES 311-319)

1. J.I. Packer, *A Quest for Godliness: The Puritan Vision of the Christian Life* (Wheaton: Crossway Books, 1990), p. 12. The story is told more fully in John Owen, *Sin and Temptation*, abridged and edited by James M. Houston, (Portland: Multnomah Press, 1983), introduction, pp. xxv-xxix.
2. Edwards, *The Life of David Brainerd*, ed. Norman Pettit, in *The Works of Jonathan Edwards*, Vol. 7, (New Haven: Yale University Press, 1985), p. 278.
3. Ibid., p. 246.
4. Ibid., p. 366.

CHAPTER 26 (PAGES 321-327)

1. John Sailhamer, *The Pentateuch as Narrative* (Grand Rapids: Zondervan Publishing House, 1992), pp. 103-104.

CHAPTER 27 (PAGES 329-339)

1. Reported in the (Minneapolis) *Star Tribune*, July 22, 1993.
2. This quote comes from Dabney's compelling essay on the necessity of good works (including sexual purity) in the light of free justification by grace through faith, Robert L. Dabney, "The Moral Effects of Free Justification," in *Discussions: Evangelical and Theological* (London: The Banner of Truth Trust, 1967, orig. 1890), p. 96.
3. "The Anatomy of Lust," *Leadership*, (Fall 1982), pp. 43-44.

CHAPTER 28 (PAGES 341-351)

1. See the January issue each year of *International Bulletin of Missionary Research*.
2. Albrecht Vogel, "Decius," in *Schaff-Herzog Encyclopedia*, Vol. 1, (New York: The Christian Literature Co. 1882), p. 620.
3. *First Things*, Issue 48, (December, 1994), p. 82.
4. *National and International Religion Report*, Vol. 9, No. 5, (Feb. 1995).
5. *Christianity Today*, Vol. 39., No. 2, (Feb. 20, 1995), p. 58.
6. Charles White, "Small Sacrifices," *Christianity Today*, Vol. 36, No. 7, (June 22, 1992), p. 33.
7. Taken from the Foreword to Herbert Schlossberg, *Called to Suffer, Called to Triumph* (Portland: Multnomah Press, 1990), pp. 9-10.
8. For a fuller treatment of the purposes of suffering in the Christian life and especially how it relates to the completion of God's purposes in world evangelization see John Piper, *Let the Nations Be Glad: The Supremacy of God in Missions* (Grand Rapids: Baker Book House, 1993), Chapter Three.

CHAPTER 29 (PAGES 353-367)

1. See Ernest Becker, *The Denial of Death* (New York: Free Press, 1973).

2. For example, *The Nicene Creed; The Westminster Confession of Faith*, Chapter xxxiii, "Of the Last Judgment;" *The Belgic Confession*, Article xxxvii, "Of the Last Judgment;" and *The Second London Baptist Confession of Faith*, Chapter xxxii, "Of the Last Judgment."

3. Quoted from Philip Schaff, *The Creeds of Christendom*, Vol. III, (Grand Rapids: Baker Book House, 1977, orig. 1877), pp. 435-436.

CHAPTER 30 (PAGES 369-383)

1. Jonathan Edwards, *Dissertation concerning the End for Which God Created the World*, in *The Works of Jonathan Edwards*, Vol. 1, (Edinburgh: Banner of Truth Trust, 1976), p. 100.

2. See Oscar Cullman, "The Immortality of the Soul or Resurrection of the Body," in *Immortality and Resurrection: Death in the Western World—Two Conflicting Currents of Thought*, ed. Krister Stendahl, (New York: The Macmillan Co., 1965), pp. 9-53.

3. Edwards, *End for Which God Created the World*, p. 120.

CHAPTER 31 (PAGES 385-399)

1. I stress one last time: this is not the whole of faith, but the heart of faith. Faith is more. See, for example, the overview essay by B. B. Warfield, "Faith," in *Biblical and Theological Studies* (Philadelphia: The Presbyterian and Reformed Publishing Co., 1952), pp. 404-445; and the extended meditation by Jonathan Edwards, "Concerning Faith," in *The Works of Jonathan Edwards*, Vol. 2, (Edinburgh: The Banner of Truth Trust, 1976), pp. 578-596.

2. See especially Chapters Fifteen and Sixteen.

3. Jonathan Edwards, "Concerning Faith," in *The Works of Jonathan Edwards*, Vol. 2, (Edinburgh: Banner of Truth Trust, 1976), p. 583; italics added.

4. For the connection between past and future grace see Chapters Seven–Nine.

5. For a similar spiritual dynamic, see the great sermon by Thomas Chalmers (1780-1847), "The Expulsive Power of a New Affection" in *The Protestant Pulpit*, ed. Andrew Watterson Blackwood, (Grand Rapids: Baker Book House, 1977), pp. 50-62.

6. See Piper, *Desiring God*; Piper, *The Pleasures of God*.

7. See the Application Chapters Three, Six, Ten, Thirteen, Seventeen, Twenty-One, Twenty-Four, Twenty-Seven.

8. "Miscellanies", #4, in *The Philosophy of Jonathan Edwards from his Private Notebooks*, Harvey G. Townsend, ed., (Westport, Connecticut: Greenwood Press, 1972, orig. 1955), p. 209. See also pp. 139, 244 for other complaints about the inadequacy of language.

9. "[Self-love] may be taken for...[a person's] loving whatsoever is pleasing to him. Which comes only to this, that self-love is a man's liking, and being suited and pleased in that which he likes, and which pleases him; or, that it is a man's loving what he loves. For whatever a man loves, that thing is...pleasing to him...And if this be all that they mean by

self-love, no wonder they suppose that all love may be resolved into self-love." *The Nature of True Virtue* (Ann Arbor: The University of Michigan Press, 1960), p.42f. See also *"The Mind,"* in *Scientific and Philosophical Writings,* Wallace E. Anderson, ed., *The Works of Jonathan Edwards,* Vol. VI, (New Haven: Yale University Press, 1980), p.337; *Charity and Its Fruits* (London: The Banner of Truth Press), 1969, pp. 159f.

10. Edwards, *True Virtue,* p.45.

11. Edwards, *Charity and Its Fruits,* pp. 157f.

12. Ibid., p.164.

13. Edwards, *True Virtue,* p.77.

14. Norman Fiering, *Jonathan Edwards's Moral Thought in its British Context* (Chapel Hill: University of North Carolina, 1981), p. 196.

15. Edwards, *Charity and Its Fruits,* p. 159.

16. Ibid., p. 160.

17. *Miscellanies,* #530, p. 202.

18. Fierring, *Jonathan Edwards's Moral Thought,* p. 161

19. Clyde A. Holbrook, ed., *Original Sin, The Works of Jonathan Edwards,* Vol. III, (New Haven: Yale University Press, 1970), p.144; Charity and Its Fruits, p. 174.

20. John E. Smith, ed., Religious Affections, *The Works of Jonathan Edwards,* Vol. II, (New Haven: Yale University Press, 1959), p. 249f., my emphasis.

21. *Miscellanies,* #530, pp. 204f; see also Fiering, *Jonathan Edwards's Moral Thought,* p. 160.

22. See Jonathan Edwards, *Treatise on Grace,* Paul Helm, ed., (Cambridge: James Clarke and Co., 1971), p. 49f.

23. Fiering, *Jonathan Edwards's Moral Thought,* p. 162.

24. Smith, *Religious Affections,* p. 242.

25. Ibid., p. 241, italics added. See also Edwards, *The Nature of True Virtue,* p. 44.

26. Edwards, *Treatise on Grace,* p. 48f.

27. Edwards, *Charity and Its Fruits,* p. 161f.

28. Ibid., p. 164.

29. *Miscellanies,* #397, p. 249.

30. See Chapter Twelve on the connection between love to God and faith in God as motives for obedience.

31. Edwards, "Concerning Faith," p. 586.

32. *Miscellanies,* #448, p. 133; see also #87, p. 128, and #332, p. 130 and #679, p. 138.

33. Edwards, *End for which God Created the World,* in *The Works of Jonathan Edwards,* Vol.I, (Edinburgh: The Banner of Truth, 1974), p. 120.

34. Edwards, *Charity and Its Fruits,* p. 161.

35. Edwards' "Resolution #6," in *The Works of Jonathan Edwards,* Vol. I, (Edinburgh: The Banner of Truth Trust), p xx. "Resolved: To live with all my might, while I do live."

36. I owe this quote to Don Westblade, who transcribed the unpublished sermon of Edwards (from the Jonathan Edwards Project at Yale University) on Canticles 5:1, with the doctrine stated: "That persons need not and ought not to set any bounds to their spiritual and gracious appetites."